Forty Acres

EARTHBOUND

— AND —

HEAVENBENT

Elizabeth Porter Phelps and Life at Forty Acres
(1747–1817)

Elizabeth Pendergast Carlisle

SCRIBNER
NEW YORK   LONDON   TORONTO   SYDNEY

SCRIBNER
1230 Avenue of the Americas
New York, NY 10020

SCRIBNER and design are trademarks of
Macmillan Library Reference USA, Inc., used under license
by Simon & Schuster, the publisher of this work.

For information about special discounts for bulk purchases,
please contact Simon & Schuster Special Sales:
1-800-456-6798 or business@simonandschuster.com

Designed by Kyoko Watanabe

Text set in Adobe Garamond

Manufactured in the United States of America

1   3   5   7   9   10   8   6   4   2

Library of Congress Cataloging-in-Publication Data

Carlisle, Elizabeth Pendergast.
Earthbound and heavenbent : Elizabeth Porter Phelps
and life at Forty Acres (1747–1817) / Elizabeth Pendergast Carlisle.
p. cm.
Includes bibliographical references (p.) and index.
1. Phelps, Elizabeth Porter, 1747–1817. 2. New England—Social life and customs—
18th century. 3. New England—History—18th century. 4. Hadley (Mass.)—
Biography. I. Title.
CT275.P5885C37 2004
974.4'23—dc22
[B]
2003054478

ISBN 13: 978-1-4165-6964-0

For Ashley, Heather, Caddy,
Meredith, Andrew, Elliott, Will,
Tim, Katie, Samantha, Jack, Caley
and Paige

community builders to come

CONTENTS

THREE GENERATIONS OF PORTER-PHELPS-HUNTINGTON FAMILY

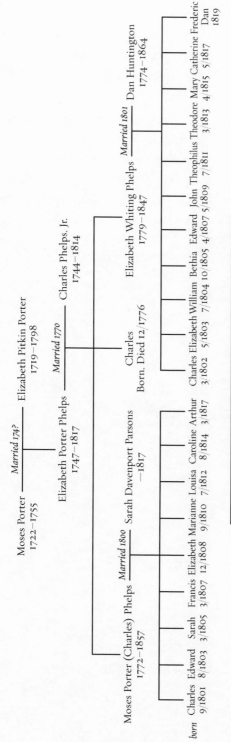

Moses Porter — *Married 174?* — Elizabeth Pitkin Porter
1722–1755   1719–1798

Charles Phelps. Jr. — *Married 1770* — Elizabeth Porter Phelps
1744–1814   1747–1817

Charles
Born. Died 12/1776

Moses Porter (Charles) Phelps — *Married 1800* — Sarah Davenport Parsons
1772–1857   –1817

Elizabeth Whiting Phelps — *Married 1801* — Dan Huntington
1779–1847   1774–1864

born

Charles	Edward	Sarah	Francis	Elizabeth	Marianne	Louisa	Caroline	Arthur
9/1801	8/1803	3/1805	3/1807	12/1808	9/1810	7/1812	8/1814	3/1817

Charles	Elizabeth	William	Bethia	Edward	John	Theophilus	Theodore	Mary	Catherine	Frederic	Dan
3/1802	5/1803	7/1804	10/1805	4/1807	5/1809	7/1811	3/1813	4/1815	5/1817		1819

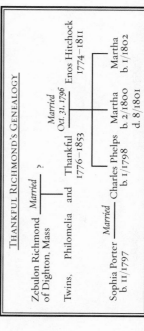

THANKFUL RICHMOND'S GENEALOGY

Zebulon Richmond — *Married* — ?
of Dighton, Mass

Enos Hitchcock — *Married* — Thankful
1774–1811   *Oct. 31, 1796*   1776–1853   and   Philomelia,   Twins,

Martha	Martha
b. 2/1800	b. 1/1802
d. 8/1801	

Charles Phelps — *Married* — Sophia Porter
b. 1/1798   b. 11/1797

Earthbound
and
Heavenbent

The faithful heart does not like to ramble about without a homestead. It needs a fixed spot to return to, it wants its square house. . . . Human beings live there, and invisible rings are created by human radiation; they enclose and invite, delimit and open gates . . . and into which we enter to receive the gift of its song.

FROM CHRISTIAN NORBERG-SCHULZ IN
The Concept of Dwelling

PREFACE

C LOSE TO the Connecticut River and set back from the road that runs north out of Hadley, Massachusetts, stands a house called Forty Acres. Built in 1752, it is a graceful blend of Georgian and Federal architecture. Lilacs and mock orange grow close to the foundations, tall shade trees shadow the roof, meadows slide gently down to the river. An eighteenth-century vision stands realized, a dream of shelter for succeeding generations, of seasoned elegance and growing prosperity emerging from a productive farm.

Born in 1747, Elizabeth Porter Phelps spent all but her first five years at Forty Acres. Her remarkable life spanned three wars, a major uprising, and the emergence of a nation. During that time, alterations to the house reflect aesthetic and practical changes in the occupants' lives. Rooms in the house, spared from overzealous restoration, retain traces of the family members who lived within its walls.

Another record exists in the wealth of family papers preserved and passed from generation to generation. Diaries and letters re-create the ordinary and extraordinary; they make audible individual voices. They put flesh on the bones of history. Phelps's papers create for us a vivid picture of a brief time when people were united by mutual needs, a common religion, and a belief in the existence of a "promised land." This belief tied them to their land and to the close-knit community that they created. It was a succoring community, its foundation the seventeenth-century covenant in which the inhabitants promised to watch over one another.

In many ways, the world described by Elizabeth Phelps has disappeared, but as we explore that world, we find ourselves on surprisingly familiar ground: lives disrupted, in some cases extinguished by war, threatened by rampant epidemics, destructive natural catastrophes; people overworked, men torn between public and private aspirations, women yearning after food for the spirit; marriages unsettled by lack of communication, depression, financial loss, prolonged absence, anxiety for children's welfare.

One cannot gain an accurate sense of what it was like to live in eighteenth-century New England without recognizing the ways in which Calvinism continued to influence people's thinking, particularly among farming communities. Though the single-minded Calvinism of seventeenth-century Puritans does not characterize the religion of all eighteenth-century New Englanders, its enduring strength can be seen in the multiple revivals that occurred well into the nineteenth century. Millennial dreams were nourished from meetinghouse pulpits. The dissensions that arose in the late eighteenth century within the Congregational Church kept theological debate alive among clergy and laity alike.

Whether the inhabitants of early New England were pious believers or not, everyday life was suffused with signs of the divine intention. Responding to that intention demanded both an active and a contemplative life, one in which love of one's neighbor was demonstrated through acts of kindness, and the love and fear of God through meditation and prayer. For the devout to fulfill both demands produced inner conflict. Writing was a way in which Elizabeth Phelps could explore this dichotomy in her own life.

The contents of a house—beds, tables, chests of drawers—can be bequeathed from one generation to another. But what about ideas, principles, creeds; can a house nurture and preserve a family legacy based on these intangibles? Can those convictions be passed from generation to generation like teapots and shawls? Elizabeth Phelps's story provides one answer to these questions.

Chapter I

A Foundation Laid

*"May I remember thankfullness for
such a good habitation."*

THE HOUSE is a cosmos with its own harmony and order. Its rooms, stairs, windows, doors, its textures, colors, odors, sounds all form that cosmos—rubbed surfaces, nut brown wood, pungent ashes, creaking floors. Houses order our lives. They command specific perspectives from which we view the universe. The juxtaposition of room to room directs our steps. Ceilings decree our sense of stature. Light circles about the house, making morning and evening places of the interior and, moving on, leaves behind shadowy corners. Fires on the hearth draw and fix our gaze. Windows pull us outside the house. Corners enclose and turn our attention inward. This is the shaping work of the house and the builder's bequest to succeeding dwellers.

Within the house the inhabitants place their possessions, move them about; objects cared for, mended and polished, speak of personal habits and preferences. Rooms expand and contract in response to their occupants' changing needs. Chairs regroup accordingly. Footsteps create worn paths, fires darken hearths, oil from fingers mingles with the wood of tables, door jambs, and bedposts. Sounds reverberate, rearranging the atmosphere: a voice calls out a name, lids bang down on pots in the kitchen, upstairs a shoe drops. Dwelling and dwellers engage in an unceasing dialogue.

Except the Lord build the house,
they labor in vain that build it.

PSALM 127

I

This story begins with a house and a vision made concrete by that house. It is the story of the life of Elizabeth Porter Phelps, but the vision belonged first to her father, Moses Porter, scion of one of the most prosperous families to settle in Hadley, Massachusetts. In 1659 a group of families, led by the Reverend John Russell, moved up the river from Windsor, Connecticut, in search of a new beginning for their community. Unanimous in their dissent from the Windsor congregation, they were fortunate in selecting the rich, alluvial plain where the Connecticut River makes a radical dogleg turn, forming a peninsula and embracing a large tract of land with its fertilizing waters. This land had been occupied by the Norwottuck Indians, its population diminished by an epidemic of smallpox in 1633. An agricultural tribe, the Norwottucks were responsible for the cleared tracts that awaited the white settlers.

William Pynchon, the founder of Springfield, Massachusetts, negotiated the purchase of the peninsula for the settlers. The new arrivals did not dally in erecting a protective ten-foot-high stockade around these desirable fields and the community that depended on them. The next generation of Norwottucks regretted the loss of control over their land, eventually becoming hostile when the English settlers demanded that they surrender their weapons. Rather than agreeing to do so, the Indians abandoned their village and moved seventeen miles northward, joining the Pocumtucks in an expedition against the Deerfield garrison in 1675.[1]

The settlers brought with them the foundation on which the community would be built. The meeting congregation drew up a covenant, signed by its members. A product of seventeenth-century New England, covenants continued to be written down and signed, even into the twentieth century.[2] Agreeing to "covenant together in faith and love, and promise in love to watch over one another," the document provided ethical as well as theological underpinnings for New England settlements.[3]

Puritan ideals of community prevailed through much of the eighteenth century, particularly in the interior rural villages of New England where commerce was not yet a way of living and thinking for the majority of the population. These ideals had been expressed in seventeenth-century sermons, lectures, and in the writings of prominent leaders such as Cotton Mather and John Winthrop. Though Winthrop's life ended a century before Moses Porter began to build his house, the principles set forth in his sermon delivered aboard the *Arbella* continued to be preached by eighteenth-century ministers and restated in their congregations' covenants:

> we must be knit together in this work as one man. We must . . . rejoice together, mourn together, labor and suffer together: always having before our eyes our commission and community in the work, our community as members of the same body.[4]

In *As a City Upon a Hill,* Page Smith writes:

> The covenanted community of New England represented the most intense community experience of modern times. . . . It was intensely communal in that it turned inward toward the interior spiritual life of the community; it was, however, remarkably dynamic, creating surpluses of human energy that were discharged unceasingly against an intractable environment.[5]

It is this combination of introversion and extroversion that accounts for the persistent tension between thought and action among the pre-Revolutionary communities of New England, between the nourishment of the spirit and the fulfillment of the promise to others. Covenant commitments, whether adhered to or not, permeated community consciousness, outlasting the paper on which they were inscribed.

Each of the early Hadley settlers received a house lot of eight acres; strips of plow land, meadow, wood, and swamplands were distributed among the settlers according to their wealth.[6] Among these settlers was the Porter family, whose members were to occupy positions of leadership for generations. The Porters were one of seven prominent families in Hampshire County with close kinship ties with one another. Substantial land holdings brought them positions in local government and the military, as well as representation in the General Court, the state legislature. Samuel Porter, the first Porter to settle in Hadley, increased his holdings significantly within two decades of his arrival. Tax lists from the 1680s reveal that his assessments were among the highest in the town. Aside from his land holdings, which increased as his assessed worth brought him larger portions of the communal land divisions, he became involved in trade. His son, also called Samuel, followed in his father's footsteps, increasing upon his inheritance and becoming one of the wealthiest men in Hampshire County. He made numerous perspicacious land purchases through the years, which earned him a prominent position in town and county government and eventually a position on the Governor's Council. He also continued his father's involvement in trade and moneylending. Samuel Porter II died in 1722, leaving an estate of more than 10,000 pounds, one of the largest in the county.[7] He was able to bequeath equal portions of 1,200 acres in Brookfield, Massachusetts (thirty miles east of Hadley), to each of his seven children, sons *and* daughters, the latter each receiving legacies of 400 pounds as well. In addition, any increase in the value of his estate was to be divided seven ways, thus ensuring a certain amount of affluence for his female descendants.

Three of Samuel II's children made socially and politically advantageous marriages, another means of assuring the family's continuing affluence and influence. One such marriage was between Moses Porter's father, Samuel III, and Anna Colton of Longmeadow. It was Samuel who built the house in 1713 where Moses Porter grew to manhood. The house occupies a central position facing the Common, across from the meetinghouse. It still stands, one of the most arresting of all the substantial houses that line West Street in Hadley. Born in 1722, Moses was the sixth of seven children and the second son, his elder brother Samuel thirteen years older. A graduate of Harvard College, Samuel was minister of the church in Sherborn, Massachusetts. Thus, on their father Samuel's death in 1748, the homestead and farmlands fell to the younger son, his elder brother inheriting undeveloped land from the second precinct of Hadley (South Hadley) and the township of Northfield.

The early houses of Hadley were constructed according to a common plan. Whether two or four rooms, one or two stories (or three in the case of the Porter homestead), the rooms clustered around a large central chimney, the second story and attic reached by a steep turning staircase compressed within the interior entry. The chimney was both physically and psychologically the center of the dwelling, the pulsing heart of the house. The hearth acted as a centripetal force, drawing the inhabitants inward for warmth, sustenance and fellowship. Whether or not everyone pursued the same task, activities were communal undertakings. Privacy was not a consideration; safety, along with the productivity that came from people working together, was.

Just as the chimney served as the focusing center of the house, the meetinghouse functioned as the heart of the village. Both house and community sought enclosure as a defense against the dangers of the surrounding wilderness, a desire that continued to be pertinent to the New England frontier until the 1740s. Deaths among area settlers from Indian raids in nearby villages (Colrain, Deerfield, Northfield, among them) occurred as late as May 1746.[8]

The Hadley house where Moses Porter was raised conformed to the traditional central-chimney plan just described, though its size signaled the prominence of its builder, Samuel Porter. (Hadley tax lists of 1731 show Samuel Porter's real estate to exceed that of all other residents.[9]) Two large rooms on the first floor of the house open out from the small entranceway with its narrow, turning staircase. The room on the right, later embellished with raised paneling and a scalloped china cupboard, functioned as a formal parlor. The room on the left, with its broad hearth, served as a workplace, kitchen, dining room, and certainly in the winter, a sleeping room. Feather beds were portable and easily carried to the place where the warmest fire burned. The absence of privacy reflected a prevailing way of life, not a lack of means.

Moses Porter's marriage in 1742 to Elizabeth Pitkin of East Hartford reaffirmed family connections with the prosperous Pitkins, since 1660 of Hartford, though, like the Porters, previously of Windsor. Moses' uncle,

Eleazar Porter, had married Sarah Pitkin, cousin of Elizabeth, in about 1721. The Pitkins were major landowners in the East Hartford area, occupying eight houses along its Main Street in the 1700s.[10] Pitkin wills reveal large families and extensive property: house lots, pastures, bush lots, plow lands, fulling mills, a clothier's shop, corn and sawmills, as well as substantial tracts of land in neighboring communities.[11] It was clearly a close-knit family. Bequests went to married brothers and sisters as well as the children of the deceased.

The only child of her father's second wife, Elizabeth Whiting, Elizabeth Pitkin brought to her marriage a considerable dowry. Her father died in 1732 or 1733 when she was thirteen or fourteen years old, leaving an estate valued at 1,425 pounds, 15 shillings, and 9 pence, a handsome sum for that time and place. Two of her five stepsisters died without heirs shortly after their father's death, the estate then divided among the remaining four daughters and their mother. Elizabeth Pitkin is cited individually in her father's will to receive specific items entrusted to him by her deceased maternal grandmother, Rebecca Russell, until her granddaughter reached the age of eighteen.[12] One senses an aura of continuing prosperity and protective familial ties surrounding the young Elizabeth.

The dress that family lore identifies as Elizabeth Pitkin's wedding gown confirms the family's affluence. The complex weave fabric, a silk brocade, was probably Dutch or English in origin, its pattern a product of the 1730s.[13] Flowers and foliage of varying shades of rose, blue, and yellow are woven onto the green and white ground. Whether the dress was originally made for Elizabeth Pitkin's wedding from a prized piece of fabric kept for such occasions or remade from an earlier garment remains a mystery, but the quality of the cloth and refinement of the design suggest that the dress was created for an important family event. Dresses such as this one were itemized in wills, their value earning them particular mention along with pieces of furniture and oxen.

In 1719 Cotton Mather counseled newly married couples to appear in their wedding clothes on the Sunday following the ceremony. As weddings were seldom performed in the meetinghouse, it would be the couple's first "public" appearance. According to historian Sylvester Judd, this custom was referred to as "coming out groom and bride," and endured for more than a hundred years.[14] The bride also wore the dress when making and receiving the ritual calls expected of newlyweds. Certainly Elizabeth Pitkin's wedding dress would have been worthy of its role in introducing another Pitkin to the people of Hadley.

Visiting in such finery must have presented challenges in 1742: no sidewalks existed in eighteenth-century Hadley and the paths along the road were often blocked by piles of manure, mud, and puddles, forcing pedestrians into the street along with cattle and horses. Barking dogs, geese, and ducks crisscrossing the roads added to the hazards. One octogenarian, reminiscing in the mid–nineteenth century, described the noise made by the geese outside the meetinghouse as deafening, causing him to lose "many fine sentences" of the sermon.[15]

It is probable that the young couple first lived with Moses' parents, Samuel and Anna (Colton), in the family homestead on West Street. A spacious third floor may have provided an apartment for them; several pieces of furniture belonging to Elizabeth and Moses, including a four-poster bed, were shortened, perhaps to adapt to the lower attic ceiling. When Samuel Porter died in 1748, and Moses inherited the family homestead, he sold it to his cousin, Eleazar Porter. Sylvester Judd heard from a Porter descendant that Moses soon built his own house on an adjoining lot, "because his Pitkin wife did not like to live with old people." Whether this explanation is true or a prejudicial judgment by an in-law is impossible to discern. We do know that Elizabeth Whiting Pitkin, Elizabeth Porter's mother, lived with her daughter and son-in-law until her death in 1753.[16]

II

It was not many years after building a new house for his wife next to the family homestead that Moses decided to move out of Hadley Village, breaking a century-old pattern of construction. His Hadley house then became his mother's home.[17] Between the years 1747 and 1753 Moses had acquired at least fifteen separate pieces of land in addition to those received from his father's estate. He also purchased a seventh part of a sawmill in 1753. These purchases represent a significant departure from the traditional system of land holdings in which strips of arable land surrounding the house lots were portioned out to the residents, and, for a time, farmed according to the open-field system. This system served to limit the area that the settlement encompassed, keeping the farmlands within close range of the farmers' dwellings. It also limited the growth of the population when a single farm could no longer sustain multiple families of succeeding generations.[18]

In moving out of the village, Moses Porter was able to create a more efficient, centralized farm with greater possibilities for expansion. By 1752, his land holdings amounted to 640 acres, then considered to be a very large estate.[19] One scholar has estimated the average New England farm at this time to have been about one hundred acres with only a small portion in cultivation.[20] A number of Moses' land purchases were clustered together in the vicinity of Forty Acres, an area lying two miles north of the village of Hadley. The move distanced the family from the sight, sounds, and reassuring lights of neighbors' dwellings, as there were no houses between Hadley Village and Forty Acres. Yet community ties remained strong. Moses was a Hadley selectman. Relatives and friends occupied the houses along West Street, which was also the site of the shop owned and managed by Eleazar Porter, and the meetinghouse, together bringing the family over the two-mile distance almost daily. Moses was one of two owners of a carriage in all of Hampshire County (which then included what is now Berkshire County). Described as a chaise, it was a light, open, two-wheeled vehicle drawn by a single horse. Most people in this part of New England relied on walking and riding on horseback.[21]

Moses Porter's new house sits on a ridge of land overlooking the great serpentine river that defines the Connecticut Valley. Across from the front dooryard, the ground rises gently, culminating in Mount Warner, a short distance to the north. The land behind the house drops down into a broad fertile plain that bordered the Great River, as it was then called. Across the water can be seen the town of Hatfield, its church bells audible to the family at Forty Acres. Aesthetic, as well as practical considerations must have attracted Moses to this site.

The designation "Forty Acres," originally applied to this tract of land outside the village proper, no longer literally described the much larger area that comprised the farm. Naming the house was another way in which Moses Porter set his dwelling apart, perhaps emulating English rural gentry. Not only the unification of his holdings, but the plan for his house departed from the norm established among earlier generations of Hadley residents. Forty Acres turns the traditional plan inside out. Two chimneys flank the north and south walls of the house. A spacious central hall sweeps from the front to back door, providing room for a broad staircase and handsome newel post. This plan, its origin in the mother country, was exported via pattern books as well as English architects themselves. Today called Georgian for the then reigning monarch, it reflects the end of the need for feudal defenses and the beginning of classical influence.

The central-hall plan had begun to appear in prosperous coastal communities such as Portsmouth, Newburyport, and Boston, but only a few examples were to be found in the interior before 1752, the construction date of Forty Acres, and none known to have been in Hadley.[22] A more immediate source for this plan may lie in one of several houses that began to appear in the Connecticut Valley around 1750, one built for the Reverend Eliphalet Williams of East Hartford, a neighbor of the Pitkins.[23] The radical departure from tradition in the construction of the house and in Moses Porter's choice of building site, as well as his selling of the family homestead, says much about his ambitions for himself and his family. He was a visionary, recognizing the possibilities in another system of farming and a new mode of architecture.

Not every aspect of the new house's design, however, is innovative. Janus-like, it looks backward and forward in architectural time and reflects both creative and practical thinking. Moses duplicated the medieval hewn overhang that appears on his father's house, which provided additional space in the upstairs chambers. He also retained the side door located on the southwest corner of the house. Both of these feaures were characteristic of early eighteenth-century houses in the region, modeled after houses in southeastern England.[24] The new location of the chimneys made possible two corner fireplaces, back-to-back, on both sides, providing a hearth for each of the four ground-floor rooms. Four fireplaces represent a substantial investment, as masonry was costly and increased the property taxes.[25]

The most visible innovation to passersby, accustomed to the unpainted board siding or wooden clapboards of Hadley houses, was the rustication of the east, north, and south facades of Forty Acres.[26] Simulating stone, rustication most often appears on structures of a considerably grander scale, such as George Washington's Mount Vernon home, rusticated in the 1770s.[27] Among the nearly twenty documented eighteenth-century houses with rusticated siding, most of them in coastal areas, Moses Porter's house is one of the earliest and the only one known of its kind in the area.

The painstaking process that produced rustication reflects the desire to emulate English manor houses, most often built of brick or stone. It demanded skillful joiners and painters. In western New England, wood was plentiful, brick and dressed stone were not.[28] We, in this century, are apt to think of such simulations as cheap substitutes for the real thing, but the popularity of graining, marbleizing, and trompe l'oeil in the eighteenth century indicates that the art of imitation was admired for its own sake. The transformation of wood into stone must have been an impressive display of the painter/joiner's mastery of his medium, his own form of sorcery. Rustication on the Porter house involved feathering or beveling the top and bottom edges of each board to form sharp tapers. Overlapping boards created the appearance of V-shaped lime mortar joints when painted white. Vertical scoring of the boards every two feet of their length produced the effect of uniform stone blocks. Red-brown paint, simulating Longmeadow sandstone, was then applied and sand thrown against the wet paint. Such a precise and complex process was not inexpensive.

The builders further enhanced the illusion of stone by incising "segmented pediments" into the boards above the windows and "flat arches" above the doors, references to the classical motifs revived in stone during the Italian Renaissance and adopted by English architects. A drawing reconstructing the house as it would have appeared when first built reveals a blocklike structure.[29] The roofline and overhang create sturdy, horizontal accents, although the overhang belies any pretense that the house was built of stone. The house's elegant simplicity, with its flat, but clearly defined decorative detail, owes more to the English Renaissance than to the Middle Ages, and announces a new attitude toward dwellings for eighteenth-century America.

The central-hall plan of Moses' new house also defined domestic space in new ways. With the central chimney plan, rooms fold into one another. Inhabitants must pass through front rooms in order to gain access to rooms in the rear. The later plan provides separate access to each room from the central hall, dividing public from private spaces. Formal rooms for receiving guests in the front of the house are clearly separated from work spaces in the back. Bedrooms, no longer passageways to other rooms, have their own entrances with doors that may be closed.

This plan creates private spaces that invite withdrawal and reflection; their separation from clearly defined work spaces fosters other activities:

writing, reading, and meditation, the latter two encouraged from the pulpit in Calvinist New England. Numerous small fireplaces make it possible to retreat from the kitchen-workroom, the center of domestic activity.

Moses Porter's new house responded to changes that had taken place in rural communities by the mid–eighteenth century. A safer environment had relaxed defenses, making it possible for the house to open to its surroundings. Greater affluence brought the desire for external display: substantial size, an impressive doorway, classical ornamentation that derived from older, well-established civilizations. Wealth also brought the pursuit of gentility; work demanded one kind of communal space, visitors another.[30]

Independent reading had become a desirable activity following the Reformation and the parallel growth of literacy. Beginning in the sixteenth century, personal libraries began to be found in European houses other than just those of the wealthy, more frequently in those of Protestants than Roman Catholics. Settlers brought these libraries to New England where reading was part of the daily routine, both as a group and as an individual endeavor.[31] The single most important volume was, of course, the Bible; sermons and meditations on the Scriptures were common as well. The emphasis was on careful rather than voluminous reading. A sermon published in Boston in 1767 warns the reader not simply to "scan the text and then set it aside. Better not to read at all than to read in that way . . . and when you have finished you must mull over what you have just read."[32]

Such admonitions presuppose a congregation that is not only literate, but one whose members are able to command the time and a quiet place for close reading and "mulling." Yet neither the time nor the place were readily available in most early New England homes. The gradual rise in literacy in New England by the mid–eighteenth century, most notably among women, created a demand for quiet corners.[33] As always, innovations in the structure of houses respond to changes, not only in the way people live, but in the way that they desire to live. The design of a house is a design for living.

Moses and Elizabeth Porter were no doubt aware of the functional advantages of the central-hall plan. Divisions between rooms facilitate divisions between people and activities: the mistress of the house from the servants, serving tea to callers from bread-baking, reading from sausage-making. Such divisions were never as sharply defined in rural areas of eighteenth-century New England as socially ambitious families might have desired, but houses such as Moses Porter's made withdrawal from the workplace more feasible.

III

The roof-raising at Forty Acres most certainly drew a great many villagers on May 27, 1752, and provoked speculation as to the practicality of this new plan. Who would wish to live so far away from neighbors? From the meetinghouse, the Porter store?[34] Who would wish to travel that rutted path in all weathers to visit relatives? Will those smaller chimneys on the house's north and south ends keep them as warm as would have a central chimney? Certainly not! But roof-raisings were social events, and the unusual location for an unusual structure would have drawn the curious as well as the expected helping hands.

Moses, his wife, her mother, and their small daughter Elizabeth moved into their new home on December 5, 1752, close to the shortest day of the year and the onset of winter. One wonders if the mother and daughter missed the passing of neighbors in the village, children playing on the common, the reassuring candlelight from other houses.

Two and a half years after moving into his new house, Captain Moses Porter was called away from his farm to take part in the French and Indian Wars, leaving mother and daughter even more isolated. As captain of the Hadley company, he joined the regiment under the command of Colonel Ephraim Williams, the destination Crown Point, a French stronghold on Lake Champlain in upstate New York.[35] A child standing by the side of the road in Hadley witnessed his departure and, years later, described him as "looking like a splendid and commanding figure to country eyes." An inventory of the clothing worn by a lieutenant in Colonel Williams's regiment during the same campaign details the splendor of those uniforms:

> good plain cloth great coat; new camblet scarlet jack[et] coat, double breasted; new German serge waistcoat; good leather breeches almost new; good new striped Holland shirt; pair of yarn stockings; new felt hat; good barcelona silk handkerchief; a pocket compass; pair brass shoe buckles; pair same buttons . . .[36]

Captain Porter's uniform was undoubtedly even grander, suitable to his higher rank.

At first Moses' family was optimistic that victory would occur in a matter of months, certainly before the end of 1755. "Your little daughter [then eight years old] sends her duty to her fond father," Elizabeth Porter wrote, "and says that when three months is out she intends to look out for him all day."[37] But Crown Point was not to be taken until 1759, four years after his departure.

The soldiers made slow progress toward Crown Point, a significant target, as it was from here that the French launched their raids on the New York and New England borders. Major General William Johnson led the 3,500 Colonial troops, consisting of farmers, tradesmen, and artisans. It was his first military command. They carried heavy artillery, ten large cannons. At a strategic site about fifty miles north of Albany, Johnson ordered the construction of a fort, later known as Fort Edward. He left 500 men there to continue construction while the remaining troops pushed toward Crown Point, among them Colonel Williams's regiment.[38]

Elizabeth and Moses Porter's correspondence during the summer of 1755 reads as a woeful tale of failed communication. Only one of Moses' surviving letters responds directly to comments in one of his wife's letters:

> I Received yours of the 14 of July [on] 19 of the same which was such a cordial to [me] as I had not had since I left you . . . You hinted something of being [alone] even in company I am very sensable of it my [self] but I believe you have a double portion of it.[39]

Subsequent letters from both of them record frustration. From Moses:

> disapointed as to letters from home there has been within this two or three days some hundreds of letters brought to us . . . but none from Forty Acres; I take ever oppertunity to write hoping therby to stir you up to the use of pen.[40]

In his final letter, his thinly disguised anger surfaces:

> I determine not to Give any of you much more trouble unless I can hear whether my letters are Read or whether they are burnd with-

out reading. . . . I might think that if you knew the satisfaction your single letter gave me you would certainly miss no opportunity to wright to me . . .[41]

Four dated letters from Elizabeth Porter to her husband survive, all written in the month of August. One, undated, refers to General Braddock's defeat in Ohio during the month of July and may have been written soon after that event. In that letter she tells of deserters from the army who try to break into the house, "milk our cows devour our corn destroy our garden and are often about the house in the night." There were still no houses between Forty Acres and the village of Hadley in 1755. Moses' dream of a pleasant dwelling, removed from other houses and surrounded by acres of productive land, could not have included his extended absence from home.

Just as Moses Porter begged for letters from home, Elizabeth Porter made desperate pleas for letters from her husband:

It is now about three weeks since the last letter I received was writ and I begin to fear that you are going to put in execution your thretning which I pray if you have any pitty for me you would not do.

There is similar anguish in her final letter to Moses, written August 29, 1755:

I write letter after letter and send them to the likeliest place that I know of for conveyance but it seams they fail as yet but I cant refrain write I must though you never have them.

The denouement of this sad correspondence between Elizabeth and Moses Porter occurred on September 8, 1755. The commander of the French forces, Baron von Dieskau, had heard of the new English fort under construction, protected by only a small contingent of Johnson's army. On September second, he sent 1,500 soldiers to mount a surprise attack on the fort. Johnson, who had arrived at Lac Sacrement (which he immediately renamed Lake George), learned of the French plan and dispatched more than 1,000 men to defend the fort under the command of Colonel Williams. "Old Hendrick," a Mohawk chieftain and adviser to

Johnson, protested that the numbers were too small to fend off the French attack and "too large to sacrifice." He was to be part of that sacrifice. En route to the fort, they were ambushed by the French. Colonel Williams, along with the Mohawk adviser, fell while rallying his men. Forty-six members of his regiment were slain, among them Captain Moses Porter.[42] Colonel Pomeroy, a survivor of the "Bloody Morning Scout," as it came to be called, described the aftermath of the battle in his journal:

> Tuesday, Sept. 9. This a fair hot day. We are about the melancholy work of burying our dead that were killed here in the camp yester-day.

On the next day he reported having returned to the site with a large group of men to bury another 136 bodies.[43]

Among the family papers is a letter from Moses' great-grandson to his niece in which he tells of that "resplendent" uniform becoming "a prey to the savages." He adds: "There were rumors of cruelties in the kind of death he endured that were almost too shocking to be believed." Whether true, unfounded rumor, or exaggeration, this account of Moses' death became part of the family lore.[44] Yet this description of the Bloody Morning Scout ignores the presence of French soldiers while singling out

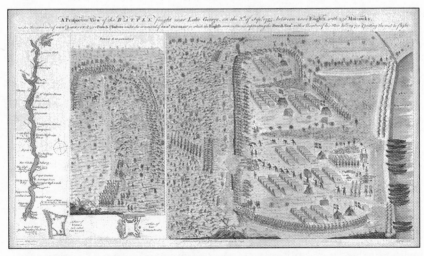

A Prospective View of the Battle fought near Lake George on the 8th of Sept. 1755 (Courtesy of Historic Deerfield, Massachusetts. Photography by Amanda Merullo.)

Indians as the foe, nor does it pay tribute to the Mohawk "savage" who tried to prevent the catastrophe.

It was not until the fourteenth of September that the news of Moses' death reached Hadley. Family tradition has preserved a vivid account of the event that was to alter permanently the course of Elizabeth Pitkin Porter's life. While putting little Elizabeth to bed, she heard a rap on the wooden shutter of the first-floor northeast chamber window. Sliding it to one side, she met with her husband's Indian guide, who, without speaking, passed Moses' sword through the window. One can imagine the turbulent emotions that weighted the silence. She knew at once the significance of this act.[45] It was only the sword, a sad relic of a lost battle, that came back to Forty Acres.

IV

What Elizabeth Pitkin Porter had regarded as a temporary period of loneliness and insecurity was now a wasteland stretching ahead, unending. Moses had engaged Caleb Bartlett, a distant relative, to manage the farm in his absence. Bartlett remained for several years, living in the house.[46] Daniel Worthington then came to the family's aid. A descendant of one of the early settlers, Nicholas Worthington of Hatfield, he appeared to enjoy a close relationship with the family, accompanying Mrs. Porter on some of her journeys in search of health and driving her daughter Elizabeth to and from Hadley and on berrying expeditions in the surrounding countryside. His age fell halfway between that of the mother and the daughter, which may have prevented him from being considered a logical replacement for the deceased father. It was also possible that Mrs. Porter was not interested in remarriage. Unlike many widows, she did not depend on a husband for financial security. With no male heir, the house was hers to live in or dispose of as she pleased.

Worthington was perhaps surrogate father for the little girl, who felt a strong affection for him. He stayed with the family until 1771, his departure noted in her diary: "altho I tho't I parted with him Chearfuly, how insensably did the tear steal down my cheek."[47]

References to Elizabeth Pitkin Porter's poor health make routine appearances in her daughter's diaries. "My mama made a visit at the Doctors" is a recurring entry during the course of her mother's long life. A

year before her husband's death, the Reverend Samuel Porter wrote to his
brother Moses expressing concern for Elizabeth Porter, having heard that
"she remains in a weak low state, but was something comforted to hear
latly by Mr. Chandler that she is getting something better."[48] Dr. Richard
Crouch, a prominent and active physician of Hadley, had patients in a
number of towns in the upper Connecticut River Valley. He kept a journal until his death in 1761, recording visits to patients, their maladies,
and the medicines he prescribed. Among his patients were members of
the Moses Porter family. His visits began in Hadley Village on February
1, 1747, and were "for wife mostly."[49] One of the medicines prescribed
by Dr. Crouch for a member of the family in 1753 was laudanum, a form
of opium. At the same time he prescribed thirty doses of "hysteric," a
medicine designed to treat bouts of hysteria as well as the uterine disorders that were believed to be its cause.[50] It seems clear that these pre-
scriptions were intended for Elizabeth Pitkin Porter, as her eventual
addiction to opium is recorded in her daughter's diary. In 1784 a diary
entry mentions a visit from a Hadley woman who seems to have functioned as a "paramedic" among the people of Hadley. "Old Mrs. Alixander came here with view to persuade my mother to leave off taking
opium but in vain—she took it before night the next day."[51]

Colonial doctors prescribed opium for a number of maladies, among
them coughs, diarrhea, malaria, smallpox, syphilis, insanity, "female
complaints," and as an all-purpose anodyne.[52] Opium was available "over
the counter" as well. In a letter of 1690 to Nehemiah Grew, M.D.,
Samuel Lee claims physicians in Massachusetts "use the London dispen-
satory at pleasure or any other, tyed to none."[53] A letter written in 1766
to an English supplier requests a number of medicines for the use of the
writer's family, among them liquid laudanum, a tincture of opium.[54]

Opium varied in potency from supplier to supplier, which may
explain the differing attitudes of Colonial physicians toward its use, some
cautious, some enthusiastic.[55] In the latter half of the nineteenth century,
concern for the frequency of opium use gave rise to scientific research,
which continued into the twentieth century. One study of 171 cases
found that, despite differences in susceptibility, a single large dose could
disrupt the patient's mental condition for a matter of weeks. The same
study reported symptoms in chronic users—muscular weakness, languor,
impaired memory, apathy, melancholia. Among the withdrawal symptoms noted were restlessness, anxiety, insomnia, delirium, and hallucina-

tions.[56] Another side effect discovered among habitual female users was cessation of the menses.[57]

Elizabeth Pitkin Porter indeed suffered from many of the symptoms listed above. Opium was most likely available to her as early as 1747. Her husband's absence during the French and Indian Wars and his subsequent death must have made it all the more difficult to resist recourse to the drug. Moses' widow may not have been endowed with the necessary stamina needed to bring to fruition his ambitions for Forty Acres. In one of his letters, Moses chides his wife: "I could have been glad to ha[ve] seen a Little more of the Hero in your letter" (July 22, 1755). She replied: "You must not expect masculine from feminine."[58] Perhaps Moses had witnessed acts of heroism among women close to the battlefields. Nevertheless, war produces female as well as male casualties and Elizabeth Pitkin Porter was one of them.

She did not succumb to chronic illness without a fight, as evidenced in the one existing letter to her daughter, written from Middletown, Connecticut, on September 22, 1765. In it she discusses her quest for a cure:

> how long I shall be upon my Jorney I cant tell, I shall endeaveur to follow the directions of Providence for the recovery of my health, I hope I aint worse then when I left you. I wish I may return in a Comfortable state of health.[59]

Her daughter's diary reports that this journey is one of several in which her mother set out on horseback to watering places, "gone into a Journey in hops of recovering her health."[60] She tried various watering places, Coldspring (now Belchertown, Massachusetts) and eleven days later, Stafford Springs, Connecticut, "to go too a Pool there very much famed for cureing disease."[61] She visited Pitkin relatives in Hartford.

Despite this energetic pursuit of health, Mrs. Porter continued to suffer bouts of depression, acute anxiety, frequent visits to and from the doctor. In another time and place, she might have closed the door on the outside world, but the community not only sustained Mrs. Porter, it elicited acts from her that engaged her in its day-to-day existence.

The religion of communities such as Hadley, reenforced by written covenants, gave continuing structure to people's lives through its rituals: bimonthly Communion services, fasts in the planting season and in times of crisis, the Sabbath Meeting that began the week with two sermons to be reflected upon during the week, Thursday evening lectures, and in each home, family prayers twice a day.

During the time of her illness, Mrs. Porter continued to make numerous calls on ailing relatives and bereaved neighbors in Hadley and in nearby Amherst, Sunderland, Northampton. She also gave of herself in teaching. We learn from an adopted granddaughter that it was Mrs. Porter who taught her two granddaughters to read and spell.[62] The twelve-year-old Elizabeth Pitkin's signature, along with her mother's, appears on a probate court record at a time when many females, including several of the young girl's stepsisters, signed documents with an X. That the daughters of the affluent Pitkin family could not all sign their names may seem surprising, but writing was regarded as an unnecessary skill for women, even a dangerous one.[63] Reading, on the other hand, was essential if one were to respond to the preacher's admonitions to meditate upon the Scriptures. Although the ability to sign one's name did not necessarily mean that one could write, Mrs. Porter's letters to her husband display more than basic writing skills, and the work of her two pupils testifies to her success as a teacher.

Mrs. Porter must also have initiated her daughter's education. Early in Hadley's history, provisions were made for educating its children. In April 1665, the town voted "20 pounds per annum for three years, towards the maintenance of a school master."[64] A bequest from Edward Hopkins, an Englishman wishing to promote education in the "foreign plantations," financed the school from its inception.[65] For the first hundred years, however, class schedules and attendance were irregular. The curriculum, which stressed the study of Latin and Greek, was designed to prepare young men for the college.[66] A coeducational school made a brief appearance in Hadley when Elizabeth was twelve years old. On January 7, 1760, thirteen pounds, six shillings, and eight pence were voted to the schoolmaster Josiah Pierce for schooling, a five-month session for boys and four months for girls. On the sixteenth of June of the same year, however, the money had not been disposed of and the same amount of money was voted, but for "boys & girls . . . to be instructed together."[67] After 1760, this school disappears from town records, and it is therefore likely that Elizabeth was educated by her mother. Moses Porter's inventory at the time of his death mentions books and "a collection of 30 pamphlets."[68] His father's store in Hadley had sold "Primers, Psalters,

Testaments and Bibles."[69] And Elizabeth Pitkin undoubtedly brought books with her from Hartford, along with the Bible bequeathed to her by her grandfather Pitkin.[70]

Nevertheless, Elizabeth Pitkin Porter remains a shadowy figure. Her daughter, cousins, friends, doctors were attentive; as the years passed, however, she seemed to dwell more and more at the periphery of the household, farm, and community. A letter written tongue-in-cheek from a member of the household describes her at the age of seventy-six as "safely stowed away in a farther corner of the house."[71]

Moses Porter's mantle then fell on the shoulders of his sole descendant, his daughter Elizabeth (referred to as Betsey in her youth). It is her diaries, begun shortly before her sixteenth birthday, and later her letters, that record for more than fifty years the shaping work of the house at Forty Acres. During those years two more wars would darken the land and local insurrections would threaten western New England. In their wake came radical changes that had economic, political, philosophical, and social implications.

At Forty Acres there are births and deaths, the latter sometimes premature, though seldom unexpected. There are personal crises. There are celebrations. The house grows. Its occupants increase in number. The farm's produce multiplies. Although two miles from Hadley, Forty Acres becomes a center for a network of surrounding communities, and the medium through which the family upholds its personal covenant with an expanding world.

Chapter II

~

PLEASURES OF THE PEN

*"Wednesday came here Miss Pen and
Miss Polly to help me quilt."*

EIGHT YEARS after the death of Moses Porter, his house stands solid, his trees grown to a height of eighteen feet. Their shadows dapple the light and project intricate patterns on the south wall of the house. On the other side of that wall, the young Elizabeth sits at Moses Porter's desk in the parlor. A Sabbath silence fills the house, stills the weekday routine in the surrounding fields. Inside Elizabeth's head, phrases from Mr. Woodbridge's two sermons intermingle with images of Mrs. Oliver Warner's new bonnet, which she could not help admiring.

She places a sheet of foolscap in front of her, picks up a pen, and begins her Sabbath journal, October 16, 1763, one month before her sixteenth birthday:

> Mr. Woodbridge preacht from Genesis 20 [39] chapter, 9 verse. How then can I do this great wickedness and sin against God. And also from Luke, 14 chapter, 17 verse Come, for all things are now ready.

She repeated the texts, chapters, and verses several times on the way home (her great-aunt Sarah Porter's advice), so that she could write them down correctly—not entirely successfully. She contemplates the paper partially covered with her own carefully wrought script and experiences a new sense of possession. It will be her book.

Why did you not wish me single thats the life for me.
LETTER FROM ELIZABETH TO MISS PEN,
JUNE 11, 1769

I

The decision to keep a journal required a greater commitment from an eighteenth-century writer than it would from a present-day sixteen-year-old. A more parallel endeavor now would be calligraphy. Steel pens did not exist until the mid–nineteenth century. It was necessary to carve a nib from goose, raven, or crow quills, using a penknife. Poorly executed nibs produced blotches and uneven script, and even well-cut nibs needed frequent sharpening. "O my dear," Elizabeth wrote to her closest friend:

> I've been pestered prodigiously to make a pen & needs think how happy you was in having a brother to go too in that need as well as many others.[1]

She may have mixed her own ink, another task requiring precision and patience. Paper was expensive and necessitated a two-mile trip to the Porter store in Hadley. She also needed imported powdered pumice or sandarac with which to sprinkle each page and prevent the ink from spreading.[2] And then there was the problem of light. Time for writing would most likely be in the evening, requiring candles for many months of the year, and even in the late hours of summer months: "My Candle acts like a fool," she explained in closing a letter to Miss Pen. (June 9, 1769) Later entries in her diaries record her involvement in the lengthy procedure of candle-making. Certainly, she did not burn candles casually.

As with calligraphy, there are levels of expertise in handwriting. At the time, penmanship was a craft and a way of earning a living for scribes employed to copy manuscripts and documents. Elizabeth's writing was not of this quality, but she did have a penchant for small flourishes, spirals, and curlicues in her letters, suggesting practice on her part as well as pleasure in the act itself. Her devotion to her diaries is reflected in her careful sewing together of pages into volumes.

One wonders if Elizabeth imagined an audience for her diaries. Many diary and journal writers betray an interest in a future audience with remarks such as "whoever may read these words." Her entries contain no such self-conscious asides. There are, however, occasional clarifying phrases as to the identity of a person referred to: "she was the widow Kneeland of Boston," "She that was Eunice Pomeroy." This specificity, as well as her recording of Hadley births, marriages, and deaths, suggests that she saw herself as undertaking the history of her community.

Congregational pastors encouraged the faithful to record each Sunday's sermon texts, drawn from the Scriptures, so that they could become the subject of meditation during the course of the week. The immediate

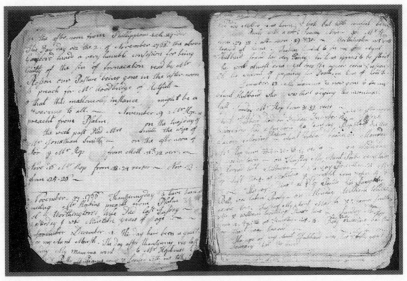

(Courtesy of Amherst College Archives and Special Collections)

model and incentive for this exercise may have been her mother's first cousin Sarah Pitkin Porter, whose *Interleaved Almanac* recorded the preacher and text faithfully for a number of years.[3] Visits between the two cousins were frequent, and it seems likely that the sixty-one-year-old Sarah Pitkin Porter felt a grandmotherly responsibility for this fatherless child, living with a chronically depressed mother. Sabbath sermons encouraged parishioners to view each biblical verse as weighted with meaning. New England parsons employed a form of exegesis of a biblical text as a basis for their sermons, a method of analysis demanding a close, word-by-word examination of a text. Single verses produced the substance for a two-hour sermon, both Sunday morning and afternoon: "Be not overcome of evil, but overcome evil with good" (Romans 12:21), or "Better is a dinner of herbs where love is, than a stalled ox and hatred within." (Proverbs 15:17)[4] The brevity of the text and the exhaustive examination of its meaning facilitated the post-Sabbath reflections of the listeners. The preacher's repetition of the text in the course of delivering the sermon ensured that listeners would commit it to memory. In his book *New England Saints,* Austin Warren points out that the preacher was "an educator as well as a shepherd of the flock." His sermons, "sequentially written and closely reasoned," then argued among members of the congregation during the ensuing week, provided them with a liberal education.[5]

The clergy, most of them graduates of Harvard or Yale, were well educated, often taking students under their wings for instruction along with their pastoral duties. Once established in a particular church, they tended to stay there for life. One of the most revered and learned New England parsons, Nathaniel Emmons, D.A. (married to one of Elizabeth's friends and cousins), was pastor in Franklin, Massachusetts; he turned down the possibility of the position of chief professor of Theology at the newly founded Andover Seminary, saying that "he preferred to remain a preacher to farmers."[6] Elizabeth was to prove as earnest a listener as any of the farmers in her congregation.

For more than two years, Elizabeth faithfully recorded the sermon texts and only the texts. It was a major catastrophe in Hadley that produced an expansion in the contents of her journal. A fire in 1766 consumed the house of the Reverend Samuel Hopkins, a close friend of the family at Forty Acres. Everyone escaped, including Hopkins's mother-in-law, Sarah Porter, and his stepchildren, Elizabeth's cousins, but nothing remained of their possessions.[7]

March 23, 1766. (The next Sunday after the remarkable Deliverance of Mr. Hopkins and his family from the flames in which their house was immediately consumed the Thursday night before.)[8]

Mr. Hopkins chose relevant texts, the first Sunday following the disaster from Job: "Naked came I out of my Mothers womb and naked shall I return hither: the Lord God Gave and the Lord hath taken away; blessed be the Name of the Lord;" the second Sunday from Matthew: "Lay not up for yourselves treasure upon Earth where Moth and rust corrupt and where thieves break through and steal." (Elizabeth's transcriptions) No calamity, however close to home, was without grist for the preacher's mill.

Gradually more and more local events fill the spaces between Sabbath sermon texts in Elizabeth's journal. On October 26, 1766, she records the death of Samuel Gaylord's wife, Submit (Dickinson), following the delivery of a stillborn child, six months after the couple's wedding. The next Sunday Elizabeth notes, "the above Gaylord made a very humble confession for being guilty of the sin of fornacation read by Mr. Rosson . . . so that this malloncolly instance might be a 'warning to all.'" (November 2, 1766)[9]

Births, deaths, natural disasters, visits received and visits made, expeditions, and domestic chores now appear:

Last Monday Came here Mrs. Crouch and in the afternoon Joseph Elixanders wife. On Tuesday Mr. Hopkins came here and made a good long visit. Wednesday I received a visit from two young Ladies that came from Hatfield Sally Chancy and Polly Little. In the Eve Mr. Oliver Warner with his wife and two of the Williamses called upon us in their return from Hatfield. (February 15, 1767)[10]

Entries such as this one occur regularly in what then becomes a personal diary. The house appears as a vortex, pulling in relatives and friends for tea or dinner, passersby for lodging.

The location of the house close to roads running east to Amherst, north to Sunderland and beyond, south to Hadley Village, and a short boat ride westward to Hatfield linked Forty Acres with a circle of surrounding communities. The only dwelling for several miles, its striking facade and ample proportions drew travelers seeking shelter at nightfall and in approaching storms that sometimes kept them there for several days. "Monday an old stragling woman was here. Tuesday night a Girl from Killingsly lodged here." (July 23, 1769)[11]

Mrs. Porter and her daughter were seldom without company. When one or the other was away for several days, a relative or friend came to stay with the one who was left behind. Sarah Porter often spent several days with her widowed cousin. Elizabeth's close friends and relatives, Polly Porter and Penelope Williams, were frequent guests. There were live-in servants, several slaves, and young women who came for extended periods to do clothes work. And in the background was the solid figure of Daniel Worthington.

If location brought many people to the doorstep of the house, it was the inhabitants who opened the door. Lengthy visits to relatives, neighborly calls on the sick, and watches at the bedside of women in labor and the dying were common practice in eighteenth-century New England. Such customs served to knit communities together, but the Porters' social status, so emphatically declared by the house itself, conferred additional responsibilities on Elizabeth Porter and her daughter.[12]

An interesting illustration of this sense of obligation appears in Elizabeth's diary on September 11, 1768: "Monday about 9 o'clock at night came here Sarah Goodrich with her sister Betty Daughters of Josiah Goodrich." The specificity as to the late hour and the particular branch of Goodriches alert us that this is something other than a social call. She continues:

> Betty being with child had no setled place of abode therefore my mother was a going to set her spinning for her a week or two she not expecting to lie in this three months.[13]

Sarah Goodrich wakened Mrs. Porter and Elizabeth in the middle of the night as "Betty was so poorly." Worthington went immediately to town and brought back Aunt Porter and a midwife. The baby lived "not an hour," and was buried the next day following a funeral service. Betty remained in their care for three weeks before her sister came to take her away—home, one hopes.

Massachusetts law defined sexual intercourse out of wedlock as criminal. In the years 1766 to 1770, twenty women in Lincoln County, Maine, appeared at the Court of General Sessions related to fornication

and paternity suits. (Maine, at this time, was a province of Massachusetts, and therefore under its laws.) Martha Ballard, a midwife in Hal-
lowell, Maine, delivered 106 first babies between 1785 and 1812. Of
that number, 38 percent were conceived out of wedlock.[14] Unmarried
women were encouraged to identify the child's father during delivery,
thus insuring the child's future support. Such confessions in the midst of
duress were accepted as true. When the couple subsequently married,
both took part in the confession before the meeting congregation. Submit Dickinson Gaylord, having died in childbirth, left Samuel Gaylord
to confess alone.

Elizabeth's diary records a "rousing" sermon on the Sunday following
Betty Goodrich's miscarriage, the Reverend Hopkins's principal target
not the unfortunate mother, but the accused father, who "professes not
to own it." (September 18, 1768)[15] Furthermore, Hopkins "reproved all
iniquity but specially the sin of lying." Fornication was a breach of the
community code of conduct, a breach rectified only by public confession
before the meetinghouse congregation. A more serious crime against the
community was one in which the perpetrator not only lied but refused
responsibility for his actions.

The public nature of the confession and absolution required by the
Church did not diminish the number of premarital pregnancies, which
increased in the second half of the eighteenth century, particularly following the Revolution.[16] Elizabeth's diaries continue to record admis-
sions to fornication during the Sabbath meeting along with restoration
to the confessors of their "former Priviledges."[17] Fornication and bearing
children out of wedlock did not bring excommunication if confessed,
though it may have brought a fine in the civil courts; nor did it necessarily bring social ostracism.

Samuel Gaylord, a highly skilled joiner, married again, this time
Penelope Williams (Miss Pen), daughter of the Reverend Chester
Williams, whose inventory at the time of his death exceeded that of
Moses Porter. Gaylord's previous confession to fornication prior to his
first marriage did not prevent him from securing the hand of a member
of one of the most prominent families in Hadley. The couple named
their first child after Samuel's former wife, Submit Dickinson Gaylord.
When the child died at the age of two, they gave the same name to their
second daughter. The desire to erase Samuel's past breach of conduct
from the community's memory did not appear to be a motivating force

for the Gaylords. His "very humble confession" reinstated him in the eyes of the community, as well as a child by his second wife paying tribute to the memory of his first wife by bearing her name.

Betty Goodrich's sudden arrival at Forty Acres, late in the evening, suggests that she was ousted from the house where she had been living. Marriage had not followed her discovery that she was pregnant as it did in many cases where a full-term birth followed six or seven months after the wedding. When Betty found herself without shelter, it was to the people of Forty Acres that she and her sister turned. Mrs. Porter's decision to "set her spinning" fleshes out her character as both practical and compassionate, imbued with female concern for one who found herself ostracized and subject to public humiliation.

II

Young hired women came to tailor for extended periods, but their presence did not exempt the young Elizabeth from plying her needle: "helpt quilt upon a brown coat for Molly Dickingson all Thursday night." Working on brown material by candlelight on a dark November evening may have provoked the emphatic "all Thursday night." "Fryday I helped Miss rebeckah Dickingson make a gown for me." (November 20, 1768)[18] Quilting parties appear again and again in diary entries, mixing companionship with the important task of providing warm padded garments and bedclothes against New England winters. Elizabeth quilted for various members of the Porter family, for her great friend Miss Pen, and for names that otherwise do not appear in her diaries.

Another task both social and practical was berrying. "Tuesday Miss Pen, Miss Joanna Williams and Miss Patty Gaylord came here. Worthington went with us to shew us a spot of wortleberries [blueberries], they Drank tea with me here." (August 6, 1769) She describes expeditions for strawberries and cherries in June, huckleberries, blackberries, and dueberries (bramble berries or possibly gooseberries) in July, wortleberries, peaches, and plums in August and September, raspberries and chestnuts in October. She does not mention apple-picking, perhaps because the apple orchard known to be at Forty Acres in later years was already planted and did not require traveling.[19]

And then there were outings to learn to sing. Elizabeth prefaced her first entry of the new year, January 31, 1768, with an apology to her diary:

> There has been a long while that I've not kept account of the texts and other things as I ought to have don—I've been greatly engaged in learning to sing. One Mr. Stickney came to teach us—he arrived here 26 of December. Many things have happened worthy of my notice."[20]

Singing schools in the 1760s were devoted to the improvement of congregational singing of the psalms. As such, Elizabeth's outings for this purpose could be seen as a pious activity. In *The Sweet Psalmist of Israel*, published in Boston in 1722, Thomas Walter described singing as:

> A means provided by the God of Nature and the Author of all Religion, to dispel and drive away the evile Influences of Satan, but also to prepare the soul for the Reception of the Inspiration of the Holy Spirit.[21]

Nevertheless, there is a secular ring to her enthusiasm for this new venture that comes through the diary entry and doesn't quite explain her failure to record the Sabbath texts for a period of two months.

After a little prayer of repentance, she records a gathering of friends and a sleigh ride into town for the singing meeting. She then remains true to her pledge to record faithfully all those things "worthy" of her attention, and singing meetings appear regularly among them. Sarah Pitkin Porter, in her *Interleaved Almanac*, describes one of these gatherings that encompassed more than voice lessons:

> Thursday. A lecture of some kind at Hadley. People went over from Hatfield. . . . Fine singing, a good sermon, good beef and rich gravy. A great multitude in the evening was gathered at the singing school. Hatfield singers shined upon anthems. Hadley never shined so well: the town was alive and appeared with spirit.[22]

In these last years of her girlhood, Elizabeth's diaries depict a rural idyll, material for a novel by an American Jane Austen. It is only in a letter written many years later that she confessed to periods of her girlhood when she "felt lonesome and low."[23] For Elizabeth, fatherless and companion to a chronically ailing, depressed mother, there must have been periods when even callers and expeditions into the countryside could not lift the gloom that settled periodically on the house. In the diaries, neither loneliness nor self-pity intrudes on her detailed listing of the week's events. Visitors, chance meetings, errands, and domestic tasks mingle with each other. The prevailing tone is one of bustle and zest. The belated confession of loneliness and low spirits casts a different light on the early diaries, revealing a young woman's wishful construction of life as she would have it.

III

It is in Elizabeth's letters rather than the early diaries that she first reveals her inner thoughts, her anxieties, and her sense of fun. They convey a strong sense of her presence. She spells inconsistently, standard spelling not yet established. When confronted with a difficult word, she resorts to a phonic approach as when she sounds out the place-name *Hocanum* as "hauk a numb." (May 3, 1772)[24] It was not until 1783 that Noah Webster's *The First Part of a Grammatical Institute of the English Language* would be published and hailed as the first step in unifying the language of the new nation. She had a grasp of correct grammar, sometimes ignored in favor of expressiveness. She drew upon a vocabulary enriched by regular infusions of the language of the King James Bible. The dash appears frequently (often with a graceful flourish). Sentences run into each other, conveying breathless enthusiasm or urgency. A phrase such as "pestered prodigiously" makes its point through alliteration; there is lyricism in the repetition of the vowel *e* in the phrase "just at the edge of eve." Her tendency to jump from one subject to another plays havoc with a logical progression of thoughts, but reveals her impetuous nature. Whereas the diary entries are terse, to the point, often abbreviated, the letters are expansive, introspective, spontaneous. She had an ear for the expressive possibilities of language and the ability to create a warm speaking voice, one directed at a specific listener.

Nine letters to Penelope Williams survive, eight written in 1769. Her friend's replies are not among the family papers, though references to them appear in Elizabeth's letters. Single sheets contain communications written on different dates. Some letters may have been written over a period of time, others were possibly returned with their replies, so that unused space could be used and sent off again. Letters, as opposed to social gatherings, provided the opportunity for an exchange of confidences. Miss Pen was not absent from Hadley when some of the correspondence between the friends took place in the winter of 1769. Diary entries record visits from her friend within a day or two of writing to her.

Although she had several close friends, her first cousin (once removed) Penelope Williams appears to have been the closest. Miss Pen's father, the Reverend Chester Williams, died when she was eight years old, a loss that she shared in common with Elizabeth. Her mother, Sarah Porter (daughter of Aunt Sarah Porter), then married Hadley's fourth minister, Samuel Hopkins. Miss Pen was two years older than Elizabeth, an age difference that explains the addition of "Miss" to her name, in deference to her superior age, though it is more likely that Elizabeth wished to amuse her friend with this note of mock formality.

In these letters to Miss Pen, Elizabeth discovers the power of words to seek out and authenticate her feelings, and her friend's responses fuel extended conversations. The letters afford a close look at an intimate friendship between two young women in Colonial America. A diary entry of March 12, 1769, mentions that her friend is ill; like most of Elizabeth's early entries, it is brief and matter-of-fact. Her letter to Miss Pen on March 19, on the other hand, reveals the profound anxiety that she had felt during her friend's illness and her joy with the news that she is recovering:

> O how thankfull ought I to be that your Life is spared . . . may our friendship grow stronger & stronger & we be mor & more united our hearts be knit together by the strongest ties of Friendship: tho I'm unworthy of your Love I know my dear I have it from your own goodness not from my desert for were it to be Detirmined by that I must soon dispair—Yes my dear you Love me did I not see the tenderest effection sparkle in your Eyes this day when I enterd the Room, O my friend I was not so ungratf[ul] as to feel no emotion, know my dear Love was in my heart if it was not in my eyes—how unwelcome was company just then I longed to have expressed my satisfaction & Joy for your recovery by tears at least—how cruel was it to forbear taking your hand but indeed I durst not altho I really tho't I had a right to do that.[25]

Her fear that her friend might die was not unwarranted in this time when death came suddenly on the heels of high fevers, "fits," and diseases such as smallpox and scarlet fever. Elizabeth confined her rejoicing to a letter, believing any overt expression of that joy to be unseemly in company.

Biblical phrases were at Elizabeth's beck and call, but the expressiveness with which she disclosed her feelings in these letters called upon other sources. Images from romances intermingle with those from the Bible. Forty Acres houses a large number of books, a number of them published in the early 1700s. Elizabeth's letters refer to specific titles, among them Richardson's *Clarissa*.[26] Years later her son remembers that she was "a most indefatigable reader. . . . Her reading embraced almost all subjects, but was directed more especially to novels—better letters—and Theology."[27] The present family library possesses only a few novels, less likely to be given the care necessary for survival than the theological works. Novels were printed with paper covers, some then given leather or wooden covers, depending on the owner's desire to preserve them; others, passed on to friends and relatives, may have been read until they fell apart.

Epistolary novels, such as Richardson's *Pamela* and *Clarissa*, were popular in England and in her colonies. At once sentimental and didactic, these books validated the expression of feeling while advocating the moderation and restraint necessary to avoid flouting social conventions. Both *Clarissa* and *Pamela* pay homage to the chaste woman, at the same time that they sanction the written expression of women's private feelings.[28]

Barbara Benedict, in her study of eighteenth-century literature, *Framing Feeling*, observes:

> Certainly, sentimental fiction does celebrate internal experience as the source of knowledge and feeling as the very process of morality. At the same time, the stylistics of sentimentalism persistently shape this celebration of feeling to social ends.

Women's feelings, Benedict argues, were given serious attention, but in their challenge to the social order that existed in the eighteenth century, they were necessarily subjected to constraints.[29] Elizabeth's reluctance to express her love for Miss Pen through any physical gesture while others were in the room demonstrates that those constraints were operating in Hadley, Massachusetts, in 1769.

The abbreviated wording of the diaries suggests moments stolen from the domestic and social round. Elizabeth's ostensible concern was to record the Sabbath text followed by the week's passing events, those "outward visible signs" of her attempt to live an attentive, useful, and righteous life. The diary entries take on the solemnity and purposefulness of the Sabbath texts that preceded them. Texts such as "Thy soul thirsteth for God, for the living God: when shall I come and appear before God" (Psalm 42: 2) do not lend themselves to levity or idle chat.

Letters, on the other hand, are avenues for self-expression, for self-exploration, even for gossip. To Miss Pen she writes: "They say John Coo[ke] drives on very fierce down street the Widow ay to be sure the Widow."[30] A letter to Miss Pen visiting in Boston includes a practical request:

> Dear I send you by Mr Porter two Dollars & beg you to get the Brown tafety handkerchief my mother & you talked of, if you can find such an one—Likewise a black alamode for mother pretty good & large too . . . Now if ever I learn to spell tafety you know I am a superiour speller. (May 27, 1769)[31]

Elizabeth also found it possible to air her fears for her own spiritual health with this compassionate, understanding friend. In January 1769, she was twenty-one years old, an age by which many women had formally joined the Church, enabling them to participate in the Sacrament of Communion. "O that I were fit to Join the Church; how differently it appears to me to Look forward to a Sacrament from what it does to you." (January 22, 1769) Miss Pen joined the church in 1766 when she was twenty-one years old.[32] In Elizabeth's eyes, her friend was well along the road to salvation, while she was in grave danger of damnation.

> Another Sacrament I've turn'd my back upon Christ & his Church . . . O how read[y] the Devil & our own wicked hearts are to intimate to us that we shall never find mercy. (Letter to Miss Pen, February 26, 1769)

Joining the church involved a public declaration of one's Christian convictions and commitment in front of the meetinghouse congregation. It is clear that Elizabeth took this declaration very seriously. Self-scrutiny convinced her that she was not sufficiently dedicated nor worthy of church membership.

> Oh this flattering deluding world how it steals our hearts from God—Oh my dear I hate my self because I dont hate my self no more. Never had one more reason to abhor themselves yet few are so in love with themselves. (Letter to Miss Pen, March 18, 1769)

Such self-flagellation may strike us as neurotic, a symptom of an unhealthy state of mind, but similar protestations are not uncommon among eighteenth-century diarists and letter writers.[33]

Sporadic religious revivals occurred in the valley, bringing public confessions of sin and declarations of newfound faith. About the time that Elizabeth was writing to Miss Pen, Seth Coleman, a young student at Yale, described one revival in the neighboring town of Amherst. Coleman recorded the congregation's response to the Reverend David Parsons's sermon:

> Every one present seemed deeply affected; there was scarcely a dry eye in the room. Many were in deep distress for sin, ready to cry out, "What shall I do to be saved?"[34]

Events such as this one would not have escaped notice in the surrounding towns. Elizabeth and her mother had close ties to Amherst, occasionally drinking tea with the Parsons family and attending church in Amherst. The emotional charge created by revivals in the area was bound to spread and capture the susceptible. In Elizabeth's case, revival fever did not bring a conversion experience, but rather, increased anxiety. Dissensions that had removed Jonathan Edwards from the Northampton pulpit in 1750 continued to exist in the Connecticut River Valley. Revivals were regarded by some as dangerous in their unleashing of emotions difficult to control. Older citizens of Hadley and the neighboring towns still had strong memories of a time when emotions ran high and dissension was rife. The rousing English evangelist George Whitefield preached in both Hadley and Northampton in 1740 and again in 1745, fanning flames ignited by Jonathan Edwards. Hatfield leaders refused to allow Whitefield in their pulpit, but that did not prevent townspeople from traveling to Hadley to hear him, and it was said that "when he preached in Hadley, his voice was heard in Hatfield."[35]

The Reverend Samuel Hopkins does not appear to have had evangelical aspirations. Nor did he agree with those who continued to endorse Jonathan Edwards's strict views on readiness for Church membership. Edwards believed that conversion must take place first before receiving Communion, whereas Hopkins saw Communion as an aid to conversion. Elizabeth appears to have accepted Edwards's stringent requirements for Church membership rather than Hopkins's "half-way Covenant." News of the Amherst conversions must have increased her desire for a conversion experience and intensified her apprehension as to the state of her soul: "I hate myself because I dont hate my self no more." In the same letter, she prays "for the Holy Spirit to be power'd out upon me."[36]

Religious revivals come in waves; one in the mid–nineteenth century that swept through Mount Holyoke Seminary may shed light on Elizabeth's state of mind. It occurred during the time in which the poet Emily Dickinson was enrolled at that school. Gathered together in a school assembly, students and faculty rose from their seats, one by one, to profess their religious beliefs. Emily tried to summon up the feelings and convictions that appeared necessary for a commitment to Christ, but could not and remain true to herself.

> Abiah, you may be surprised to hear me speak as I do, knowing that I express no interest in the all-important subject, but I am not happy, and I regret that last term, when that golden opportunity was mine, that I did not give up and become a Christian. . . . I am one of the lingering *bad* ones, and so do I slink away, and pause and ponder, and ponder and pause . . . *you* know of this depth and fulness, will you try to tell me about it?[37]

The poet's "wrestling with angels" parallels Elizabeth's inner struggle. Neither young woman was capable of an unquestioning commitment. For both of them, a habit of introspection and absolute honesty prevented them from being swept along by the prevailing wind.

Elizabeth's letters to Penelope Williams were not entirely occupied with her struggle toward salvation. "O dear what would I give to see you or rather what would I not give," she wrote to her friend, who was visiting in Roxbury, Massachusetts.

Why did not I take a tender leave of you as I ought in a parting Manner: as from my side the dearer part is torn: the rest lies bleeding & but lives to mourn. (Letter to Miss Pen, June 11, 1769)[38]

References to letters received from her friend make clear that Elizabeth's devotion to Miss Pen was requited. In the above letter, she continued:

indeed my dear I can hardly expect your love but to have you tel me you love me with all your heart guess how I bore it—not without a flood of tears.

Similar declarations of love and concern between sisters and friends appear in many letters of the time.[39] Such declarations between two young women whose relationship was unlikely to have been an overtly sexual one may sound extravagant to present-day readers.[40] Often responses to perceived crises, Elizabeth's letters provide a glimpse of a passionate nature that does not dissipate with age. While they are replete with protestations that have the ring of eighteenth-century novels, one does not doubt her sincerity. The novels provided her with the vocabulary needed to articulate strong feelings. There are even signs of jealousy when she writes: "I took a great deal of notice of your more than ordinary affectionate behaviour of Miss Patty too." (June 13, 1769)

A note of mischief appears in the letters following Miss Pen's recovery of her health:

Now Im all shut up Ive nothing to say, struck Dumb, a great deal I long to say but yet cant say one word, once in a while can fetch a good hearty Sigh & set & set & Look on my paper. I never. . . . O by the way you will be sure to come home by my Weding, my Weding did you ask? ay mine—But by the account I hear there is some probability of one before mine I intend to tell you either the man or the Girl & leave you to find out the other Timothy E-st-n. (June 9, 1769).[41]

Although she did not mention her future husband's name in this letter, Miss Pen seems to have known his identity. Elizabeth's next letter to her friend thanks her for her wishes of happiness "with the best of men," but chides her: "Why did you not wish me happy single thats the life for me." (June 11, 1769)[42]

It is a rather surprising remark for a young woman who has just agreed to marry her suitor, or possibly it masks—humorously—underlying apprehensions. In a letter of October 17, 1791, Hannah T. Emery of Exeter, New Hampshire, announces her forthcoming marriage to a friend:

> The die is about to be cast which will probably determin the future happiness or misery of my life. . . . I have always anticipated the event with a degree of solemnity almost equal to that which will terminate my present existence.[43]

Such qualms are not unusual following a momentous decision, especially if, as we discover, the decision is made without family support.

No mention of her engagement or approaching wedding appears in Elizabeth's diary until almost a year later when, on May 13, 1770, she drops this announcement into the midst of her weekly routine: "Sunday this day I was published to Mr. Charles Phelps—Mr. Hop from Matthew 23 and 8. Tuesday I went into town to quilt."[44] "Publishing" notified the community-at-large of a forthcoming marriage by posting the banns or announcement of the date on the meetinghouse door.

The name Charles Phelps had appeared only rarely in the diaries during the months, weeks, and days preceding the wedding. When she does refer to him it is in the same manner in which she notes down visitors, her watches with the sick, quilting, and berrying expeditions. The names of John Chester Williams and his younger brother Nathaniel also appear from time to time in the diaries.

Who was this successful suitor for the young Elizabeth's hand, daughter of both a Pitkin and a Porter? Mrs. Porter hired Charles Phelps to manage Forty Acres several years before the couple's engagement. The previous managers, Caleb Bartlett and Daniel Worthington, had had close connections to the Porter family. The latter lived at Forty Acres during his tenure; Charles Phelps did not. The marked absence of any mention of him in Elizabeth's diaries, until shortly before their marriage, suggests a more distant relationship between him and the Porter family.

IV

The Porters of Hadley were firmly established as "River Gods," along with other Connecticut River Valley families: the Williamses, Ashleys, Dwights, Stoddards, Partridges, and Pynchons.[45] The offspring of these families tended to marry within this group. The Porters were related to the prominent Northampton Stoddards through marriage to the great-granddaughter of Solomon Stoddard, and daughter of Jonathan Edwards. When not forming alliances with local gentry, men and women were willing to travel in search of a suitable mate, someone of similar "caste." A number of Porter women married clergy, whose education and position of leadership in the community gave them similar status to that of affluent families, whatever the ministers' economic position. Graduates of Harvard and Yale colleges, the Porters occupied commanding posts in the community and in their military regiments.[46] Marrying within this circle, consolidating the ownership of property among themselves and retaining control over community affairs helped to maintain an elite status with its attendant economic and civic power.[47]

Among the family papers is a reference to "a man by the name of Williams" as having been selected by the Porters to marry Moses Porter's daughter. The writer comments that he "moved in the best circles of society but had not much else to recommend him."[48] The most likely Williams referred to was John Chester, the brother of her close friend, Miss Pen. He was a graduate of Yale College, a lawyer, a member of a powerful family (and a relative). A number of years later, another diary-writer, Rebecca Dickinson, who often came to Forty Acres to sew, referred to this same Williams:

> the last night died at hadly the wife of Chester Wiliems aged forty three years. She was lovely in her life and happie in her death I hope. She has been married Seventeen years a most agreable women deserved a better husbend then she had . . . God has called her to great tryals the loss of her health for the last seven years of her life the loss of goods which I hope weaned her from the world her husband has been in jail for more then a year.[49]

Williams was incarcerated for failure to pay his debts, a not unusual penalty for this default, but probably not condoned by Hadley "River Gods." Elizabeth refused to be influenced by the Porters' concerns for status, but rather she chose the dictates of her heart.

Judd reports that Charles Phelps was "said to have been previously engaged to a Goodrich [Sarah, daughter of Aaron], who later mar. Daniel White."[50] Who broke the engagement and when is not recorded. Visits from Sarah Goodrich to Forty Acres appear a number of times in Elizabeth's girlhood diaries, but not after the Phelpses' marriage. Engagements, often formalized before the meetinghouse congregation, were not lightly terminated. The names of Charles Phelps and Sarah Goodrich both appear on Reverend Hopkins's list of new members of the church for 1766. Declarations of readiness for church membership often occurred shortly before or soon after applicants entered into marriage. Sarah's marriage was recorded in Elizabeth's diary in 1772: "Daniel White married to Sarah Goodrich—Dolly [Charles's sister] the only one of our family asked to wedding."[51] What upheavals lie behind that comment?

Charles Phelps's name first appears in Elizabeth's diary in June 1768 when Worthington went to Hartford to bring Mrs. Porter home from a visit with her Pitkin relatives. In his absence, Phelps stayed at Forty Acres. The following week his name appears again, accompanying a party that includes Elizabeth on a strawberrying expedition. "Charles Phelps carried Esq. Porter's wife in a chaise Lawyer Porter carried his wife, Pen and Patty, Nabby and Polly and me" (June 26, 1768), an unusually detailed accounting of the way in which members of the party were transported. On October 3, 1768, she went "into town at Mr. Phelps to twisting," probably a communal gathering in preparation for weaving.

Phelps is not specifically mentioned for some time after these appearances, although Elizabeth recorded various events that include male friends: "Just at the Edge of the Eve three Gentlemen came over to wait on the Ladies home with a slay—all spent the Eve here returned at 9." (February 12, 1769) These omissions may be more revealing of Elizabeth's feelings than casual mentions of his name among her weekly listing of visiting friends. Or is it possible that Sabbath journals, written by unmarried daughters, were subject to a mother's scrutiny? That the Porters did not approve of Elizabeth's choice of suitor appears in several memoirs of family descendants, which may help to explain his absence from both letters and diaries.

Parents expected to play a role in the selection of their children's mates, particularly the father, and in the event of his death, the appointed guardians, in Elizabeth's case, Eleazar Porter, Esq. and Samuel Marsh, married to Moses Porter's sister Phebe.[52] Elizabeth must have summoned considerable courage to reject the Porter clan's intentions for her future. One wonders if she found it possible to turn to Miss Pen for support in this matter as Williams was Miss Pen's brother. Obviously, if he were intent on marrying Elizabeth, he soon recovered from the disappointment and married the unlucky Lois Dickinson several months after the wedding at Forty Acres.

One of the reasons behind the Porter disapproval of Elizabeth's choice may have been Charles's father, Charles Phelps, Sr. Born in Northampton in 1717, he moved to Hadley in 1743 or 1744, where he lived on the "back street," now Middle Street. Residences of Hadley's "first families" at that time were on West Street, the houses lining the Common. Phelps was descended from one of the families that arrived at Dorchester, Massachusetts, in 1630. A family member who remained in England was private secretary to Oliver Cromwell.[53] Phelps's great-grandfather was among the first settlers of Northampton in 1655. Nevertheless, in the eyes of the Porters, he had none of the criteria for membership in the Hadley elite at that time: kinship with the "River Gods," a degree from Harvard or Yale (although his eldest son Solomon, later ordained, graduated from Harvard in 1762), or a prominent position in local government. Even his appointment to the bench by the Massachusetts governor did not compensate for the absence of these all-important qualifications. There was an altercation between Moses Porter and Charles Phelps, Sr., in 1750 in which Porter appealed a previous judgment against him in favor of Phelps. The jury decided in Moses' favor and awarded him 9 pounds and the court costs.[54] In 1759, eleven Hampshire County justices of the peace, among them Elizabeth's great-uncle, Eleazar Porter, resigned their positions "en masse because serving with Charles Phelps, a recent gubernatorial appointee to the bench, would put them in such company as [they] never inclin'd to keep.'"[55]

Phelps Senior's physical appearance must have made him difficult to ignore. Six foot three inches in height, with a heavy build, he had a loud commanding voice and a love of fine clothes and flashy accessories.[56] As a youth he followed his father's trade of bricklayer, but in his mid-thirties he took up the practice of law, a profession that provided him with a respectable channel for an inordinate love of debate. A number of incidents in which the elder Charles Phelps played a key role suggest that he possessed a contentious personality. He was noted for having "soon developed a reputation for a pompous, exceptionally long-winded style at the bar."[57] In a letter to Governor Clinton of New York in reference to the senior Phelps's involvement in the controversy over Vermont statehood, John Jay made a telling remark. Phelps had been useful in putting the issue before Congress, he wrote, but needed to be "properly directed . . . easily done by encouraging the good opinion he entertains of his own importance!"[58] His law practice brought him more notoriety than respect. A case that received considerable publicity was one in which he defended a group of young dancers accused of disorderly conduct at a local tavern.[59]

Phelps's penchant for taking positions seen as antisocial by the community resulted in his break with the Hadley Meeting in 1760 over the issue of qualifications for admission to full Communion. He publicly endorsed Edwards's belief that conversion should take place before Communion, rejecting the Hadley minister's acceptance of the Halfway Covenant.[60] In eighteenth-century Hadley, one's relation to the Church was a deciding factor in one's relation to the community. In 1762, he was dropped from the county commission.[61] It may have been these events, as well as the attitude of his fellow Justices, that led him to leave Hadley in 1764 for New Marlboro in the New Hampshire Grants (later to become the state of Vermont). His son Charles stayed behind.

Phelps's tendency to take strong adversarial positions was to bring considerable misery to him and his family in later years when he led the opposition to Vermont statehood well beyond the time in which the cause was clearly lost. The Vermont controversy arose some years after his son's marriage to Elizabeth, but the elder Phelps had already caused enough "ungentlemanly" turbulence in Hadley to bolster the family view that Elizabeth was marrying "beneath her rank and standing. . . . Among other groundless apprehensions it was feared that he [Charles Phelps, Jr.] would squander her estate."[62]

Shortly before his marriage, Charles traveled to Boston to buy a carriage. Elizabeth recorded his return: "in the after- noon Mr. Phelps and I took a Ride into town in the new chaise he got at Boston." (May 20,

1770) The young couple certainly attracted attention trotting through Hadley in a new one-horse shay, the extravagant purchase perhaps raising eyebrows along West Street. Carriages were still a rare sight in Hadley in 1770. Judd reports one chair (or chaise) owned by Elisha Porter in 1763, another belonging to Dr. Kellogg in 1768, both well established citizens of Hadley. Such display by a young man may have seemed to echo the ostentation of his father in the eyes of the disapproving Porters.[63]

With Elizabeth's marriage, letters to Miss Pen cease, possibly seeming inappropriate, her confidences to be reserved for her husband. In her new role as Mrs. Phelps, mistress of Forty Acres, the time to take up her pen would not be plentiful.

Yet the desire to write was now unquenchable, and so the diaries continue. The satisfaction that comes from letter writing, thoughts and feelings explored in private, written down and exchanged, responses poured over at leisure, would reappear when distance provided the need to compose a letter.

Chapter III

~

CROSSING THE
THRESHOLD

*"Just six minutes before six in the morning
I was safely delivered of a son."*

ALONG THE Great River in mid-June, remnants of spring linger in multifarious shades of green. Just before dawn, the mist that hovers over the river and dew-soaked ground lends the house at Forty Acres the quality of a dream. Whippoorwills and the resident great horned owl have ceased calling, and now warblers, phoebes, and wood thrushes take up their songs. To the east, a pale apricot hue stains the sky just where it touches the peak of Mount Warner. The windowpanes on the front of the house give back the light, which slowly intensifies. The yellow sun disk appears suddenly and wakens the sleeping house to its solid and tangible self. Insects fly in and out of the mock orange that surrounds the house, drawn by its heady sweetness. From behind the barn a cock sounds a reveille. A horse tethered in the pasture, raises his head expectantly. A door opens, then closes. Early morning sounds— the rhythmic up-and-down of a pump handle, splashing water— reverberate from the side of the barn. Two women on horseback ride into the yard. The south door opens, voices call greetings. The air vibrates with purpose and anticipation. It is Elizabeth's wedding day.

I gave my hand where long before I placed my heart.

ELIZABETH'S DIARY, JUNE 14, 1773

I

Under a rare mid-week heading in her diary, Elizabeth solemnly announces: "a few minutes before 4 oclock I gave my hand to Charles Phelps." (June 14, 1770)[1] The specificity of clocktime lends an emotional charge to the brief statement. The diaries of her girlhood are dutiful records, matter-of-fact, with only very occasional hints of the writer's feelings. It is not until after her marriage that some indication of the inner turbulence preceding her wedding appears in her diary. On the Phelpses' first anniversary, she wrote:

> Blessed be that Providence which made us for each other and at last
> *thru many difficulties* [my emphasis] united us in a bond which . . .
> welcome and sweet as it is Death will break. (June 9, 1771)[2]

Was she romanticizing the courtship period in retrospect? An entry on the third anniversary suggests that resistance to their marriage was of some duration: "three years are past and gone since I gave my hand where long before I placed my heart." (June 13, 1773) If Elizabeth had evidenced a particular attraction to Charles before 1768, the probable year in which he began to work for Mrs. Porter, it is unlikely that he would have been hired.

Once the date for their marriage was established, relatives rose to the occasion and observed the customary ceremonies. Charles Phelps (now

"Mr. Phelps" in the diaries) moved up to Forty Acres from Hadley at the end of May. Preparations for the wedding begin to appear: "Bekah Dick. came home with me—made me a dark brown ducape for my weding Gown and a light brown tafity for Dolly." (June 3, 1770) The simplicity of the fabric for her wedding dress, a plain-woven stout silk cloth, contrasts with the elaborate brocaded silk of her mother's wedding gown. The dark color and sturdy fabric of Elizabeth's wedding dress may reflect practical considerations that were not a primary concern for Elizabeth Pitkin's family. The gown was to be altered twice for her use, in 1788 and again in 1812.[3] A family memoir, which describes Elizabeth as "comely in person, tho of less than the average height, and in later life somewhat inclined to a full figure—tho not corpulent," provides a reason for alterations.[4]

Two days before the wedding, Elizabeth's Aunt Marsh (Phebe Porter) and Lawyer Porter's wife arrived to help with preparations. Her cousin Polly Porter and Charles's sister Dorothy Phelps were "Bride maids." Thirty couples attended the wedding, all sixty guests returning the next day for dinner. Then ritual calls began: "Monday Lawyer Porter and his wife called upon us—many visitors this week." (June 17, 1770) The following Tuesday "Mr. Hop [the minister] made the weding visit." (June 24) Weddings, rarely performed in churches at this time, were community affairs. Once realized, the marriage of Elizabeth Porter and Charles Phelps was sanctioned by the community and the Reverend Mr. Hopkins's visit bestowed the Church's blessing on the couple.

Following her marriage to Charles, Elizabeth duly records her husband's comings and goings and numbers him among her blessings:

> whence is the many good things I enjoy but from the goodness of God while others are poor and can hardly tell where or how to get a support through the world, my table is plentifully spread with good things—God has given me a careful and kind provider in my Husband.[5]

While "a careful and kind provider" is not the romantic description one expects from a bride, Elizabeth's choice of words suggests that she has a new sense of security. She laments the departure of Charles, "my dear husband," when he leaves for Boston to sell cattle, and rejoices on his return: "Mr. Phelps came home. Blessed be the God of all my mercies . . . He's come in safty."[6] In marking her first anniversary, she refers to "the kindest of husbands."[7] "How welcome a meeting," she exclaims, when her "Dear and welcome Husband came home" from yet another trip to Boston.[8] Charles is also a dutiful son-in-law, accompanying Mrs. Porter to Hartford and then returning to bring her back three weeks later. "Kind," "tender," "affectionate" are words that continue to preface Charles's name for a number of years, words that evoke an image of a serene, contented, if not passionate, relationship.

In November, several months after their wedding, Elizabeth wrote, "Satterday I moved my Bed into the Bedroom." Remarkable as the first mention of the placing of furniture in her seven years of diary keeping, this entry prompts speculation as to the difficulty in establishing territorial prerogatives for the young couple in the family homestead. Which room is designated as "*the* Bedroom [my emphasis]"? She refers to "my bed," but not "my bedroom." Where was her bed before? Did the couple not sleep together until now, or have they taken over what was the "master" bedroom? Is Mrs. Porter's position in the household altered by her daughter's marriage? Who was to hold the keys to chambers, cupboards, and chests, their possession an identifying sign of the mistress of the house? Such keys are mentioned in a letter as in Elizabeth's possession, but only after her mother's death.[9] There are no clear answers to these questions, but it is certain that there were numerous adjustments to be made with the arrival of a new head of the household, replacing the order that had existed for fifteen years.

Sermon texts disappear from her diary for lengthy periods in the latter half of 1770. In a few instances she recorded the preacher, but left a blank space for the text, as if she expected to enter it later when a member of the household returned from meeting. The distractions of marriage appeared even greater than the singing lessons of 1768!

Wed . . . in the after-noon Mr. Phelps and I went to Mr. Chester Williams Weding to Loice Dickinson of Hatfield. Thursday Miss Pen was married to Mr. Sam'll Gaylord. Timothy Eastman to Anna Smith, Eaneas Smith to Mary Dickinson, Hannah Montague to one Isaiah Carrier of Belchertown—so much for one day at Hadley." (November 11, 1770)[10]

Weddings continued to abound, and when there was a hiatus in those gatherings, it was funerals that brought people together.

In January 1772, Elizabeth and Charles journeyed to Hartford to visit Elizabeth's Pitkin relatives and to New Haven to see her girlhood friend, Polly Porter, now Mrs. Jonathan Edwards (her husband a clergyman and son of the great preacher and theologian). At Forty Acres, the procession of callers continued to increase:

> Thursday Mrs. Warner and her sister Miriam Church here—Mrs. Parsons and Mrs. Woodbridge here. Fryday Esq. Porters wife [Susannah, daughter of the elder Jonathan Edwards]. Betty Williams here, Mr. Lyman of Hatfield here. Mrs. Parsons, Mrs. Woodbridge went home.[11]

Changes in the weekly list of events in her diaries reflect changes in Elizabeth Phelps's daily routine. Before her marriage, she recounted berrying expeditions, quilting parties, occasional gardening—pastoral pleasures that evoke images of a New World Arcadia, somewhat qualified by days spent working in relatives' households. At that time, she made frequent visits to the homes of female friends, who returned the visit often for several days. In 1767, she mentioned 107 visitors. In 1773, after her marriage, the number rose to 132, but more marked were the increased references to people coming to work, to harvest, and to make clothes.

"Monday we killed hogs" (December 27, 1772); "Monday began to make Soap" (March 28, 1773); "Monday we had twenty five Reapers." (July 17, 1773) Monday appears to be the day, after the laborless Sabbath, on which ambitious tasks were undertaken. Such entries do not appear in the girlhood diaries. These activities, noted for the first time in the diaries, reflect a new sense of proprietorship, of responsibility on her part. Elizabeth, in becoming Mrs. Phelps, also became the virtual mistress of Forty Acres.

II

In the spring following the Phelpses' marriage, new construction announced Charles's ambitions for the farm, now fully under his direction. Hard on the heels of his marriage, he made a series of land purchases: in September 1770, he acquired five acres, in January 1771, eight more, and in February of that year, yet another eight acres. All of these properties are described as "lying in the skirts of Forty Acres."[12] Charles Phelps was completing the expansion and consolidation of the land abutting Forty Acres begun by Moses Porter. He continued to purchase land for the next thirty-five years. When he had exhausted the possibilities of local acquisitions, he bought farms, lots, houses as far away as Cumberland County, New York, and southern Vermont.[13] One imagines that Moses would have applauded his son-in-law.

Between 1752 and 1771, the house remained unchanged. Maintaining the farm in its original condition would have posed quite enough challenge for Mrs. Porter, and temporary managers would have had little incentive to expand. In the spring of 1771, the house acquired an ell; outbuildings began to multiply.[14] Included in the ell was a spacious kitchen with an ample hearth and working space, replacing its predecessor containing the small corner fireplace, which then became a second, less formal parlor. These changes expanded the possibilities for entertaining, which in turn necessitated greater work space. Clearly, the impact of this expansion to the house, as opposed to the farm, fell primarily on Elizabeth. At the same time, the accompanying increase in farmland brought with it a greater workforce and more people to feed. By November of the same year, there was a woodshed, and the following February, an additional well dug near the barn.[15]

The Porters' fears concerning Charles soon proved to be unfounded. Prior to his marriage, his name does not appear on town records as holding offices. As his father's second son, he would not expect to inherit a substantial portion of his father's land holdings, particularly as he chose not to follow his father to the Grants, in what later became Vermont.[16] There is, however, one interesting land purchase by the young Charles Phelps that must have taken place before his marriage. He owned a tract of land in the neighborhood of Southampton, Massachusetts, in common with three other men: Ebenezer Pomeroy of Northampton, Oliver Warner of Hadley, and John Hancock of Boston.[17] The bold signature of the latter, familiar to every American schoolchild, appears on the document of July 19, 1770, when the land was divided among the owners into four parts. Ebenezer Pomeroy was a member of a prominent Northampton family, his grandfather, the king's attorney; Oliver Warner appears on the tax rolls of Hadley in 1770, his holdings placing him among the eight most affluent families of the town; John Hancock, even

prior to the American Revolution, was a prominent and prosperous figure in New England, known for ambitious business ventures.

This early land speculation and the association with older and more
established members of the Connecticut River Valley communities suggest considerable ambition and acumen on the part of Charles Phelps.
His marriage to Elizabeth gave him access to the large farm that, as a second son, primogeniture had deprived him, though the house and land
passed to his mother-in-law and wife.

Charles's orderly account book creates an image of a hardworking,
conscientious, and fair-minded citizen. The only one of his account
books known to have survived dates from 1805 until the end of his life,
and records "dialogues" between employer and employee in the form of
work performed in return for goods acquired.[18] On the left-hand side,
marked debtor, appear items purchased from the Phelpses: pork, cheese,
molasses, vinegar, wool. On the right-hand side, marked contra, are
listed the hours worked by the employee: "driving plow and looking up
sheep," carting ashes and dung, one day's reaping, thrashing oats, and
fanning or winnowing wheat. A reckoning took place after several
months or at the end of the worker's tenure. When both sides balance, a
large X covers each of the two pages.[19]

Accounts with friends are equally specified, such as the one with the
joiner Samuel Gaylord, a frequent visitor to Forty Acres and married to
Elizabeth's close friend, Miss Pen. It was he who was responsible for
much of the woodwork inside the house, as well as chairs, tables, coffins,
and fence repairs. Charles sometimes paid him in cash, but also in services and goods, such as "use of boar to 2 sows," 13 shad fish, 10 bushels
of wheat. Another item that appears frequently in accounts with neighbors is "sundries from your book," a witness to the trust relationship that
existed in these exchanges.

From John Hibbard, Phelps acquired the use of a bull "to 12 cows,"
revealing the scope of his dairy operation in 1808 (as well as the vigor of
Hibbard's bull). The Phelpses pastured their neighbors' cows, for which
they charged a fee, and, in turn, were obliged to pay for damage done by
their livestock to other people's fences. Charles built a number of small
houses on Forty Acres land that he was able to rent or to offer as housing
for hired help, one with a garden and an acre for broom corn to Thad-
deus Hibbard for $14 a year.

In later years, the town paid Charles for serving on the General Court, as well as supervising work on bridges and roads. He was one of the largest taxpayers in Hadley, and thus redeemed some of those taxes by undertaking a broad range of responsibilities on behalf of the town. Entries in the account book suggest that the Phelpses kept a kind of company store for employees. On the debit side appear items such as: felt hat, tobacco, India cotton, molasses, cider, gloves, shawl, and shoes. In a letter to a member of his family, Charles mentions having "just finished the Shop," a term that he applies in the same letter to Dr. Porter's store, which was a commercial enterprise.[20]

There are only a few accounts in Charles's records that appear to be unsettled, one for Thomas Williams, a black man who bought a wide variety of goods from the Phelpses, primarily food, but also leather, a pipe and tobacco. From the kind and amount of debts that he incurred, it seems clear that he was supporting a family. Another unbalanced account was with a young woman, Polly Randall, who worked for the Phelps family for sixteen months.[21] On the debtor side of her page were purchases for gloves, wool, a shawl, shoes, and several visits to the doctor. There were also items such as pork, cheese, butter, and sugar, which she then took home to her aunt in Pelham. The agreement was that she would be paid $1.00 a week. By the end of her tenure at Forty Acres, she owed $25.98 minus $19.00 unpaid wages, leaving a balance of $6.65. No X indicates a settled account. Perhaps Charles decided that these two cases merited clemency on his part.

III

Growing up at Forty Acres, an only child with an ailing mother, Elizabeth must have moved gradually into the role of housekeeper. Yet the change in status that came with marriage was necessarily sudden; on June 13, she is Elizabeth Porter, on June 14, Mrs. Phelps. Not only her perception of herself, but the community's view of her position changed. As a married woman she was now called frequently, often in the middle of the night, to the bedside of women in labor, the sick and dying: "Lawyer Porter's wife taken in Travel the night before Delivered about four oclock this afternoon of a Daughter stillborn—watched with her. Satterday came home." (October 14, 1770); "In the night I was called up—Snells wife in travel—I got home Fryday after-noon all well."

(January 7, 1776) The Phelpses had built a house on their mountain lot for Snell and his wife Molly in 1774, who came to Forty Acres from time to time to weave.[22] The call on a January night was most likely over the snow-covered trail that ascended Mount Warner, easier if moonlit, treacherous if in the middle of a storm. Only rarely does Elizabeth note down weather conditions, in her mind irrelevant where women in labor were the issue.

Marriage brought other new concerns: "Thursday been in some trouble on account of some temporal affairs but to the [sic] O Lord I cry. Fryday found unexpected redress." (March 22, 1772) "Temporal affairs" may translate into "money problems" as scarcity of specie was a perennial problem for New England farmers. The Hampshire common pleas court dealt with large numbers of cases in the early 1770s that concerned disputes over land titles, and most of all, unpaid debts.[23] Whatever the Phelpses' problem, it was of short duration.

It is difficult to discern from the diaries exactly how many people Mrs. Porter and then the Phelpses employed, but names of servants appear more frequently after their marriage. In 1773, three women arrived to do clothes work: spinning, weaving, and tailoring. One of them, unnamed, came in February specifically to weave; Tabby Clark came for several days in April, June, and September; Sarah Smith in December, both Tabby and Sarah hired for tailoring. Some young women came for extended periods. Eunice Pomeroy arrived from Amherst in August of the same year and stayed for two months.[24]

We know from the inventory of Moses Porter's estate that he owned slaves.[25] The document lists "negro man and negro girl" following the enumeration of his land holdings. Elizabeth refers to both of these slaves in her diary of 1768, Zebulon Prutt having run away from her mother, who then sold him to Oliver Warner "for fifty dollars," and Peg, who went back and forth between Forty Acres and the homes of Porter friends and relatives.[26] On one occasion, she left in order to look after the wife of Colonel Partridge's slave, who had just given birth. (October 4, 1768) In 1767 Elizabeth remembers the birthdays of Peg's children, Rose, who was six, and her younger sister, Phillis, two.

Where did all these people sleep? Six bedrooms (referred to as chambers) existed in the original house, two on the ground floor containing fireplaces. (The existing fireplaces on the second floor were added some years later.[27]) The construction of the 1771 ell created a garret with adequate space for several cots. There was certainly room, if not always warmth, to accommodate hired servants and slaves, as well as visitors. If the slaves slept beneath the same roof, it is probable that they ate at separate tables.[28] There is as yet no archaeological evidence as to the size and situation of outbuildings prior to the 1770s. For slaves to reside within the main house in New England was not unusual. Often purchased at a very young age, slaves frequently shared in the family life, including instruction of the household's children in reading, along with the young white servants.

Another responsibility that now became Elizabeth's was the health of servants, some of whom seemed accident-prone: "This night our Little Boy Simon Baker Broke his toes at the saw mill." (November 5, 1770) Several months later he cut his foot. But disease also demanded her attention. In January 1773, Simon contracted "quincy" (tonsillitis). What must be an almost complete compendium of diseases afflicting New Englanders in the latter half of the eighteenth century runs through the pages of the diaries: the colic, the itch (scabies), rattles (croup), throat canker (diphtheria), consumption (tuberculosis), King's Evil (scrofula), pneumonia, whooping cough, measles, childbed fever among them. A small partitioned wooden box exists at Forty Acres, believed to have belonged to Elizabeth Phelps. Lingering odors suggest that it once contained herbal medicines, the box a veritable pharmacopoeia. With handles, it is useful for carrying as well as storing and conjures up an image of Elizabeth's bedside visits, bringing soothing remedies along with moral support. Later correspondence evidences a lively interest in medicinal concoctions. There is no reason to believe that she acted as a midwife, but rather as a woman of means endowed with a strong sense of social responsibility and curiosity concerning physical disorders.

Natural disasters took on new meaning for her when they threatened the security of her household:

Wednesday a very Remarkable experience of Divine preservation. A flash of Lightenin came Down our Ketching Chimney almost filled the Room with the Flame—Three persons in the Room, viz. Beriah Smith, one Bascomb of Amherst (accidently here) our younest Negro Girl Phillis. All shocked but none hurt—no person but those that have felt it can conceive the Noise the terrible Noise when it strikes the Dwelling where we are. . . . The Lightning melted the

tramel, hand iron, shovel and a spike left on the edge of the floor
near the hearth. (July 12, 1772)[29]

Lightning was the cause of a considerable number of house fires in the
days before lightning rods and some fatalities when people were hit
directly. In Calvinist New England, electrical storms were seen as manifestations of God's wrath. A number of churchmen criticized Franklin's
invention of the lightning rod, which the inventor describes in "Poor
Richard for 1753," believing it to be a sacrilegious refusal to see God's
hand in the event.[30] The Phelps family offered thanks at the next meeting for their miraculous survival.

In the spring of 1772 Peg departed for what seemed to be the final
time:

> this Day our Peg who has Lived with us near 18 years of her own
> Choice Left us and two children and was sold to One Capt. Fay of
> Benington with a Negro man from this town all for the sake of
> being his wife. (April 3)[31]

The use of the passive voice, "was sold," is ambiguous. The phrase "of her
own Choice" implies that Peg was no longer in bondage. In the previous
August, Elizabeth had reported that "Peg went out for herself."[32] Who
then benefited from the sale? Perhaps her marriage to a slave automatically included her in the sale of her husband, though it is surprising that
she would forgo her freedom, "all for the sake of being his wife," a phrase
that reveals Elizabeth's vexation with their former slave.[33] Peg's two children, Rose now eleven, and Phillis seven, continued to live at Forty
Acres. Children of a female slave became the property of the master
under whom they were born.[34] Now both of Moses Porter's slaves were
gone from Forty Acres, leaving behind a young generation of slaves.

Another slave, Caesar, came to Forty Acres with Charles Phelps.[35]
Charles purchased him in March of 1770 from his father, now living in
New Marlboro, for 66 pounds, 13 shillings, 4 pence. Caesar first appears
in Elizabeth's diaries on May 26, 1771: "This day [Wednesday] Mr.
Phelps set out with Cesar to sell him. Thursday returned with him."
Boston was the chief trading site in Massachusetts. If Charles set out for
Boston, he must have changed his mind en route, as Boston was ordinar-
ily a two-day journey. Or did Caesar convince Charles that he should keep

him? In either case, Caesar was back at Forty Acres for the time being, and continues to appear in the diaries, primarily when his health is an issue: "Last Tuesday cesar froze his finger." (December 22, 1771) "Thursday very much surprized with Cesars hand . . . he has had a terrible Swelled hand this month." (June 4, 1775)[36]

Caesar did leave Hadley in 1776, but neither to go free nor to another owner. Charles Phelps, Sr. had written to his son in February 1776, suggesting that Caesar come to New Marlboro to work for him. His hand continued to be a problem and Phelps believed that he could develop tools adapted for Caesar, making certain tasks possible. He mentioned another slave who would be living with Caesar as a source of companionship and proposed to allow him to make some maple sugar for his own profit.[37] But the escalating crisis in the Colonies was to send Caesar in another direction.

In the same letter, the elder Phelps referred to Caesar's relationship with Peg, who had gone to Bennington, not far from New Marlboro where the Senior Phelps resided, when she left Forty Acres with her new husband. "I am persuaded," he wrote, "that he is more peckish & fretful in Pegs resistance of his former Indulgences and freedom with her." He speaks of Peg's "Peremtory Denial & resistances of His—those former gratifications," which raises the possibility that Caesar fathered Rose and Phillis.

Concerns for the welfare of "our folks," which encompassed the extended family, servants, and slaves, included their spiritual, as well as physical health. When the twelve-year-old Simon Parcus came to Forty Acres as an indentured servant, Elizabeth prayed: "O may we do our Duty to him and will God bless him and us." (April 3, 1774) During his tenure, Simon became essentially a member of the family.[38] Contracts signed for the indenture of young males promise that they "be instructed in the art or mystery of husbandry," provided with "Reasonable Meat Drink Washing Lodging Physick & Nursing in Case of Sickness, and, at the time of their departure, provided "with two decent suits of apparel proper for their station in life." Contracts took care of practical considerations, but concern for the spiritual welfare of the household arose from the habit of thought expressed in the early Calvinist covenants.

To some extent, slaves shared a similar status as that of indentured servants in Colonial New England, usually without the contracted promise of an end to their servitude at an agreed-upon tenure. The Massachusetts law of 1641 gave to the slave: "all the liberties and Christian usages which the law of God established in Israel doth morally require."[39] Yet the slave trade was generally accepted as a legitimate enterprise along with lumbering and fishing, with only a few voices raised against the practice, such as that of Judge Samuel Sewall.[40] The wording of the law removed the issue of slaveholding from that of civil rights to the sacred realm where few churchgoers challenged what they perceived as the law of God. Slave-owners managed to live with the irreconcilable contradiction between what they believed to be a "divinely ordained" slavery and the Christian belief in the worth of all individuals.

As a woman, Elizabeth knew where lay the disenfranchised population's one claim to equality and that was in the eyes of God, a view that had been endorsed by theologians, including Cotton Mather, many years before. She saw the spiritual welfare of the slaves as another of her God-given responsibilities as mistress of Forty Acres. On several occasions she stayed home so that their slave Rose could attend meeting. In the diary entry that reports Caesar's swollen hand, Elizabeth prays that it be "for his spiritual good," admonishing him in the same terms with which she addresses herself when suffering from the canker.[41]

Nothing in Elizabeth's diaries questions the system of slaveholding.[42] Frequent references to her "station in life" reflect her acceptance of the existing establishment, though she held her own Utopian vision of what that establishment should be. In the early months of 1775, she was preoccupied with the illness of Phillis. The younger of the two female slaves, Phillis was nine years old when she contracted what appears to have been tuberculosis. On January 1, Elizabeth mentioned taking the little girl to the doctor, "she poorly." Her prayers that the child's life be lengthened indicate that her disease was already well advanced. Two weeks later she stayed home from meeting to look after Phillis. In February, Charles took Phillis to see another physician, Dr. Mather, in Northampton. There were more visits to the doctor in March. A six-board chest still resides in the upstairs hall, which Elizabeth brought down into the kitchen to make a bed for the little girl.[43] In this way she kept the sick child in the warmest room of the house, near the fire, and under constant surveillance. The deep chest protected her from sparks igniting the mattress and from drafts. On Sunday, April 16, the family asked the meeting to pray for Phillis, "being very low." On the following Friday, Elizabeth wrote: "a Little after eight our poor little Phillis left this world."

Several days before Phillis's death her sister Rose, aged fourteen, had given birth to a daughter. Mrs. Alien (Elizabeth Allen),[44] a midwife from Northampton, came to assist with the birth, and a slave belonging to Oliver Warner moved to Forty Acres to look after Rose for three weeks, the customary convalescent period after childbirth. The deceased little Phillis was remembered in the naming of Rose's baby and in Elizabeth's journal on the first anniversary of her death. In the absence of Peg during Phillis's extended illness, Elizabeth had become a surrogate mother. Such a relationship would account for the unusual outpouring of grief in the diary, which so often mentions deaths in very few words, recording date and cause only.

There were certainly economic reasons for the diligent care of the slaves' health by their masters and mistresses. In their capacity as productive "property," like the farmer's horses and oxen, their good health added to their owners' greater potential for prosperity. Nevertheless, there are records of close attachments between master, mistress, and slaves in Colonial New England. The historian Lorenzo Johnston Greene finds more instances of these relationships and of humane treatment in New England settlements than in the South or the northern province of New York, and accounts for it in several ways: the Mosaic Law that formed the basis of a number of Colonial New England institutions; the fewer number of slaves in the North that made uprisings unlikely; the more varied occupations of the slaves that brought them into closer contact with their masters and mistresses.[45] In the case of little Phillis, it is clear that Elizabeth played an important role in her rearing. Still, there is an ambiguity in the relationships between owners and slaves. Emotional attachments existed within the context of property ownership. However close owner and slave became, the economic implications of ownership stood in the path of true kinship.[46]

Although prominent New England leaders, Sewall and John Adams among them, denounced the practice of slaveholding as contrary to Christian teaching (let alone humane decency), it was not until 1783 that slavery was outlawed in Massachusetts. A bill proposed to the state legislature in 1767 was amended numerous times, then voted down. Several attempts made prior to the Revolution were passed in both houses and vetoed by Governor Hutchison, who declared that no authority had been granted to him by the crown to sign such a bill.[47] It would take even longer to bring an end to the slave trade. Slave trading was a vital part of the triangular system that took place between Massachusetts ports, England, and the West Indies.[48] Not until the economic, philosophical, and political changes that came in the wake of the American Revolution was slavery eradicated in all its forms in New England.

III

With the end of her intimate confessions to Miss Pen, Elizabeth confided instead in her diary. On October 13, 1771, she heard a sermon preached by Mr. Olcott in Hatfield on a passage from St. Luke's Gospel that particularly spoke to her, in which Christ admonishes Martha for complaining that her sister Mary leaves her alone working in the kitchen while she sits at Christ's feet:

> Martha, Martha, thou art careful and troubled about many things, but one thing is needful, and Mary hath chosen that good part, which shall not be taken away from her. (Luke: 10:40–42)

Elizabeth reflected on the sermon in her diary: "a charming sermon indeed—it was he taught us all our Duty—the same temper and discomposure troubled me thro the last week." Inevitably, as the mistress of a large productive farm, she identified with Martha, the grumbling workhorse. It would be interesting to know, even now, what Mr. Olcott had to say on that topic.

This story of Mary and Martha has become emblematic for the conflict experienced by women who feel torn between practical demands on their time and their desire for spiritual nourishment: the active versus the contemplative life. And for Elizabeth, living a Christian life hung on her ability to reflect on the Scriptures, to ponder their significance in her life. In a society that also valued industry and frugality, the dilemma was a real one, especially for a scrupulous and introspective woman such as Elizabeth. How could she nourish her spirit while also nourishing husband, mother, friends, servants and "twenty-five reapers"? How could she sit at the feet of Wisdom, as did Mary, while—Martha-like—she must supervise the manufacture of soap, candles, cheese, and sausages? The sermon's endorsement of Mary's contemplative life as one's "Duty" sanctioned Elizabeth's search for a more spiritual life; yet that search demanded resistance to social convention and domestic expectations, for the role of Martha was accepted as the female condition. A formal education would have endorsed time dedicated to thought, but such a prize was rarely awarded to women, and not to Elizabeth.

Eighteenth-century women had no civic powers; they could not attend Harvard College, nor could they ascend the pulpit to preach. Laurel Thatcher Ulrich notes that "hoping for an eternal crown, they never asked to be remembered on earth. And they haven't been." It was in elegies, memorials, and funeral sermons that a limited number of women received public attention.[49] Death alone brought acknowledgment of their worth.

Elizabeth had not ceased to question her readiness for that important step toward salvation—Church membership, but on February 3, 1771, she announced:

> This day Publickly Dedicated myself to God and Joined my self to his Church and Now most mercifull Father Grant me thy Grace to Honour the [sic] by an obedient Walk, may thy Good Spirit always be ready to my assistance and encouragement and now I desire always to view myself as not my own but entirely thine—may all my sins be washed away in Christs Blood for his sake may I have Eternal Life. Amen.[50]

The fervor implicit in this prayer would not, certainly could not, be maintained by Elizabeth Phelps day after day, week after week. But the commitment, so seriously debated in her letters to Miss Pen, was a serious one: her soul's arduous journey toward salvation. Following her marriage, her diaries record that journey, and the obstacles encountered along the way.

A lengthy passage appears on February 24, 1771, in which she reflects on her "neglect of Duty in a very tender branch of it." The passage continues:

> as it tends much to my comfort in Life and peace of Conscience. . . . Having been for a long time greatly troubled at the conduct of a near and Dear friend do remember I have not made my case known to him praying for his power—do therefore now plead for humility

and shame at my self Neglect now beging a merciful God to help and may I have occasion to say as in time past the Lord has helped and eased me of the heavy burden but if it may not be removed grant me patience.[51]

Who was it that she neglected? Miss Pen? Worthington? Certainly not Charles, her husband of eight months. The words "for a long time," "heavy burden," and her appeals to God "in time past" suggest that she is referring to her mother. Read in that light, the passage uncovers a darker side of her girlhood than appears in the diary references to visits with friends, berrying expeditions, and quilting parties. The likely consequences of her mother's prolonged use of opium cast a shadow over Elizabeth's early life in the large house at Forty Acres. She must have participated in her mother's bouts of anxiety and insomnia and experienced fear when witnessing spells of delirium.

Elizabeth does not provide the answer, but the increasing introspection in the diaries reveals much about the character of their author, if not the names of those who provoke strong feelings and remorse. Her relationships with people close to her become subjects for scrutiny. Rather than berating the source of her suffering, in this instance she chastises herself for neglect.

The sermon text for March 3, 1771, "whatever thy hand findeth to do do it with all thy might," is written in full rather than the usual abbreviation.[52] Her diaries reflect increased attention to Mr. Hopkins's preaching. On March 10, 1771, she heard Hopkins preach on a verse from Proverbs 17:16: "Wherefore is there a price in the hand of a fool to get wisdom, seeing he hath no heart to it?" During the succeeding week she wrote:

Wednesday morn. A sorrowful heart by my own foolishness—must always be medling. O that experience of the naughtiness of my heart serve to my humiliation and greater care . . . this day especially to be spent with more than common sobriety and reflection on my own unworthiness.[53]

Elizabeth's severe self-castigation also reveals—certainly unintentionally—engaging character traits. Meddling can be an unwelcome intrusion; it can also be an indication of beneficial interest in the welfare of others, as in her readiness to provide medicinal advice. That interest is borne out in her willingness to drop whatever task was at hand, awake at the small hours of the night, and respond to the many requests for her presence in the sickroom. She was later to become the official recorder of births, marriages and deaths for the town of Hadley, keeping careful records until within a year of her death. It is also true that she paid particular attention to the number of months between weddings and births:

> May 10, Sun. . . . Dan West and his wife made public confession for the sin of fornication—she went hardly seven months and upon our last Sacrament Day Timothy Stockwell and his wife did the Like . . . she went just seven months. (1772)[54]

Confiding information such as this to her diary may have satisfied the urge to gossip. Her resolve to behave "with more than common sobriety" suggests an effort on her part to suppress any untoward tendency for levity. Fortunately, she was unable to adhere to that resolve.

IV

There is a gap of six weeks in Elizabeth Phelps's diary between August 2 and September 13, 1772, explained subsequently in a lengthy entry announcing the birth of their son, christened Moses Porter. No mention of her pregnancy appears in the diary prior to this time, unless a reference in May to being "taken poorly" (often the phrase used to describe the onset of labor) suggests a threatened miscarriage. At that time, Mrs. Crouch, widow of the family's former doctor, came to see Elizabeth specifically.

Two days before her labor began, she rode into town in the evening to drink tea with her sister-in-law. There was no abating of her social and domestic activities in the preceding weeks. The lack of reference to the upcoming event masks the anxiety that must have preceded the onset of labor. With the birth of her healthy child, she expressed joy and relief expanding on words drawn from the fourth Psalm:

> Gladness is put into my heart and a song of praise in my mouth; mercy and Loving Kindness has been shewn me from the Lord—

the Living Mother of a Living perfect Child, wonderful Deliverance. (September 13, 1772)[55]

The high incidence of stillborn infants and of mothers' deaths in childbirth in the eighteenth century made apprehension inevitable. The day before Porter, as his family would call him, was born, the ten-day-old son of Elizabeth's cousin died. There is no sign of the anticipation and elaborate preparation that precede many desired births in this century, as if such attention might tempt Fate.

Babies had been born at Forty Acres—the children of the slave Peg and the premature birth and death of Betty Goodrich's child; yet it was twenty years before the house, conceived by Moses Porter as a family seat, became the birthing place of a member of the family.

Porter Phelps's entrance into the world was fraught with uncertainty. In the first year of his life, serious illnesses and an accident from scalding water made his survival into adulthood seem uncertain. Deaths continued to occur close to home: a cousin's infant daughter lived only ten hours, a neighbor's child, just under one year of age, died of the "rattles." Perhaps the birth of her own child made Elizabeth particularly attentive to illness and death among children of the community: "Our folks had the Measels but thro Divine Goodness all recovered," Elizabeth wrote on October 4, when Moses was just two months old.[56] Again and again the diaries record infant deaths. When one of Porter's illnesses kept her from attending meeting, she prayed: "O God, enable me to stand to what I have done in giving of it to thee in Baptism . . . we are all in thy hand as clay in the hand of the Potter." (December 6, 1772)[57] Elizabeth continued to call on the sick and bereaved, now carrying her baby with her. Leaving him behind merited mention in her diary. On November 22, 1772, she went to meeting: "I left my dear Little Son (for the first time) at home—his Dadda stayed."[58]

Work on the house continued. Charles's father came down from Vermont, returning to his old trade in order to plaster the new kitchen. Joiners arrived to finish up "our Old Ketching Chamber." (October 24, 1773)[59] These finishing touches completed the additions begun in 1771. While private spaces for reading, reflecting, and writing increased, the time to use them decreased as the house embraced a new generation.

Chapter IV

~

CONFLICT AND LOSS

Ferryman's house on the Connecticut River

Across the Common, Hadley, Massachusetts

War! The very word sends a chill down her spine. Recollections from her childhood burst through the scar tissue that time has mercifully created—the gathering of uniformed men on the common, muskets, swords, a cannon, all the tools of death assembled. Women and children cluster on the sidelines, there to see off sons, husbands, fathers. Emotions run high—excitement among the little boys who march up and down the common, shouldering sticks in imitation of a militia muster, thinly disguised apprehension on the faces of the women, an array of feelings flickering over the faces of the men, most too young to have experienced the war that killed her father.

What will happen to us, she wondered, when all the young men have gone off to battle? Will her mother's story be reenacted? Houses no longer safe havens, targets for attack, theft, fire? And the people inside? Now the village of Hadley seems distant from Forty Acres, and Boston too near, the woods to the north and east no longer a protective wall, but a place for Regular scouts to hide.

Lines from Psalm 27 that she memorized as a child are suddenly weighted with meaning and provide her with the words that she needs to stifle her fears:

Though an host should encamp against me, my heart shall not fear;
Though war should rise against me, in this I will be confident . . .
For in the time of trouble he shall hide me in his pavilion . . .
In the secret of his tabernacle shall he hide me.

My heart shall not fear, Oh Lord, deliver me from fear, she prays.

a mighty force it is said is coming against this land.

ELIZABETH'S DIARY, MAY 11, 1776

I

The uprisings in Boston, even the massacre that took place there on March 5, 1770, do not appear in Elizabeth's diary, and in the early years of her marriage, Boston was outside the sphere of Elizabeth's attention except for Charles's trips to that city's market. Yet the town of Hadley was not oblivious to the events in the eastern part of Massachusetts. Believing that the source of the problems lay with the royal deputies, the citizens of Hadley resolved at the town meeting of 1772 that "our grievances be made known to His Majesty."[1] By November of that year, the Colonists' disaffection with British rule had intensified. Samuel Adams proposed that the Boston Town Meeting establish a Committee of Correspondence directed to send letters to outlying communities, asking for their commitment to the cause of liberty.

Responses to Samuel Adams's attempt to rouse Hampshire County towns to resistance were mixed, as were the citizens' reactions to the Boston Tea Party in December of 1773.[2] Hadley residents were predominantly Whigs, and responded positively to the requests from Boston for support. Both Eleazar and Elisha Porter were officers, first in the militia, then in the Continental Army. Charles Phelps, Jr., his father and two brothers were all described as "constant in their fidelity to the patriot cause until the war ended in 1783."[3]

With the majority of influential families, in both Hadley and Hatfield, Whig in their sympathies, Tories, such as Israel Williams, were in an uncomfortable position. Although Williams, prosperous merchant and Hatfield's most prominent citizen, was firmly established as a "River God," he did not escape ostracism by his community. The British governor of Massachusetts had empowered Colonel Williams to commission officers in the local militia. After a single training under these officers in the fall of 1773, the local militia refused further training under them, forcing the officers' resignation.[4]

The restrictions placed on both trade and self-government in Massachusetts by the British Parliament's passing of the Coercive Acts in 1774 provoked consternation throughout the Colony. Local participation in government through the House of Representatives and town meetings was severely curtailed.[5] The closing of the Boston port to all seaborne trade in June of 1774 and the Massachusetts Government Act forbidding town meetings brought the entire colony to its feet and elicited sympathy for the plight of Massachusetts from other colonies. A sense of impending disaster begins to appear in Elizabeth's diaries:

> The People of this Land are greatly threatened with Cruelty and oppression from the Parliament of Great Britain—the Port of Boston is now and has been ever since the first day of this month shut up and greater Callamities are Daily expected.[6]

Leaders of the resistance to these acts sent a letter on June 8 to all the towns calling for "concrete and concerted action," specifically asking the towns to "cut off all commercial action" with the mother country by August 31, 1774."[7] Colonel Israel Williams was imprisoned in 1776 when it was discovered that he had stocked his store with a large shipment from England. His argument that his aim was purely that of profit rather than support of the British position gained his release, but he continued to be regarded with suspicion.[8]

The closing of the port of Boston further fueled patriots' desire to boycott importation from England. As early as 1765, Colonial leaders had encouraged a return to home production of clothing, which had diminished on the coast with the increasing availability of imported goods. In the rural western part of Massachusetts, spinning, weaving, and dyeing of fabrics continued to be an important part of household production, even within affluent families, well into the nineteenth century.[9] These activities could not be seen then as the protests that they were in some coastal towns, but Elizabeth's diaries reveal an increase in clothes making beyond her customary quilting of petticoats and fashioning of bonnets for herself and friends.[10] She went elsewhere to acquire new skills: "I went to Landlord Smiths to spool yarn." "Fryday went down to Mr. Thomas Smiths to get Lydia to show me how to make a pair of Breeches for the soldiers." "Mrs. Dean here in the fore-noon to shew me about some colouring."[11] Perhaps her choice for her wedding gown of dark brown ducape, a cloth French in origin, reflected the early boycott against British imports.

In October 1774, the town of Hadley voted to erect a powder house, "round in compass equal to eight feet square." Four and a half barrels of powder and a "great gun" were purchased as well.[12] In some communities, Maypoles were transformed into declarations of freedom. Hadley's pole rose to an unprecedented 130 feet, the highest liberty pole in the colony and the pride of the Whig Club that erected it.[13]

These preparations were given an emotional charge from the pulpit. On June 19, 1774, the Reverend Hopkins preached on bondage "spiritual and temporal." He chose as his sermon text, Psalm 53, verse 6:

Oh that the salvation of Israel were come out of Zion! When God bringeth back the captivity of his people, Jacob shall rejoice, and Israel shall be glad.

The governor of Massachusetts, undoubtedly in response to directions from Britain, refused to proclaim a general fast day in the Colony, customary in times of crisis, times menaced by "the Dark aspect of our Publick affairs" (Elizabeth's words). Therefore, individual towns declared their own fasts, Hadley among them. The Reverend Joseph Lyman, the minister from the neighboring community of Hatfield, preached on the appropriate goal for a communal fast, drawing his text from Isaiah, Chapter 58: "to loose the bands of wickedness, to undo the heavy burdens, and to let the oppressed go free, and that ye break every yoke."[14]

The Congregational Church had grown out of resistance, of refusal to bow to an authority perceived as subverting the Christian message. Although there were a few ministers with Tory sympathies in neighboring towns, among them Amherst, Deerfield, and Longmeadow, the majority of Congregational ministers were Whig in sympathy; some actively preached rebellion. Lyman, his church often attended by the Phelps family, drew frequently upon scriptural passages referring to the bondage of Israel as a parallel to that of the colonies. A young man recently appointed to the church in Hatfield, he is credited with turning his congregation from the Tory sympathies of Israel Williams to the Whig cause.[15]

The Colonists' pent-up anger with the British government found expression close to home. Elizabeth described her husband's journey to Springfield to sit on the Grand Jury in August 1774. He discovered on arrival that a mob had gathered, forcibly shutting down the courts. Bells summoned what was estimated to be several thousand people to a march on the Hampshire County courthouse. Their intention was to obtain renunciations of royal commissions from each of the justices. They succeeded and laid the groundwork for more mass initiatives.[16]

Tensions ran high, rumors rampant. On September 3 of the same year, Elizabeth's diary reports:

> Satterday just at night my Husband came home from town with terrible news that the army of forces which are stationed in Boston had begun to fight and were coming out into the Country spreading desolation where ever they came. The men rallied from all parts, vast numbers.[17]

The brevity of her diary entries does not reveal the images of desolation that must have filled Elizabeth's thoughts—fields trampled, crops destroyed, houses burned to the ground, indiscriminate killing—women and children as well as soldiers, the fruits of this fertile valley laid waste, and all the promise of their young family come to nothing.

In response to this alarm, Charles saddled his horse in order to meet up with the Militia. "Then," Elizabeth wrote, "did I in a good measure realize parting with my dear Husband." When he arrived in Hadley, he found that someone else had taken his gun.[18] Arms were in short supply and stored in a common armory to be available in the event of an emergency. The alarm proved to be exaggerated. General Gage, in charge of the British forces, had ordered troops inland in search of Whig gunpowder. They returned to Boston after a short foray into the countryside, but messengers had already spread the news, increasingly magnified as the word moved farther from Boston.

The meetinghouse served as a source of information as well as the place where political, economic, and military events received providential meaning. Although Hadley's Reverend Hopkins possessed a style of preaching remembered in later years as "entirely without action," even "dull and languid," he, like the Reverend Lyman, rose to the escalating crisis.[19] On November 13, 1774, he preached on the current "very dark" affairs and supported the determinations of the Association of Ministers that "each town ought to set apart some times for prayer frequently and sometimes fasting."[20]

Not only did the British governor refuse to declare statewide fasts, he would not exercise his prerogative and declare the traditional Thanksgiving Day. That he recognized the power of these religious observances to subvert royal authority is evident in his refusal. Now local congregations and the Provincial Congress, the latter independently organized by the Whigs in October 1774, declared fasts.

News took at least two days to travel to western Massachusetts from the coast, but it was possible that the news was traveling only hours in front of the British army. On April 23, Sunday afternoon, Charles rode eastward to Brookfield to bring back information regarding yet another rumor of battle. His venturing alone into uncertain territory was certainly disquieting for Elizabeth. The specter of her father's death in the French and Indian Wars could not have disappeared. Although no battles from the earlier wars took place in the vicinity of Hadley, there were a number of people still living who were able to give graphic accounts of the encounters that took the lives of both soldiers and civilians twenty years before.[21]

Charles returned safely the next day with the news: "last Wednesday the Troops and our men had a Battle, numbers lost on both sides but it seems as if we were most favoured." (April 23, 1775) In this way, Elizabeth reports the confrontation between the British army and the patriots in Lexington. Thus the war had officially begun, "a Civil war" Elizabeth calls it "in all the Horrors of it." (June 4, 1775)[22] She was not alone in seeing this battle as the beginning of a *civil* war. In the French and Indian Wars, New England farmers had fought side by side with English soldiers. All of the early settlers left family behind in England when they sailed for Massachusetts. Ties to family, however distant in place and time, and allegiance to the king, however much he misbehaved, were not easily shed.

Despite minimal training and limited access to guns and powder, more than 10,000 Minutemen from Massachusetts communities marched toward Boston following the battle at Lexington, not knowing how many experienced British Regulars they would confront.[23] Forty-six Hadley men, under the command of Captain Eliakim Smith, went to Lexington in response to the alarm and then to the vicinity of Boston where they remained for varying periods of one to five months. The names of 183 soldiers appearing on the Hadley lists during the Revolution would have included recruits from surrounding communities, as the town's census for 1776 lists only a total of 681 inhabitants.[24] Approximately sixty from the lists joined the Continental Army, at least twenty of them enlisting for three years.

Many farmers were prepared to fight under their own officers and close to home, but were suspicious of standing armies, associating them with British tyranny.[25] This attitude created recruiting problems for the Continental Army. Despite General Washington's urging, men did not want to enlist for the duration, especially as the fighting moved far from home. Both Eleazar and Elisha Porter fought in the battle at Lexington as officers in the Continental Army. Charles Phelps, on the other hand, did not join the army, nor did some of his neighbors such as Samuel Gaylord and his brother-in-law, Lemuel Warner, though they were ready to take up arms as members of the Militia when necessary. Commitments to the Militia were for short terms of three or six months. Just before the occupation of Boston in March 1775, Charles traveled to Boston with one of his hired men and a team, presumably going to the market. Subsequent trips in that directions were to Cambridge, then the northern army base. With the port of Boston closed and the city occupied, Charles's journeys to Cambridge responded to the base's urgent need for supplies. He may have seen the managing of his large, productive farm as a more effective contribution to the Revolution than joining Washington's army, and he may have found a substitute.

It was on one of Charles's trips to Cambridge that Caesar was delivered to the Continental Army. The plan to send him to Charles's father in Vermont had changed with Washington's appeal for recruits. Caesar's induction into the army with a disabled hand that had prevented him from performing certain tasks at Forty Acres evidences Washington's desperate need for more soldiers. Slaves were easier to hold to extended commitments than were independent New England farmers. Caesar enlisted for a three-year stint, perhaps preferring a status shared by free and slaves alike.

A number of prosperous farmers were able to send slaves or white servants in their place or hire other replacements. These substitutions were not needed until the summer of 1776 when volunteers no longer supplied the necessary numbers.[26] Then the Massachusetts General Court instituted the draft. Whether Caesar went in Charles's stead or joined of his own accord is unclear. As Robert Gross has pointed out, "drafts favored the rich."[27] Charles was appointed to a committee, formed in 1779, to fine those "delinquent in war service." It is unlikely then that community leaders viewed him as derelict in his military duty.

Several months after his induction, Caesar wrote to his master from Fort Ticonderoga, complaining of the officer under whom he served. He had not received the wages that were his due. This negligence affected both slave and master. Although he would receive the same wages as white soldiers, most slaves were obliged to give half, if not all, to their master.[28] The possibility of being sold at some future date was another of Caesar's concerns:

> Sir I take this oppertunity to enform you that I dont entend to live with Capt Cranston if I can help it and I would Be glad if you would send me a letter that I may git my Wagers for I have not got any of my Wagers and I want to know how all the Folks Do at home and I Desire you Prayers for me while in the Sarves and if you Determin to Sel me I want you shud send my Stock and Buckel So no more at Present But I Remain your Ever Faithful Slave
>
> Sezar Phelps[29]

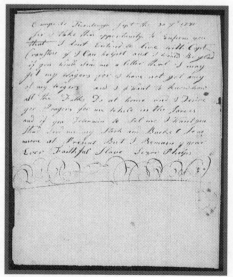

(Courtesy of Amherst College Archives and Special Collections)

The poignancy of the mention of his two possessions is intensified by his signature, Sezar Phelps. In the majority of the documents cited by the historian Greene, slaves had no last name, their signatures simply their first names followed by the word "Negro."[30] On being freed, slaves often took the surnames of their "first or favorite owner."[31] Whatever the Phelpses' feelings toward him, Caesar expresses a warm attachment to his owners. He undoubtedly chose his words carefully in this letter, which is an appeal, but his desire to know "how all the Folks Do at home" and his request for prayers ring true.

The letter raises questions as to Caesar's education. Was it written by a white soldier for him or was it in his own hand? The handwriting is legible, embellished with extravagant loops at the bottom of the page; the message is clearly articulated. Joshua Boston, a former slave of Colonel Eleazar Porter and a soldier in the Revolution, could read and write.[32] Part of the obligation that slaveowners in New England felt toward their slaves included reading instruction to enable them to read the Bible by themselves. Writing instruction was not automatically joined to that of reading, but a number of slaves acquired that ability, useful in their diverse occupations in Northern households. When eventually freed, those ex-slaves who had learned to write were in a better position to establish their own businesses. Ironically, free Negroes had fewer economic opportunities than slaves because of social prejudices, confining them largely to domestic service.[33]

Despite the possibilities for flight during the Revolution, the slaves at Forty Acres remained faithful to the Phelps family. Even Peg, who came and went at will, returned on several occasions. It was the indentured servants who were most susceptible to the talk of liberty. On April 4, 1779, Elizabeth reported that "one John White had run from us, stole a coat and pair of Breeches." One week later, "our Josiah Gylbert run away."[34] White runaways were more likely to escape notice than black runaways.

II

Hard on the heels of the battle at Lexington and Concord came word of defeat at Breed's Hill (usually referred to as the battle of Bunker Hill). The battle was far more costly in lives lost for the British than for the

Minutemen, but the news that ground was lost to the enemy certainly increased dread of what was to come. How long would it take for fighting to be within earshot? Another fast day in May 1775 and another sermon from Mr. Lyman: "Be not afraid nor dismayed by reason of this great multitude; for the battle is not your's, but God's."[35] Lyman's sermon did not calm Elizabeth's fears: "What is in the Womb of Providence we know not," she wrote, "great events seem to be portended." She adds her own prayer:

> if it may be thy will command a peace . . . give us not up to final Destruction, hear our prayers be entreated for us, Let us again enjoy thy prosperity and thy Blessing.

Although no battles were taking place in the immediate vicinity, British prisoners were marched through the streets of Hadley on the way to the Northampton jail. On February 19, 1776, the Reverend Lyman preached a sermon urging men to enlist in the Quebec campaign. Several weeks later, the local regiment set out for Quebec. The people of Hadley gathered on the common to see them off, knowing that their soldiers would face experienced troops on arrival.[36]

A month later Elizabeth's diary reports joyful news from a different quarter: "This day the Regulars Left Boston which they have held as their Garison this year—Glory to God." Dr. James Thacher, surgeon for the rebel forces, viewed the evacuation of British troops from Dorchester Heights. This account is one of a number of eyewitness reports recorded in a journal that covers the entire duration of the war. Thacher estimated the number of evacuees to be about 10,000, consisting of 7,575 troops, plus staff, marines, sailors, and some Tories with their families.[37] This news brought relief from the fear of more forays from eastern Massachusetts, but the threat of enemy attacks from the north and west was still very real, and would become more so as news trickled back to Hadley from Quebec.

A month after their departure in early March, the American soldiers arrived on the Quebec Plains of Abraham, where they found deep snow and an outbreak of smallpox. Details of this expedition reached the ears of Hadley residents as members of the regiment found their way back to Hadley. Soldiers, of necessity, inoculated each other, an undertaking fraught with danger. The serum consisted of matter drawn from a pustule on an afflicted person, which was then injected into the arm of the person to be inoculated.[38] A soldier from Hadley described the situation: "no doctor—no medicine except butternut bark pills." Several men from the area contracted smallpox in Quebec and some died.[39] War and pestilence go hand in hand. During the French and Indian Wars, disease destroyed more people than did the enemy, a fact that would not have been forgotten in the twenty-year interval. The high incidence of fatalities from smallpox did not end inoculations, which in turn often produced severe reactions, occasionally death. In 1776, when the slave Zeb Prutt contracted smallpox during the Quebec expedition, his return to Hadley was a source of alarm. The prevalence of the disease in a number of military camps during the winter of 1775–76 provoked rumors that the British and the Tories were using smallpox as a weapon against the revolutionaries. General Washington voiced the same fear in a letter to the President of the Council in September 1775.[40]

On November 3, 1776, Elizabeth expressed her anxiety concerning the disease:

> Sacrament day we all went to meeting in the time of the first prayer my Husband came in and told mother and me that there was a number of parsons [sic] in Capt. Marshes House taking the Small-pox by inoculation, then pasing and repasing continually—we all of us Left the meeting and some others. thus were we deprived of the ordinance of the Lords Supper—pardon O Lord. O Lord forgive.[41]

This rapid exit from the meetinghouse was undoubtedly caused by the "pasing and repasing" of the inoculated persons who had not been quarantined. In the evening the family at Forty Acres watched the flames rising from the Hatfield "pox house," set on fire by people opposed to the use of inoculation. Its destruction necessitated a new place for those inoculated until they recovered. They stayed with the Reverend Lyman until a house was located in which they could remain under quarantine, this time in Hadley. Confinement was sometimes extended. Judd describes his uncle Jonathan's convalescence and interesting treatment from an inoculation, also in 1776: "For some days J.J. took physic and hasty pudding . . . left Chesterfield Nov. 12 after a confinement of 29 days."[42]

III

Another possible reason for the family's anxiety at the appearance of the disease was that Elizabeth was about to give birth to her second child, although again no mention of the coming event appears in the diary. The entry on November 26, 1776, her twenty-ninth birthday, begins with a prayer: "may I dayly walk with God and have a preparedness for all events."[43] Her second son was born on December 3, 1776. "All events" included the possibility of death. Laurel Thatcher Ulrich describes "preparedness" for women at this time as twofold:

> On the one hand she had to arrange for a midwife, ready a warm and convenient chamber, prepare childbed linen for herself and clothing for her infant, and plan refreshment for the friends invited to attend her. But she knew . . . she might "perchance need no other linen shortly but a winding sheet, and have no other chamber but a grave, no neighbors but worms." Her primary duty, then, was preparing to die.[44]

Elizabeth fell ill shortly after her delivery, perhaps from childbed fever, "fearful whether I ever should recover," she wrote some days later.[45] On the evening of December 8 the baby had a seizure, rapidly growing worse. The Phelpses summoned the Reverend Hopkins who baptized him Charles. He died a few hours later.

The Thursday following the baby's death was Thanksgiving Day. "We have a great many mercies to be thankful for," she wrote on that day. This stoicism contrasts with her expression of grief when little Phillis died. With the frequency of infant deaths, bonding between mother and child must have been tentative in the early weeks of a baby's life. The warmth and capacity for close attachments evidenced in diary references to her husband and in letters to Miss Pen remained under check in the first months of her children's lives.

Healing came from an unexpected place. Several weeks after the death of their second child, she wrote: "one Richmond brought his child here about a fortnight old—the mother had twins and Left 'em when about one week old—she Died." (December 29, 1776)[46] The way in which Elizabeth referred to the father suggests that he was unknown to her, and a subsequent entry identifies his residence as the town of Chesterfield, eighteen miles away.[47] Undoubtedly the news of the death of little Charles Phelps had traveled.

Had the Phelpses' reputation for providing a port in the storm, both literal and figurative, reached his ears? Or is it possible that some intermediary thought that a baby girl might bring solace to the family? Judd believed that the father was in search of someone to suckle the twins.[48] All three reasons may have played a part in the arrival of the infant. Three days later, however, the Phelpses heard that the child's mother had suffered from the "itch," a highly contagious form of scabies. As Elizabeth was not yet recovered from her illness, the family felt that it was unsafe to keep the baby. They took the infant to Oliver Bartlett, another prominent Hadley citizen, where the baby's twin sister was being cared for. At that time, Mrs. Bartlett had a child whose baptism was fifteen months before the birth of the twins, and she may have been breastfeeding him, though it is also possible that one of her servants had given birth more recently.

It is clear that Elizabeth was uncomfortable with her decision: "now Lord I make it my prayer that I do my duty fully however hard." (January 5, 1777) Two weeks later Charles brought the child back where she remained until Richmond reclaimed her on February 3. But by February 5 Charles and Elizabeth set off for Chesterfield to bring her home again, "for we feared it would suffer." (February 2, 1777) Had she perhaps let down her defenses and allowed the beginning of an attachment to take place? Richmond's name makes only one more appearance in the diaries, in April of the same year: "Mr. Richmond came to see his Babe for the first time since we brought it home."[49] Little Thankful was there to stay, her name perhaps a poignant reference to her survival in the face of her natural mother's death. Although the process for legal adoption was not established in Massachusetts until 1851, the Phelpses essentially adopted her as their daughter, though she would keep Richmond as her last name.

Zebulon Richmond, the baby's father, was not a native of Chesterfield, but came from Dighton, Massachusetts. Richmond men held prominent positions in the town government and served in both the local militia and in the Continental Army under George Washington. Zebulon was eighteen when he enlisted in the army in 1775, along with his younger brother, Nathaniel.[50] What brought the brothers westward from Dighton is unclear, their brief stay in Pelham presumably to enlist in the Continental Army before moving to Chesterfield.

It was perhaps a sign of the turbulent times that Thankful was not returned to her relatives in Dighton. It is possible that Zebulon's family did not know of the twins' birth. The absence of any mention of the death of the mother and the birth of the twins, or of the parents' marriage in Chesterfield's *Vital Statistics* is unusual, as births and deaths were customarily recorded in church documents. If the twins were born out of wedlock, a possibility considering the youth of the father, their birth may not have been reported to the pastor or the town officials. Thankful's twin, Philomelia, did come to Forty Acres several times. She may not have fared as well as her sister. She was passed from the Bartletts to John Chester Williams after the death of his wife; he eventually moved to Randolph, Vermont. Philomelia disappears from the diaries before Thankful is fully grown.

Another arrival in the Phelps household by a very different avenue was John Morison. The diary entry for March 23, 1777, mentions "one of the Highlanders . . . sent by Coll'l Porter to live here."[51] Following the evacuation of the British troops from Boston, two transports from Scotland arrived in Boston Harbor. Unaware of the British evacuation from Boston on the preceding day, two hundred and sixty-seven Highlanders were taken prisoner as they disembarked from their ships.[52] One can imagine the stupefaction of those Scottish soldiers as they came ashore, kilts swinging, bagpipes wailing, and found who it was that awaited them on the wharf. Among the prisoners was John Morison, who came to Forty Acres soon after he was taken captive.[53] The recruiting of soldiers from the rural New England communities created a severe shortage of farmworkers and seriously affected the planting and harvesting of produce. Very soon after the first shots were fired in Lexington and Concord, farmers petitioned the local Committees of Safety for permission to employ British captives in the fields.[54]

Morison brought to Forty Acres extensive experience as a gardener in his homeland, an accomplishment he may have made known to Elizabeth's cousin Colonel Porter, who served in the Continental Army. At the time that Morison began to work for the Phelps family, however, he would have been seen as a much needed replacement for the loss of hired hands to the army, his horticultural talents put to use at a later date. The gardener's rapid absorption into the extended Phelps family is evidenced by a journal entry on August 17, 1777: "None of the family at meeting but John (the Regular captive) and Josiah Guilbard (he was bound here a year ago last winter).[55] With such freedom to move about independently, it is clear that he was happy to stay at Forty Acres. Although there are occasional references in letters to the gardener's bouts of drinking in later years, he was a trusted employee, his signature witnessing an indenture document of 1807 along with that of Charles Phelps.

Births, deaths, and events related to the house and farm temporarily supplant diary references to the Revolution, now in full swing, and inevitably the rumble of war reappears; "Last Wednesday Simon Baker and Jonas Kelsey having enlisted in Army left home." (April 20, 1777) Both had been indentured to Charles Phelps, the accident-prone Simon in 1765 at the age of ten. As his indenture was for ten years and nine months, he had stayed on as an employee.[56] In the summer of 1777, they were stationed close enough to make occasional overnight visits to Forty Acres.

At the end of the week of July 6, 1777, Elizabeth wrote: "very bad news this week our forts at Ticonderoga given up to our Enemies hand."[57] Dr. Thacher was present at this battle and describes the week-long struggle to resist the advance of the British army and the Revolutionaries' eventual capitulation when ammunition ran out. The defeat was unexpected and "has given to our cause a dark and gloomy aspect."[58] On July 13 of that year, Elizabeth reported: "great part of Militia went to the Northward last week."

A month later the family awakened at 4 A.M. to the ringing of the Hatfield meetinghouse bell: "an alarm from the Westward—many men set out to go . . . all seems confusion." (August 17, 1777) The following week she explained:

> The event of the late alarm was that the Enemy sent out a party to come and destroy the out parts but the people rose and the Lord so ordered it that they met with a great defeat drove 'em back to a wonder not unto us but to the Lord be the Glory.

A few weeks later there was another alarm: "O Lord we tremble." (September 14, 1777)[59]

The "trembling" must have continued for nearly five weeks until the news of Burgoyne's surrender at Bemis Heights, some sixty miles south of Fort Ticonderoga, reached Hadley on October 19. Elizabeth's joy and relief surpassed her capacity to put her feelings into words: "Oh wonderful, wonderfull Words cant express our adoration and Praise! . . . I desire to fall down in astonishment!"[60] For the people of New England, this victory was the major turning point in the war, ending the threat from the north and west, and resulting in an alliance with France. On October 29, the family, except Elizabeth, who remained at home with the baby Thankful, turned out to watch the defeated Regulars pass through Hadley. Although Elizabeth makes no mention of the presence of General Burgoyne in Hadley following the surrender, there are several accounts of his having been housed at the home of General Elisha Porter. In appreciation for that hospitality he is said to have presented his host with one of his swords. He was then marched through the town en route to Boston.[61]

IV

Two Thanksgivings were celebrated in the fall of 1777, the first on November 20, and the second on December 18. The second feast day was possibly a response to the defeat of Burgoyne and his army in October. On the December date, Mr. Hopkins preached from Exodus 15, Moses' and Miriam's victory songs: "Sing ye to the Lord, for he hath triumphed gloriously; the horse and his rider hath he thrown into the sea." His choice from the Scriptures underlines the connection made by the clergy throughout the war between the bondage and release of Israel, and that of the Colonies.

In the midst of these celebrations, another rather surprising example of Forty Acre hospitality occurs. On October 14, 1777, "one Mr. Bartholomew" appeared on their doorstep. Arriving from a town called Skenesborough, in New York (now known as Whitehall), he was in search of a place to live. The Phelpses offered him and his family a house that they had built on Mount Warner in the fall of 1774. They invited the Bartholomews for the second Thanksgiving celebration of the year. Their name appears several times in the ensuing weeks until February 22, when returning from meeting, Elizabeth and Charles found Mrs. Bartholomew waiting for them. She was there to tell them that her husband had been taken off by the constables under a warrant "for being a 'Tory.'"[62]

Skenesborough, in its proximity to Ticonderoga, had been a refuge for wounded American soldiers after the surrender to the British. It was also a place where supplies for the army were gathered and troops assembled, and therefore not hospitable to anyone with Tory sympathies. It was this environment that forced the couple to move eastward in search of a place to live.[63]

Following her husband's incarceration, Mrs. Bartholomew continued to be a frequent guest with her children at Forty Acres. Sheltering anyone identified as a Tory would not have been applauded by the community, though Elizabeth makes no mention of any repercussions from her neighbors.

Hospitality at Forty Acres transcended political affiliations or, for that matter, economic and social sanctions, as in the case of the expulsion of an unmarried pregnant woman from her employer's home. There are no records of the community taking action against the Phelpses following these gestures of hospitality. Perhaps their position of prominence provided them with an immunity not available to every citizen of Hadley.

While the operation of the war had moved southward, its presence continued to be evident in the number of military titles that appeared in the diary entries: "Wednesday Col'll Chapin of Hatfield, Major Murry, Lieut. Elisha White and their wives . . . all here for a visit." (January 27, 1779)[64] On Friday of the same week, Mrs. Bartholomew was back to help Elizabeth make breeches for the army, an act that may have helped to erase her former association with the Tory cause in the minds of local Whigs. Mr. Bartholomew reappeared in May 1779, no longer imprisoned. The Bartholomews moved on "up country" in February 1780 and a family named Hibbard, who figure frequently in the later diaries, moved into the mountain house.

The peace that Elizabeth prayed for was not yet assured, but the spring plantings could now take place with less anxiety and the harvest could be anticipated with greater confidence. She was able to put her children to bed at night without fearing that the bells from Hatfield would sound an alarm before morning. The house standing alone on the road out of Hadley, which had seemed so vulnerable, was once again a sturdy shelter. Now the promise that lay in the farm and the fertile fields of the Connecticut Valley returned.

Chapter V

~

A Tumultuous Time

*"the clock struck three just after
I went to bed."*

THE HOUSE is silent, its occupants asleep. But as wooden houses do, it stirs, sighs, settles. For a generation it has engaged in a dialogue with its surroundings. What wakened her in the still, early-morning hours? No child cries, no wind buffets the windows. Then the clock strikes four. Elizabeth turns onto her back and stares through the bed curtains into the darkness. At first it is impenetrable, but gradually solid forms emerge—the bedpost, chest, chair, its outline blurred by the shawl draped over its back. Small sounds invade the quiet—scurrying feet. A mouse, perhaps. Listening, she can hear her bedmate breathing, and the child close by, their inhaling and exhaling not quite in harmony. It is cold and she moves closer to the warm body next to her. She drifts into sleep. A sharp rap on the south door pulls her back into wakefulness. Slipping out from beneath the covers, she wraps the shawl around her shoulders and feels her way through the darkness to the door. A caller at this hour, she knows, is in need of help.

With the door closed, the house surrounds a finite space, its occupants wrapped in the protective cocoon of sleep. Open, the threshold becomes a crossing into a world of infinite space, unpredictable possibilities—a neighbor dying, a woman in travail, a house burning, Solomon in trouble. . . . It is difficult to step out into the winter night, but from somewhere come the covenanting words: "We . . . promise in love to watch over one another."

O Lord bring order out of Disorder

ELIZABETH'S DIARY, SEPTEMBER 24, 1786

I

Once more a hiatus in the diary entries—this time seven weeks—announces a birth. On February 3, 1779: "Safely Delivered of a Daughter about 4 o'clock all comfortable, tis of the Lords mercy." A month later, Elizabeth was able to breathe more freely after a bout of high fever:

> Tuesday I came out into mothers Room tarried all Day and had a Living babe too to be thankful for and to carry with me, when I lay in last I went empty. (March 7, 1779)[1]

The birth of Elizabeth Whiting (to be called Betsey) completed the family, the immediate family.

The decade that follows this happy event is a turbulent one. The source of the turbulence is no longer the War for Independence, which has moved southward, but clashes arising out of local concerns, particularly those leading to Shays' Rebellion. There are family crises, losses, and extraordinary responsibilities, at least one of them a threat to the safety of the family, all of which test Elizabeth's mettle.

Once again Elizabeth took on the role of surrogate mother. "Wednesday Pene came here to Live." (December 10, 1777) Pene (Experience) was Charles Phelps's seventeen-year-old sister. In July of that year, Elizabeth's father-in-law had written to Charles, asking him to take her into his household, in the hope that there she would be brought "under due Government and taught what is reasonable in every respect by you Mrs. Porter and Daughter" until she was eighteen. He qualified his request by adding: "if Mrs. Porter inclines," and thanked her for her many past kindnesses.[2] The senior Phelps may have been quarrelsome, but he had courtly manners. The senior Mrs. Phelps had died on September 11. The responsibility would be primarily Elizabeth's to see that Charles's sister acquired the domestic and social skills necessary if she were to marry satisfactorily, in other words, "make a good match."

Charles's older sister, Dorothy, lived in Hadley with her husband, Lemuel Warner, but it was to Charles and Elizabeth that the senior Phelps turned rather than to his elder daughter when looking for a home for Pene. Undoubtedly Elizabeth instructed Pene in both the kitchen and the parlor. Such "apprenticeships" under the guidance of a woman known for her industry, social graces, and piety were seen as the best way to prepare young women for their future roles as wife, mother, and housekeeper. By the spring of 1780, the diaries begin to record Pene's social life: quilting, "cherrying with young company," a visit to Northampton, and many calls on friends in Hadley. Elizabeth's riding into town "on errands" included Pene, another means of introducing her to the local society.

A more troubling obligation for the Phelps family was that of Charles's brother Solomon, an obligation that often fell to Elizabeth. Two years older than Charles, he was known to share his father's love of extravagant dress, and was somewhat profligate in his expenditures. Solomon graduated from Harvard in 1762, and returned seventeen years later to receive his master's degree.

By 1764 his family had moved to New Marlboro in the New Hampshire Grants, where Charles Phelps, Sr., and Solomon began the construction of their "log college," Solomon to be its preceptor. In 1769 he received a commission as attorney-at-law from the governor of New York. During the Revolution, however, he turned to preaching. It may have been this change of profession that caused him to pursue the master's degree so many years after his graduation from Harvard. He was offered the pulpit in Winchester, New Hampshire, but declined. He did preach from time to time, traveling as far as Cornwallis, Nova Scotia.[3] The few surviving letters written by Solomon portray an intelligent, intellectual, and affectionate son and brother. A letter written to his father from Harvard reveals his questing intellect as well as power of expression:

> Some have considered definite Space as the receptacle, or rather the Habitation of the Almighty but the noblest & most exalted way of considering this Infinite Space, is that of Sir Isaac Newton, who calls it the Sensorioum of the Godhead—were the soul separate from the Body & with one glance of thought, should start beyond the Bounds of the Creation; Should it for millions of years continue its Progress through Infinite Space, with ye same activity, it would still find itself within the Embrace of its Creator, & encompassed round with the Immensity of the Deity.[4]

Astronomy had been a part of Harvard's curriculum almost from its inception. The emphasis in the seventeenth century was to discover the divine purpose in natural manifestations such as comets, viewed as prophetic warnings, often of the wrath of God. Gradually, in the course of the eighteenth century, astronomy was studied as a source of scientific information.[5] Solomon was able to fuse his interest in science with his belief in and understanding of the deity, though this more rational view of the heavens may not have sat well with congregations in the hinterlands.[6]

Solomon's visits to Forty Acres appear frequently in Elizabeth's diaries; he often came for extended periods. At the end of May 1780, Charles went to Boston as deputy to the General Court and stayed for two weeks. During his absence, Elizabeth wrote: "Satterday had a mighty fray with Sol." (June 4, 1780) On November 26 of the same year, after Solomon's return to Marlboro, there was even more ominous news: "We heard Brother Sol Broke his skull with an ax last Tues." Charles then brought him to Forty Acres so that he could be under the care of Dr. Kellogg in Hadley. On December 17, Elizabeth reports that his wound was healing. He was still in Hadley in January 1781, when he "began to grow crazy" and once again hit himself in the head with an ax. In desperation, they chained him up for several days.[7]

This episode is the first of several severe bouts of insanity during which the Phelpses looked after Sol. By the fall of that year Sol had become uncontrollable: "this Eve. my husband had a most dreadful Fray . . . with Brother Soloman he very crazy." (October 20, 1782) A week later Elizabeth wrote that Sol, who had been restrained with chains in the barn, broke loose, then was chained again in one of their outbuildings. Charles was gone from home when Sol freed himself a second time and entered the house: "hurt none of us—praised be God." (October 27, 1782)

With three young children (ten, five and three years old) and a frail and aging mother under her care, as well as servants, Elizabeth's consternation was understandable. Solomon often wandered to places some distance from Forty Acres. This reference to potential violence explains the use of chains to restrain Sol, though today it seems an appalling treatment of someone suffering from insanity. Other families in the area also resorted to chaining when a relative was deemed "crazy." Preserved Bartlett of Northampton was confined by chains, escaped, and disappeared. "An alarm was made; the drum beat and the bell was rung—she was found dead in Mill river."[8]

Mental illness was little understood in the eighteenth century, treatments for specific forms of insanity unknown. Philadelphia physician Benjamin Rush, who practiced from the mid 1770s until his death in 1813, was one of the first authors to refer to insanity as a disease.[9] Theories as to the causes had ranged from satanic possession to personal responsibility arising from "moral irregularities" or "excess passions" in the victim's way of life.[10] Physicians' testimony as to a patient's mental condition was not considered reliable evidence in court, as it was deemed "opinion" as opposed to "fact," or "behavior." No asylums for the care of the insane existed until well into the nineteenth century, when they were often established in the face of vociferous objections from the community.[11]

Isolating and restraining the afflicted person most certainly exacerbated the condition. The Phelpses resorted to all the known treatments available to them: a physician's care, isolation and, perhaps as a last resort, chaining. These varied approaches reflect the conflicting views as to the origin of insanity. If the cause were physical, then a doctor's care was needed, if the result of the individual's moral "irregularities," punishment was appropriate. If the afflicted was viewed as a menace to the community's safety and tranquility, chaining ensued and town officers were summoned. Rebecca Dickinson of Hatfield reported being terrified for two nights "by a Distracted man his name is Solomon Phelps."[12]

The end to Solomon's tragic tale came in the spring of 1790, a year after his father's death:

May 16. Sun. . . . Saw a man. one Wells, who came from Brattle-
borough—said he saw one of the Jury of Inquest who sat upon the
body of Brother Solomon last Monday who was found dead with
his throat cut.[13]

His demise must have evoked in Elizabeth a mixture of sadness, horror,
and perhaps an inadmissible relief. Yet, as with the death of her second
child, her recording of this occurrence is brief, suggesting her reluctance
to dwell on the event. She follows this announcement with a formulaic
prayer (augmented only by an exclamation mark): "O Lord may his
death be sanctified to us all!" She then moved onto matters at hand: "Dr.
Edwards preached in Hadley. Tuesday Brother Warner had his house
raised."

The details of his death appear in Benjamin H. Hall's *History of
Eastern Vermont*:

In the spring of 1790 he disappeared, and it was some time before
it was discovered that he had gone into a woodlot, lain down
between two hemlock logs, and cut his throat.[14]

Suicides were condemned as a form of premeditated murder. Those who
died by their own hand were often buried outside the churchyard on
unconsecrated ground, and some Congregational ministers would not
officiate at the funeral of a suicide victim.[15] The Phelps family cemetery
occupies a plot of land in the midst of the Marlboro farm. Surrounded
by a stone wall with tall shade trees on one side, it sits in the center of
once-cleared land now invaded with a forest of younger trees and saplings.
Four small stones are clearly marked. Three additional gravestones were
carved a number of years after the deaths that they record. None of them
refer to Solomon, though it seems likely that he would have been buried
in the private family cemetery near his mother's grave. There is evidence
of buried stones, perhaps one of them once marking his grave.[16]

II

Hadley's proximity to the Connecticut River brought numerous advantages to those with farmland along its banks, but was also the source of

tragic accidents. Drownings appear in the diaries even more frequently than fires. The strong current of the Connecticut River, so advantageous for traders shipping southward to ports such as Hartford and New York, took its toll in human lives and continues to do so. No bridges crossed the Connecticut River in the vicinity of Hadley until 1806. In all seasons when the river remained open, four ferries transported residents back and forth between Hadley, Northampton, and Hatfield daily.

When the river was frozen, walkers and wagons crossed the ice as late as the month of March, often a time when thawing had begun. Elizabeth recorded one narrow escape for her son Porter, crossing the river to Northampton in the winter with Colonel Porter. The diary does not explain the details of what happened, but later in the same week she wrote of John Morison's misadventure when he and a companion fell through the ice while crossing the river; his companion slipped under the ice and drowned.[17]

A distant river was responsible for a tragedy that struck very close to home for Elizabeth Phelps. She wrote in her diary on June 30, 1782:

> Monday . . . Just at Dark Sam'll Porter came here and brought the Maloncoly News of Mrs. Edwards Death—said she was Drowned watering her Horse he went in too far.[18]

While waiting for her husband, Polly Porter Edwards had driven the chaise in which she was riding to a small river intending to water the horse. A precipice at the water's edge caused the horse to pull her into the river, which was over her head.[19] What follows Elizabeth's announcement of her friend's death is a prolonged lament for the loss of her girlhood friend.

> Oh Omnipotent Jehovah: Oh Lord God Almighty: Holy and Righteous—thou hast taken away my dear friend, the companion of my Childhood and Youth. . . . may this perfect a good work in me if any is begun and if I am still in the Gall of Bitterness and bond of inquity [sic].

A lengthy entry under April, 27, 1783, describes another extraordinary accident, happier in its outcome:

Fryday Pene took the Little Girls went to Brother Warners. . . . Satterday my Husband went after' em put the Young Horse into the Chaise—just as they were coming over the Bridge the Horse took a fright—went so far to the edge that off he fell—but it was so ordered that he Left the Chaise on the Bridge and sliped out of it himself to the great admiration of all—yet the Jirk was so great that it threw both of the girls out and a bunch of bushes that grew not far from the bridge prevented their falling to the Ground—they hung there safe till my Husband took care of 'em—put the Horse into the Chaise all got home without any considerable hurt.[20]

As with all catastrophes, including those averted, Elizabeth turned to God, this time with praise and a prayer that she "take a suitable notice" of His mercy.

A different threat to the children's safety, at least in the minds of their parents, lay in the still untamed wilderness bordering on the fields of Forty Acres. Returning home from the Sabbath meeting, the Phelpses discovered a number of their sheep and lambs slaughtered by wolves. "But thanks be to God tis not our house Lambs."(May 4, 1783)[21] In March 1785, Hadley paid a bounty of 4 pounds for each wolf killed. Two wolves roamed the northern part of Hadley, not far from Forty Acres, as late as 1805, and residents complained of their howling in the night.[22]

Death came twice to Forty Acres in the early 1780s. In March 1781, the Phelpses' slave Rose, sister of the lamented Phillis and mother of the latter's namesake, died. Why she died is not clear. Her name appears in the diaries from time to time as a member of family outings. In August 1780 she had accompanied Mrs. Porter on a watermelon-eating expedition at the Alixanders. In December of that year, Elizabeth recorded that she was "more poorly," and the family arranged expeditions to improve her health. "Riding out" when in poor health was a common practice endorsed by "doctor books" such as Dr. William Buchan's *Domestic Medicine: or, a Treatise on the Prevention and Cure of Diseases by Regimen and Simple Medicines,* in the family library. In January, Rose had a chance for a sleigh ride to Northampton and went, but a few days later, Elizabeth wrote: "Rose a very ill turn—tho't she was a Dying but got better. Mr. Hop came and prayed with her." (January 21, 1781) Then on March 14, "a little after sunrise our Rose Died."[23]

A year later, Rose's six-year old daughter Phillis became ill. In February 1782 Charles took her to see Mr. Arams, "he a seventh son," in Muddy Brook, just south of Deerfield, suspecting that she had "King's evil" (scrofula, a form of tuberculosis).[24] Charles brought her a second time to be "stroked," a treatment that derived from the belief that anointed kings, and in their place, seventh sons of seventh sons, could cure this disease by stroking the neck of the afflicted.[25] When "stroking" failed to cure Phillis, the Phelpses returned to their doctor, then another, and finally the parson, Mr. Hopkins.

Peg, who had "gone off free," returned to look after her granddaughter, now seriously ill. She was there for ten days when Elizabeth reported that Phillis was very bad. She died the next day:

> she was a very prety Child, I hope she sleeps in Jesus, being washed in his Blood. Oh Lord grant it may make a sutable impression on all our hearts . . . enable us that have the care of 'em to discharge our Duty faithfully.[26]

The funeral was held at Colonel Porter's house in Hadley. Equal in the eyes of God, slaves were sent on their way to the next world with as much ceremony as their owners, though their graves were seldom given a stone marker. "There be of those that hath no name," as the author of Ecclesiasticus observes. The funeral taking place at the home of a prominent citizen would have brought a larger number of the community to add its blessing for the dead child.

Once again, Elizabeth's attempts to nurse one of her slaves back to health had failed. Now all of Peg's descendants were deceased, none of her offspring able to take advantage of the abolishing of slavery in Massachusetts in 1783. The first Phillis died of tuberculosis; the cause of Rose's death is unclear, but the identification of scrofula in her daughter establishes the presence of another form of tuberculosis among the Phelpses' slaves. These three deaths raise the question as to the care that they received. Were they undernourished, ill-housed? Lorenzo Johnston Greene's research suggests that, with some exceptions, slaves in New England were better clothed, fed, and cared for when ill than those in the other Colonies, particularly in the South; yet illness was prevalent among Northern slaves.[27] He poses the radical shift in climate as one cause for the frequency of sickness, particularly respiratory diseases. This reason would seem most applicable to first generation Africans or newly arrived slaves from the South, but a less convincing explanation for the illnesses of Rose and the two Phillises.

A more likely contributing factor to their poor health comes from the practice of trading less robust slaves to the North.[28] Labeled "refuse" persons as unfit for the arduous labor demanded of them in the West Indies and on Southern plantations, they fetched lower prices and were more affordable by farmers of moderate circumstances. Whether Peg or a previous generation qualified as such a person, her family succumbed to tubercular infection in several forms, which the Phelpses did not contract.

III

Another upheaval for the Phelps family was the dissension over Vermont statehood, which escalated rapidly with the end of the war. Charles Phelps, Sr., had acquired extensive land holdings in the New Hampshire Grants, making him the largest landowner in New Marlboro, and a powerful voice in the growing conflict.[29] When New York began granting land to new owners in the neighborhood of New Marlboro, the senior Phelps switched his allegiance to Massachusetts, fearful that his own holdings were in jeopardy. Phelps made numerous trips to Philadelphia to petition the newly formed Congress to annex the territory to the Bay State. In a letter to George Clinton, Governor of New York, John Jay claimed that Phelps had engaged in duplicitous attempts to obtain allies from New Hampshire, Massachusetts, and New York, each believing that the disputed territory would be joined to their state.[30] The promised support from those states was at best provisional, however, and did not assure Phelps that his land would remain untouched by would-be usurpers, among them Ethan Allen and the Green Mountain Boys, stout supporters of Vermont statehood.

In a letter written in 1775 to his brother in Hadley, Solomon expressed enthusiastic support for the Revolutionary cause, but went on to rail against his neighbors from the disputed territory, who wished to form a new state:

> Our county is now in a critical situation—the People in general are almost ready to *revolt* from New York—such consummate

knavery, and *Ignorance* is blended, in our Magistrates, that they are insufferable.[31]

He, like his father, appears to have feared that a break from New York would threaten the considerable family holdings that had made them the leading landowners in Marlboro. Solomon's vituperative language in his letter to Charles testifies to the intensity of his feelings and the extent to which he viewed the campaign for statehood a personal affront. Although he eventually concurred with the Vermont party, neither the senior Phelps nor his son Timothy joined Solomon in this support. The father first endorsed New York's claim to jurisdiction over the New Hampshire Grants. He held positions conferred on him by Governor Clinton of New York: justice of the peace, the commissioner to administer oaths of office, and assistant justice to the court.[32] Timothy Phelps, as adjutant of the New York regiment of Minutemen, and later High Sheriff of Cumberland County, backed the New York claim for the territories.[33]

These events were taking place at some remove from Forty Acres; nevertheless, their repercussions eventually found their way to the Hadley Phelpses' doorstep. Father Phelps arrived on September 13, 1782, bringing news of the "great commotion there about a new State got to Bloodshed but none Killed yet as we know of."[34] Timothy Phelps, part of the commotion, had been banished from the Vermont territory. In December, Elizabeth wrote: "Last Tuesday Brother Timothy came here again fled from home," suggesting that he had tried to return to Vermont, only to be ousted once more. He tried again in January 1783 and was jailed in February. Eventually released from prison, he continued his resistance to Vermont statehood, fleeing to Hadley yet another time to avoid arrest.

The senior Phelps had managed to escape when his son Timothy was first incarcerated in 1783, but the troops who pursued him "plundered his home, took his 'silver hilted sword,' and confiscated much of his library." The greatest loss for Charles Phelps, Sr., was his library, which encompassed works on law, religion, history, and philosophy. Ironically, his law books were used in the 1784 revision of Vermont's laws. He eventually managed to regain 145 books, still a substantial library for a frontier community. Despite repeated efforts, he was unable to retrieve most of the property confiscated by the Vermont government, and was able to bequeath to his heirs but a fraction of what he had once possessed.[35]

On January 18, 1784, Elizabeth wrote: "Monday Five men came to take Brother Timothy—they abused my Husband and took Tim—went off. We had a most dreadful fright." The Vermont troops had mistaken Charles for his brother. Recognizing their mistake, they seized Timothy and set off for Vermont. Charles, with several members of the Massachusetts Militia, pursued them to Deerfield and fined four of the captors for violation of Massachusetts sovereignty, though they were unsuccessful in securing Timothy's release.[36]

The "commotion" was ongoing. Just weeks later Charles set off for Bennington "to get Father out of gaol"; he had been sentenced to sixty days' incarceration.[37] His release was granted following his "volluntarily" swearing allegiance to the State of Vermont.[38] To the end of his life, however, the senior Phelps refused to endorse the statehood of Vermont, signing his will, years after Vermont had been granted statehood, Charles Phelps "of New marborough late in the County of Cumberland and Province since State of New York."[39]

Charles Phelps, Sr., was an independent spirit. Quixotic is another word that comes to mind; he did indeed tilt at windmills. His "Log College" was never completed nor students enrolled, the Utopian scheme reduced to grassy ruins. Yet his willingness to risk his wealth and freedom to a cause that he believed in lends his character a heroic dimension. He vigorously supported the Revolutionary cause, yet his resistance to Vermont statehood allied him with Conservatives and Tories associated with the Yorkers party, as did his religious affiliation with the New Side Scots Presbyterianism.[40] On the other hand, he championed the farmers' cause that incited Shays Rebellion, uniting himself with a radical faction. He expounded in public on issues of law and government and wrote angry pamphlets denouncing the Allen brothers and the Green Mountain Boys. Having lost his fight against Vermont statehood, he did not abandon his desire to involve himself in issues affecting the welfare of the new state. His propensity for strong and enduring convictions was a legacy that he passed on to his sons, though his namesake Charles chose to use that legacy in less controversial ways.

IV

On March 7, 1784, Charles's twenty-four-year-old sister Pene married Caleb Cooley and went to live in Longmeadow, just south of Springfield,

Massachusetts. "We had a pretty Weding," the diary announces.[41] The satisfaction that the Phelpses felt in seeing their charge happily "settled" was short-lived. In a matter of months after their wedding, Caleb Cooley fell ill, bringing the couple back to Hadley so that Caleb could live under the Hadley doctor's care. The couple spent part of December at Forty Acres, returning to Longmeadow at the end of the month. On February 13, 1785, Elizabeth began the week's entry: "This morning Mr. Phelps and I set out to go to Brother Cooleys Funeral."[42] Several days later they brought Pene and her baby home to Forty Acres. Although Pene visited her in-laws in Longmeadow during the following August, she remained at Forty Acres until her second marriage to Aaron Dickinson of Hatfield in July 1786.

Elizabeth Porter's health also claimed her daughter's attention. A diary entry of September 12, 1784, is a variation on an ongoing lament during these years: "Tuesday mother up to Mr. Worthingtons she is in one of her low turns."[43] It was at this time that her mother's friend Mrs. Alixander, a frequent visitor to sickbeds, came to try to persuade Elizabeth Porter to stop taking opium. She was unsuccessful. In November, Elizabeth reported that her mother was very depressed, "did not get out of her bed this day."[44] The next week Dr. Wells came to see her and spent the night. He concluded that her condition was not dangerous, but that she needed diversion. The following week her daughter described her as "quite lost."[45]

"Diversions" for Mrs. Porter were plentiful at Forty Acres. Friends came for dinner, tea, and for extended stays. Strangers came to lodge: "Wednesday . . . one man and two Women, one 88 years old all Lodged here." (January 20, 1782)[46] "One Mrs. Chapman traveling on foot from Hebron to Westminister stayed here." (April 3, 1785)[47] It is difficult to calculate the exact number of people who arrived at the Phelpses' doorstep, as Elizabeth occasionally resorted to generalities such as: "just at night Coll'l Moore and his son and others here, Lodged." (July 6, 1783)[48] A count of those *named* reveals more than 200 visitors in most years between 1780 and 1800.

Forty Acres was undoubtedly not the only house that opened its doors to strangers, nor were Charles and Elizabeth Phelps motivated simply by hospitality. Small almanacs, printed in Boston in the latter part of the eighteenth and early nineteenth centuries, list houses available for lodging along all the major roads out of Boston. Hadley was not on the main east-west road from Boston to Albany nor the north-south route leading to Montreal, but alternate routes included Northampton, Hadley, Sunderland, and Amherst. In each of these towns the names of prominent families are listed as accommodating lodgers, presumably for a fee: Pomeroy and Lyman in Northampton, Kellogg in Hadley, Hubbard in Sunderland, and Warner in Amherst. Places where travelers might find bed and board must have been passed along by word of mouth, as well as advertised in newspapers and almanacs. A Frenchman traveling through New England in 1780 was referred to a private home in Litchfield, Connecticut, by a friend who assured him that he "should find better 'accomodation' there than at the local taverns."[49]

A survey of a number of the almanacs containing lodging information in the last quarter of the eighteenth century does not reveal Forty Acres as a place to lodge.[50] Nevertheless, Elizabeth's diaries mention large groups of people traveling through who do lodge with them: "at night there came here two Famillies moving up to New Labanon from Norwich—Twenty persons in all." (October 18, 1778) What sounds like an even more daunting number appears in an entry of March 9, 1783: "three Waggons loaded and Lodged here."[51] Elizabeth's use of the word "lodged" when referring to unidentified persons suggests that they were paying guests.[52] She did not use that word when referring to extended visits from friends and relatives, nor to strangers described as poor and homeless or victims of calamities that turn up on their doorstep:

> Monday at night a traveling Woman came here going on foot from Oinion River to Coventry in Connecticut—her Husband killed about 9 weeks ago by a fall tree . . . stayed Tuesday rainy she did not go on.[53]

It would be unlikely that they expected wayfarers such as these to pay for their stay at Forty Acres. Judging from the numerous references in the diaries to lodgers, the Phelpses did not need to advertise.

Often Elizabeth returned home from a visit in Hadley to find callers seated in the parlor or kitchen. Formal invitations were delivered by hand only for special events such as weddings. Letters could warn of a proposed extended visit, but the delivery of mail was erratic and unpredictable. A full and flexible larder was necessary to accommodate the waves of visitors: "Satt. Mr. Hop. and wife Mr. Lyman of Hatfield and wife Mr. Austin

and wife with a great number of others Dined here, 15 besides our own."
(October 19, 1788)[54] Such hospitality required the managerial skills of an
innkeeper, and at times she was just that. In a letter written some years
later, Elizabeth reveals her awareness of differences in the lodgers' social
status: "Our gentry are at supper," she announces, as she puts down her
pen in order to prepare their bed "and set some with 'em too."[55] There
were occasions when Elizabeth must have offered her hospitality reluctantly: "Sun. I tarried at home because of a stranger here who we thot not
proper to leave with the others." (September 13, 1778)[56]

At times, the Phelpses gave shelter to people who would seem to have
been candidates for "warning out." In February 1784, Elizabeth describes
the arrival of the constable with a warrant for people temporarily housed
at Forty Acres. "Fryday morn the Constable came and took a woman and
four children from here they came here last week."[57] "Warning out," a
procedure by which transient individuals and families unable to demonstrate economic self-sufficiency were removed from communities, had
been in operation since the seventeenth century. In the 1720s and 1730s
the General Court enacted "entertainment" laws, prohibiting transients
from living in a town for more than twenty days, unless approved under
special circumstances. These laws served to warn citizens against long-
term housing of such people. The economic stability of the community
depended on limiting the number of new settlers and ascertaining their
ability to support themselves. It was not only the elderly who made up the
migrant population. Younger sons were often compelled to seek land in
adjacent communities or to travel to newly opened territories to the north
and west in order to find their livelihood.

A 1767 statute was designed to shift the responsibility away from the
constable and onto the transients themselves, requiring them to report to
the selectmen on arrival in town. If the intention was to eliminate the
practice of "warning out" throughout the state, it failed. Records reveal
that more than 200 people were "warned out" of Northampton in 1791,
29 in Hadley.[58] In 1794, the General Court rewrote the laws pertaining
to poor relief and settlement rights, bringing to an end the "warning out"
of transients. The new statute transferred the responsibility for care of the
poor to the town for three months. At the end of that period, town officials were to return the transients to their legal residence, its whereabouts
often a subject of dispute.[59]

In 1774, Forty Acres acquired a farmhand named Timothy Buggy for a period of three months. It is one example of how the town of Hadley dealt with the problem of "undesirable" residents who did not respond to "warning out," and threatened to become a financial burden to the town in case of illness. A document drawn up by the selectmen and overseers of the poor cited Buggy, who had been living in Hadley for several months, as

> a Person of able Body to work and Labour, and has no Estate other-
> wise to maintain himself, yet lives Idly, mispending his Time in
> loitering and Intemperance, and uses or exercises no daily lawful
> Trade or Business to get his living by.

Hadley laws destined him for the House of Correction or Work House unless he was "bound out to Service to such Person or Persons as we shall judge suitable." In this case, Buggy was bound out to Charles Phelps, who was then directed to turn over Buggy's wages to the selectmen at the end of three months "to be . . . disposed of according to Law."[60]

Civil actions were the province of male officials; provision of food and shelter that of women. At this time, when women had no direct power in the making and execution of laws, their command of the house and its larder made it possible for them to mitigate, for a brief period of time, the hardships caused by the practice of "warning out."

V

By 1781, new disturbances were developing that would replace Hadley citizens' preoccupation with the Revolution, creating new causes for anxiety. Once again, as in 1775, people of this region resorted to demonstrations. The object of the earlier demonstration was to shut down the courts appointed by the king. This time the crowd was there to "contemn all authority," though there was also "a great number to uphold it." (June 16, 1782) Elizabeth feared bloodshed. "Thou canst put thy Hook in their Nose and thy Bridle in their Jaws and turn them back," she prayed, drawing upon a verse in Isaiah and the second book of Kings. The fervor of her prayer was undoubtedly caused by Charles's presence at the scene of the clash. He did not return until 2 A.M. on June 17 when the insurgents dispersed.

"All authority" included locally elected officers of the courts who were enforcing the payment of the debts many farmers accrued in consequence of the interruption to farm production during the war. The person initially responsible for organizing the uprising, Samuel Ely, was imprisoned, then forcibly released by three men holding military titles, who in turn were imprisoned. Elizabeth's cousin Elisha Porter was sheriff of Hampshire County at this time. Invited to send a committee to meet with the rioters, he declined, but the next day acceded to the insurgents' request to release the three soldiers in return for handing over Samuel Ely. Writing with the advantage of hindsight in 1855, Josiah Holland criticized General Porter for his leniency; he believed that such clemency laid the groundwork for what, a few years later, erupted into Shays Rebellion.[61]

By 1786, tensions had seriously escalated. The Court of Common Pleas empowered creditors with the right to demand payment in hard money. Daniel Shays of Pelham was one of the many farmers being pressured to settle their debts in this way. Nearly 3,000 debt cases were brought before the Hampshire County Court of Common Pleas between the months of August 1784 and August 1786. This figure represents a 262 percent increase over cases presented in the two-year period between 1770 and 1772."[62] Once again, the courts became the target of an uprising.[63]

> Monday my Husband set out for Springfield—publick affairs seem
> to be in a confused situation. many are gone to prevent the sitting
> of the Court and many are gone to uphold the Court. O Lord
> bring order out of Disorder. (September 24, 1786)[64]

Thursday she recorded his return—"no lives lost." On Thanksgiving, she devotes a number of lines in her diary to this conflict, expressing ambivalence as to which side is justified: "There has been a great deal of Disturbance of late among the people, how it will terminate God only knows. . . . I am not able to Dictate, I know not what is right and best."[65]

In retrospect, one can see that the disagreement that ended in armed conflict was brewing even before the American Revolution. The majority of the western Massachusetts population were farmers; doctors, lawyers, clergymen, and merchants also farmed. An informal system of local exchange existed in communities, often in the form of barter, "direct swaps of work or goods considered to be of equivalent value."[66] Other times a looser arrangement existed: produce exchanged for labor to be fulfilled at a later date, deferred payment. Charles Phelps's account book contains both kinds of exchange: a bureau and table from Oliver Pomeroy of Northampton for beef and rye from Forty Acres; a bushel of rye for Joab Bartlett in exchange for reaping and carting ashes and dung.[67]

As commerce grew between inland and coastal settlements and between foreign countries and the States following the end of the war with Britain, such systems were no longer feasible. Merchants needed specie to conduct foreign trade, but for many farmers, settling their debts in any form was impossible. Pressure from creditors was not the only problem they faced. The General Court, in order to reduce the public debt, raised taxes, predominantly poll taxes, especially burdensome for farming families.[68]

But not all farmers experienced these hardships. Those who had been able to increase their productivity to the point where they harvested more than their family consumed were looking for markets for the excess produce. Charles Phelps was one of these farmers, evidenced by his trips to Boston markets mentioned in the diaries as early as February 1771.[69] Inevitably, his interests paralleled, to a degree, those of the merchants. He was also increasingly allied with local and state government. In 1774, Charles held the position of selectman and was reelected twenty times in the course of his life. In 1780, he went to Boston for two weeks as deputy to the General Court. Although he would also be faced with the difficulty of settling debts with cash, his affiliations with town government and the courts provided other possibilities for dealing with temporary debt. In addition, the Revolution brought Charles, unlike many of his farming friends, an increase in dependable, experienced help in the persons of the Scottish John Morison and a Hessian soldier, Andries. He was in a good position to realize profits from his surplus in this postwar period of scarcity. These advantages joined his interests with those of the powerful establishment.

For Elizabeth, however, the issues were not as clear. She expresses her quandary in a number of ways: "This has been a confused day," she wrote on January 28, 1787, as the government troops occupied Hadley. "A confused time" prefaces her entry announcing the departure of the army for Petersham.[70] There are no prayers of thanksgiving following the defeat of the insurgents in that town, as there had been with the defeat of

Burgoyne, nor are there pleas to God on behalf of one side or the other. All that she felt she could do was to leave the matter to God and pray for "peace and good order." Whereas Charles responded with alacrity to the first sign of an actual insurrection in January by bringing aid to the government troops, Elizabeth seemed distraught and nonpartisan. Certainly there were friends and neighbors, sympathetic with the insurgent cause, whose beds she had sat by during illnesses and childbirth. Charles's positions of authority in the community put distance between himself and many Hadley citizens. Although social prominence came with Elizabeth's position as Charles's wife and as a member of the Porter family, there was a leveling effect in the chores that she shared with her neighbors: the quilting and exchange of expertise in the making of breeches and bonnets. Her close contact with hired girls from the hill towns such as Pelham that produced most of the insurgents would have awakened her sympathy for their cause.

Once again, Charles provided support for the Militia, this time in opposition to some of his neighbors:

> Thusday Morn my Husband set out with sleighs to help the men to Springfield which are raised in this town for support of Government . . . it Looks as Dark as Night, a very great Army is coming from Boston and some are Collecting upon the other side. It appears as if nothing but the imediate interposition of providence could prevent Blood. (January 14, 1787)[71]

The following week Charles went again to Springfield, having slaughtered two oxen for meat to give to the Militia. He was unable to pass through the insurgents to the courthouse and returned, but succeeded in delivering the beef the next day.

Only four years after the cessation of the war against Britain, the people of Hadley once again lined the streets to watch the army march into town, three thousand soldiers led by General Lincoln. On the previous Sunday, word had spread that "Mobs" (capitalized by Elizabeth) were gathering in Northampton and Amherst, the former passing through the lower end of Hadley to join the Amherst insurgents. The confrontation between these opposing forces occurred about twenty-five miles to the east at Petersham on February 4, when Lincoln's 3,000 men surprised the Shaysites, 2,000 in number, in the midst of a severe snow storm early on a Sunday morning.[72] The next day Charles delivered supplies to Lincoln's army in Petersham.

Elizabeth's fear that there would be bloodshed was realized, and more were to fall from both sides during the ensuing weeks. Thirty of the rebel farmers were killed or wounded in a battle near Sheffield, Massachusetts, on February 27, 1787.[73] Ongoing skirmishes claimed the lives of both rebels and government soldiers from Worcester to the New York border until the month of June when they finally came to an end with the defeat of Shays Rebellion.

In June, Massachusetts Governor Bowdoin, believed by Shaysites to be the principal source of their problems, was toppled from office in the state elections, and replaced by John Hancock. Although, predictably, Hancock proved to be a supporter of mercantile interests, while governor, he reduced taxes and court fees and enacted exemption laws, easing some of the burden on farmers. Habits of local exchange continued in western Massachusetts, witnessed by Charles Phelps's account book of the early 1800s.[74]

In retrospect the uprising can be seen as doomed from the start, though it did purchase time for some farmers to settle their debts. Shays Rebellion is just one of the visible signs of change that would gradually erode the close-knit community that fostered the barter system. Ironically, support of the government's repression of the insurgency by people such as Charles Phelps hastened the demise of the way of life that had once been the ideal of these Connecticut River Valley farmers.

Chapter VI

Chapter VI

FOSTERING HEIRS

"here to dine . . . twelve in all."

A PROMISE OF new life comes to the house with the birth of children. Nights are broken by infant cries—ongoing watches over a feverish child. Lullabies counterpoint the rhythm of a rocking cradle.

Toys turn up in unexpected places: rag dolls, then a whistle, wooden sword, hoop, drum. Caches of dried flowers, birds' nests, odd-shaped stones, arrowheads, acorns appear in corners of the house once swept clean. There are spills to wipe up, bruises to rub, torn clothes and hurt feelings to mend. Young soprano voices, shouts of protest, of laughter, the staccato of running feet on the stairs, in the hallways, mingle with the ongoing liturgy of adult domestic routine.

The strongly built house embraces this new life, absorbs its music, and responds with its own anthem, nurturing yet another generation.

be not trifling and vane in your behaviour associate
yourself with the Virtuous and Wise.

LETTER FROM CHARLES PHELPS TO PORTER,
DECEMBER 11, 1787

I

The single branch that stemmed from Moses and Elizabeth Porter was
sending out shoots. The family of Elizabeth and Charles Phelps was not
large for eighteenth-century New England, but its future was more secure
than it had been at the time of Moses Porter's death. Running through the
diaries during this period of war, insurrection, and family crises, are intermittent references to the Phelps children and their progress.

As he approached the age of seven, Porter appears more frequently in
his mother's diaries: "Fryday I and Porter attended a Lecture before the
Sacrament." (July 25, 1779)[1] The next week we read that Porter carries
his mother into town "of errands," the verb *carries* indicating that her son
was in the driver's seat. Both entries place Porter in a more adult world.
The age of six or seven for boys was traditionally marked by a change in
costume, from the unisex robes of infancy and early childhood to
breeches and frock coat or, later in the century, trousers and jacket. The
latter costume was a modification of the clothes adopted when petticoats
for boys were set aside in the early 1770s. This clothing, designed for
youths between the age of seven and fourteen, represents a change in attitude toward the rearing of boys, recognizing an interim stage in their
development.[2] The less formal long trousers and jacket allowed for more
freedom of movement than the adult costume of breeches and frock coat,
and made possible rough-and-tumble play.

No early portraits of Porter exist to indicate which costume he wore at the transitional age of seven, although his petticoats may have been put aside at the age of five when Lydia Smith came to Forty Acres "to make cloaths for Porter."[3] Elizabeth's diaries reveal the Phelpses' ambitions for their son, beginning at an early age. In the spring of 1780, they sent the seven-year-old Porter to live and attend school in Northampton. Their plan was for the rigorous grammar school preparation necessary for Porter to enter Harvard College, whereas many Hadley sons had a more practical preparation for life in the Connecticut Valley.[4]

Porter's parents made rare visits to him at school. Elizabeth took the two little girls to see him in February 1782. He returned to his home for Thanksgiving and at the end of the year. When Porter came home for short visits, he assumed new responsibilities. Elizabeth sent her nine-year-old son to Amherst to pick up a young woman hired to weave at Forty Acres. Whether he drove the chaise or brought his passenger back in the pillion seat, he was in charge.

In February 1784 the eleven-year-old Porter went farther afield for his education, to school in Westfield for a short time only. His parents must not have been satisfied with this school, for in August of the same year they sent him to Hatfield to live with the Reverend Joseph Lyman, pastor of the church in that town. A grammar school, by definition one that emphasizes the study of Latin and Greek, was established in Hatfield in about 1754.[5] It was Lyman who had preached revolution from his pulpit, despite the presence in Hatfield of the Tory, Israel Williams. Educated at Yale University, Lyman graduated with high honors in 1767 and returned there as a tutor for a year. He came to Hatfield in 1772, and like many clergy at that time, took in boarding students along with his pastoral responsibilities. Now close to home, Porter visited his family frequently, bringing with him fellow students who boarded with Mr. Lyman. According to Sprague's biography of the Hatfield minister in *Annals of the American Pulpit,* the Phelpses' choice of mentor for their son was a wise one:

His mind was formed after no ordinary model. His Maker had originally impressed upon it the stamp of greatness. The idea of force was that which first seized you, as you contemplated his intellectual powers, and especially as you witnessed their development in the ardour of discussion.[6]

In addition to Porter's Hatfield schooling, he often accompanied his father to sessions of the court in Springfield and in Northampton, where he witnessed a murder trial. On another occasion, Elizabeth accompanied them there to hear "one Norton tried for murder." (April 30, 1786)[7] Subsequent letters from father to son point to law as the profession that Porter's family desired for their only son.

Just a week after his fifteenth birthday, Porter set off for Cambridge with his father to enroll in Harvard College. In recording his departure, Elizabeth gave him his full name, Moses Porter, a formality that signals solemn occasions in the diaries. She concludes this entry with a prayer for her son, asking God to "remember him in mercy for soul and Body— take possession of his heart." (August 12, 1787) The move from western Massachusetts to Cambridge was a radical change for their fifteen-year-old son, who would no longer be under the watchful eye of the Reverend Lyman.

In a Polonius-like letter, Charles advises his son on a number of matters a few months after his departure:

Dec. 11, 1787. I would recommend to you, to be particular in learning to write, these long Evenings—much time may be lost in foolish company. If you intend to make a scholar, you must be a careful improver of Time—you must consider you are arriving to a State of Manhood, and are now establishing your Character as a Scholar— be not trifling and vane in your behaviour associate yourself with the Virtuous and Wise—and you will guard against indecent or profane language—and always remember you have Business to transact between God and your own Soul, every day read your Bible—and learn to be [a] sober virtuous youth.[8]

Porter's account book demonstrates his desire to follow his father's admonitions with diligence. He lined the paper to make a ledger and began immediately on arrival to enter his purchases: "cash paid for Homer, two volumes—12 shillings"; "Ca[e]sar, one volume—6 shillings"; "Art of speaking—5 shillings"; "Horace one volume." Even minor purchases appear in the pence column: four pence for a watermelon and three for a bottle. Despite his careful accounting there is, inevitably, an unaccountable sum at the end of the page: 1 pound, 3 shillings, and 3 pence— "cash paid for different things & at different times."[9]

For Porter living in Cambridge and close to Boston must have been a heady experience. Several acquisitions soon after his arrival at the college indicate his awareness of urban fashion and diversions. Immediately following his visit to the barber to whom he paid 1 shilling, he purchased a cane, duly noted: 1 shilling, 6 pence. When cold weather arrived, Porter bought skates for 3 shillings, 4 pence. In the second quarter he found a more expensive barber who charged 3 shillings to cut his hair, and by the summer of his second year, 12 shillings. Purchases of books are interspersed with expenditures for cherries and ale (6 pence), for lemons on numerous occasions (undoubtedly, a rare luxury in western Massachusetts). In the first quarter of his senior year, 2 shillings, 8 pence, for pipes, tobacco and wine. For a pair of shoes that cost 8 shillings, he bought a pair of buckles for 18 shillings. Few items appear in the pound column of his ledger, but he entered 2 pounds, 8 shillings for the dancing master, presumably for a series of lessons. Clearly Porter was learning about the world of fashion as well as the Greek and Latin classics.

In the spring of 1789, Elizabeth was preoccupied with Porter, now in his third year at Harvard. During the week of April 12, she reported a visit from Porter. The return from a journey by members of the family always elicited a thanksgiving for their safe arrival: "common Providence takes a kind care of his body. O Lord may thy especial grace find his soul."[10] The following week Porter set off once again for Harvard, obliging his father by taking cattle to the market on his way back to Cambridge. The sale of this livestock was important when it was necessary to produce the quarterly payment of 50 ounces of silver for his tuition.[11]

Elizabeth's anxiety for Porter now seems to reach beyond what might be expressed in a routine prayer:

> Lord I leave him with thee—surely he is in good hands, thou wilt do right and tho he prove a base wicked creature. Only teach me true submission if he must be a cast away, yet is it not in thy power Heavenly Father to save even him? The Glory and the praise shall be thine. Yes Lord and Glory and praise shall be thine if he is not saved. O may I be fitted for all events.[12]

Subscribing to the Calvinist doctrine of the "Elect," Elizabeth spread her fears regarding her own worthiness of salvation to her children. Perhaps some of the expenditures recorded in her son's account book appeared to her to reflect an unseemly interest in worldly things. She had a store of biblical phrases in her memory: "Their foot shall slide in due time" (Deuteronomy 32:35), "every man is vanity" (Psalm 39:11).[13] Inevitably, her personal prayers incorporated words such as these and gave powerful expression to her fears for Porter. Many years later, when an old man, Porter described his mother's religious views as rigidly Calvinistic.[14] He attributed to her the dark images of God that stayed with him throughout his life.

If Elizabeth worried and prayed about her son, it was Charles who kept up a regular correspondence with Porter, admonishing him, sometimes gently, sometimes severely, to serious study and upright behavior. A substantial package of letters, labeled "from my father," suggests their importance to Porter. The few surviving letters from Elizabeth to Porter during his college years are primarily concerned with practical matters: purchases to be made, clothes to be repaired. After returning from enrolling his son at Harvard, Charles wrote:

> 31 Aug 1787 . . . I hope you will behave yourself so as to get the Esteem of your Tutor . . . and behave yourself with decency and good order in the Family—you will keep yourself clean, should always wash in the morning.[15]

A month later he cautioned Porter not to go out in the evening air without his "surtute [overcoat]" and to "use no bad Language." (September 22, 1787)

During his first year at Harvard, Porter had not taken rooms at the college, but expressed a wish to lodge on the campus the next year, to which Charles replied: "I have no Objections if you will mate with a sober Virtuous, Reputable—scholar." (June 29, 1788).[16] This cautionary note may have arisen from the reputation associated with the college residences. A remark in Clifford K. Shipton's *Sibley's Harvard Graduates* concerning Elizabeth's cousin Elisha Porter, who graduated a generation earlier, may reflect a well-established view of the dangers of campus life:

> He [Elisha] won a *detur* [a prize of books awarded annually at Harvard College] and kept out of trouble, which was the easier because he was not in residence the last five quarters of his undergraduate career.[17]

Fatherly advice continues during the summer of 1789: "you will remember to behave according to your station, and not be guilty of a little, mean action." He cautioned Porter against card playing, and closed his letter with a very Calvinist reminder: "as your life is uncertain, be diligent to make your calling and election sure."

Nothing in Porter's account book substantiates his father's worries that he might be engaged in gambling. But during his last two years at Harvard, he did frequently hire a horse and chaise and occasionally recorded dinner for two. A significant purchase in November 1790 was a violin for 1 pound, 10 shillings. He had already learned to play the violin prior to that time as purchases of violin strings appear earlier among his expenses. He may have desired a better instrument. On the back of his account book, he carefully copied the music for several hymn tunes, followed by diagrams of the vibrations of stringed instruments.

Charles's advice to his son concerns the welfare of both body and soul: "use no bad language," "every Day read your Bible," "you informed us of your illness, you will be carefull and not expose yourself to take cold and get a relaps." The letters, often signed "I am my dear son your Affectionate Father," convey warmth as well as concern, high expectations of his son's behavior, and apprehensions for all the possible threats to those expectations.

In sending Porter to Harvard, his parents placed him under the influence of philosophers and theologians whose teaching exposed him to the thinking of Deists, as well as such writers as John Locke and Jean-Jacques Rousseau, who, counter to Calvinist thought, believed in the perfectibility of human beings. Did his parents' worries about their son arise from ideas that he brought home and discussed with sophomoric enthusiasm? Nearly thirty years before this time, his uncle Solomon had written a letter to his father from Harvard that interwove his Calvinist faith with Deist thought.[18] Eighteenth-century Deists rejected Revelation and the Christian Mysteries as a source of knowledge of God, believing human reason to be the means by which such knowledge is attained. The Deistic God was a distant God, detached from His creation, impervious to prayer. Such beliefs undermined the foundations of Calvinism.

Earlier in the century the ground was laid at Harvard by scholars such as Edward Wigglesworth and his son for the liberalizing of the strict Calvinist Congregationalism. Samuel Eliot Morison describes the elder Wigglesworth as "one of the first theologians in New England who dared publicly to challenge the 'five points of Calvinism.'" Morison sees both Harvard and the Congregational Church "broadening down from primitive Calvinism to eighteenth-century Deism or Unitarianism."[19] But in the Connecticut River Valley, Calvinism continued to hold many church members in its sway. In the 1780s, New Light revivalism was preparing the way for the Second Awakening, its base at Yale in New Haven. Ideas as well as goods traveled up the river and found fertile ground among the inhabitants. Theological developments in the Massachusetts capital produced unease among those reared in orthodox households, and the developments in Connecticut were welcomed as a counterforce to the threat from Cambridge. In Elizabeth's eyes, this threat amounted to apostasy.

Despite his parents' concern for his spiritual and scholarly development, Porter graduated second in his class (1791), was elected to Phi Beta Kappa, and on the occasion of his being awarded the master's degree from Harvard (in course), gave a valedictory oration in Latin.[20] This accomplishment should have allayed his parents' anxieties as to his academic achievements, though no mention of these events appear in the diaries nor are there any congratulatory letters in the bundle of letters preserved by Porter. Praise of that sort may have been feared for its encouragement of vanity.

The impact of Charles's letters on his son is evidenced in an endearing and amusing way when Porter took pen in hand to write to his sisters. In the fall of his year of graduate studies at Harvard, he wrote the following letter to his sisters Thankful and Betsey, then fourteen and twelve respectively:

Cambridge October 10th, 1791
    To Thankful and Betsey severally. I shall no longer write to you in the language of childhood and youth, but shall address you as a person of understanding—a person just coming forward in life, to take a place among the rest of mankind. You at present know little, and I may almost venture to add—nothing, of the world, of which you are now going [to] make a conspicuous, and, I hope, a worthy part. Though I am but poorly qualified to advise you; yet, considering your total inexperience, my advice may, perhaps, be of some consequence in warning you to avoid those errors into which numbers of your sex have so often plunged themselves. These lines may

possibly induce you, now at your first appearance among mankind, to look around you, to be cautious in forming intimacies in your friendships, and to be circumspect in your manners and deportment. Lay aside all childish and juvenile amusements, and copy your conduct from those whose behaviour is most easy and graceful.

Consider, likewise, that these are the most precious moments of your life, that you have now an opportunity of laying up in your mind that knowledge which will be useful to you in every possible situation in life. You cannot be too careful to improve the flying moments as they pass. Remember that time once past cannot be recalled. If you do not now strive to get wisdom, think, what must be your sentiments and feelings, as age advances? when you shall be called forth into company. You will then be obliged to sit mute and silent in some bye corner and utterly unable to join in any conversation that passes. But, if by chance you should have a word to put in, you would deliver it in such an awkward, disagreeable manner as to embarrass yourself, or make the whole company feel for you, and pity you. But, on the other hand, if you replenish your mind with the maxims of virtue and knowledge, now while it is in your power, you will be enabled to acquit yourself with ease and dignity in every action; you would command the love and esteem of the good and worthy; and as you smoothly pass down the still current of life, will secure yourself the approbation of your own hearts, and the affection of mankind. If you improve these hints, you shall hear from me again. The bell now calls me to dinner, and I here bid you both an affectionate adieu.

Moses Porter Phelps [21]

It was at this time that Porter's sisters were sent to school in Amherst, in Porter's words, "just coming forward in life." He was nineteen, conscious of his achievement as a graduate of Harvard, embarking on advanced study. He was feeling worldly wise and empowered to take on the role of mentor to his younger sisters. A number of his admonitions reflect those that he received from his father, but with a subtle difference, sometimes attributable to the gender of the recipients. Both father and son stressed caution in forming friendships, and serious application to study, but Porter seemed more concerned that they comport themselves gracefully in company. He advised them to learn the art of conversation, whereas Charles Phelps admonished his son to "guard against indecent or profane Language." There is concern for "polish" in Porter's letter that does not appear in his father's letters, which endorse the fundamental virtues of hard work, steadfast character, cleanliness, avoidance of anything unlawful, vain, or trivial. Porter had acquired a measure of urbanity that he wished to pass on to the younger members of his family. No further letters written in this vein have survived. Perhaps Porter felt that he had provided sufficient counsel to launch Thankful and Betsey into polite society.

II

Elizabeth's diaries tell us very little about the education of Thankful and Betsey. Sylvester Judd tells us more. He records lengthy conversations with Thankful toward the end of her life. It is she who credits Elizabeth Porter with having taught her and her sister to read, spell, and write. Elizabeth's diary of May 25, 1783, mentions leaving Thankful in town to go to school, though years later Thankful remembered only having attended school in Amherst. Perhaps, at the age of six, she begged to return home to Forty Acres, as mention of "the two little girls" being together appears in late summer entries, or possibly the Phelpses were dissatisfied with the school in Hadley. It may be at that time that Elizabeth Porter took on the early schooling of the two little girls.

Thankful and Betsey, aged fourteen and twelve respectively, set off for school in Amherst in July of 1791. No record of Amherst private schools of that time exists. There were undoubtedly Dame Schools designed to teach very young students a rudimentary knowledge of reading and writing. At the time that Thankful and Betsey were growing up, town schools were primarily for boys. When girls were included, they were relegated to the early hours of the morning, such as 5 A.M. to 7 A.M. during the summer months.[22] Thankful later told Sylvester Judd that she and Betsey were taught "various branches" by a man.[23] Soon after the girls entered school, Elizabeth reported a visit at Forty Acres from the Amherst schoolmaster, Mr. Harris, who must have set up a private school as there was no academy in Amherst until 1814.[24]

Betsey's and Thankful's writings demonstrate exceptional facility with language, evidencing familiarity, not just with the King James Bible, but other forms of literature as well.[25] They wrote poetry that reflected an understanding of poetic forms, and read novels popular among their contemporaries in England, which influenced their own writing.

While in Amherst they resided with the family of Dr. Cutler, a physician married to one of the prominent Northampton Pomeroys. The house still stands on Amity Street, its original location close to the center of the town.[26] It was a new experience for the two girls, accustomed to two-mile walks or rides to see their Hadley friends. The Cutlers had six children, among them two daughters, Esther and Susan, close in age to Betsey and Thankful, who then became close friends. Cutler had taught his children himself, including his daughters. Son of a Harvard-educated minister, he must have received a good and classical education from his father, who most likely took in additional students. In Cutler's memoirs, written in 1811, he wrote that he had moved with his family from Pelham to Amherst in 1787.

> There I educated my children and when they had received their education and came to adult age it gave me great pleasure to think that if I should be taken away that they *all* [my emphasis] were put into a capacity to support themselves.[27]

Robert Cutler appears to have had some of the qualities that drew the Phelpses to board their son with the Reverend Lyman in Hatfield. "As to religion," he wrote, "I have called myself a Calvinist and a Congregationalist and hope and trust I am a Christian." Among his papers are six pages of fine script, a lengthy "covenant with God" that he wrote in 1782 at the age of thirty three.[28]

At Amherst, Betsey and Thankful acquired an education not readily available to girls in western Massachusetts at this time, except through parents or tutors willing to devote themselves to female students. Elizabeth's pleasure in reading and, as she declares in later letters, in writing, certainly was a shaping force in the rearing of her children. Both daughters had access to the house's substantial library, and were part of the family circle when books were read aloud in the evening. The effort that the Phelpses made to ensure a serious education for their daughters sets them apart from the majority of parents, even some urban dwellers who had greater access to private schools and tutors willing to take on female students. A letter written in 1782 by the Bostonian John Eliot reflects what must have been a pervasive attitude toward women's education:

> We don't pretend to teach ye female part of ye town anything more than dancing, or a little music perhaps . . . except ye private schools for writing, which enables them to write a copy, sign their name, &c., which they might not be able to do without such a privilege, & with it I will venture to say that a lady is a rarity among us who can write a page of commonplace sentiment, the words being well spelt, & ye style & language kept up with purity & elegance.[29]

More examples of Betsey and Thankful's writing skills have survived than those of fancy needlework. The qualities that John Eliot believed to be a rarity in women's writing appear later in their letters and poems. That they achieved this level of skill must be attributed, in part, to Elizabeth and Charles's recognition of their potential.

Betsey and Thankful's "course of study" was more varied than Porter's single-minded academic, then professional program. Extended visits to family friends and relatives were seen as another way of enriching their daughters' experience, especially when those relatives lived in more urban areas. Just before beginning school in Amherst, Betsey spent a month with the Reverend Hopkins's daughter Jerusha, married to the Reverend Samuel Austin, a pastor in Worcester, Massachusetts. Betsey visited her brother in Cambridge on several occasions where she met Sarah Parsons, who would eventually move to Newburyport and invite both Betsey and Thankful to visit her there during the summer of 1794. Porter kept Betsey abreast of current Boston fashions: "I want those silk stockings my brother left at home for me," she wrote to her mother from Boston in 1797, "they are very much worn now by the ladies."[30] Silk stockings represented a substantial outlay on Porter's part. Jane Austen, born just four years before Betsey, wrote to her sister in 1796, lamenting her inability to afford such a luxury.[31] Another Boston purchase appears in a letter from Betsey to Porter:

> my *pudding* or neck cloth, was not dislik'd tho' ma said I should frighten some out of the house of worship—however I believe they withstood the shock—for I heard of no disturbance.[32]

Porter is also the one who brought her a "guittar," on approval, which purchase she then justified in a letter to her mother:

> the price is twenty dollars—and I think I can save so much from the expences of dress etc. . . . perhaps Pa will think it money thrown away—but I Hope to make such proficiency, as to be able to charm away his long tedious winter evenings—but stop, I forget that his *favorite* employment is *nodding*—yet I think he, and the rest of you will sometimes listen to me. [33]

Trips to Boston were often shopping excursions for both mother and daughter. Letters going back and forth between Hadley and Boston are replete with requests and questions as to the precise desires of the purchasers; "does Mrs Shipman want earrings or ear-drops?"[34] Italian silks, florentine slippers (with "Court heel"), "Muslin for a pretty handsome frock," were to be had in port cities such as Boston.

The number of visitors to the Phelps family continued to increase. The list included young people who came for extended visits: children of the deceased Polly (Porter) Edwards, Gaylord and Hopkins children, and Warner nieces and nephews. Porter brought friends home from school and college. The diaries portray a house filled with people: Elizabeth's contemporaries, youths, and the elderly. Forty Acres hummed with activity: spinning, weaving, candle, soap, and sausage making. A number of women came to "fix a bonnet." Elizabeth was renowned for her millinery expertise. "April 11 [1790]. Fryday Mrs. Pierce here for her bonnet I made for her."[35]

For eighteenth-century young women of rural New England, the training acquired in their own home was essential if they were to acquire the skills that would turn them into good housewives. The girls went to spin at their cousins' houses, who returned the favor two weeks later, mitigating the labor with companionship. When Elizabeth wrote, "Satt. we made almost 6 hundred candles," (October 30, 1790) the *we* surely included both girls.

But all was not labor. Winter brought sleigh rides and balls, where Betsey and Thankful danced minuets, cotillions, Irish jigs, and reels.[36] Summer brought expeditions to pick peaches, plums, and berries. There were sailing outings to Stoddard Island in the Connecticut River for picnics. Trips to seamstresses necessarily increased: "Wednesday Betsy at

Dr. Cutlers to get the damask she has been colouring for cloaks" (October 27, 1793); "[Betsey] and Thankful at Capt. Chiliab Smiths to get their wild boar gowns made." (November 17, 1793)[37] One wonders if such gowns were peculiar to frontier living!

Charles and Elizabeth desired attributes in their children that were associated with gentility, which they saw as appropriate for their position in the community. Both Betsey and Thankful had their mother's experience of the Singing School, under the same instructor, Mr. Stickney, as well as dancing lessons. Not only Porter possessed musical instruments—a violin, a flute, as well as drums—Betsey played her "guittar," and eventually, Thankful, the pianoforte. In 1799 the Thanksgiving celebration included music: "In the evening Mr. Woodward, Mr. Martin, Mr. Erastus Smith here—had fine music."[38] None of these accomplishments, however, were to stand in the way of their development as pious Christians.

III

Porter continued to be a constant source of concern for Elizabeth. His comings and goings provoked prayers in ways that her daughters' peregrinations did not. "Fryday Porter got home again—common Providence takes a kind care of his body. O Lord may thy especial grace find his soul."[39] Her diary sounds a similar note several years later when Porter completed his studies in Cambridge: "When I got home found Porter come. Lord may mercies & troubles all keep me humble." (May 27, 1792)

Porter then decided to go to Newburyport to study law under Theophilus Parsons, Esq., a prominent lawyer in that prosperous city. Charles was able to arrange for his son to board with Lawyer Parsons as well, and continued to send him letters of advice:

Give yourself Time every Day to read the Scriptures or some Religious books—and learn divine Wisdom—as well as the Laws of your Country. (August 19, 1792)[40]

Porter remained in Newburyport until a few months after the expiration of his clerkship in January 1795. During his residence there he had come to know Sarah Parsons, niece of his mentor, Theophilus Parsons. Sarah lived in Boston with her grandmother until the latter's death at the end of 1794 and then moved to Newburyport, bringing the two young people together in close company for the months before Porter left to open his own practice. Friendship between the two families extended to other members; Thankful and Betsey spent a month with the Parsons family in the summer of 1794. At that time Elizabeth wrote to Betsey from Hadley intimating that Porter's father was considering providing his son with "a handsome supply of money" with which to establish himself in the practice of law.[41]

A letter from his father, written on December 31, 1794, indicates that Porter had entertained the possibility of setting up his practice in Northampton. Charles responded to his choice of town:

> But as Land there is not to be purchased short of 400 Dollars an Acre—and there being four offices in Town—and almost every Town except Hatfield of any great respectability that side the river has an Attorney in it—I think the chance for business in this side the river has the preference—I think all things considered that Hadley will be the most advantagous place—but I wish not to controul you.[42]

The father's desire to see his son settle in Hadley surfaced from time to time in letters and the diaries. This sentiment was not shared by Elizabeth who wrote to her son in 1799: "the fond father I suppose wants the son near him—but the ambitious mother wishes him a better place."[43] When Porter was admitted to the Massachusetts Bar in April 1795, he elected to practice law in Boston. By this time he and Sarah were engaged to be married. Sarah had grown up in Boston, which may have influenced Porter's choice as to where he would practice law, as well as his memories of happy years in the more urbane environment of Cambridge. An incident that occurred in June 1795 reveals a characteristic that may shed some light on Elizabeth's anxious prayers for her son. A party was organized for a group of young people from Newburyport to attend an ordination in Haverhill. In his memoirs, Porter, looking back over more than half a century, confessed that he did not know what possessed him, but he invited another young woman to accompany him in his chaise, leaving "Miss Parsons to get a seat with her Uncle's family as best she might." He offered a not entirely satisfactory explanation:

A morbid and depressing sensitiveness has *always* marked my feelings . . . I have never been able at any time wholly to escape from
the withering influence of a strong, tho somewhat singular, pro-
clivity to self-depreciation, and a tendency, at least, to magnify, if
not multiply my actual deficiences.[44]

Porter speculated that this tendency caused him to shrink from any public display of his affection for Sarah. On return from the ordination
party, Porter called on his fiancée and met with a chilly reception and
what seemed to him to be a final farewell.

After several months in his Boston office with no clients, he removed
to another part of Boston, where he practiced until April 1799. During
the year following his estrangement from Sarah, rumors abounded as to
other suitors for her hand. In the fall of 1795, Porter visited his family
and accompanied his sisters to a ball, apparently still alienated from his
former fiancée. On May 5, 1796, Betsey wrote to her brother in Boston:
"O how happy if a certain person could receive you with satisfaction—
or rather, happy if you had never forfeited their favor."[45] The letter closes
with her hope that he be "rewarded in a *good wife.*" It is a sisterly wish
that failed to conceal her belief that he had lost the best possibility for
that to happen.

In May 1796, Charles Phelps went to Boston as Hadley representative
of the General Court, taking Elizabeth with him. While there, Elizabeth
expressed a wish to visit an old friend now living in Newburyport and, as
Porter had no pressing business, he drove her there in his chaise. Was this
a mother's covert plan to restore her son's relationship with Sarah? If so,
she was successful, and the couple were once again betrothed. In July
1796, Betsey wrote teasingly to her brother:

I was quite surprised to hear that you had made another visit . . .
how did she receive you with a frowning aspect—or with a smile
upon her sweet face?—do hasten the time when hymen's silken
chain shall unite you in the most sacred bonds to the woman you
so much love and esteem.[46]

Weddings now were in the air at Forty Acres. Betsey wrote to her
brother again in September of the same year:

You recollect, in your letter by my father, in June you requested me to tell you whether *Miss Richmond* [Thankful] was soon to be married—I cannot tell how soon—but I think it probable within a year or half that time—I need not tell you the happy man is MR HITCHCOCK—he has apply'd to my father, and obtain'd his consent.[47]

Enos Hitchcock was living in Northampton when Thankful met him. Trips across the Connecticut River to that town had appeared from time to time in Elizabeth's diaries: "The girls to a Ball at Northampton in the Eve." (November 22, 1795) In the letter of September 11, 1796, Betsey wrote to Porter in a mocking voice that she often used with her brother:

Mary [Thankful changed her name about this time] & myself propose spending this week at Northampton, at the hospitable house of Capt. Lane—you know what a slanderous place Northampton it is—& I almost dread to enter it—there are some who never *know* us—& there are others who *appear* to be quite our friends—they live in style there—and you cannot wonder that we wish to enlarge our acquaintance beyond the bounds of Hadley.[48]

It was a little more than a year after this visit that Thankful married. The name Hitchcock began to appear in Elizabeth's diaries of September and October 1796, followed by the announcement: "Thankful set out with Mr. Hitchcock for Boston & Providence." (October 25, 1796)[49] An entry under November 6 explains the "unchaperoned" expedition:

Jest at Eve Mr. Hitchcock & Thankful came home—they were married at Providence last Monday by his Uncle Dr. Hitchcock minister there—Lord bless 'em.

The next few references to her adopted daughter were as "Daughter Hitchcock" or "Mrs. Hitchcock," but then the name "Thankful" reappears. Weddings customarily were at the bride's home, but occasionally Elizabeth mentioned their having taken place at the meetinghouse.[50] Relatives of Enos Hitchcock, one of them a Congregational minister, lived in Providence. The presence of blood relations may have outweighed Thankful's claim for a Forty Acres wedding. The Phelpses' absence at the ceremony was not extraordinary considering the distance, nor did it imply a lack of interest in the bride's welfare. A more significant indication of Elizabeth's concern for Thankful was in the preparations of her wardrobe on the day before her departure: "Monday Lucinda Noble here to alter Thankful's surtout."[51] Surtouts were long, loose overcoats with layered capes around the shoulders. Worn by men since 1680, they became fashionable for women after 1790. Elizabeth Phelps made sure that Thankful was stylishly dressed as the bride of Enos Hitchcock.[52]

The Hitchcocks returned to Forty Acres to live until Enos established himself in business. The family gathering for Thanksgiving was therefore still complete. Unlike weddings, this holiday was a celebration to which members of families were willing to travel distances in order to be together. In 1796, President Washington announced that Thanksgiving would be celebrated on Thursday, December 15. Porter came home on Tuesday evening.[53] Now happily reinstated as the betrothed of Sarah Parsons, he spent Thanksgiving evening writing her a long letter that creates a lively picture of the extended family at Forty Acres:

> While my father & Mother have crossed the river over into Hatfield to pass the Evening with Parson Lyman and his wife—while my Grandmother is safely stowed away in a farther corner of the house, wrapt up in rather noisy slumbers to be sure—while my sisters (for Mary has not yet left the family) are tripping it away at two miles distance to the sprightly sounds of a rustic *twi-tweedler*—while Lydia & Polly have prevailed upon Seth to put the team horses into the old sleigh and are at this moment (I suppose) enjoying all the transport of a *Thanksgiving Sleighride*—while John, the Scotch gardener, by the kitchen fire side (I'm sure of it for I just look'd in) is managing the "Gentle Shepherd" as well as could be expected, considering the hour, and the quantity of *ungentle spirit* that he has to manage at the same time—While all this is going on about me— here in an inner room—of which the greatest ornament is an old family clock at my left hand corner—the hour pointer of which just borders upon ten—before an old fashioned desk which once belonged to my maternal Grandfather sits the form and figure of a man—the heart with all its tenderest sensations, which alone form an existence worth possessing—where are they? bound within the silken coster that encircles the lovliest of her sex—[54]

I arrived here on Tuesday evening—& had the pleasure of finding my friends in health—To the many affectionate enquiries after
you I answered *comme il faut*—bless me! what am I about? However you will have it in English—I told them everything that a
heart, filled with love and Thee, dictated as proper to be said on the
occasion. . . . I wish I was in Summer Street—but why do I talk? I
am in Summer Street—a Bumper is by me . . . the clock strikes
ten—I toast my Beloved Sarah—and may she sometime bestow a
tender thought upon her faithfil—her absent Charles.[55]

Porter here refers to himself as Charles, a decision that he appears to have
made himself, as his parents were slow to adopt the change. His letter,
along with the "sermon" written to his sisters, reveals his finesse with the
written word. He creates vivid images of a winter evening at Forty Acres
for Sarah, and then, with the reference to the "silken coster" (hangings
surrounding beds), slips in a discrete allusion to what was most on his
mind.

For a year and a half after Thankful's marriage to Enos Hitchcock, the
couple lived at Forty Acres. In April 1797, Charles Phelps accompanied
Thankful on a furniture-buying expedition to Northampton and the
Hitchcocks went together to Springfield on a similar expedition.[56] The
Phelpses supplied Thankful with furniture as well as a wardrobe. Carpets
were rare in Hadley before 1800, according to a member of the Porter
family reminiscing with Sylvester Judd, and those that did exist were
made of cloth or rags. There was an imported carpet at Forty Acres and
Thankful's adopted parents gave her a similar one, "all in one piece with
a border." She also had a piano. It is not certain when she acquired it, but
subsequent developments suggest that it was early in her marriage.[57]

Not until the following spring, however, did they have a place to put
their belongings. Enos Hitchcock's frequent trips away during the couple's stay at Forty Acres must have been in search of that place and the
employment that would support it. In March 1798, Betsey wrote to
Porter with the good news that Thankful's husband, Enos, was now
employed and the couple about to settle in a home of their own:

Capt. Hitchcock [Enos's father] has bought a good house and store,
in Brimfield—for our brother—and two or three men set off this
morning with her furniture.[58]

With Mr. and Mrs. Hitchcock went Charles Phelps Hitchcock, born January 28, 1798, "about one o'clock on Satt—after a severe travel." Dr. Cutler came to assist with the birth rather than a midwife, and Mrs. Shipman gave the neighborly assistance so often supplied by Elizabeth. Doctors assisting at births became more usual in urban areas toward the turn of the century, but midwives continued to play the major role in rural areas.[59] Although the Phelps family applied to doctors in the case of injury or illness, it was with the birth of Thankful's baby that the first mention of a doctor attending a woman in childbirth in Hadley appeared in Elizabeth's diaries. It may have been the difficulties associated with the birth, never specified, but an ongoing concern for Thankful, as well as the family's close association with Dr. Cutler that brought the doctor.

The arrival of Charles Phelps Hitchcock ushered in the fourth generation of the Forty Acres family, but his departure was imminent, producing a wistful note in Elizabeth's diary:

> April 8 Sun: . . . At thy table dear Lord once more & the heart felt satisfaction of both my daughters with me. . . . Mr. Hitchcock's son this day christened by the name of Charles Phelps—Lord he is thine & I rejoice in it. Dearly do I love him—but Monday morning early he & his mother & father left us to go to live at Brimfield.[60]

Betsey accompanied the Hitchcocks and their last load of furniture to Brimfield from where she wrote to Porter:

> a fortnight has pass'd since Mary and I with our *little charge*—left the abode of our infancy—our sister—has now got nearly settled— just setting out on the voyage of life—no wonder if she feels anxious for her fortunes in this boisterous sea. . . . This town I find much pleasanter than I expected,—tho' the inhabitants are unpolish'd and rather more *rustical* (if possible) than those of Hadley.[61]

Betsey's sojourns in Boston and Newburyport had provided her with a yardstick by which to measure sophistication, and another perspective on her birthplace as well as Thankful's new home.

With the departure of two of her children and periodic absences of the third, expressions of lonesomeness began to appear in Elizabeth's letters to her children. The nest was not completely empty, however, with the arrival of Mitte. This child came to Forty Acres in December 1791 when she was six weeks old. Her mother, seventeen-year-old Susannah Whipple, was unmarried and in need of a place to live and work.[62] Taking in Susannah and her child provided Elizabeth with a much-needed source of domestic labor: "Wednesday Susa washed all the chambers I the windows." In November of the following year, Elizabeth and Betsey quilted a winter coat for Susannah. It seemed that she was there to stay, but in the end, only for two and a half years. On March 16, 1794, Elizabeth reports that the Reverend Hopkins came to marry Susannah Whipple (three months pregnant with her second child) and Samuel Blodget, who also lived and worked at Forty Acres. Two weeks later the Blodgets and Mitte left and went to reside elsewhere, but in July Mitte was back living at Forty Acres "most of the time" without her mother. In the summer of 1794, a letter from Elizabeth to Betsey in Newburyport is mostly taken up with Mitte, now nearly three years old:

> you may be sure she is writting with me now, she asked me cant i get in letter to besse *ma'ma* . . . I asked her one moment ago what I should tell miss Betty—she got down out of her chair & came looked me right in the face with an earnestness which almost surprised me—& said these words of her own accord without any telling—tell besse I keep or wear dat pette ting in my bosom near my heart.[63]

Several anecdotes in which Mitte holds the central position reveal the extent to which she had engaged Elizabeth's affections. She, in turn, addressed Elizabeth as ma'ma, the underlining of the word revealing its significance for the writer: "indeed i think she is a great deal of company for me—I love dearly to hear her talk."

Elizabeth's next letter to Betsey in Newburyport perhaps explains Mitte's separation from her natural mother, at least temporarily: "Susa is about yet I fear she will not hold till you get home tho so that you may watch with the little basket."[64] Two weeks later the diary reports that Susa gave birth to twins. "The little basket" may refer to Elizabeth's portable container for medicinal herbs, entrusted to whomever was appointed to "watch" beside the woman in labor.

Elizabeth's delight in the little girl Mitte provides a glimpse of her responsiveness to children, absent from the abbreviated diary entries that are primarily witnesses to her diligence. And her affection for Mitte is returned: "she is so fond of me, I cant leave her at all."[65] References to Mitte in diaries and letters characterize her as affectionate, intelligent, and headstrong, a challenge that Elizabeth takes on gladly, extending her period of child-rearing.

Chapter VII

SOME NEW SORROWS

*"never anybody loved to be at the head of a
great business better than he does."*

AUGUST IN the valley of the Great River brings quiet days of ripening and—gradually—of drying. It is a time of yield—tomatoes, melons, peaches, and the slow reddening in the apple orchard—small harvests that promise a life of plenty for the winter.

But August also brings the insistent, rasping chant of the cicada, the withdrawing moisture from leaves, here and there an untimely swatch of scarlet in a green maple tree. A shift in the wind brings an unexpected drop in temperature and calls for a fire in the clean parlor hearth. It is a chill, slight and ephemeral, that nevertheless warns of autumn, the gradual dying down of the valley's abundant growth.

The contrary moods of August provide a metaphor for the vagaries of the human condition, when in the midst of halcyon days of harmony, darkness suddenly enfolds the spirit. A cold weight constricts the heart. Then, not the ordered, fruitful farmland, but the dense woods across the road, entangled undergrowth, and wounding stabs of broken twigs describe the soul's landscape. Sun-filled fields and ripening grain seem a mockery, the dark forest on Mount Warner, a refuge.

a sore tryal I have been tryed with

ELIZABETH'S DIARY, APRIL 27, 1788

I

"What lies with great weight on one's mind, is apt to get into the pen," Elizabeth observed in a letter to Betsey.[1] And it was first in the spring of 1788 that her diary revealed a new preoccupation that was to be an ongoing source of sorrow:

> This day the fruit of Gods House has been sweet to my taste. I hope I am not finally given over to hardness—a sore tryal I have been tryed with the week past; not of death but a Living affliction—one which perhaps will Live with me as long as I live ... very carnel and stupid have I felt my self of late—tis for my humbling—and I am bowed down greatly; I go mourning all the day—when I view it coming from the first cause the hand of God I feel more calm but when I look upon it from the second cause which is a tender con-nection it cuts me to the heart.[2]

She accuses herself of being "carnel and stupid." Both words appear fre-quently in eighteenth-century writings with somewhat different mean-ings from present-day usage: carnal in the literal sense of corporeal, rather than sensual or sexual.[3] Elizabeth used this word on a number of occasions, often following Sacrament days. Trapped in the flesh, she felt unworthy and incapable of the transcendent experience that she expected from the Communion Meal. *Stupid* is another word that she applies to herself, particularly on the Sacrament Sundays, its common meaning in the eighteenth century that of insensibility, a deadening or paralysis of one's faculties, moral indifference.[4] The state of mind expressed by the word *stupid* had been a theological concern for many centuries, referring to spiritual apathy or *acedia,* the sin much feared by medieval monks.[5]

Although she did not identify the source of her anguish, her reference to the "second cause" points to someone close to her, and the intensity of her emotions, to her husband. "The first cause," she says, comes from "the hand of God," sent perhaps to test her faith. Such a trial she can accept, but the second cause, "a tender connection," cuts her "to the heart." The doctrine of first and second causes would have been familiar to eighteenth-century congregations.[6] Elizabeth found it possible to bow to the will of God, but to forgive the earthly agent of a painful wound, one so deep that she believed it would stay with her for the rest of her life, she found more difficult.

The trouble continued to occupy her thoughts. On June 29, 1788, she wrote: "This day Sacrament day—Lord how much I need trouble to bring me near to thee."[7] On August 31:

> Thursday I spent the after-noon alone in the Woods. Some have bitter portions in the vale of tears—O Lord let me not be given over to a hard heart.

Elizabeth's retreat into the forest that surrounded Forty Acres is unusual. She was a social being. Only extreme distress would have sent her in search of solitude, the dark, dense woods emblematic of her state of mind. The plowed fields and John Morison's garden were signs of an ordered life that she could not claim as hers on that day when she felt that she had lost her way.

Elizabeth marked her birthday in her diary each year with a prayer. On November 23, 1788, an unusually long petition begins with a reference to her unspecified trouble:

> This day forty one years old—one year more is added and a pecular one it has been—many mercies I've had and some new sorrows.[8]

Her reference to "new sorrows" implies the presence of others in the recent past. The diary entries for 1787 and 1788 shed no light on the causes of her grief. There are deaths noted, but only the gradual decline and death of the unfortunate wife of John Chester Williams receives more than perfunctory attention.[9]

A letter stored with those written in her girlhood to Miss Pen foreshadows the state of mind expressed in the above entries. Written in the spring of 1787, Elizabeth's letter begins: "My Dear friend. Formerly when I felt lonesome & low, I used to find great satisfaction in writing to you—why may not I try it now?"[10] There were frequent meetings between the two old friends, but as in the sixties when she was writing to Miss Pen, she found it more possible to discuss her most private feelings in writing than in person. The letter is unsigned and does not appear to have been sent and returned, kept perhaps for possible delivery at some future date, as she suggests toward the end of the letter: "I rather think I shall carry it with me sometime, & deliver it my self if I think it will do."

Early in the letter Elizabeth recalls her youthful confessions to Miss Pen concerning her spiritual condition, but also raises questions as to the health of her marriage and perhaps that of the Gaylords:

> I suppose you are able to guess at my present feelings by your own—but my dear can we not say, tis good to feel low sometimes; to be still & sit alone, to take a vew inward & upward; to see our infirmities & even our trials & afflictions together with the perticular dispositions of providence for our reformation, trial, & amendment. . . . do not we lose much comfort & benefit we might gain, because we do not keep sight of the first cause—many things may disturb us here because we see them from second causes.[11]

The closing paragraph contains a mysterious reference to her mental condition:

> I could wish for a favour from you but I fear shall not have it.— excuse a thousand faults, I guess I had better go to bed & see if I can sleep this night—whether I write any more depends upon my feelings—Adeiu for the present you know I am a peice of a Widow.

Absence does not account for the phrase, "a peice of a Widow." Even Charles's position as delegate to the General Court did not take him to Boston for visits of more than two weeks. Several years later, she refers to Charles's absence of not quite three weeks as the longest separation of their marriage.[12] Her sense of widowhood must have arisen from feeling forsaken. If, as she suspected, her friend was experiencing a similar feeling of emotional desertion, recourse to her companion might bring solace. Whatever the "favour" was that Elizabeth had considered asking of her friend, she dismissed the possibility, perhaps because she felt it would be unseemly on her part.

Elizabeth prayed her way through this period of alienation and anguish and, for at least a time, the rift seemed to have healed. But in the summer of 1794, she confided to her diary that the pain and anger that she expressed in 1788 had returned:

> Oh what a day and what a night was the last. Good God help me compose my spirit, teach me what I ought to do, for Jesus sake. . . . what a week of wonder and amazement—such feelings—Lord help me. Surely now I can truly say I am at thy feet in anguish of spirit. I said surely the bitterness of it is past when to a new tryal. O God support thy poor distressed handmaid. Dear Jesus turn it for my good. May my husband find it works for our good as all troubles do for them that love God. From this time forth may we live heavenly, may this bitter cup prepare us for divine food. May we never turn again to folly.[13]

Ten days later Elizabeth and Charles called on the Reverend Hopkins. Whether it was for pastoral counsel or merely a social call is not stated. Three days after their visit to the pastor, on August 3, she wrote:

> I hope I have had communion with thee father and with the saints & sweet friendly communion with my dear husband. A new life we hope to live by the grace of God.

Toward the end of the month, Elizabeth and Charles together kept a day of fasting and prayer, but on Saturday night: "new discoveries—bitter! Cruel." (August 24, 1794) Elizabeth's birthday entry summarized this period of anguish and unhappiness:

this day forty seven years of age—when I view the occurences of the past year how am I filled with amazement, the wormwood and the gall, my soul hath them still in remembrance & is humbled in me. I think it is for my real good that I have such peculiar trials.[14]

Old Testament verses from Lamentations provide her with the words that she needs to express her state of mind.[15] Whatever provoked the pain and sorrow of these outbursts, neither the diaries nor any existing letters pinpoint the precise cause. Her use of the word "discoveries" implies specific acts on the part of Charles rather than ongoing dissension. She does not exonerate herself when she prays, "may we never turn again to folly," which may refer to her response to the discoveries.

Were the "discoveries" then incidents of sexual infidelity? Several decades earlier, members of the "River Gods" had been defendants in paternity suits.[16] Adultery and fornication were still considered causes for public confession in the meetinghouse, a practice that continued in Hadley until well into the nineteenth century.[17] If the couple's visit to the Reverend Hopkins concerned their marital problems, and possibly infidelity on the part of Charles, the Reverend Hopkins may have been willing to substitute a private confession and penance for a public admission at the meeting. Was there a double standard that allowed a prominent citizen to escape exposure? Only a general conspiracy of silence would obliterate every trace of such a breach of behavior in the deacon and justice of the peace, positions that he now held. The recurring references to "discoveries" over an extended period of time suggest that there was more than one woman involved. That she or they may have worked at Forty Acres would make possible liaisons less visible to the community at large, though not to Elizabeth. Only the birth of a child would threaten exposure if the woman attempted to take her employer to court. Such an act would have been daunting for a hired servant, and no record of a paternity suit against Charles Phelps exists.

There is the possibility that Elizabeth's perception of infidelity did not imply specifically a physical relationship, but reflected the high standards to which she held herself and her family. And jealousy can be deluding. Still, the person who emerges from the diaries and letters appears to be a woman of common sense. Introspective as she was, she was careful to scrutinize her own thinking and behavior before that of others.

Elizabeth's circumspection in regard to her relationship with Charles appears to have buried forever the origin of her suffering. Her refusal to name names reveals her sense of propriety, of what is appropriate to declare in writing. It was acceptable to record one's struggle with anger, hurt, and sorrow, but not acceptable to inscribe names on paper that might fall into the hands of future generations. Writing was not casual in the eighteenth century. As with deeds, contracts, and wills, the written word committed the writer for all time.

The anniversary entry for 1795 appeared to bring to an end this unhappy period in Elizabeth's life:

> June 14 . . . This day twenty five years since we were united in the marriage relation and how tender the feelings of this day—how softened my heart.[18]

Five years later, however, on October 5, 1800, the sorrow returned:

> This week had a tryal similar to those I had July 1794 tho not so great degree yet—I think I may truly say that the Lord has tryed me in the tenderest spot and blessed be his name. I hope tis not in vain. Surely it has been a means of weaning me from all earthly enjoyments & shewing me a good in God. But when I feel only the channel thro which the chastisment comes then sorrow like a flood is ready to overwhelm me. When I view the tender connection from which my grief comes a sharp sword seems to pierce thro my very heart. . . . I have hoped that this cause of sorrow might cease but now dear Lord if it is best to continue it I hope I submit.[19]

In this entry she again makes an oblique reference to first and second causes, the latter coming from "the tenderest spot," a wound to the heart. In a letter to Charles, written in 1802, she comes closer to identifying a specific cause of her misery than in any diary entry. Writing from Litchfield to Forty Acres, she closes the letter with an admonition: "I leave all, under providence, to your wisdom & care, only dont introduce Judith [probably the Phelpses' hired help] . . . remember, *faithfully* remember your *faithful* wife."[20] Her emphasized words imply, by indirection, faithlessness on the part of Charles.

In 1807, the problem reappears: "Satt. night a singular night remebered the trouble I had jest 13 years ago the wormwood & the gall, my soul hath them still in rember[ance]."[21] Nor was the discord between them a temporary disaffection. On a torn piece of paper placed among the pages of the diary for 1810, she vents feelings that lie somewhere between anguish and rage:

> Oh what a trying scene, this Lords-day morning introduced July 29, 1810—many, very many the like trials have I been called to bear from the hand of God, but oh dreadful to my heart thro—one who is, or should be my best earthly friend.[22]

Why did she keep this carefully dated loose piece of paper? So easy to destroy, its presence within the pages of the diary increased its chance of survival, though it is possible that one of her descendants placed it there. Putting her distress into written words may have helped her to gain distance from the emotions that were consuming her. Writing gave her the assertive voice that she needed to authenticate that experience. A marriage such as Elizabeth desired can not have been common in the eighteenth and early nineteenth centuries. In a patriarchal society where parents were involved in selecting spouses for their children, where considerations other than love played a significant role, and where women were assigned a subordinate position in the household, the relationship that Elizabeth dreamed of would be difficult to forge. Growing up without a father from the age of seven, she had little time to observe the relationship of her parents and considerable time to imagine an ideal union. Her expectations of Charles may not have been unusual in a young woman, but Elizabeth carried them, along with her demands on herself, into maturity and beyond. She wished for a true partnership, not only through mutual "good service,"[23] as she referred to their community responsibilities, but through harmony of thought and feeling. She had hoped for a soul mate.

What was it then that held them together during these turbulent years? Supports for their troubled marriage came from several sources. Although Charles bought the house from his mother-in-law, Elizabeth *owned* the house in another very real sense. It had nurtured her childhood and had been a solid presence when her mother was absent or suffering from depression. She knew its nooks and crannies, and found quiet places that she made her own. The house cradled her children. It was a homestead, the center of family life, and would house future generations. She described it as the "mansion house of our forefathers," an extravagant claim for a fifty-year-old house, but one that revealed her dynastic ambitions for her descendants.[24] It was to be a dynasty based on religious principles rather than temporal power (though she would not have rejected the latter for her son), one that she hoped would secure for her children and theirs a place in heaven.

Then there was the Forty Acres family, the household that comprised the servants living under their roof, as well as relatives who came under Elizabeth's charge. There was the community, that of the meeting and that of the town. In both, Elizabeth and Charles provided "good service," and received friendship in return. For the pious, the covenant on which the community was founded still held sway. Finally, the Phelpses were partners in business, Charles running the dairy farm, Elizabeth producing cheese.

Elizabeth's identity was not solely that of "Mrs. Phelps." She possessed an uncommon sense of independence that appears in her references to "*my* station in life [my emphasis]."[25] She inherited land from her parents, which gave her some control over a portion of their property. She was born into a prominent family. She possessed managerial skills as well as expertise in the manufacturing of cheese and making of bonnets. While she did not possess the authority of her husband in civil affairs, she exercised another kind of authority that extended beyond her family into the community. She was constantly called upon to respond to personal crises, and in at least one instance, a communal crisis.

Elizabeth's "station in life" brought with it responsibilities. Her gender brought limitations. It may be the latter as well as the former that provoked from her a rare complaint. The eighteenth-century novels and essays in the Forty Acres library advocate, directly and indirectly, compliance with the social hierarchy, which includes deference to the husband's wishes.[26] Elizabeth complied, but not without protest. By recording her protests in her diaries, and occasionally in letters, not only did she unburden herself of all that disappointed and enraged her, she was able to preserve these feelings as part of her personal history. Just as she desired to record the births, deaths, and disasters occurring in the community of Hadley, she wished to tell her own story, all of it.

II

A community crisis that involved Elizabeth occurred in August 1793 when she embarked on "an extraordinary errand." The Hampshire Association of Ministers summoned Elizabeth to Sunderland, along with her friend Mrs. Shipman, to serve on a "Mutual Council." The next week she noted a visit to Mrs. Shipman's house to meet with the two pastors, Mr. Hopkins and Mr. Lyman, "there to take account of some facts relative to Mr. Lyon Minister of Sunderland." (August 25, 1793)[27] A month later, she wrote:

> Tuesday Morn Mr. Hop came here I went with him to Sunderland respecting Mr. Lyons cause—home at night. Had a very sick night, violent pain in my head and back.[28]

At the end of that week, Elizabeth reported: "Mr. Lyon is silenced."

The Reverend Asa Lyon, twenty-nine years old, was a graduate of Hanover College (now Dartmouth), and was noted for his learning in the field of astronomy. He was called to Sunderland in 1792 as associate to the Reverend Ashley and ordained there in October of that year.[29] It was less than a year after his ordination that the council was called to consider accusations concerning his behavior.

Councils grew out of Associations of Congregational Churches and Ministers, the Hampshire Association founded in 1731. Most of the concerns considered by the association were questions for debate concerning the interpretation of the Scriptures. On the same day that Mr. Lyon's case was under discussion, a question concerning the law of Moses was raised: why was it that the period before the purification of women could take place was twice as long after the birth of a daughter as a son?[30] Unfortunately, the answer is not recorded. "Cases of conscience" with which individual clergy were grappling were also reviewed and advice offered when appropriate. Occasionally, the association was a recourse for congregations that wished to register complaints against their pastors or settle disputes within the congregation. The association would then decide if a particular case should be brought before an ecclesiastical council composed of clergy and lay members from the church.

In the case of Mr. Lyon, the association decided in the affirmative and appointed the Reverend Samuel Hopkins of Hadley as moderator. Other members of the council were to be "mutually chosen" by Mr. Lyon and the church "to hear and form judgement and decision upon the matters of criminal conduct of which Mr. Lyon is reported to be guilty." He was accused of "immoral and scandalous conduct, by falsifying the truth and by certain lewd and lacivious actions."[31] If the defendant refused to participate in this process, then the council was instructed to call in people from neighboring churches. It is at this point that Elizabeth and her friend were summoned. After a number of meetings, Mr. Lyon was "convicted of several immoralities and scandalous offences disqualifying him from the Gospel ministry." He was then deposed from his "sacred office."[32]

The council expressed hope that Mr. Lyon reform his ways, atone for his sins, and meet with forgiveness, but not in Sunderland. Furthermore the town had some trouble in reclaiming the homestead and land given to him when hired. Forgiveness must have been granted in South Hero, Vermont, where he went on leaving Sunderland. After preaching for one year, Lyon organized the church that he led for the next forty-five years. The final words on Mr. Lyon in a Sunderland history were charitable, allowing that he was "a remarkable man in some respects," perhaps referring to his knowledge of astronomy.[33]

Although women could not be ordained, nor speak from the pulpit, nor serve as deacons, their judgment was valued in cases such as this one. The Association of Ministers may have wisely recognized that female opinions would be valuable in cases involving women as victims. Elizabeth Phelps and Mrs. Shipman must have been respected for their sense of fairness and ability to make sound decisions, although the ordeal cost Elizabeth one of her severe sick headaches.

Women of Hadley, reminiscing in later years, described the Porter women of Elizabeth's generation as workers, but it was Elizabeth that they singled out as "industrious."[34] In his memoirs, Porter remembers his mother as "reserved and silent" when among those that she did not know intimately.

> In mixed society she was cautious and guarded in her conversation, and I never heard her speak evil of any one. The law of kindness dwelt always upon her lips. . . . among her friends and familiar acquaintance she was free and communicative, and ready to sustain her share of the conversation.[35]

How tempting it would have been to decline appeals for assistance that pulled her out of the enclosed circle of old friends and family. Yet her sense of obligation to community, underlying so many passages in her diaries, would have made such a refusal impossible.

Elizabeth's complaints about the amount of work that fell to her alone were often accompanied by lamentations for the lack of food for the soul. Like Martha, she was "careful and troubled about many things," while recognizing that "the better part" belonged to Mary. It is in such grievances, however, that she reveals the principles that ordered her life:

> surely I have had a wrong temper of late—what is it material whether our time be spent in making cheese or making shirts,—it is apparently the dictate of providence I should do the business which is allotted for me, & may I not find as much communion with my saviour, think of heaven as freely, exercise as much love & benevolence to my fellow mortals (perhaps more kindness & pity) as when sitting in my parlour . . . these are not words of course, I really think, but dictates of my heart—& a heart too which has been shamefully riseing against my occupation & business in life. [36]

"Dictates of [the] heart," she believed, have greater power than mere words. Yet she recognized that emotion might lead her in a direction that, rationally, she would not choose to follow. If indeed her business was the "dictate of providence," she needed to find a way to reconcile the heart's desires with the will of God. "The pursuit of happiness" was not a goal that Elizabeth believed appropriate. Willing surrender to God's will was. Personal suffering, she recognized, could increase her compassion for her fellow human beings, perhaps experienced more profoundly while churning than sitting quietly at her father's desk in the parlor. With one exception, the diaries record her compliance with what she perceived as God's will, and that exception—try as she might—was her relationship with her husband.

III

Charles Phelps has left no diaries and few letters (beyond those to his son). They are reserved in content: "you know I am as poor a hand at letterwrighting—as at visiting," he wrote to Betsey. None of his letters to his wife shed light on the rift in his relationship with Elizabeth. Beginning, "my dear wife, and closing, "I am your affectionate Husband," they are formal, seldom exhibiting spontaneous expression of feeling. When they do, however, they are all the more convincing for their rarity. During Elizabeth's absence in Boston at the birth of Sarah and Porter's first child, Charles wrote frequently. "It is lonesome and I think much about you," he complained.

> I have been to NHampton and have received a Treasure—the receipt of your letters gives me real Joy—but how thankful ought we to be to the Supream Being for our mercies—I have been rather gloomy this some Time. [37]

His son Porter paints a gentle portrait of his father as a man of honor, just, and calm. He was a highly respected member of the community, one who took a leadership role in a number of community undertakings, who served as a justice of the peace, and deacon in the church. The Porter family's fears that he might squander the family estate had long since been allayed. Charles would serve as executor for General Porter's estate in 1796, certainly a strong indication of the deceased's confidence in his honesty and his judgment.

In 1792, Charles Phelps was appointed to the first of several tenures as justice of the peace, bringing with it the title Esquire. In 1797, Elizabeth's diary reports "a large court" at Forty Acres.[38] Charles had purchased numerous chairs, a number of them crafted by Samuel Gaylord, which were put to use on these occasions, as well as for the teas at which Elizabeth presided. In his position as justice, Charles conducted a variety of hearings pertaining to offenses against community harmony: any breach of Sabbath Day observances, profanity in public places, fornication, lewdness, or disorderly conduct. In addition he was empowered to perform marriages, serve as referee in civil disputes ("references" in Elizabeth's diaries), issue search and arrest warrants, license tavern keepers, oversee the Militia draft, break up riots: in short, "all matters relative to the conservation of the peace."[39] The justice's jurisdiction was limited by the amount of money involved (in civil actions, "not exceeding the value of four pounds"). He punished by fines "all assaults and batteries that are not of a high and aggravated nature." Despite these limitations, the position of justice of the peace gave to Charles considerable power in the affairs of Hampshire County, and led to his appointment to numerous committees involving construction projects: a bridge across the Connecticut River, the new turnpike to Boston through Pelham, and the county jail. The latter, to be built of stone, replaced one built of squared logs, "very insecure, and from it many prisoners escaped." Built in 1773, "it answered its purpose for about twenty-seven years, holding securely all prisoners who were willing to remain within its walls."[40]

Elizabeth's diaries record Charles's frequent absences to "lay out roads" in the hill towns: Ashfield, Heath, Colrain, Worthington. While under British rule, the Colonies had received little support for the improvement of interior roads, thus reducing competition with imports from the mother country. After the Revolution there was a surge in road building with the backing of farmers and merchants, both of whose interests were served by improved traveling conditions.[41] Laying roads in these areas involved surveying, the clearing of forests, and the extensive labor that produced passable surfaces for wheeled vehicles. The miles of low stone walls that line New England thoroughfares and meandering back roads represent hours of hard labor. Winding in response to the demands of both terrain and landowners, the roads traverse hills, valleys, and streams. Charles's contribution was undoubtedly that of surveying and mapmaking rather than actual physical work, his age (and perhaps his status) exempting him from such labor. His surveyor's instruments, the transit and chain used for measuring, are stowed away in the house's attic.

A strong sense of propriety on the part of both Elizabeth and Charles must have preserved the appearance of a serene and solid marriage. Both of them occupied positions of responsibility in the community, Elizabeth's lacking an official title, and both served as arbiters in matters of discord. That Charles valued Elizabeth's companionship and felt affection for her would not have compensated, however, for the absence of the faithful, single-minded devotion that she so desired.

IV

Elizabeth's sorrow at this period of her life did not quench her thirst for new experiences. She found time for excursions to see friends, to Franklin to hear the renowned preacher, the Reverend Nathaniel Emmons, to inspect turnpikes in the making, to admire the newly made canals in South Hadley, and the "curiosities" at Dartmouth. The latter consisted of mementos from Captain Cook's travels with the addition of a stuffed zebra from a philanthropic (and whimsical) Englishman.[42] She traveled to Byfield to examine the first incorporated woolen factory, built in 1794.[43] She was undeterred by long rides on horseback. Another diary entry describes what appears to be an excursion for pure pleasure:

> Fryday morn Dr. Porter & Major Porters wives Mr. Strongs wife & I set off for Dalton—Mr. Phelps went with us. Satt. he came home—we women rode around the country into Pittsfield.[44]

Charles accompanied them as far as Dalton and then returned home. The women remained for several days, lodging with relatives, the Ashley Williamses, and when they left, Mrs. Williams rode with them for ten miles, an act of friendship and courtesy. They proceeded without a male escort. Their journey on horseback over forty-three miles of county roads, rutted and full of small stones, or perhaps along the incomplete turnpike from Pittsfield to Northampton, was not just a leisurely afternoon outing, but an adventurous expedition.[45]

Under the week of May 6, 1798, Elizabeth noted in her diary:

> Wednesday Fast day . . . This is a continental fast appointed by the President of the United States John Adams on account of the dark aspect of our publick affairs with France—War is greatly threatened.[46]

On that day Mr. Hopkins preached on Psalm 44:26: "Arise for our help, and redeem us for thy mercies' sake." Only fifteen years after the Revolution had come to an end, the possibility of armed conflict once more hovered over the young nation. This time the problem arose from the French refusal to receive American envoys seeking to negotiate an agreement concerning trade between the two countries. A French decree stating that any neutral vessel carrying English goods or arriving via an English port was a "good prize," subject to confiscation.[47]

Fasts had been declared routinely during the Revolution, but were not authorized in subsequent years by President Washington, raised in the Anglican rather than Calvinist tradition. He proclaimed national

Thanksgiving Days twice only in the course of his administration, the first time in response to urging from a joint committee of the First Congress. The penitential language of the Colonial fasts returned with President Adams, who asked his countrymen to "acknowledge before God the manifold sins and transgressions with which we are justly charged as individuals and as a nation."[48]

New Englanders were accustomed to annual fasts held on a weekday during the spring, coinciding with the planting of the fields.[49] The belief in the fundamental degeneracy of the human race outlived Edwardian Calvinism and called for communal penance when war threatened to erupt, its outcome seen as hinging on the direction of God's wrath. Fasts consisted of two services at the meetinghouse, including both preaching and prayers. Most of the congregation went without food until after sundown, and certainly Elizabeth Phelps was among the abstainers.

The country was divided between those who saw England as their natural ally and those who did not wish to break with their old friend, France. New England Federalists belonged to the former group, and among them was the Phelps family. Repeated threats from foreign powers serve to rouse people to expressions of patriotism. The Federalist party under the leadership of Alexander Hamilton was growing in importance during the 1790s and had a strong position in New England. In August 1798 Betsey went into town to Colonel Porter's "to assist making the Federal Flagg—did not make it."[50] (August 12, 1798) The next day, however, Betsey was hard at work altering a gown with the help of Elizabeth's friend, Mrs. Shipman. Gowns may have seemed a more imperative need than flags to nineteen-year-old Betsey at this stage in her life. Nevertheless, two weeks later she wrote to Porter's fiancée, Sarah Parsons:

> I sometimes feel my own bosom fir'd with the glow of Patriotism— & would do all in my power to animate those over whom I have the least influence—there Sarah—am I not Federal? pray don't tell any body that I write politics—for they say 'tis not feminine—yet I think our sex is interested in the cause of liberty. (August 27, 1798)[51]

Summertime along the Great River muffled the rumbles of war in 1798, at least for the young. Elizabeth's diary depicts a rustic pastoral at Forty Acres. The Hitchcocks returned for a visit in July. On August 1, a large party of young people, with picnic baskets, sailed to an island in the river to drink tea. In the same month, Porter brought his fiancée home for a stay of several weeks. Porter, Sarah, and Betsey, with a group of friends, made an excursion "up the mountain" (September 16), the time of apple picking.

The previous week Elizabeth had written that her mother was "poorly," an oft-recurring word associated with Elizabeth Pitkin Porter, now on the verge of her eightieth year. For the next two Sundays Elizabeth stayed home from meeting to look after her mother, a sure sign of the gravity of her condition. Visitors began to arrive: the Reverend Mr. Hopkins, Mrs. Gaylord, the Widow Porter, Mrs. Walker. Mrs. Gaylord returned to watch the night of September 29, and Charles's sister, Dorothy Warner, the next night. "Sunday evening many people here to see her."

> Tuesday morn five o'clock appeared more distressed—grew worse & worse till about a quarter before eleven then expired without a groan. breathed shorter & shorter. . . . Mrs. Gaylord came just at her last gasp.[52]

The community gathered around the dying Elizabeth Porter, as it had in her widowhood, through her chronic illnesses and the terrors of opium addiction. Mrs. Gaylord and Sarah Parsons laid out the dead woman, a somber initiation into duties that were to come with the latter's membership in the family. A message brought Thankful back from Brimfield the next day. On the following day, in what seems a fitting final chapter to her life, the body of Elizabeth Porter was placed in a boat and conveyed down the Connecticut River to a wharf close to the meetinghouse, and then carried across the field to the cemetery. Her last journey was down the same river along which Elizabeth Pitkin had traveled northward from Hartford to begin her life as Elizabeth Porter. Betsey, having begun a journal in 1798, noted the death of her grandmother:

> last week on Tuesday—a quarter before eleven—my grandmother left this world she passed a gloomy & uncomfortable life here O may I hope that she has exchanged it for one infinitely glorious.[53]

Inevitably the rhythm of life at Forty Acres resumed. Friends and travelers arrived on the doorstep. The Hitchcocks returned to Brimfield,

Porter and Sarah to Boston and Newburyport respectively. Elizabeth prepared for Thanksgiving Day.

> one is missing of our family who will never return, every year since
> my birth have I kept Thanksgiving with my mother till this but no
> more—a long farewell.[54]

As the third generation began to disperse, the promise of future children gave to the house a new function, both practical and symbolic. It
was to become a gathering place, a lodestone drawing family members
back to this source. Not only in the family, but in the nation, a new era
was beginning, one that expanded the commercial possibilities for farms
such as Forty Acres and found expression in architectural forms. Despite
the ongoing discord between Elizabeth and Charles, the house and surrounding buildings expanded yet again, announcing still greater ambitions for Forty Acres.

Chapter VIII

⌒

"This Great Cathedral of a House"

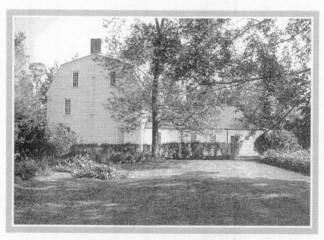

*"a great deal of business done here—
the new roof raised on the old house."*

THE FAMILY dwelling, having settled into the ground above the Great River for nearly fifty years, stretches and reaches outward into the north garden and south toward the great barn, then upward. A gambrel roof now rides on top of the old structure, declaring its manorial stature. Outbuildings continue to multiply—an enclosed woodshed, corn barn, tan and cider-mill houses. Sheep graze within a fenced yard east of the barn and not far from the house. The elm trees have soared beyond the rooftops and, in summer, spread a green gauze tent over the compact colony of buildings. In the winter the elms stand as stark sentinels guarding the approach to Forty Acres.

The old house has shed its Georgian dress and put on apparel suitable for the New Republic. Gone is the medieval overhang, the painstaking rustication. White clapboards shine through interlaced branches, and a new portico leads to the main door fronting on the road that runs between Hadley and Sunderland. Sidelights break through what was the large double doorway, bathing the central hall with morning light. The back of the house has acquired a long veranda overlooking fields of wheat, rye, corn, and beyond—the wide, winding river. This west side of the house exposes the sturdy, broad pine boards—nailed flush, one on top of the other—that sheathe the entire house. The afternoon sun warms the orange-brown wood and the benches nailed to the wall. Trestle tables await the harvest celebration of the ongoing cycle of sowing and reaping.

Horses, oxen, and the large dairy herd pasture to the east of the road and beneath the wooded hillside. From that hill, the viewer looks down on what seems a peaceable kingdom, a dream realized, and like all dreams, ephemeral.

such confusion, you would not know this solitary antique
habitation; the house is undergoing a complete repair.

LETTER FROM BETSEY PHELPS TO SARAH PARSONS,
JULY 18, 1799

I

Changes in the lives of the Forty Acres family found visible expression
in the expansion of the house. Structural and decorative alterations to
the house were ongoing. Samuel Gaylord, with two apprentices, had
begun refurbishing the Phelpses' house interior in 1775, working inter-
mittently over the succeeding eleven years to cover the pine board
sheathing with plaster and Georgian woodwork. Mr. Billings came in
January 1782 to put a fireplace into Elizabeth Porter's upstairs bedroom,
surely a response to her increasing bouts of depression during which she
kept to her room. The original kitchen had become the family sitting
room in the early 1770s, reserving the front parlor as a place to receive
callers. One corner of the sitting room must have been Elizabeth's, with
its connections to both front and rear of the house. It was the likely place
for her father's desk, mentioned in Porter's Thanksgiving letter as residing in an inner room, along with an ornamental clock.[1] From the window to the south, Elizabeth was able to see the arrival of callers on foot,
horseback, or by carriage and greet them at the south side door, most
frequently used by both family and visitors and opening directly into the
sitting room. Through the room's west door was the kitchen with a large
cooking fireplace, its capacity much increased from the small corner
hearth of the original kitchen. This new configuration of rooms allowed
her to withdraw from the center of activity, yet remain within calling

169

distance. The distinction between public and private spaces implicit in the original plan was now further defined. Although the diaries make no claim to Elizabeth's role in the design of changes and additions to the house, the alterations from the original plan were most clearly adapted to her particular needs. Work outside as well as inside the house continued; in March 1782 Elizabeth noted that "our folks begun to get Timber for a Barn." Two months later the preparations were complete; a brief diary entry summarizes what would seem today the work of months:

> Monday we had a great number of men here to raise a new Barn, move an old one and a House—all done and safely thro the mercy of God. (May 26, 1782)[2]

Only a community of people accustomed to working together could complete an undertaking such as this one in a single day. No wonder that Elizabeth saw divine intervention at work.

Samuel Gaylord's renovations of the interior of the house in the 1770s and 1780s transformed Forty Acres into a fashionable Georgian dwelling.[3] The dark walls were plastered, painted, and embellished with wainscoting, chair rails, moldings at baseboards, ceilings, around windows and new paneled doors. These additions produced interesting complex patterns of light and shadow; they softened the angles between floor, wall, and ceiling and countered the verticality of the walls with stabilizing horizontal lines. The painting of the walls was the result of an involved process, in which the base pigment was a strong color softened by a glaze. Analysis of the hall paint reveals the first layer to be Prussian blue overlayed by a verdigris glaze.[4] Blue paint was rare, the most expensive color in the eighteenth century.

The resulting Georgian elegance further distinguished the house's work areas from its leisure places. Forty Acres expanded in tandem with the expansion of the country. The community in which the Phelpses functioned grew, in many cases taking them out of the house, but also bringing that wider world to their doorstep. The list of guests on one day in February 1787 included "visiters from ten different towns," including Hartford and Wethersfield, Connecticut.[5]

Following the Revolution, the desire for Georgian houses and civic buildings began to give way to new influences from England. There was a search afoot for a style that would express something of the spirit of the new republic. Builders imported English pattern books by Batty Langley, Peter Nicholson, and others, which then found their way to the New England interior. The neoclassicism of the English architects of the period was also characteristic of the work of Charles Bulfinch, Asher Benjamin, and Samuel McIntire, New England's leading architects. East Coast merchants, in close touch with England and enjoying a period of affluence, were anxious to own houses that would represent the most recent architectural developments and proclaim the owners' position in their communities.

Excursions to visit their son, friends, and relatives kept the Phelpses abreast of these developments and fed Charles's desire to enlarge and transform the house and outbuildings. When children leave home, the incentive to enlarge the homestead and to increase its uses is apt to disappear. The reverse was true of Forty Acres. The farm was becoming more and more productive, Charles's position in the local and state government more prominent, and now that the Phelps children had reached adulthood and marrying age, an enlarged family was inevitable. And so Forty Acres underwent further radical changes, both inside and out.

In December 1794, Charles wrote to his son in Newburyport with a request:

I wish you to send me the dimentions of Mr. Parsons Barn as I expect to build something of the kind early in the spring—and I think Mr. Parson's pleases me better than any I have seen—you will not omit the height & weadth of the Chaise room.[6]

In the spring Elizabeth's diary duly notes: "Monday had our Chaise house raised."[7] Constructed in between the house and the 1782 barn, it was of substantial proportions, its most striking feature a large central entranceway framed by pilasters supporting an arch with keystone, in imitation of stone or brickwork. Both its white clapboard and the architectural details around the door and windows were characteristic of the new Federal style.

This structure was just the beginning of the series of additions and renovations that took place during the 1790s. A new enclosed woodshed replaced what had been essentially a simple covering roof. Betsey wrote to her mother from Boston in November 1797:

This morning when I awoke and heard the rain and wind beating against our windows—I turned to Mary [Thankful] and began to tell her how I presumed this South wind had wet our shed—before I tho't that it was demolished, and I hope a low building reared in its stead.[8]

The building she refers to is low and long, extending from the 1771 north ell to the new chaise house. Next to the south wall of the house is yet another kitchen, followed by the now enclosed woodshed and a barn-like space for storing corn.[9] Small arches duplicate the chaise house entranceway across the entire addition. These repeated arches with their simplified classical detail produce a rhythmic counterpoint to roof angles and corners, creating harmony and grace in this practical extension of the house. The design for these additions may have derived from the barn that Charles Phelps had seen at the home of Theophilus Parsons in New-buryport, but the application of that design to connecting structures must have come from Charles himself, or perhaps father and son together.[10] Porter Phelps had an eye for architectural design. In a letter to her brother, Betsey requested that he send a plan for a meetinghouse.

The good people of Hadley talk a great deal of building one—& as I have seen specimens of your talents that way—I should like to see one of your construction.[11]

It is likely that Porter was enlisted in the design of these buildings, as his memoirs testify to his involvement in the changes in the house proper that took place in 1799.[12]

The south ell kitchen did not replace the existing one built in 1771. In its separation from the house proper, the new kitchen may have served as a summer kitchen, accommodating the large numbers of farmworkers to be fed, as well as an increased production of cheese. This kitchen contains the largest fireplace opening of any in the house and connects with two small rooms, one containing a pump, the other storage shelves.[13] There is evidence that walls have been moved to accommodate changes in the family's use of these peripheral spaces. A small room adjoining the new kitchen is identified on a family-drawn map as the cheese room.[14] The entire addition made possible the increased production that now exceeded the needs of the Forty Acres household, the surplus to be marketed. Elizabeth was in business, producing cheese for the Boston market, as well as local customers.

The work on this elaborate extension took six weeks to complete. In the midst of the construction, Elizabeth added a hasty note to her diary: "We all in confusion, the hearths laying." (October 22, 1797) As there is only one hearth in the new addition, the plural noun suggests that old hearthstones were being replaced with the same Longmeadow stone used in the south ell kitchen.[15]

On November 19, Elizabeth reported that work on the woodhouse had been completed. Construction must have moved from north to south, the kitchen and related rooms completed first. Two weeks earlier Elizabeth wrote to Betsey, visiting in Boston, describing enough work to keep two kitchen fires going:

> this day we have been hard at it I can tell you. made a cheese—churned—got dinner for between 20 & 30 persons, made between 20 & 30 mince-pies—Mrs. H. [Thankful] has been a bed a long time—tho' tis now but about 8 but we shall all be rested by the morning I hope.[16]

The twenty or thirty people fed must have included workers involved with the construction, the mince pies baked in anticipation of Thanksgiving.

II

Once again, Charles served as deputy and representative to the state government, this time for two years, 1798 and 1799, just as further renovations were under way at Forty Acres. Two terse entries in Elizabeth's diaries give little sense of the upheavals that must have occurred in order to bring them about: "The latter part of this week a great deal of business done here—the new roof raised on the old house." The disruption of the domestic routine is reflected in the next sentence. "I hope I learn something by all." (April 28, 1799) One imagines her throwing up her hands with vexation at what had been wrought.

It was not simply a matter of covering the roof with new shingles; a gambrel roof replaced the former pitched roof necessitating a change in the structure. Essentially a double pitched roof, gambrel roofs had begun to appear in the Connecticut Valley in the mid-eighteenth century.[17] This roof significantly increased the house's livable space. The double pitch made possible the addition of a third story almost equal to each of the two floors beneath. It also enhanced the house's claim to manorial status among the residences of the Connecticut Valley. Gambrel roofs were associated with civic as well as domestic buildings, the Springfield Town Hall and the State House in Hartford.[18] The period in which these roofs were in high fashion had passed, however, suggesting the practical benefits to be the principal incentive. In or out of fashion, the gambrel roof at Forty Acres produces pleasing lines. The sharp angles of the pitched roof are softened, the eye's progress toward the peak slowed.

Approaching the house from either the south or the north, one is struck by the harmony of mass and line. The 1752 overhang of the second floor has disappeared beneath the clapboards; the roof's eaves project over the facade, creating a strong shadow that emphasizes the amplitude of the house's new covering. The effect is of a sheltering ark. Narrow cornerposts and cornices at the roof's edge trace the exterior of the house's facade. Wooden lintels and thin moldings outline the windows, the moldings producing strong vertical accents against the fine horizontal lines of the slender clapboards.

In his frequent travels to Boston, Newburyport, and Springfield, Charles saw the homes of prosperous merchants. The architect, Asher Benjamin, was building houses at this time in Greenfield, Massachusetts, often visited by both the Phelpses.[19] Builders working in rural areas parted slowly with traditional construction habits and styles, but the spirit of the new republic that Thomas Jefferson wished to see shaping the country's architecture was beginning to appear in the Connecticut River Valley.

The renovations at Forty Acres include a number of features of the new Federal style: a pedimented portico, dentils beneath the eaves and surrounding the pediment, and louvered blinds. The portico, projecting out from the east facade, invites passersby inside in a way that the previous large double door, flat against the facade, did not. The single paneled door has made room for the addition of side lights, opening views and sending light into the central hall. Beneath the side lights are panels containing an understated cartouche-like design.

The exterior appearance had been important to Moses Porter, its rustication certainly one of the most time-consuming operations in the construction of the house. The emphasis was on enclosure and solidity, attributes of the English manor house. The renovations of the 1790s put Forty Acres in tune with the spirit of the Federal era. These transformations were the work of an intuitive designer (or designers) who amalgamated Colonial and Georgian attributes of the house with Federal additions and produced a harmonious whole. The house's wooden construction is now undisguised. Whether the renovation of the house was solely under Charles's direction or a collaboration of father, son, and builders, it testifies to an innate sense of the beauty that comes from an economical interplay of form and function.

Once again, the house's interior, as well as the exterior, underwent radical changes: "Satt: pulled down our chimney at the south end of the old house." (June 2, 1799)[20] This chimney had originally provided hearths for the parlor and the first kitchen that was later transformed into the family sitting room. These two rooms joined together created a single room, thereafter referred to as the "Long Room." The south exterior entrance now opens into a hallway. One fireplace on the south wall replaces the two corner hearths and projects out into the room, creating recessed spaces on either side. The mantel is centered in the south wall, measuring from the classical arch that creates an alcove at the east end of this room. Classical detail outlines both the mantelpiece and the archway. Chair rails along the walls repeat the motif that appears on the mantel. The same restraint that characterizes the exterior of the house appears in the details of the Long Room. A subtle segmentation of space in the alcove and recessed areas defines intimate places within the long, rectangular room. Elizabeth's diaries record multiple uses for this room: ceremonial occasions, family reunions, sleeping quarters, meetings of the court, as well as a place in which to find the solitude to write letters and entries in her diary.

The greater capacity for entertaining provided by the Long Room demanded a larger kitchen, even further removed from those spaces dedicated to gatherings of family and friends, meetings of committees and the court. The original ell of 1771 now extends northward to provide for a spacious kitchen, increased pantry space, and access to the keeping room in the south ell. Although clearly designed for work, the kitchen is finished with the wainscoting, chair rail, and moldings that appear in the remodeled Long Room. Plaster covers the beams, producing clean angles where ceiling and walls join. These details bring the kitchen and the Long Room into the Federal era, and distinguish it from the simpler south ell kitchen, the latter's simplicity identifying its function as part of the working farm.

The ample fireplace of the north ell kitchen accommodates large cooking pots suspended from a trammel, a baking oven, drying rack, and the necessary long-handled utensils needed for cooking over an open fire. Pewter plates that came to Forty Acres with Elizabeth and Moses Porter line the mantel and were used by the family, according to Thankful, for many years after Charles and Elizabeth's marriage.[21] The long pine table, another legacy from Moses Porter, occupies the center of the room, its burnished surface testifying to years of rubbing. There is room for a dough box and spinning wheels in the corners, as well as an armchair, making it possible to spin, knit, or knead bread while the oven warms and the pot simmers.

This new kitchen eased the extensive annual preparations for the Thanksgiving feast. Elizabeth's anticipation of that feast appeared weeks, even months ahead of the day in her diaries, and the holiday increased in importance as her children began to leave home.

Many of the preparations were done by Elizabeth herself; "this day— I began & had done my pies .22. or .23."[22] (November 15, 1805) Her desire to bring family home at Thanksgiving provided her with increased energy for the week-long preparations. Kitchen fires must have burned constantly, the scent of cinnamon, cloves, nutmeg, drying apples pervading the back rooms of the house. As this feast day is now, it was then a family ritual, but a sacramental one as well, which merited a prayerful paragraph in the November diaries. Many years later, a grandchild re-created the scene in the kitchen at Forty Acres prior to that celebration:

> Truth obliges me to say that it began like the old Jewish feast of the Passover, with a great slaughter; not of lambs, however, but of equally innocent chickens; and, must I confess it? on the Sunday evening of Thanksgiving week. . . . in those days Sunday was universally regarded as beginning at sundown Saturday and ending at sundown on Sunday. . . . Monday was devoted, of course, to the weekly washing and nothing must interfere with that. Tuesday was the great day for the making of pies of which there were from thirty to fifty baked in the great oven. . . . Two kind of apple pies, two of

pumpkin, rice and cranberry made out the standard list to which additions were sometimes made. . . . Wednesday was devoted to chicken pies and raised cake. The making of the latter was a critical operation. If I mistake not it was begun on Monday. . . . The two turkies have been made ready for the spit. . . . This was done in a tin oven with an iron rod running through it and also through the meat that was to be cooked. This was the spit. The meat was fastened to the spit with skewers so that by means of a small crank at the end, it could be made to revolve in order to cook evenly. The oven was in shape something like a half cylinder with the open side to face the fire. But there was a still more primitive way of roasting turkey and one which was resorted to sometimes when our family was at the largest. Room was made at one end of the ample fireplace and the turkey was suspended by the legs from the ceiling where was a contrivance to keep the string turning, and of course, with it the turkey. On the hearth was a dish to catch the drippings and with them the meat was occasionally basted.[23]

The previous kitchen, built in 1771, is now a sitting-dining room, replacing the one absorbed into the Long Room. Its hearth was reduced in size and given a mantelpiece in the Federal style, along with enclosed beams, chair rail, and moldings surrounding doors and windows similar to those that adorn the Long Room. Numerous cupboards, at least two now dismantled, argue for the room's use for dining, although a diary entry of 1804 mentions the sitting room, clearly referring to this particular space.[24] That the room served both purposes is not surprising, as several of the rooms had multiple functions in response to expanding demands on the family.

The Federal embellishments, as well as the new "mansion" roof, do not disguise its agrarian raison d'être. The house, outbuildings, planted fields, woods, pastures, and orchards, along with John Morison's orderly gardens, create a northern version of the Jeffersonian dream. Formal gardens were a rare sight in rural western Massachusetts. Even in Southern states, where they were more common, it was difficult to find a skilled, dependable gardener. George Washington was constantly in search of an experienced gardener, often resorting to indentured servants. He hired and fired ten gardeners between 1762 and 1797.[25] Hadley gardens tended to be modest extensions of the family's vegetable plots. Until

Morison's arrival, Elizabeth's diary references to gardening are sporadic and casual, appearing primarily before her marriage. An exacting and professional gardener, Morison laid out the gardens to the north of Forty Acres in the form of a rectangle, subdivided by paths into four parts, a circular rosebed at the center, the whole lined by fruit trees on the long sides.[26] Family letters going between Boston and Hadley contain Morison's demands for very particular seeds.

Travelers approaching Forty Acres from the east, among them Timothy Dwight, looked down from Mount Warner on this formal design in the midst of plowed fields and stretches of woodland. A decade after the renovations to the house were completed, Dwight, then president of Yale, traveled through the Connecticut Valley and described Forty Acres in *Travels in New-England and New-York*:

> This estate lies on the eastern bank of the Connecticut River, and contains about six hundred acres, of which about one hundred and fifty are interval, annually manured by the slime of the river. . . . The interval is universally meadow, and of the best quality. The remainder of the farm is remarkably well fitted for every kind of produce suited to the climate, abounds in pasture, and yields an inexhaustible supply of timber and fuel. It is also furnished with every other convenience. . . . The scenery, both near and distant, is eminently delightful; and within very convenient distances all the pleasures of refined and intelligent society may be easily enjoyed. In a word, this estate is the most desirable possession of the same kind and extent within my knowledge.[27]

Dwight's references to the beauty of Forty Acres were certainly, in part, a tribute to Morison's labors.

From its beginning, the house has reflected both practical and aesthetic considerations, the former never sacrificed to the latter. Unlike the coastal houses of prosperous merchants that served as display cases for their wealth, Forty Acres played an active role in securing the family's livelihood. The newly renovated house's ability to feed and house still larger numbers of people reflects the Phelpses' growing involvement with the community, as well as the farm's increasing production. The various ways in which the rooms accommodated large numbers of people denote a far more public role for the Phelpses' home than is true today for the dwellings of prominent citizens. Having become retreats, they tend to be hidden from view, their entranceways seldom fronting on public thoroughfares. Certainly Charles Phelps designed the family dwelling to project an image of the prosperity that he and his wife had labored to achieve, but the restraint evident in the adaptation of the Federal style is commensurate with the reserve and circumspection evidenced in his letters to his family.[28] While the changes made to the house in the 1790s make a muted statement as to the prominent position of the family, they increase its ability to welcome large numbers of people through its doors.

III

Multiple factors motivated the Phelpses' decisions to make these changes to the house. Perhaps most pressing was their desire to provide space for their son and his family. Charles had written to Porter, who was about to leave Newburyport, expressing his desire that he return to practice law in the Connecticut Valley.[29] Porter at first complied with his father's wishes. Writing his memoirs many years later, he recounted having closed his law office in Boston on April 1, 1799, and returning to Hadley:

> where I was occupied till late in the autumn superintending the alterations and repairs of my father's home to render it convenient for the accommodation of two families, as I proposed to bring my wife there in the spring.[30]

The third floor would provide ample room for an apartment for the young couple, or perhaps ultimately for the older people. Porter continued to reside with his parents as renovations proceeded.

The long-awaited marriage of Porter and Sarah Parsons is given the same spare treatment characteristic of such events in Elizabeth's diaries. At the end of 1799, she reports Porter's departure with Betsy for Newburyport, but it is not until January that we learn the reason: "Charles married to Sarah D. Parsons this first day of this year."[31] Porter returned soon after the wedding, perhaps to continue work on the house. A letter from Betsey to Sarah, written in July 1799, intimates that the question of the young couple taking up residence at Forty Acres had been a subject of discussion, yet to be resolved:

We are all in health—but in such confusion, you would not know this solitary antique habitation; the house is undergoing a complete repair—and may I not hope you will soon make it your dwelling? pardon me, my Sarah—it is a subject, which has too long, I think, been treated with reserve—Charles [Porter] has been long expecting an answer to a letter he wrote, some time since—he has partly told me its contents—and upon your decision, I believe his hopes now hang.[32]

Sarah's answer must have been in the negative. In her diary entry of March 9, 1800, Elizabeth announces: "Our son set out for Boston this morning to reside there."

The finishing details were never applied to the third floor. The wood sheathing and overhead beams remain uncovered. There is an attic feel to the space. A remark in Porter's memoirs reveals both his and Sarah's reluctance to leave the urban society of Boston for the rural life of Hadley.

Sarah (as with most members of this family, she has a nickname—Sally) spent the summer of 1800 at Forty Acres. An entry in her diary is brief and somewhat ambivalent: "I have visited at various places in Hadley and past my time more pleasantly than profitably, I fear—"[33] Was she bored, or is she regretting what may have seemed an extended period in which the young couple were not making serious decisions? Uncertainty as to the future site of their residence lingers at the end of the summer when they have returned to Boston: "went to housekeeping the first day of September—and how long we shall continue so heaven only knows."[34]

In January 1799, a new name appears in Elizabeth's diaries—Mr. Huntington, who replaced Mr. Hopkins in the Hadley pulpit for a single Sunday. The day after the Sabbath, he came for tea along with Patty Dwight, related to Timothy Dwight. Betsey's diary also records his sermon text, but unlike her mother, she elaborates: "Mr. Huntington gave us two excellent sermons."[35] She then continues for two pages, summarizing the sermons, space she did not give to Mr. Hopkins's sermons. Huntington was a graduate of Yale, and protégé of President Dwight, who credited himself with suggesting that his student introduce himself to the Phelps family. Dwight had drunk tea at Forty Acres in May 1798 and admired their attractive daughter. Matchmaking was not the prerogative of females alone! A few months after their initial meeting, Dan Huntington returned to Forty Acres two days in a row, only to find that Betsey was visiting her sister in Brimfield. He was not to be deterred. The following Monday Betsey returned to Forty Acres, accompanied by Mr. Huntington. Subsequent entries record longer visits, including a week's stay with the Phelpses in December 1799 when again he preached in Hadley. As with all the previous family courtships, Elizabeth's diaries are silent on the implication of these visits, though their frequency, so carefully recorded, alert us that a courtship is in process.

In February 1800 Betsey went to Brimfield for an extended stay, and Elizabeth joined her there the day before the birth of Martha Keyes to Thankful. When Betsey returned to Forty Acres with her nephew Charles Hitchcock, Dan Huntington was waiting for her, but it was not until the following September that there is any evidence that his persistent courting bore fruit. A letter from Betsey to her father, written during one of her visits to Boston, is almost exclusively concerned with proposed expenditures for her trousseau. After making a round of Boston shops and artisans, the letter concludes: "it is quite a disadvantage not to have money I find."[36]

Farmers from Western Massachusetts continued to be plagued by the scarcity of hard currency. Barter was still the major form of local exchange in rural areas, even among prosperous farmers.[37] It was not until the Phelpses needed to make a number of purchases at a distance from Hadley that they experienced the embarrassment of inadequate means of payment.[38] Betsey's letter spells out her problem:

> Mr. Smith from whom I could purchase things to the amount of 150 dollars will credit, if you pay him common interest from this time till next April—Nichols and Poor, who have the best cottons in town will credit only ninety days . . . I suppose for my china, glass, crockery and silver, I must pay the money—my cabinet work, I think I can procure here cheaper than at Northampton, but that is not material—I shall likewise want some money for clothes—Thus Sir, I have stated the matter—and knowing your circumstances, I think it best, all things considered for me to write to our friends at L—d [Litchfield] and gain his consent, to defer all preparation on my part till next spring—perhaps it will be difficult, but he is a reasonable man, and I can at least make the attempt.

Elizabeth's diary makes no mention of these financial difficulties, nor any further references to Daniel Huntington until close to the end of the year.

The final week of the year 1800 was one of preparation. With no preliminary announcement, the diary breaks the news:

> Dec. 28 . . . Fryday night Charles [Porter] & Sally [Sarah] got here from Boston. Wednesday the Waggons came from Litchfield for Betsy's things. Went before night. Soon Mr. Huntington, Mr. Gould, Mr. Smith came. Thursday Jan 1 1801 jest at night our friends came in & about 7 Mr. Huntington & Betsy were married. Lord bless them. Fryday morning the Litchfield people left us & took with them our dearly beloved daughter, hush every anxious thot.[39]

Charles Phelps must have found some way to satisfy the Boston merchants, apparently avoiding the petition to Dan Huntington.

Family tradition places the wedding ceremony under the alcove arch at the east end of the Long Room. No descriptions of the event exist, but certainly Elizabeth and Charles gave their daughter a wedding comparable to their own, and now in a more spacious setting. Betsey's circle of friends resided in surrounding towns as well as Hadley: Amherst, Hatfield, Northampton.

Now all of the Phelps children had left the sheltering embrace of family and Forty Acres. Their absence would bring Elizabeth more frequently to the desk in the Long Room or to the table in front of the kitchen fire to communicate with them.

Chapter IX

~

ONCE AGAIN THE
PLEASURES OF A PEN

*"harvest day, & there are now in our stoops more
than .20. eating supper."*

MIDNIGHT, she thinks. The clock in the hall agrees. She places another log on the kitchen fire and pushes the table close to its warmth. All the other hearths in the house are cold. The mighty March wind pummels the northwest corner of the house. On the pine table sit a candle, a sheet of foolscap, a box of sealing wax, a container of newly made ink, and a pen. The fire leaps high and deepens the surrounding shadows that conceal the wood box, the spinning wheel, the cooking pots, and the pewter plates on the mantel. The light from the candle focuses her attention and creates a place from which the mind can travel distances, backward and forward in time. She sits down to the pleasure of writing. "My dear child," she begins and inscribes the letter M with the flourish of an attenuated loop. Once this first letter appears on the paper, words crowd one upon the other and she writes rapidly lest a thought be lost. A falling log breaks the silence. Her candle sputters and goes out. She replaces it with another, and now the only sound is the scratching of her pen as it moves rapidly across the paper. The fire has died down to a few embers. She is cold. An owl calls faintly, gradually moving closer to the house. She holds a wafer of wax over the candle flame, then seals her letter.

Hadley March 16 1801 monday eve—8
Dear Eliza I dont believe you take half the pleasure in
writing to me, as I did in writing to you—for I had
quite as live [sic] write as work.

LETTER FROM ELIZABETH TO BETSEY

I

The fervor with which Elizabeth had taken up her pen to write to her girlhood friend returned when all of her children left home. The expanded house now provided her with a number of retreats where she could "visit" with each one of them: the desk in the Long Room, a table in front of the kitchen fire, the small desk in the keeping room behind the dining/sitting room. Her satisfaction in this new call upon her energy and time appears in a letter to Betsey: "you must know I have got all my writing apparatus into the long room, my letters & papers make the table & room look like a writing office almost."[1] There is a wistful note in the addition of the word *almost* as none of these places could be identified as her private "office."

In a letter to her husband in 1776, Abigail Adams expresses delight in the temporary possession of such a room, ending on a similar note:

I have possession of my aunts chamber in which you know is a very conveniant pretty closet with a window which looks into her Flower Garden. In this closet are a number of Book shelves, which are but poorly furnished, however I have a pretty little desk or cabinet here where I write all my letters and keep my papers unmollested by anyone—I do not covet my Neighbours Goods, but I should like to be the owner of such conveniances. I always had a fancy for a closet with a window which I could more peculiarly call my own.[2]

The letters that went back and forth between Elizabeth and Betsey during the years that followed her daughter's marriage to Dan Huntington are replete with information about day-to-day life in early nineteenth-century households of the Connecticut Valley. They encompass a wide variety of topics: child-rearing, housework, farmwork, accidents, journeys, mental and physical illness, politics, scandals. Such details put flesh on the bones of our skeletal view of the past.

Elizabeth's letters also run the gamut of her feelings: pleasure, loneliness, curiosity, anxiety, melancholy, humor. She dispenses with letter-writing conventions in her impatience to put pen to paper. "Why betsy," she begins one letter, "the more I write, the more I want too [sic]." Her style is pithy and colloquial:

> Fryday .4. o clock—your father is gone to meet the meetinghouse committe, & I jest eat some dinner (which by the way dont sit overwell) & now for writing about the weather which in general I have little to do with as anybody.[3]

Writing in the midst of one day's chores, she communicates a breathless sense of bustle and frustration:

> I've jest done my mondays stepping about & now when I'm ready to set down to work, theres so many things to do, for my heart I dont know which to set about first . . . Elisha suffers for his frock made—your father must have some new stocks—my old check'd aprons are scandalous,—all last weeks mending is not finish'd yet & plenty more—good-day the clock strikes 3.[4]

"Mondays stepping about" was first and foremost laundering, a communal affair that must have enlisted all the available house help, as well as Elizabeth's supervision. Then follows a list of tasks that demands her attention alone. "So many things to do." The diaries provided her with a place to record the making and receiving of visits, "social work" as one historian has labeled this activity.[5] Letters, on the other hand, relay news gathered during those visits, as well as the life of the house that was hidden from the Long Room company. They are conversations, conveying a strong sense of the presence of the person addressed as well as the addresser, an implied dialogue. Like many conversations, they flit from one subject to another. Letters were delivered by relatives, the preferred carriers, friends, even strangers, and, it would seem as a last resort, the government postal service, the nearest office situated across the river in Northampton. Although sealed, letters traveled a rough road and often passed from one traveler to another, making their confidentiality uncertain.

Advice and admonitions dominate the letters written soon after Betsey's marriage. Elizabeth was not yet ready to relinquish her maternal responsibilities:

> well to begin with your Girl—you must see to & really do a great deal about the house-work your-self, to tell you the truth I fear for you in that spot, as much as anywhere—you dont like to take hold right sharp.[6]

In response to a letter from Betsey, Elizabeth replies with reassurances:

> the love & friendship of your husband will continue long as you live I trust—but that very perticular attention will likely in some degree abate—your father said when we were there, these was your days of Courtship—for I do think the poor man had as odd a time of Courting as ever one had.[7]

A remark that appears in one of Betsey's letters may explain this last comment. In reference to Mr. Huntington's plan that they visit Hadley and Brimfield, she exclaims: "What do you think I have got to tell you of this husband, whom I had once almost refused."[8]

Elizabeth did not hide from Betsey the sorrow that she felt at their separation. She and Charles visited the newlyweds in Litchfield, Connecticut, several weeks after the wedding, and complained in a letter, "never did home appear so gloomy as now."[9] Few letters omit a plea for a visit from the Huntingtons or from their daughter alone.

Even Charles Phelps joined Elizabeth in schemes that would bring the Huntingtons to Forty Acres:

never yet once have we *enjoy'd* Mr H. at Hadley & according to your plan we are to have very little of his time now—pray my dear children contrive somehow to give us more—your father wishes to have him preach at Brimfield if it could be so.[10]

Preaching at Brimfield would bring the Huntingtons together with the Hitchcocks, and fill the pulpit vacated by the departure of their present minister, who, like the Reverend Mr. Lyon of Sunderland, was decommissioned after a twelve-day meeting of a counsel. "But to return," the letter continues, "we must not only claim our son to preach here [Hadley] but to spend considerable time among the friends." She proposed a fortnight as "short eno'." When that letter failed to bring the Huntingtons to Forty Acres, she tried another approach:

I told John [Morison] how you wanted some of his garden—& your father being present said I must tell you it was the best way for you to spend the summer here—Mr H. would preach a great deal better without you—fine advice.[11]

Elizabeth's declarations of loneliness were matched by what is clearly homesickness on the part of Betsey. After her parents' first visit to Litchfield, she wrote to her mother describing a visit to her "chamber" in order to shed tears in private, while looking longingly at the road along which they travelled back to Hadley. Elizabeth replied:

now as to your *Chamber visit* I have tho'ts of saying to you as we sometimes do to children if you are such a naughty Girl we must not come again.[12]

These letters record the close relationship between mother and daughter, each appearing to be the other's confidante.

Betsey, in turn, wrote to her mother for advice and for solace. Although expressions of her devotion to her husband are frequent: "appropo of harmony—it still subsists between my husband and me—indeed I think it increases," the pull toward Forty Acres remains powerful throughout their correspondence.[13] In July 1801, she sent a wistful letter asking if the harvest was over:

that used to be a joyful time, and I hope it is this year—you remember how pleasantly we spent it last year—Sally [Sarah] was with us, and partook of our rustic amusements.[14]

Betsey's homesickness gives to such memories a romantic cast, not diminished by Elizabeth's accounts of unremitting labor:

what a busy week we had last week—about .15. men the whole time night & day—but we can do anything if we do but think we can—last Satturday we churn'd made the cheese got all the dinner in the pots.[15]

Dinners during that season at Forty Acres were served to large numbers: "harvest day, & there are now in our stoops more than .20. eating supper."[16] The last day of the harvest brought family and hired hands together for a celebration, its highlight the "reaping cake." Preparations for the cake involved as many members of the extended family as could be induced to enter the kitchen. Elizabeth referred to that event in an August letter to Betsey, undoubtedly rekindling her daughter's nostalgia:

did I ever tell you our reaping-cake observations—the monday before our harvest day we bak'd the cake & you may well think what conversations we had—that among some other similar occurrances perhaps the anniversary will never pass unnoticed.[17]

Elizabeth's grandson Theodore remembers this annual celebration terminating in the harvest "shout," an invitation to the farmer to provide liquid refreshment for all the harvesters.[18]

The pull toward Hadley apparently had spread to Dan Huntington as well. In a letter of April 10, 1801 (little more than three months after the wedding), Betsey recounts a conversation with her husband in which he muses about the possibility of retreating to Hadley, where he would have greater leisure for study, thereby increasing his usefulness; "then I," she adds, "could comfort the declining years of my honour'd parents—and spend the remaining part of my life in that dear spot."[19]

Another of the Phelpses' plans for bringing their daughter home was for the entire family to be inoculated with the smallpox vaccine, using their tanning house in which to quarantine those inoculated. In the late fall of the previous year, Dr. Cutler had inoculated Betsey, her parents, and a number of their servants with kine (cow) pox, a new form of inoculation by serum taken from cows suffering from a mild viral skin disease. Discovered in England in 1798, it was still regarded with suspicion, both as to its effectiveness and its safety as a preventative. Inoculation of any kind met with considerable resistance; however, the town meeting passed a resolution for one to be held in the spring of 1801. That Elizabeth and Charles proposed yet another inoculation, this time with the smallpox serum taken from a diseased person, evidences their doubts as to the efficacy of the kine pox serum.[20]

Elizabeth had some qualms, however, remembering that Betsey had expressed reluctance to undergo that experience once again:

> I'm almost sorry it was proposed to have it here by us, because if it should not hit your fancy to be innoculated it might hurt your visit."[21]

Once the symptoms of the disease appeared, the patients were quarantined, the Phelps household in their tan house, and about fifty others from Hadley in a new house constructed for that purpose near Forty Acres. They remained confined until the pustules disappeared, their bodies washed, and their contaminated clothes exchanged for clean. Nevertheless, there were instances of people dying after inoculation, and when Charles experienced a severe reaction, the family's concern was justified. He had been inoculated twice, a week apart, apparently thinking the first had not taken:

> Mr. Phelps took a large dose of salt peter for salts—had a dreadful day—vomited once about 2, then the Dr. Left him but his distress increased to such a degree we sent again for him.[22]

Betsey arrived from Litchfield and was inoculated on May 1. She continued to make a round of calls with her mother during the following week until she developed symptoms, at which point she was quarantined in the tan house:

> Wednesday night Betsy had a very ill night—in the morning of Thursday her symptoms were alarming—sent for Dr. Colman got here about 1, staid till near night.[23]

Unable to walk, she was confined to her bed for a week following her release from the tan house. Two days after returning to her parents' house, she set off with her husband for Boston. They got as far as Dr. Cutler's in Amherst where she was unable to continue and returned to Forty Acres for another week of convalescence.

Betsey recorded her experience in a poem, "Lines written in May 1801 during a confinement with the Small Pox," in which she writes of "the gloom of death," "scarce one bright ray," and beseeches God "to save her flesh from death."[24] There is, perhaps, a certain amount of poetic over-statement in this poem, but death from smallpox continued to be a very real possibility, whether from inoculation or direct contact with the disease.

Another of Betsey's poems follows the one written in the smallpox "hospital," perhaps celebrating her return to health, in which she pays homage to the "Whip Poor Will," a woodland bird not heard in Hadley Village, but in the woods near Mount Warner, the vicinity of the tan house.[25] The two poems have been preserved along with two others, one an acrostic based on her husband's name, a classical poetic form popular in the seventeenth and eighteenth centuries. Her poems evidence a sophisticated knowledge of literature, one that she must have gleaned from her intermittent schooling in Amherst, from libraries at Forty Acres, and the Boston and Newburyport homes that she visited. She also had the advantage, during formative years, of an older brother at Harvard, who returned for vacations with books and conversation that would have stimulated her desire to learn. Elizabeth, on the other hand, had had no brother, not even one to make her a pen.

There is an interesting contrast between the mother's style of writing and her daughter's. Elizabeth's letters seem to be spoken thoughts and feelings, transcribed as they enter her head and spilled onto the page. Betsey's reveal forethought, "emotions recollected in tranquility." Both mother and daughter were readers. They sent books back and forth between them, but the impact of their reading on their written expression differs. Betsey writes more consistently in complete sentences, she develops thoughts in paragraphs, she uses fewer colloquialisms.[26] The influence of the novels and poems that she read as a young woman can be felt in her choice of words and the cadences of her writing:

> I have been giving your letters which we received this day another
> perusal—but why this air of melancholy? alas it cuts me to the heart,

and the tears are streaming from my eyes while I write—"don't for-
get us," you say[,] it is an injunction altogether unnecessary.[27]

In another letter moistened by tears, she reassures her mother: "but do not
be surprized—or grieved—it is a luxury sometimes to indulge melancholy."[28] Betsey's poems reflect the Romantic poets' attitude toward
nature, an attitude that distances her from the exigencies of farming:

> *Sweet bird awake; renew thy gentle lay,*
> *And warble still from night till dawning day—*

and

> *Beneath a cloud, with scarce a glimering way,*
> *I walk forlorn, and wander from my way—*[29]

It is Betsey who referred to her Hadley home as "Pleasant Hill" in letters
to her future sister-in-law Sarah, perhaps preferable in her mind to the
agrarian "Forty Acres."

Tears stream from Elizabeth's eyes as well, but they provide only brief
interruptions to the flow of her thoughts: "how strange it is the tears will
stream when I have a letter from you on reading it—tis all right feel all
you feel, enjoy all you enjoy."[30] It is likely that both mother and daughter read Richardson's *Clarissa,* mentioned in a letter from Elizabeth to her
son, but for Elizabeth the message rather than the medium seems to have
had the greatest impact.[31]

Gossip very occasionally found its way into Elizabeth's letters, providing lively interludes for the more serious business of advice and lamentations.[32] One instance is a woeful tale of a bride left waiting at the altar, or
at least upstairs in her chamber *with the groom,* both in their wedding
clothes. Just before they were to descend to the parlor for the ceremony,
the groom, "wringing his hands in great distress," confessed that he did
not love her enough to marry her. Elizabeth's description of the denouement testifies to her ability to re-create a scene that she had not witnessed
herself, but had heard described by another:

it soon took air something was the matter—& one must step up, &
another till the whole were pretty well collected in the brides appart-

ment. which was a place of great confusion—Mr Gillet beging for tenderness & pity to be shewn him, as he really suffer'd greatly, & none seem'd dispos'd to say much to molest him but Mrs Spring who gave him a piece of her mind—Mr Coffin beg'd the Company to pertake of the Supper which was in readiness of which Mrs Hop's mother was presidentess in all respects as Mr Coffin is a widower a sad sorrowful meal was attend[ed] tho' not devour'd—Mr & Mrs Spring took home with them the faint-hearted Gentleman.[33]

On occasion, Elizabeth's sense of fun extends to the solemn subject of sermon texts. In a letter to Betsey concerning a sermon at the Hadley meeting, she writes:

I must jest tell you, Mr Woodbridge yesterday, preach'd the same sermon I wrote to you about in my last . . . he told us he did it by perticular desire—who's we can guess.[34]

Along with her preoccupation with journeys between Hadley and Litchfield came concerns about the weather, the condition of the roads and the Connecticut River. Powdery snow provided the ideal travelling conditions, making a smooth surface over the rutted mud so prevalent then in New England:

I think a sleigh will run here considerable well—I am almost ready to wish we could hear how the road is your way . . . but if there is no snow we must be silent.[35]

Although she was constantly on the lookout for a good snowstorm to prepare the roads for easy traveling, it could be too much of a good thing. Sometimes, particularly on trips to Litchfield, Elizabeth and Charles were obliged to get out of the sleigh so that the horses could plunge their way through drifts: "they would spring (we had the best horses) & jump & try with all their strength to get thro', & yield & lie down—then up & at it again."[36] Some years later Elizabeth and Charles Phelps, with Betsey and Dan Huntington, were able to travel the ninety miles to Boston, usually a two-day trip, in a double sleigh over a well-packed snow covering, leaving at 8 A.M. and arriving at 4 P.M. The purpose was twofold, to visit Porter and Sarah and for both Betsey and Dan to have teeth put in.

Apparently Boston's reputation as the place to go to solve problems corporeal was already established.[37]

Roads were sometimes hazardous. Elizabeth worried that Betsey would have trouble traveling from Litchfield to Hadley unaccompanied by her husband. The shortest route was through the wilderness of western Connecticut, which necessitated crossing two mountain ranges. It was less traveled than the road from Hartford that ran along the plains on the east side of the river. A map of 1795 shows a series of roads running north and south in western Connecticut, and very few running east and west.[38] The Phelpses traveled to Litchfield by way of Westfield, Massachusetts, where they turned west, crossing the mountains over narrow roads, sometimes no more than bridle paths.

> If you think no one can come from Litchfield to help your journey over the rocks & mountains, your father & all of us think it best for you to come by Hartford . . . I durst not have you attempt coming over that dreadful stony way alone, for I walk'd on foot & your father led the horse several times down thos steep precipes.[39]

A letter from Elizabeth describes other hazards—mud and losing their way. It was "heavy wheelng," the mud so deep "we almost stuck fast." In addition, "there was no moon, & the roads bad in many places." On this journey, the Phelpses lost their way until they met a wagon carrying local people who led them to a nearby tavern where they spent the night:

> what a relief it was to my mind you can hardly conceive . . . my fear & anxiety was soon quieted . . . but as to the tavern we found very good entertainment indeed, & the people very assiduous to please.[40]

II

Elizabeth and Charles were now traveling in three directions: to Litchfield, to Boston, and to Brimfield. The two-day journey to Boston was made in the family chaise, with a stopover near Worcester with friends or in lodgings. Elizabeth often made the one-day trip to Brimfield on horseback:

dont you think that last week on Thursday I mounted on a pillion behind Reuben [an indentured servant] a few moments before .8. we alighted in safety on the step stones of Mr H: hitching-door, to the no small surprize of them both—indeed I dare[d] not put off no longer all things consider'd—for I had .2. or .3. letters since you left us of the same nature as the one you saw.[41]

Thankful is a constant concern in the letters that go back and forth between Forty Acres and the Litchfield parsonage:

Cap't Smith & wife have been going to Brimfield ever since we came home & tis proposed for me to [go] with 'em but the weather looks now very forbiding, & really the time seems long since I was there & I fear for my daughters feelings too—do you write to her.[42]

In her next letter to Betsey, she mentioned having received a letter from Thankful: "it appeared to me rather gloomy moving, the tears run like rain when I read it."[43] Elizabeth did manage a trip to Brimfield two weeks later and wrote to Betsey from there telling her how pleased Thankful was with the prospect of a visit to Litchfield in August. "It *has* been sad times here—you can hear the perticulars I hope soon."[44] If Betsey did hear the "perticulars," no written account of them survives. At the end of the same year (1801), Elizabeth wrote to Betsey: "I feel for our daughter at B-d if she could only have one thing."[45] One can only speculate what that "one thing" was. A letter from Betsey the next year may narrow the possibilities, but doesn't point to the specific source of the problem; "what troubles she had to bear," she wrote of her sister, "troubles of the mind I mean."[46] There is a letter from Thankful to Elizabeth, along with two of her poems, which supports her mother's view of the prevailing mood at Brimfield:

Brimfield March 18, 1801 You ask me how I feel? I feel much better than I did before I received your kind letter—hard tho'ts sometimes arise that I have few friends or none.[47]

Thankful misses her sister in Litchfield, now living a three-day journey distance from Brimfield: "when I shall see her I know not, *she is lost to me now*." She closes her letter with an appeal for a visit from her mother: "I hope I shall see you very soon for I wish to say a great many things which I cannot write."

Several poems written by Thankful have survived, and like Betsey's, they testify to her knowledge of verse forms and Romantic poetry. Thankful worked over her poems, crossing out a word and trying another. The rhyme scheme is regular, and her efforts to retain a consistent meter almost succeed. There is a hymn to the seasons in strict sonnet form. In a poem composed in 1800, she pines for Forty Acres:

> *When far from this abode*
> *Of happiness and love,*
> *These walks by me untrode*
> *Thro' distant walks I rove*
> *Should I revisit this dear place*
> *This faithful wind*
> *Shall call to mind*
> *Those scenes which time can ne'er efface.*[48]

Written in the early years of her marriage, the poems surprise by the strength of her feeling as opposed to the gentle melancholy of Betsey's poems. One line from the sonnet, crossed out and replaced by another, refers to "our bitter past." Another poem is more a prayer than a poetic reverie:

> *This sad suspense, my trembling anxious heart*
> *Seeks aid from heaven; O guide my doubting mind*
> *And thro' this critical important hour*
> *Kindly direct me by thy skill supreme—*
> *No human wisdom can dispel the Shades*
> *That hover round my dark, uncertain way.*
> *On thee alone, Omnipotence I place*
> *My firm unshaken trust; O let my hope*
> *Remain, forever feed on Thee—*
> BRIMFIELD APRIL 28 1799[49]

In these lines she did not try to rhyme. There is a sense of urgency in "this critical important hour" that a regular rhyme scheme and meter might diminish. Future events reveal that these evocations of unhappiness in Thankful's poems were not simply passing moods.

The unexplained "sad times" in Brimfield are not alluded to again in letters or diaries until the end of 1803, when a specific problem gave rise to anxiety concerning the Hitchcocks.

In July 1801, Charles Phelps traveled to Brimfield as Thankful had written that the eighteen-month-old Martha was very sick. She died two days later and was buried on the Sabbath. Nevertheless, the Hitchcocks' trip to Litchfield went as planned. On their way home they passed through Hadley to pick up little Charles, who had been with his grandparents for an extended stay; "he is in haste to go home," Elizabeth wrote to Betsey, "to see where Martha is buried up." An unexplained remark follows: "from the moment we heard of her illness if he had been taken I think they would have felt quite differently."[50] This conjecture is never explained, but implies some unnamed problem associated with little Martha or perhaps the Hitchcocks' stronger attachment to a son and heir than to a daughter.

III

Earlier in this same summer, a letter from Porter recounting another death as a result of a duel took Charles to Boston in haste.[51] For the family it was a shocking affair, a dramatic end to a young life and a serious threat to their son's business prospects. After deciding to give up the practice of law and live in Boston, Porter, backed by Sarah's merchant uncles Eben and Gorham Parsons, had entered into a business partnership with Edward Rand. Rand traveled abroad extensively and established trade connections in Europe and Africa. He had recently been captured by pirates in Tunis, who detained him for several months.[52] On Rand's return from this adventure the two young men formed a partnership, their business located on Long Wharf, Number 28, in Boston.

Porter described this catastrophe in his memoirs:

Late in the afternoon of Saturday, June 13 . . . Mr. Rand met me in State St. and taking from his pocket-book a parcel of Bank Bills observed that as he should probably go out of town in the morning, I had better take charge of them—it being then too late to deposit them in Bank. I took them and he passed on. It was the last time I ever saw him.[53]

The duel took place at Dorchester Point, just south of Boston. A boarder from Rand's boardinghouse summoned Porter, who went there to claim his partner's body. He, with Gorham Parsons and several friends, buried Rand late that night in the Granary Burying Ground near the Boston Common.[54] The choice of hour and the haste with which he was interred must have arisen from their desire to protect their friend's reputation from the stain that would come with his acquiescence to an illegal act. Outlawed in Massachusetts since 1719, dueling met with general disapproval in New England, the body of anyone who died during a duel "appropriated to anatomical demonstration."[55] There was also a "shared oath of secrecy" among the participants that protected many duelists and their seconds from discovery and prosecution.[56] This particular duel was an "affair of the heart." A man named Miller had challenged Rand to the duel, the cause believed to be a "lady from Rhode Island." Miller, his second, and Rand's brother, the victim's second, all fled Massachusetts following Rand's death. Miller was indicted for murder, but escaped incarceration by exiling himself to New York. Duelists did not always attempt to kill their opponents, obtaining satisfaction from the risks involved in confronting each other with weapons. Porter, however, implies that Miller may have intended to end Rand's life:

> It was reported at the time as a fact, stated by the sentinels at the fort, that Rand had the first fire and missed, and that then Miller took deliberate aim, (which *may* or *may not* have been true).[57]

Duels as a recourse for settling disputes were more frequent in America and in the North than has been assumed.[58] The most famous encounter, between Alexander Hamilton and Aaron Burr, occurred three years after the affair with Rand.[59] Alexis de Tocqueville made a distinction between European and American duels, the former concerned with points of honor, the latter, he maintained, fought in order to kill one's opponent. De Tocqueville was mistaken. The code of honor was very much in place among the ruling elite in America. "Honor was the core of a man's identity, his sense of self, his manhood."[60] Hamilton accepted

Burr's challenge, but decided that he would withhold fire, thus defending his honor and, at the same time, adhering to his moral principles that denounced dueling.

At the time of the Burr-Hamilton duel in 1804, Timothy Dwight, still president of Yale College, preached a public sermon on the subject of dueling. Not only was it a violation of the Sixth Commandment, he argued, it encouraged "passionate displays of 'wrath and revenge,'" inappropriate behavior for rational, educated gentlemen.[61] In *Travels in New-England and New-York*, Dwight dedicates a chapter to "Learning, Morals, &c. of New-England" in which he endorses the right to bear arms: "Every man is, or ought to be, in the possession of a musket," he pronounced.[62] Muskets equip their owners for public service in the Militia. Dueling, on the other hand, he could not justify. In lectures to his students at Yale, he repeatedly held up such combats as examples of the social consequences of sin.[63]

Dwight apparently did not know of the duel between Rand and Miller, though he claimed to have heard of five other duels having taken place in New England, and though he was related to the Porters.[64] The secrecy surrounding the burial of Rand and the disappearance of the parties involved appear to have minimized the publicity surrounding the event, preventing it from coming to the ears of the New England public-at-large. Sudden death was not a new experience for the Phelpses, but the melodramatic circumstances of this death had a particularly strong impact on Charles. Elizabeth wrote to Betsey: "never did I see your father so shocked at any death before . . . from the moment he read the letter his heart inclin'd toward Boston."[65] Dwight's reasons for denouncing dueling would surely have been shared by Charles Phelps.

Soon after this event, Elizabeth's thoughts turned from her son to his wife. Letters between Elizabeth and Sarah had been concerned with Elizabeth's proposed visit to Boston and what seems to have been some doubts on her part as to a mother-in-law's welcome. Sarah was expecting a baby. Reassurances arrived from both her son and his wife, laying her misgivings to rest. She wrote to Betsey describing the welcome that she received on her arrival in Boston:

> my lovely daughter opened her door & bid us a hearty welcome— the table was set for dinner & every preparation made for a third person—even the meat was veal that mother might be suited.[66]

Sarah declared that Elizabeth's arrival had removed any thought of danger in the approaching birth. Elizabeth, on the other hand, worried that their optimism would not prepare them for possible disappointment.

On September 18, a son was born to Sarah, yet another Charles, and Elizabeth sat down to write to Betsey. The description of his birth is typical of Elizabeth's diary accounts of births except that a doctor assisted her, more common in urban areas than in rural Hadley. Visiting relatives there to welcome the baby lent the event a festive air:

> Sally [Sarah] had the warning I always had—but felt very ill— about 12 perceived herself something unwell—we sent Jack to call Dr Rand—about 2 he came—sat & chatted awhile then left us— came again before 6—the three Aunts step'd in,—& a long time before 8 we had a fine *boy* how different from poor Mrs H: . . . (by the way two uncles & charles have been in & seen our son already) the nurse here & all still by a little after 10 is not this too charming, Sally appears as well as we could wish—the perticular difficulty Mrs H. labour'd under, we are very agreably sure there is not the least sign of here.[67]

(Along with Thankful's unidentified troubles, she had prolonged labors and the "perticular difficulty," perhaps hemorrhaging following delivery.) Gatherings such as the one that surrounded the birth of Sarah's baby were the rule. They were occasions on which to bring together female friends and relatives around the woman in labor; births were communal rather than secluded events. Support rather than sanitation was the concern, the dangers of infection from bacteria as yet unknown.[68] The Scottish doctor, William Buchan, censures this practice in *Domestic Medicine* as "that ridiculous custom which still prevails in some parts of the country." He believes the women to be the cause of numerous problems, crowding the house, getting in the way of experienced attendants, creating unnecessary noise, and "by their untimely and impertinent advice, do[ing] much mischief."[69] His predictions were not realized with the birth of this baby. Although the Phelpses owned Buchan's book, the doctor's prohibitions did not change the customs surrounding childbirth at Forty Acres, nor for the Boston family. It is interesting that, since the last quarter of the twentieth century, we have moved away from the antiseptic isolation of delivery rooms to recognize some advantages in the earlier system.

Elizabeth made additions to the letter during the succeeding week, the last one beginning "good news still," as if crossing her fingers. She went on to sing a grandmother's praises of her new grandchild, her fears set aside. Before closing the letter to Betsey, she described her plan for bringing everyone together at Forty Acres for Thanksgiving:

> give my love to your beloved & ask him if I may have you, a little while before thanksgiving, to help me prepare for him, & our other friends.[70]

IV

In these early years of the nineteenth century, Elizabeth's diaries contain fewer references to women coming to the house for extended stays to do house and clothes work than those of the late 1700s. The letters of both mother and daughter are preoccupied with the search for dependable servants. "My girl is a homebody," Betsey complained, "and rather stay there, in rags and poverty; than live out, and earn something for herself—she intends leaving us a week from today—what I shall do then is uncertain."[71] Several months later she wrote: "Candace the girl who is with me I believe will stay two or three weeks more—after that I think of looking again for a little one."[72] Servants came and went after short stays with the Huntingtons. Betsey counted ten different girls that worked for her in the first nine months of her marriage.[73] Both women were particularly pleased when they found a young black girl to work for them, as they believed that they were more willing to work hard. "I am my own negro," Elizabeth complained to Betsey when the heavy housework fell to her alone.[74]

In her letter of June 12, 1801, Betsey recounted, with some pride, her role in entertaining the Association of Ministers meeting at Litchfield. At just one of the association events for which she and Dan were responsible, nearly forty Congregational ministers came to dine:

> I have lived so far, and the worst of this association, I hope is over, after all that Mr H told me of not providing dinner for the whole, I have had it to do—all day on saturday I was at work making pies

and cake . . . and all the meat, for this day's dinner to cook, as it was
tho't best to have a cold collation.[75]

Her concluding remarks on this undertaking refer to her husband:

Our company is all gone. Mr H bids me tell you he is tired almost
to death, and that I beat him all to nothing in going thro' difficulty—tis true, I stand it beyond my own expectations.

The Huntingtons were subject to unexpected visitors and lodgers as well,
much as was Forty Acres, but for different reasons. Travelers without
lodging referred first to the minister's house, always located near the center of villages and towns. In addition, Mr. Huntington decided to take
on boarding students, one way in which clergy and their wives could
supplement their modest incomes.

Colonel Chester's son is coming, soon I suppose—perhaps I shall
be afraid of this *high Blood* but they wish him to be treated with
severity, as he is a great rogue—We should not have undertaken
this business had we not the prospect of good help—a black girl in
town.[76]

In her next letter, she reassured her mother:

Our boarders are not troublesome; Mr Mills who was expelled
[from] Williams Colledge, is really a well meaning young man—
very accomodating, and steady—Mr Chester is a meer boy,
about fifteen, and as unstable as the wind—he is rather noisy and
dirty. [77]

So much for the anticipated "high Blood"!
    Elizabeth clearly found satisfaction in enumerating her domestic
achievements to Betsey as well. The making of cheese is a constant preoccupation in Elizabeth's letters, referring to herself on one occasion as
"the old dairy maid:"

I must tell you of last Satt:—about .3. in the morning I wak'd
with the sick headach grew worse puk'd a number of times—but

knew I must get up. which I did towards .6.—skim'd my milk being oblidg'd to stop, go to the door & puke a number of times—but at last got my cheese set could do no more, took to my bed.[78]

Writing to Betsey on a winter evening, she described alternating knitting on a mitten with churning.

There was a weekly rhythm to the chores that dominated Elizabeth's life: "fryday kill'd hoggs—Satt: made candles—monday try'd [the suet]—Tuesday sausages—& by Wed. I was prety well tyr'd out."[79]

There was a seasonal rhythm as well. Soap was a springtime activity. Aunt Sarah Porter set aside three days in the first week of April for that purpose, "three great kettles of soap."[80] It was also a prolonged chore for Elizabeth: "Tuesday began to make soap. . . . Fryday finished making soap."[81] Whitening (or bleaching) was a summer chore, following hard on the heels of harvesting the hay. "You can easily guess what rest it will afford," she reminded Betsey, who must have observed this process at Forty Acres at least once a year. Whitening involved steeping the linen first in a solution of lye, then for about a week in a mixture of lye and potash. Immersed in boiling water, washed, and then placed in wooden vessels containing buttermilk for several days, the linen was finally spread on the grass, sometimes for a matter of weeks.[82]

Slaughtering on a large scale took place in the late fall when the temperatures dropped, providing natural refrigeration. An Englishman who resided in the United States for the year of 1818 kept a journal in which he wrote down a number of observations on the American diet. "When the hogs are killed, the house is full of work. The sides are salted down as pork. the hams are smoked. The lean meats are made into sausages."[83] Elizabeth refers to sausage making throughout her diaries, a process that was often spread over a matter of days: "Monday killed Hogs 12 Wednesday tryed [separated] the suet." It is not until six weeks later, on January 4, that she is able to record: "Satt: finished making sausages."[84] A smoke oven exists in the garret space over the south ell and would have warmed attic residents during that season of the year, as well as rousing their appetites for ham.

In 1802, Elizabeth had only one house servant, Zerviah, who needed to go home on the day of the harvest meal, leaving Elizabeth alone with the preparations:

baking bread, two sorts & pies, & churning, & cheese, & a great deal
to do in the cheese room—about .10. men to get dinner for—so I
felt griev'd & kept on work—the next day worse than that never took
off my morning cloaths till they were taken off to go to bed.[85]

Changing clothes in midday in order to receive visitors was the mark of
a lady of leisure, however deceptive for women like Elizabeth, who were
laboring in the back of the house before sitting at the tea table in the
front.

Chores do not crowd out advice in her letters. Responding to Betsey's
news concerning the boarders, she wrote:

your boarders I hope will do well, put on patience—remember
every situation has its trials & temptations—dont be too anxious to
get rid of trouble. only let us be persuaded which is the path of duty
& then go on our way rejoicing.[86]

Elizabeth did not always manage to rejoice, allowing herself an occasional grumble when help was scarce: "why . . . now in the decline of life
we are so embarrass'd."[87] She also lamented the lack of visitors, and the
pile of fifteen to twenty pair of stockings to mend, a task that would have
been more pleasant in company. "Such a letter of complaint seems more
like my mothers language than what I generally allow in myself."
Nowhere else in letters or diaries did Elizabeth refer to this tendency in
her mother, and this time only to castigate herself.

Writing for Elizabeth and Betsey was a form of reflection, an accounting of oneself, sometimes the only possibility for that necessary pursuit
of intentional living.

Chapter X

~

BINDING THE TIES

"I have got my paper in my lap by the kitching fire."

S NOW SWEEPS across the western mountains of Massachusetts, plunges into the valley and falls on the Great River. Snow covers the dried brush, wipes out animal and bird tracks, and piles up against fences and farm buildings. Snow clings to tree trunks, roofs, and rides on the wind, buffeting walls and windowpanes. Contours of the house blur. Ground and sky fall away. Uprooted, the house floats free, a sturdy vessel riding the storm.

The next morning, the people in the house wake to a world white and still. Paths from the house and the road to the village have disappeared and in their place is a pristine surface that has smoothed over otherwise bone-shaking stones and frozen ruts, inviting would-be travelers. Sleighs glide over these white surfaces, pulled by horses made frisky by the cold, sharp air, and the bells that adopt the rhythm of their gait.

Winter is unpredictable, isolating. It can bring blizzards, sleet, muddy thaws, all of which confine. An unanswered letter brings anxiety to the sender. Then—unannounced—the world is transformed. Distances are diminished, the journey to distant children possible. It is the blessing of snow.

were the powers of flying given to me—by tomorrow
night probably you would see the old croak poking her
gray head in at some one of your doors.

ELIZABETH'S LETTER TO BETSEY,
JANUARY 24, 1802

I

Letters continued to go back and forth between mother and daughter
with the regularity of a shuttle, weaving a tapestry of labor, local news,
and loving concern for each other. In a letter to her mother soon after her
marriage, Betsey wrote in the margin of the final page: "What I write to
you my father must receive—somethings will not be proper for him to
hear perhaps, if so omit to read them to him."[1] Nothing in that letter
would seem to be "improper" for her father's ears, unless it is her remark
that she rides to meeting in a man's saddle every Sabbath during the bad
weather. Would he have found that shocking or plucky? Perhaps she was
warning her mother that in future letters she might want to discuss with
her physical aspects of her relationship with her husband or possible
pregnancies.[2] Yet, surprisingly, even those subjects do not seem to have
been barred from "polite conversation" among men.

In the midst of her preparations for the Ministers' Association,
Betsey complained of feeling sick; "Mr H—said he thought I had
more of my nervous affection than I have ever had." References to her
"nervous affection" appear in several letters, usually coupled with the
return of her "common complaint," which follows and "carries off"
the former, seeming euphemisms for premenstrual syndrome and
menstruation, less precise but more descriptive. In a letter written June
12, 1801, Betsey mentions a visit from Mrs Wolcott, a new Litchfield

friend, who passed on to her secondhand gossip that she thought might be of interest:

> she told me that President Dwight was at ther uncle Chester's, and gave them to understand that my constitution was ruined by taking the Small-pox at a very *improper time*—You know we suspected he was deceived in that way.[3]

Timothy Dwight, Dan Huntington's tutor while at Yale, took credit for having brought the young couple together, and now evinced interest in the establishing of their family. His concern was premature, but his desire to see his former pupil as the head of a substantial family would eventually be more than satisfied.

Betsey continued to complain of the aftereffects of the smallpox inoculation that may have delayed her discovery that she was indeed pregnant. This news evoked an eager response from her mother, although she veiled the object of her interest, perhaps because of the uncertainty as to the letter carrier:

> there is now twenty questions I want you to answer, which I dare not ask—you can guess what they are—for you can exactly tell what I wish to know—only can you commit it to paper thats the thing.[4]

In a letter of February 17, 1802, Betsey tells her mother that she has written to her sister-in-law Sarah, "and let her into the *fatal secret*—." The birth of a child was a social occasion, but the condition leading to the birth was to be kept secret as long as possible. Was it superstition, a feeling that to announce the coming birth too soon courted disaster? Or was it modesty? Remarks during subsequent pregnancies suggest that it was the latter reason. It is an attitude that continued well into the twentieth century, until feminist movements and increased study of human sexuality have sanctioned open discussion of the various phases of reproduction.

In her next letter, Betsey worries that her mother will not come soon enough, expressing "some qualms, and pains & uneasy feelings . . . and I hope you will be here in time to make all right."[5] Charles Phelps Huntington was born May 24, 1802, and Elizabeth arrived in time for his birth. And now there were even more pulls to Litchfield:

I think how can I bear to have all taken from me not only children but those dear little ones, which they bring jest long eno' to make us love 'em, & then away they go—& leave us here to tug & toil.[6]

But no "toiling" was too much if it would bring the entire family home to Hadley.

The gathering of all their children at Forty Acres brought cousins together and inevitably passed along whatever childhood disease one of them was harboring at the time, eliciting more advice from Elizabeth. When Betsey's baby was exposed to whooping cough and measles, she passed on the remedies applied by Betsey's friend, Mrs. Hopkins, for her child's whooping cough: "I believe she has given it elixir—& puke very constantly." She advised letting the disease take its course as the best remedy, and cautioned: "I long to tell you, to be ware of Drs. . . . they had a great deal too much doctoring at Brimfield by what I hear from Mrs Ward."[7]

Yellow fever was raging in Boston at this time, another cause for worry. A secondhand account of the disease came by way of a letter to Colonel Porter informing him of the death of a friend. In a letter to Betsey, Elizabeth describes the plight of the victim's wife following his death:

instantly as soon as he was dead she & her black girl took chaise & fled for fear of being sent to the hospital—that when she got to her friends none dare receive her into their houses.[8]

A month later she reports on health in Hadley:

it is not very sickly here but a number have died—twice there has been three buried in a day, mostly children.[9]

The numerous small gravestones in New England cemeteries testify to the fragility of children's lives in this era. A study of American mortality rates between 1750 and 1880, a relatively stable era in relation to numbers of deaths, reports: "between one fifth and one third of all children died before age ten."[10] Two of the Phelpses' three natural children had reached maturity, but now there were grandchildren whose lives seemed always at risk.

In December 1802, Elizabeth's letter to Betsey reveals her daughter's second pregnancy: "how glad you get along unsuspected—what a pretty thing could you get near thro'—so—do try—the longer the better."[11] Not quite "near thro'," Betsey reports in a March letter that her condition is known by her Litchfield acquaintances, but asks her family not to tell her Hadley friends as yet.[12] Elizabeth Porter Huntington was born on May 8, 1803, less than a year after her brother Charles. The Phelpses arrived the day before and remained in Litchfield for a month until the baby was baptized.

Their return to Forty Acres was not, this time, to an empty "gloomy" house, for their son, his wife, and child had come to Hadley to reside, "blessing to each other," Elizabeth wrote in her diary (May 1, 1803). Porter's return would seem to have satisfied his father's long-held wish. He was not returning to practice law, however, but to wait out the turbulent period of skirmishes and piracy on the high seas. Problems with England were still unresolved, and France continued to threaten trade between the United States and Europe. The previous fall, Betsey had written to her mother:

> in a letter from brother not long since he says, that "unless prospects are more favourable, some other place than Boston, and some other business than my present will contribute to the support of me and mine"—what his design in going to Hadley is, I cannot imagine he can do no business—and idleness will not suit him or my father—I fear his views as to living are so high—that he will be obliged to expend too fast considering how much it has cost you & my father to build up the estate.[13]

Although there may be a modicum of jealousy in Betsey's reaction to her brother's return to Forty Acres, passages in Porter's memoirs add substance to her fear of his extravagance. Employed as he was in trade with European countries, his fortunes rose and fell along with the volatile relations between the United States and England and France, and his expenditures followed suit.

The presence of Porter and his family at Forty Acres made possible a reunion of all three children and their families in the month of July 1803. In August, Sarah gave birth to another son, Edward, the second grandchild to be born at Forty Acres. His birth followed the pattern of most Hadley births recorded in Elizabeth's diaries. Charles Phelps brought Mrs. Breck, a midwife from Northampton. His sister, Dorothy Warner, and Elizabeth's close friend Mrs. Gaylord came from Hadley. Sarah's Boston relatives appeared on the Phelpses' doorstep within a few days, complete with a coachman and waiting woman, followed by Sarah's uncle, "Mr. Theophylus Parsons & wife & son Charles & daughter Judith in a coach & four."[14] The arrival of this prominent family from the coast would have occasioned a flurry of preparations on Elizabeth's part.

After this spate of visitors from Boston to admire a new grandson, the Phelpses' attention was demanded elsewhere. Elizabeth's diary of November 13, 1803, reports that Mr. Phelps was summoned to Brimfield as "Ward & Hitchcock are very much embarrassed in their trade."[15] A month later, in response to an urgent message from Thankful, Porter went to Brimfield in his father's stead when the latter had gone to New York on business. "We hear from Brimfield," Elizabeth wrote to Betsey, "an Act of Banskrupcy (I dont knoe how to spel it) is taken out.—the sooner they come to a settlement final, the better I think."[16]

Thankful had sent Dr. Butler, a friend who lodged with the Hitchcocks, in search of her father as the appraisers were coming to view their property. Much of the furniture had been purchased by Charles Phelps and she wished him to reclaim it. Hitchcock and his partner had gone to Boston to appear before the commissioners, one of several appointed meetings. The humiliation, along with the deprivation visited upon the partners' families, was undoubtedly intensified by the possibility of incarceration for the debtors. Elizabeth wrote to Betsey that Dr. Butler told her that Thankful "behaves with great steadiness & propriety, he thinks he never liv'd with any woman who appear'd to endeavour *always* to do perfectly right."[17] A year later, Elizabeth continues to worry about the Hitchcocks in a letter to Betsey, as they were again embroiled in debt.[18]

Another source of anxiety was Porter's son Edward. At the age of six months he began to suffer from convulsions, which continued at regular intervals. From February through the summer of 1804, Elizabeth's diary reports frequent recurrences of the seizures: "Edward had two fits Fryday & two Satt." His parents took him to different doctors, they tried home remedies—"garlic steeped in brandy"—and extended carriage rides, resorted to by all ages when suffering from chronic ailments.[19] Elizabeth's participation in Edward's care came to an end in September of 1804 when Porter and his family returned to Boston, leaving Forty Acres once more devoid of small children, and more reasons for Elizabeth to take up her pen.

II

Early in her marriage when she had but one child, Elizabeth developed a deep affection for the little slave girl Phyllis. Later, she found another child to love in Mitte. But that love brought nagging worries as Mitte was clearly an independent spirit, both captivating and prone to insolence. Mitte was terrified of storms. Elizabeth wrote Betsey that the ten-year-old read her Bible throughout a storm and then said proudly: "now I've been a good girl yesterday & today, & I shall be tomorrow, wont that be a great while ma'me?"[20] When eleven years old, Mitte went to Litchfield so that she could help Betsey through the birth of her second child. Betsey had long felt a sisterly affection for little Mitte, sending messages to her while visiting in Boston and Newburyport, saying that she missed having her as a bed companion on cold winter nights.

Both mother and daughter were concerned that Mitte receive an education, and began to teach her to read at an early age. While at Litchfield, Mitte learned to write. A piece of paper remains among the family papers on which she proudly inscribed the name of the Huntington's eldest child in large well-formed script, *Charles Phelps Huntington*. "She has likewise learnt all the commandments," Betsey wrote to her mother, "and some of her catechism—she reads every morning with Mr Huntington and John."[21]

Something of Mitte's spirit appeared in her complaint that Betsey did not allow her to visit friends as often as she would have liked. Despite her application to pious readings, Mitte's behavior continued to leave something to be desired in the eyes of Elizabeth and Betsey. Elizabeth wondered if Mitte should remain with Betsey and worried that she would misbehave and overtax her daughter's patience. Porter, presently at Forty Acres, had more than impatience, which Elizabeth described as an antipathy for the little girl.[22] Nevertheless, Mitte returned to Hadley, which saddened Betsey:

It grieves me to think she cannot stay—having been brought up in the same family I feel a tenderness for her, which her forwardness cannot overcome; what joy would it give me to see her amiable.[23]

When Mitte went back to Litchfield several months later, Betsey's letters contain new concerns for Mitte: "Almond [a male servant] and she are so very sociable when she is in the kitchen that I shall be obliged to keep her principally with me." She informed her mother that Mitte had had "the sign [yet another interesting euphemism for menstruation], you and I did not have till 14" (Mitte was now twelve).[24] Her next letter, however, assures her mother that it is better for Mitte to stay in Litchfield, rather than be exposed to the older help in Elizabeth's kitchen:

I feel as if she was not in so great danger here as she was with your girls—from some things I understood from her, Persis is a poor example for a girl of her years, & she says, Meriam was quite as bad.[25]

Whatever else was going on in the kitchen at Forty Acres, Elizabeth had more helping hands than she had had for some time.

A letter to Betsey, written the day after the Huntingtons' departure from Forty Acres with Mitte, contains a message for the young girl:

O my dear little child, how my heart achs for you, both for this world & another—sometimes I feel really in distress when I think about you, (which I do a great deal)—I feel as if I long'd to take you into my arms & fold you to my heart & entreat & beseech you to be sober & serious . . . O mitte I do hope in the power of God, yet to save you.[26]

Elizabeth asked Betsey to read as much of the letter concerning Mitte as she thought proper, and added that her "earnest desire for her good, is nearly the same as towards my own dear children." The passage following immediately after her expression of anxiety for Mitte jumps to another little girl, probably nine years old.

Ruth Dickinson has got to be a very good child, I hear—can tell the texts, & some parts of the sermons for many months past—&

the bible is her constant study—feels her lost condition & need of a Saviour.[27]

Mitte's resorting to the Bible during thunderstorms was not sufficient indication of her commitment to a truly Christian life for Elizabeth. References to the child's bad behavior appear in both Elizabeth's and Betsey's letters. Mitte was clearly spunky and self-willed, and provides an example of the rebellion that a strict Calvinist upbringing must have provoked in some children.

Elizabeth's last lengthy discussion of Mitte appears in her diary November 25, 1804, when Mitte was thirteen years old:

> I carried Mitte down to her grandmother Wests to life [sic] there. O how pitiful I feel for her. I commit her Lord unto thee. do thou dispose of her as seemeth good in thy sight. My heart melteth for the poor child, dear Lord thou knowest her case, once more I give her up to thee May I ask mercy for her & myself.[28]

Elizabeth's identification of Mitte's paternal grandmother points to her likely father. Among the Hadley Wests there is only one possible father, Daniel West, already married to Mary Cook, who was giving birth to one of his children close to the time of Mitte's birth. For this reason, Mitte's mother, Susannah Whipple, would have been unable to legitimate the birth of her first daughter.

Although the tenor of this entry suggests that Mitte has left for good, she would return to Forty Acres, and on one occasion provoke yet another cry of dismay from Elizabeth. In 1810, after an absence of six years, Mitte made a brief reappearance in Elizabeth's diary: "Mr Phelps up at Conway Submit West [Mitte] had a child there at one Mr Gray's said to be a negro, shocking affair."[29] The next week Charles and Captain Caleb Smith went to Conway "to do something about Mitte, got her in at Mrs. Blotchet's her mothers, for the present."[30]

All of the references to Mitte establish her as an independent spirit, and it seems likely that she left her grandmother West's home in Hadley of her own volition to live in Conway. In the State of Massachusetts, however, the community in which one was born continued to regard that person as one of its own.[31] Charles's account book contains an entry for $2.00 paid to him by the town for traveling to Conway to find a place for Mitte and her baby to live. Whereas these New England communities had protected themselves from excessive numbers of dependents by the practice of "warning out" would-be residents, they remained a recourse for those born within their boundaries when in need.

Elizabeth turned to prayer concerning Mitte's "misconduct." Sarah's letter to Elizabeth reveals the identity of the baby's father:

> Col'l Porter drank tea with us to Night, and he confirmed what I greatly feared to hear, by your letter I suspected, that poor Mitty [sic] was in trouble my heart sickens within me when I think of her or Prince, what will become of her I know not I am afraid it is the prelude to more of the same kind.[32]

Prince, a former slave, had worked at Forty Acres. He appears in Elizabeth's diary another time, October 14, 1804, when a child of his died and the Phelpses attended the funeral. Whether Prince was married or not is unknown.

Mitte, at this time eighteen years of age, clearly refused to be shaped in the Calvinist mold. There is no mention of an ensuing marriage, which would have been the expectation if the child's father had been white (and unmarried). According to the Massachusetts law enacted in 1786, interracial marriages were illegal: "no person by this Act authorized to marry, shall join in marriage any white person with any Negro, Indian or Mulatto." Any marriages of this kind that took place would be "null and void."[33] Massachusetts was the only state that prohibited marriage between whites and people of color.

The word "shocking" does not appear in Elizabeth's diaries in reference to other children born out of wedlock. Even when recording events that one senses she found reprehensible, she avoided language that might be construed as judgmental. She had emotionally "adopted" Mitte, offered her to God through baptism, and educated her during the time that she resided with the family. And now, in Elizabeth's mind, she had failed in her desire to set Mitte on the road to salvation. Slavery had ended in Massachusetts, but the conviction that races were not meant to interbreed would be held for generations to come. Court records reveal a number of instances of miscegenation in Massachusetts in the seventeenth and early eighteenth centuries, most of them among servants and slaves who worked side by side in field and kitchen.[34] That Mitte, a white woman, had given birth to a child that revealed her relationship with a black man was outside of Elizabeth's experience. Dedicating Mitte to God was not an adoption in the sense in which Thankful came into the family. Mitte came to Forty Acres as the illegitimate child of a servant. The difference between the "adoption" of Mitte and that of Thankful may have been one of social position, though very little would have been known about the Richmonds from Dighton, a town in southeastern Massachusetts. Although Thankful saw her sister, Philomelia, from time to time when they were little girls, that tie to her natal family eventually disappears from family papers.[35] Perhaps Thankful's "anonymity" made it easier to incorporate her into the family. Mitte's background, on the other hand, was known to the community. Mitte continued to visit her mother and her grandmother West occasionally, making the break with her own family less final.

Both Elizabeth and Betsey spoke of Mitte as someone who would help with the Huntingtons' children or work in the kitchen at Forty Acres, and Mitte was a willing worker, rising early in the morning in order to "strip" the milking cows at Forty Acres. Elizabeth's emotional investment in the children given to her care was not diminished by their inferior social position or racial difference, but their place within the family structure was dictated by those factors. As she had grieved over the death of the little slave girl Phillis, she suffered when Mitte committed an act that Elizabeth believed ostracized her from the community in which she had grown up. Mitte also must have suffered from the reaction of the woman whom she had called "Ma'me" when a child. No mention of marriage appears in the diaries, and years later Betsey continued to refer to her as Submit West.[36]

III

In 1804, Betsey was expecting her third child. Written exchanges between mother and daughter concerning concealment of her condition had been brought to an end by a visit from Betsey's neighbor, Mrs. Hooker, who called on her in the fifth month of her pregnancy:

> she saw me feed E[lizabeth]—and wanted to know how long since
> I had weaned her—there was no room to evade—so I suppose all

the good women in the street have it by this time . . . I hope I have not lost all modesty, but I am very much hardened—and no wonder.[37]

Elizabeth expressed no dismay at the frequency of her daughter's pregnancies. To have only three children, as she did, was unusual, particularly for rural families at this time.

With the birth of a child being almost an annual event in the Huntington household, much ink went into discussions concerning Betsey's success in keeping her numerous pregnancies undiscovered. From time to time a welcome note of frivolity finds its way into Betsey's letters when her girlhood interest in fashion resurfaces, though she is quick to suppress it.

As to the muff, Mr Wolcott has got his wife a new muff and tippet—the price was 55 dollars (don't mention it) it is very elegant, and *as I have rather too much pride,* I think I will not have one this winter.[38]

The Wolcotts were one of the most prosperous families in Litchfield. Although clergy were among the best educated and most prominent members of the community in which they lived, the currency needed for even small luxuries was rare, a substantial part of the minister's salary paid in the form of goods such as fireplace wood and produce. The Huntington's finances were no better in 1813. When Dan Huntington decided to take no more boarding students, Betsey's response was one of resignation: "so we must try the strength of 800 dollars."[39]

The status of clerical families required them to maintain the appearance of gentility and to spend considerable time in visiting and being visited. With her rapidly growing family and scarce help, Betsey was hard put to rise to community expectations. In the letter in which she renounces the muff, she recounts, with some satisfaction, the accomplishments of one day:

the day you went away I went about my work, and clean'd all the lower part of the house except the front room—swept eight rooms, washed and scour'd six and got dinner. . . . Yesterday I preserved my quince, in the evening made a few candles to last till Christmas . . .

went to bed about 12, rose early this morning to have the hog killed, got it all done . . . cleaned meat salted suet cut up ready to try tomorrow floor washed etc.—and I am quite a lady set down to writing.

Like her mother, Betsey labored in the kitchen while striving to preserve an atmosphere of refinement in the parlor.

Her desire to have her mother present with each birth of a child did not abate. The possibility of death was ever present in her mind when she approached that event and seemed to increase with each pregnancy. Shortly before the birth of her fourth child in 1805, a friend of hers in Litchfield died in childbirth. "I must tell you," she wrote to her mother, "how gloomy I feel a great part of the time—my prospects for futurity are dark as midnight . . . the death of Mrs Tallmadge makes me dread a certain event more than usual."[40] Her foreboding had appeared during earlier pregnancies. Describing the alteration to a dress two months before the birth of her second child, she had added, "perhaps if I live I may want to have a handsome gown made."[41] Her friends' pregnancies increased rather than decreased her anxiety:

Mrs. F. Wolcott they say is again *in the fashion,* and Mrs. Oliver expects to be sick in September. She now is so weak that she can hardly walk about [the] house, and her friends and Physician, think it very doubtful whether she lives long after her confinement.[42]

Like most of their contemporaries both Elizabeth and Betsey used the words "sick" and "ill" in referring to childbirth, whereas Martha Ballard, their contemporary and a midwife in Maine, tended to use vocabulary more familiar to us, for example: "I was Calld about midnight to John Shaws wife in Labour. She was safe delivered at 8 hour this morning."[43] Perhaps words related to maladies were felt to be more genteel, euphemisms appropriate for polite society, whereas Martha Ballard, writing in her diary, uses the vocabulary of a practitioner, and less frequently the words in common usage. Nevertheless, Laurel Thatcher Ulrich finds a certain reticence in Ballard's descriptions of details related to the birth process, a reticence also evident in one midwifery manual whose author explained that he wished to avoid giving "the least offence to the most modest Reader."[44]

In September 1805, Betsey wrote: "Mrs. Oliver is sinking fast." She had given birth to a son, "a poor little thing not like to live."[45] On October 7 Betsey's fourth child Bethia was born, and by November 1, Betsey's letters are written in a lighter vein: "You ask what I want from Boston—a pair of handsome shoes with block heels and long quarters would be very acceptable."[46] Betsey was to have seven more children, and each birth was preceded by apprehension as to the outcome. A letter to her mother in December 1810 announces her seventh pregnancy: "I am at present in a situation not joyous but grievous."[47]

Certainly Betsey's immediate uneasiness as to the actual birthing process was exacerbated by the financial concerns arising from the number of children that they were raising. Betsey told her mother that her husband had discussed the inadequacy of his salary considering the size of his family with a member of the Litchfield meeting, apparently to no avail. As early as 1805 he had expressed his desire to leave on that account, but in January of the next year, Betsey wrote that they would probably stay, "even if we have to live . . . upon bean porrige and potatoe skins."[48]

Forty Acres provided the Huntingtons with barrels of pork, firkins of butter, pails of honey, chickens and sausages, mincemeat pies, bottles of metheglin (mead), seeds for their garden, and even John Morison, the Scottish gardener, on one occasion.[49] Barrels went part of the way by the river and then across the land. In return, Betsey sent small offerings—cranberries and puddings—when she found someone traveling north as far as Northampton. A letter was a welcome extension of the person who wrote it, but produce was a tangible reminder of the abundance that Betsey associated with Forty Acres.

Hadley selectmen convened a town meeting in Hadley on May 22, 1809, to consider Dan Huntington as a replacement for the ailing Reverend Hopkins.[50] The Phelpses must have seen the election of their son-in-law as almost certain, as he had received the endorsement of the dying Mr. Hopkins. Dan had requested a dismission from Litchfield in 1809, but when he received it, it was to answer a call to Middletown, Connecticut. It was later said that the sense of the Hadley town meeting was against appointing Dan Huntington, as it would put the Porters in an even more powerful position in the community than they presently held.[51] Jefferson's desire that politics and religion occupy separate spheres had not yet won over the people of Western Massachusetts. One can only imagine the family's disappointment, as no word of this decision appears in letters and diaries.

Now that the Huntingtons were established in Middletown, it was easier and more expeditious to ship gifts from the farm's yield almost entirely by boat on the Connecticut River. The couple's journey to Middletown over the well-traveled roads along the river, rather than the mountainous routes to Litchfield, was also less arduous.

IV

Although the Phelpses' circumstances were far less straitened than those of the Huntingtons, Elizabeth was able to recount her own tales of back-breaking labor in response to Betsey's lists of chores completed:

> I rose this morning before four . . . it is now toward 11 and my cheese will soon be ready to chop the last time, we make more than we ever did, we have a great many good things, the best butter I ever made owing to the cool weather we have, fine strawberries, and *good* milk. . . . but we have some crosses, a fine field of wheat 20 acres all destroyed, with the Hesian fly or nearly. . . . Cheese, cheese, hay, hay, cooking, cooking . . . churning every other day sometimes—I have had two days now, that I have indulged myself in bed till near 5, but tomorrow morning it must be a little after 3 that the butter may be worked in the cool air . . . I do not have the time for thots and reflection, that I think I should have.[52]

"A great deal to do in the cheese room" became a recurring motif in both diaries and letters. By June of 1805, Charles decided on another kind of expansion of the cheese business to appeal to a broader market:

> Your father has propos'd several times to have a few cheeses made with all the cream in them, so now we make night milk into a cheese every night which takes up the time pretty busily till 10 or 11 & it is rather slow tonight tis not broke up yet.[53]

Clearly, Charles was aiming at the carriage trade. Elizabeth's reputation as producer of fine cheese was, by this time, well established. Mrs. Hibbard came to stay at Forty Acres in order to learn cheese making so that she could start her own business.[54] By 1813, the sixty-six-year-old Elizabeth was still hard at work in the cheese room: "we make about 3 cheeses in a week, & consequently have a great deal of butter to attend to, & you know the cheese & butter falls pretty much to my part."[55]

The mixture of pride in her accomplishments and concern that she was neglecting her spiritual life appears in these letters to Betsey and runs through the diaries as well—the exigencies of growing things: hay to be cut and stored before the next rain, butter churned before the arrival of the hot sun, workers fed at least twice a day, strawberries picked before they spoiled. Where was the time for her to read and meditate on Mr. Hopkins's last sermon with his admonitions to live each day attentive to God's divine will?

Chapter XI

Seeking the
Celestial City

"this day the raising of the meeting house was
completed . . . except the steeple."

IN OCTOBER the road to Hadley is drenched in color. Maple trees vie with each other in a parade of intense scarlet, orange, russet, gold. A slightly acrid smell rises from the leaves that crackle beneath the feet of the citizens of Hadley on their way to the meetinghouse. A momentary breeze detaches leaves from their branches, and sends them dancing to the earth. Overnight, the maple in front of the church has become a flaming torch, a trumpet call to the faithful. But some feet move slowly, reluctantly, up the stairs, turning away from this feast of color.

The climb to the second floor lofts the congregation above ground level. Distracted by so much earthly beauty, Elizabeth mounts the stairway and makes her way to the family pew. "Oh that I might not lose relish for spiritual things," she prays. Inside the hall, the dazzling white walls replace the exterior glory with another splendor. A line from her store of memorized Psalms comes to mind—"In thy light shall we see light."

One of Isaac Watts's hymns fills the meetinghouse:

> *Come, Holy Spirit, heavenly Dove,*
> *With all thy quickening powers:*
> *Kindle a flame of sacred love*
> *In these cold hearts of ours.*

The old struggle is still with her, thoughts and concerns that draw her earthward, while she tries to rise above them. "Lord," she prays, "pour out thy spirit upon my dry and rocky heart." She hears the last two lines of the hymn as if for the first time:

> *Come, shed abroad a Saviour's love,*
> *And that shall kindle ours.*

"Shed abroad"—her gaze turns sideways out through the clear glass windows and travels along the village common. Is that the answer then? she wonders.

Mr. Honest: It happens to us, as it happeneth to wayfaring men;—sometimes our way is clean, sometimes foul; sometimes up hill; we are seldom at a certainty. The wind is not always on our backs, nor is every one a friend that we meet with in the way.

JOHN BUNYAN, *The Pilgrim's Progress*

I

The active life that was Elizabeth's left little room to meditate on its significance, but travel evoked in her a philosophical bent, providing her with little allegories for life:

> the great resemblance of a Journey thro' the Country. & a Journey thro' life, struck me very forcably, yesterday, one while 'twas uneven hard disagreeable going, then better, soon perhaps draging up long gravelly hills—then a fine delightful road—anon plunged in water—but the succession of these scenes were so rapid one hardly knew we were in them till they were past—& we insensably slid along to our Journeys end.[1]

The metaphor of life as a journey, a pilgrimage fraught with misleading digressions, dangerous temptations, unexpected catastrophes, runs through Christian writing from the early Church Fathers through the nineteenth century. Forty Acres possesses a copy of John Bunyan's *Pilgrim's Progress,* a staple in most Calvinist libraries and a favorite for reading aloud. Elizabeth's diary records one such reading: "My husband read in *Pilgrim's Progress,* a welcome, welcome, Spirit divine, if I may take that comfort."(February 2, 1806)[2] Bunyan's work certainly contributed to Elizabeth's tendency to find meaningful allegories in everyday occurrences. The hills, dales, and marshes of the Connecticut River Valley provide concrete parallels for Bunyan's "Delectable Mountain," "Valley of the Shadow," "Slough of Despond." Included in a letter to Betsey containing disturbing news about the Hitchcocks, as well as anxiety about Mitte, is a passage perhaps designed to cheer both Betsey and herself:

> I have frequently seen when I have been travelling, a terrible thick fog jest ahead, a few rods more we should be swallowed up in darkness—but we ride on, & the air appears very clear & comfortable where we now are—but every moment we are expecting to get into the thickest of it—yet it remains at a small distance, till we pass the whole.[3]

Written in 1802 and 1803, these two descriptions of the uncertainties of travel serve as little allegories for Elizabeth's increasing awareness of the vicissitudes of human existence.

All three of the Phelpses' children had moved beyond the range of easy communication. Each couple was engaged in the hazards of child-bearing and -rearing, and of economic uncertainty. None of the children had the security that Elizabeth and Charles found in the land, however uncertain their harvests. To see life as a journey puts what otherwise might seem random, capricious events into a meaningful context. Journeys have destinations, and whatever the obstacles, the traveler must bear the goal in mind or succumb to meaningless sidetracks, perhaps never arriving at that place.

Although Calvinism as a ruling force in New England is generally regarded as a phenomenon of the seventeenth and early eighteenth centuries, briefly revived by the Great Awakening, its presence remained powerful in agrarian communities into the nineteenth century. In addition, the Puritan ideal of a "covenanted" community continued to influence the way in which many people lived their lives, particularly in rural areas of New England.[4] The belief in the existence of an "Elect" was slow to disappear from some New England pulpits, and from the minds of faithful members of the congregation. Such a view endorsed a social hierarchy in which each person had his or her appropriate "station in life." It is a phrase that Elizabeth uses on several occasions, seemingly not as a matter of pride, but of responsibility, and at least once, as a complaint.

The existence of this hierarchy was reflected in the seating system in

New England meetinghouses. Although the qualifications for selecting specific pews for specific families do not appear among Hadley records, those listed by surrounding towns suggest criteria that the Hadley committee may have used. Hatfield, South Hadley, and Amherst all list age and estate as two of the qualifications, a third described in different ways as "places of trust," or "usefulness."[5] Charles Phelps was a member of the pew selection committee as early as 1781, an indication of his position of trust, which, along with the size of his estate, placed him in a prominent pew. Disagreements as to pew assignments were frequent. Usurping seats assigned to town dignitaries was regarded as a profanation of the Sabbath.[6] In 1760, there was a minor insurrection when some members of the Hadley meeting refused to accept their assignment and "crowded into higher seats."[7] Four years later "persons were aggrieved (as usual)."[8] The selection committee relegated people of color to back seats in the gallery, with the exception of the highly respected Ralph Way, whom they assigned to his own pew, allowing him to bring with him "such negroes as he chose."[9]

Congregationalism was factionalized at the end of the eighteenth century, divided by doctrinal disagreements and opposing stands on the developing wave of revivalism. Inevitably, the ideas concerning self-governance and freedom from oppressive rule that had fostered the Revolutionary War found their way into congregations, producing separatist movements.[10]

These developments, in turn, gave rise to conservative reactions within the Congregational Church. Orthodox members of the congregation regarded the wave of revivalism with suspicion, seeing it as encouraging subjective experiences and validating individual emotions as opposed to reinforcing the established authority of church doctrine.

Timothy Dwight was one of the chief architects of the Second Awakening.[11] Dwight, through his position as president of Yale College and mentor of the student body that came under his tutelage, was able to establish a strong support for his particular understanding of church doctrine. He was a Federalist, his political convictions parallel to those of John Adams. Both men feared democracy for what they saw as the inevitable disruption to social harmony in its fostering of "factional rivalry, electioneering, and a general disrespect for authority."[12]

Dwight, although committed to preserving orthodox Calvinism, parted company with his grandfather, Jonathan Edwards, in certain important aspects of Edwards's beliefs. It is these departures that are particularly significant in understanding the convictions that impelled the Phelps family.[13] Like Edwards, Dwight subscribed to the belief that salvation did not come about as the result of good works. The experience of conversion was the first and most important step in the person's spiritual journey. Deviations from that belief Dwight regarded as heresies. Nevertheless, he maintained that an individual's will can be propelled in the direction of virtue by means of education and worship. Descriptions in his four-volume *Travels in New-England and New-York* are interspersed with remarks on the moral conduct of the inhabitants of the settlements that he visited: "The people of Hadley constitute a single Presbyterian congregation, and have long been distinguished for their steady attachment to good order and government."[14] He goes on to praise Hadley residents for their support of the Revolution, but also their refusal to participate in insurrections and mobs. The passage of time separated acceptable from unacceptable rebellions in Dwight's mind. The Revolution cleared the Colonies of the obstacles that lay in the way of the new country's millenarian mission, whereas uprisings such as Shays Rebellion replaced harmony with discord.

The "New Eden" was to be free of Old World corruption and conflicts such as existed between England and France. Dwight found in the Connecticut Valley a cultivated Paradise and an exemplum for young communities to the west:

> the most exquisite scenery of the whole landscape is formed by the river and its extended margin on beautiful intervals. The river turns four times to the east and three times to the west within twelve miles, and within that distance makes a progress of twenty-four. . . . The intervals, which in this view border it in continual succession, are fields containing from five hundred to five thousand acres, formed like terraced gardens, lowest near the river and rising as they recede from it by regular gradations. These fields are distributed into an immense multitude of lots, separated only by imaginary lines, and devoted to all the various cultivation of the climate. Meadows are here seen containing from five to five hundred acres, interspersed with beautiful and lofty forest trees rising everywhere at little distances, and at times with orchards of considerable extent, and covered with exquisite verdure.[15]

This passage is just the beginning of his hymn to the Connecticut Valley. In addition to the beauty of the land, he lauds the inhabitants for the traits that they held in common, their dedication to education and to worship:

> Families have not only opportunity, but the most convenient opportunites, for being present at the public worship of God. Children also are sent universally at an early age to school, and begin their education almost as soon as they can speak. In consequence of these facts, the inhabitants are better educated and more orderly than in most other parts even of New England. . . . Steadiness of character, softness of manners, a disposition to read, respect for the laws and magistrates, a strong sense of liberty, blended with an equally strong sense of the indispensable importance of energetic government, are all extensively predominant in this region.[16]

A close look at documents from this time and place certainly tempers Dwight's unbridled enthusiasm. His observations about Hadley reflect his Utopian vision of the ideal community, one that would give each of the inhabitants access to the school and the meetinghouse, both essential for the true Calvinist.[17]

The growing debate as to the role of good works as the Means of Grace in the search for salvation produced splinter groups within the New England Church. Dwight had studied theology with his uncle, Jonathan Edwards the Younger (the husband of Elizabeth's cousin and close friend, Polly Porter). He thus was early allied with an orthodox Calvinist; eventually, however, he came to straddle two positions.[18] The orthodox position held that the gift of grace was solely an arbitrary, predestined act of God with no reference to pious efforts on the part of the recipient. Dwight agreed, but also felt that proper nurture in a religious environment could ready the heart for conversion, though it would not guarantee its occurrence. This stand was viewed by some to border dangerously on Arminianism, the faction that strict Calvinists accused of preaching justification through good works, also a Roman Catholic doctrine. Another group, called Old Calvinists, heirs to the Puritan religious tradition, saw the Means of Grace as preparation for conversion, stressing a rational approach to religion over an emotional conversion.

New communities were appearing in western Massachusetts as the population grew, providing fertile soil for young missionaries, and for evangelism. Unlike the earlier settlements in the Connecticut River Valley, the new settlers did not come in covenanted groups, "inspired by the same ideals of utopian harmony and purpose," but rather as individual families.[19] Practical considerations brought them together and sometimes divided them.

Meanwhile, a more dangerous threat to orthodoxy than these internal disputes was in the making. Harvard College was producing among her students deists, skeptics, and Unitarians (the last seen as the most threatening), who returned to their homes taking their convictions with them. Yale College, on the other hand, under Dwight's leadership, responded to these threats with reinforced Calvinist zeal. Dwight instilled in a number of his Yale students missionary fervor that he found validated in the Scriptures: "Go ye into all the world, and preach the gospel to every creature." (Mark 16:15).

II

These increasing threats to the solidarity of the Congregational religion were perhaps a source of the anxiety that infuses so many of the references to Porter in Elizabeth's diaries during and following his studies at Harvard. While staying with her son and daughter-in-law in September 1801, her Sabbath notations mention attending the New South Church in Boston with Porter and Sarah and hearing the preacher, Mr. Kirkland, who was a Unitarian. John Thornton Kirkland was only two years older than Porter, graduating from Harvard "with high honour" in 1789. He began studying theology under the Reverend Dr. Stephen West at Stockbridge, Massachusetts. West's Calvinist views "found little favour in the eyes of his pupil; and, accordingly, after a short time, he went to Cambridge to continue his studies in a more congenial atmosphere."[20] His return to Cambridge brought him back under the influence of Harvard mentors.

Neither a skeptic nor a nonbeliever, Porter attended Kirkland's church on the Sabbath with his wife. Letters written early in his marriage testify to his and Sarah's religious convictions. In 1807, he wrote, "Oh— that we may all be prepared to meet together at last in that world where . . . sorrow sin & death shall never enter."[21]

But for Elizabeth, he had fallen into apostasy, and was in danger of damnation. In this conviction she apparently differed from her husband. In his memoirs, Porter describes his father's position concerning the theological controversies of the time:

> In his religious opinions my father probably ranked with the moderate Calvinists of that day. . . . But tho my father was fully persuaded of the truth of his own religious opinions, as regarded himself, he was catholic and tolerant of the opinions of others. I never heard him denounce any one for entertaining religious opinions differing from his own.[22]

Elizabeth's children believed their mother to possess more than the usual piety attributed to faithful members of the meeting. In a letter to her mother before her marriage, Betsey wrote from Boston that she planned to call on Mrs. Parsons, "a very great favorite with my brother—he says she is all that is amiable . . . as *religious* as our *inestimable mother*."[23]

Elizabeth believed one of her missions to be the raising of her children in the tradition of such Calvinists as Jonathan Edwards. Porter held his mother responsible for the specter of a wrathful God that haunted him throughout his life.

> I think she must have viewed the power and sovereignty of GOD as overshadowing all his attributes of Love and Mercy. The earliest idea that I remember to have formed of God in my childhood and Youth, represented him as a being of human form—of large dimensions—sitting on his throne—clothed with terrific power— angry with all his creatures and threatening vengeance and destruction upon the whole guilty and rebellious race of Adam.[24]

Porter confessed that, despite his later education and increasing rationality, this image remained with him and cast a shadow of despondency over his thinking. Memory is selective. It seems possible that his image of God stemmed from several sources: sermons listened to in his childhood, adult conversations overheard, books read aloud following family prayers. Whatever the source of this figure of an angry, vengeful God, its impact on Porter helps to explain his defection to the Unitarians.

In 1810, sixteen years after his ordination, Kirkland was offered and accepted the presidency of Harvard College. Although no contemporary accounts of his ministry charge him with mounting a campaign against Calvinist beliefs, he was remembered to have said "that the doctrine of the Trinity was now to be classed with the exploded doctrine of Transubstantiation."[25] A fellow student said of him: "His preaching, I believe, had scarcely a doctrinal tinge."[26] Educator Elizabeth Peabody recalled a toast that he gave at an ordination dinner to "the fundamental doctrine of the Anti-sectarian Sect—that goodness consists in doing good."[27] Such an aphorism may seem to twentieth-century ears incontestable, but to orthodox Calvinists it was subject to debate. The emphasis on behavior as opposed to Election as a sign of the goodness that leads to salvation, they believed, was leading the faithful astray.

For Calvinists, both strict and moderate, the denial of the Trinity and divinity of Christ was heretical, an attack on the very foundation of Christian faith. In a letter of 1804 to Betsey, Elizabeth mentioned having had several talks with her son on the subject. "He does not see things as some do—no nor never will unless the Spirit of God teaches him."[28] Several years later, she expressed her dismay with stronger words:

> I am distressed for him, and his, to have them poor children educated in such a dibolical system as I fear he has adopted, is a dreadful thing.[29]

Betsey appeared to be of the same mind, recalling a time when her brother was in Hadley:

> the year he lived at home, he read, and I believe prayed a great deal, but he did not read the right sort of books, and I feared he was prejudiced in favour of error.[30]

She in turn wrote to Porter and Sarah, serious letters, she informed her mother, but did not receive replies. "I fear they are displeased . . . I had at that time a great desire for their eternal welfare."[31]

These letters, written in the summer of 1807, followed perhaps too closely on the heels of a sad event in her brother's family. On February 17, 1807, Porter and Sarah's three-and-a-half year old son Edward died.

A return of the severe convulsions that he had experienced as an infant was the apparent cause.[32] Charles and Elizabeth set out for Boston several weeks later. She described a "sorrowful pleasant meeting. "I went because our dear Edward was dead, to join my tears with my children's."[33] In a letter to Betsey, Elizabeth described their meeting in detail:

we got there Satt: night about .7. all was very still, they were up two pair of stair in the nursery as the children had been a little unwel, and Sally [Sarah] the night before and that day—so that I ran directly up tap'd gently on the door—opened it, he sat on one side with the babe in his arms, daughter on the other with sarah in her lap who she was undressing, the children both complaining, you don't know daughter how malloncolly it appeared to me,—the room was dusk, when I entered, they gazed, and stared, kept them sitting, Who is here! Who is come? as the vail was all over my face—I stepped up to him, seiz'd his hand—he exclaimed Oh mother! tis my mother! . . . what a shower of tears ensued, you can *only* guess.[34]

Elizabeth's sorrow for the death of her grandson and compassion for her son and his wife eclipsed her anxiety concerning the young couple's religious convictions. Betsey reassured her mother, as well, that her brother was taking the loss of his son "like a true christian," and quoted from his letter to her:

For some days your sister [Sarah] seemed to be almost broken down—but our heavenly father will rarely impose greater burdens than his children can bear—We have repaired to him for his strength—his consolation & his grace—and hope that our prayers in some measure have been answered.[35]

Although Porter's letter reflects strong religious convictions, his mother continued to fear that he could not be a member of the Elect when he had departed so radically from the doctrines of the orthodox Church.

III

Elizabeth's preoccupation with the state of her own soul, as well as that of her children, had not diminished with time. Her youthful conviction that she was unable to seek membership in the church as she had not experienced conversion allied her then with strict Calvinist doctrine. Diary entries in later years continue to refer to the "chosen few" and sometimes to "the elect."[36]

Through Sabbaths spent in the meetinghouse and through her reading, Elizabeth was exposed to a broad spectrum of Calvinist theology. William B. Sprague's *Annals of the American Pulpit* contains a lengthy reminiscence of the Reverend Samuel Hopkins, who occupied the Hadley pulpit for fifty-four years. The Reverend Parsons Cook, born in Hadley and baptized by Mr. Hopkins, described the Hadley minister's theology as moderate, opposed to the strict view of the predestination of the Elect held by his better known cousin from Newport, also the Reverend Samuel Hopkins. The Hadley Hopkins saw the Lord's Supper or Communion as one of the means to conversion, rather than a consequent privilege of that experience, though he did not deny the belief in Election.[37] To reconcile the doctrine of the Elect with that of the Means of Grace as an avenue to regeneration, Hopkins must have believed that it was possible to prepare oneself for the reception of grace. It was the position that Timothy Dwight eventually reached.

The term "Hopkinsianism" came from the teachings of the other Samuel Hopkins, a disciple of Jonathan Edwards, who took an unyielding stand on doctrinal matters. In his sketch of the Hadley Hopkins, Cook noted that his congregations were not deprived of Hopkinsian theology, as four of the parson's daughters and one stepdaughter married clergy who espoused the stricter view and frequently preached in the Hadley pulpit.

One of Elizabeth's letters to Betsey, written in 1807, contains pure Hopkinsian doctrine:

> We must be born again pass from death to life—*yet the divine power must do the whole-free grace all*. predestination & election naturally come in view . . . the Spirit is I think evidently among us [my emphasis].[38]

Elizabeth was not, however, a theologian and there were inconsisten-
cies in her theological position. The Phelpses subscribed to various journals, among them *The Panoplist,* which was evangelical in mission while
reflecting Dwight's particular brand of social conservatism.[39] Elizabeth's
diaries and letters reveal her emotional nature, making her particularly
susceptible to the tide of revivalism that grew out of the current evangelism, spurred on by a number of Dwight's Yale protégés. A letter to
Betsey recounts what were, in Elizabeth's mind, signs of the Spirit at
work in their midst:

> there are several girls in this town, serious, Cap't Dickinson daugh-
> ter hannah, Mr Shipmans daughter betsey, Major Porters daughter
> Sukey, she seems to be quite derang'd, talks very wild at times—a
> part of her conversation is upon Salvation & being saved, some call
> it hystericks—I know not what it is.[40]

Distress was seen as a sign of receptiveness to an awakening on the part
of the sufferer. Elizabeth's account of the illness of Charlotte, her cousin
Dr. Porter's wife, suggests that it was psychological in origin.[41] The letter
describes a very emotional meeting with the young woman, who was
thirty-two and mother of four small children. Clearly distraught, Charlotte spoke in half sentences, alternating exclamations, "oh what a
tryumph of mercy" with despairing cries, "oh it cant be—no never."
Elizabeth wrote of her cousin:

> the awful descriptions she gave of the tho'ts that are every moment
> in her mind is eno' to make ones hair stand upright—& that it is
> no devil she is as sure as of her own life—she knows it is her own
> heart.[42]

Her diaries record a number of prayer meetings about this time concerning Charlotte Porter, whose condition worsened in the ensuing weeks.
These meetings rallied a community of women around her in an attempt
to bring healing, as it did with the physically sick and dying. She was not
subjected to the treatment applied to those identified as suffering from
mental illness, as her disturbance was seen as a promising prelude to a
conversion experience.[43]

Similar cases of mental distress appear in the diaries and letters during this Second Awakening, two involving people for whom Elizabeth felt a strong affection: Mrs. Hibbard and Lawyer Porter, a cousin. The latter had fallen into debt and attributed this condition to his sinfulness: "I have been such a monster in sin that mercy can never reach me," he stated repeatedly.[44] Mrs. Hibbard, a contemporary of Elizabeth's and a friend of many years, appears in the same letter:

> Mrs Hibbard has been very much derang'd has made several attempts to do herself mischief the razor has been found at the head of her bed, and several other matters very alarming, but now is much more composed—appears to be ditirmined to seek for mercy ever an interest in the Redeemers purchase.

However complex were the reasons for the mental distress of these two people, they themselves clearly ascribed it to the depraved condition of their souls.[45]

During the Great Awakening of the 1740s, a number of cases of "distraction" were reported. At that time Ebenezer Parkman, minister at Westborough, Massachusetts, recorded seven attempted suicides among members of his congregation between 1749 and 1755, some eventually successful.[46] Revivals made converts, but in their wake fostered morbid brooding in those who felt weighed down with a sense of irredeemable sin.

Sabbaths set aside for receiving the Sacraments provoked particularly searching self-examination in the diaries of both Elizabeth and Betsey, and they were not alone among diary-keepers.[47] On June 1, 1800, Elizabeth wrote: "Communion day but full of darkness and fears, can it be that I am a child of God and heir of heaven, how insenseable of the dreadfulness of being found a reprobate, stupid & dead." Writing to her mother, Betsey, in turn, refers to herself as a "sinful worm," lamenting the infrequency with which she found time to pray.[48]

By 1807, the revival fever had spread throughout western New England. In a letter of that year, written over a period of weeks, Betsey described several incidents of revival enthusiasm in Litchfield: "more new instances of conviction have come to our knowledge in this time, than there has in the same length of time, since the awakening began."[49] Dan Huntington's sermon preached primarily to the youths of the congregation reduced them to tears. "Mr H—saw Mary on Thursday—he thinks he never saw any person in more distress—surely this displays the wonderful power of Divine grace." Betsey then goes on to describe the previous Sabbath:

> Mr Ward of Danbury preached here . . . his text was in Hosea . . . during the second singing 5 or 6 of the [illegible] were so affected that they were forc'd to sit down, and Mr Roberts the chorister was overcome and sat down a thing which he condemned and ridiculed Ann Stone only two sabbaths before.

Dan Huntington was credited with the conversion of three hundred young people as he traveled among the towns of Litchfield County to preach in their pulpits.[50]

Not all reactions to the wave of revivalism were of the nature of those described above. Elizabeth's diaries contain increased references to Charles's involvement in church-related affairs. He was a leading member of the Missionary Society, frequently conducting meetings at Forty Acres. As a deacon, he also preached at The Mills (now North Hadley), which appears to have been the center of the local revival movement. During the declining years of the Reverend Hopkins's life, Charles often replaced him in the Hadley pulpit, reading sermons from his own library and from journals such as *The Panoplist*.

Charles's response to this Second Awakening was a more active role in the church, as deacon and occasionally preacher, and as head of the committee to build the new meetinghouse, begun 1808. The many civic offices held by Charles, as well as his position as deacon in the church, were probably viewed by the community as "outward visible signs" of the grace with which the Elect were believed to be endowed. Elizabeth, on the other hand, looked inward for signs that she was on the road to salvation. It is a difference in their thinking that, for Elizabeth, became a serious obstacle in their relationship. In 1807, she marked their wedding anniversary with the following words:

> thirty seven anniversaries have I seen of our wedingday—my feelings this day have been tender, & solem—when I remember, what my expectations were before I married respecting a life of religious conversation, & mutual enjoyment of the things of God—I am almost ready to sink in discouragement—my husband has treated

me with that reserve & distance which I little expected—but probably the cause is in me—he finds not that inducement to converse upon experimental religion perhaps, which is requisite to a free union & endearing interchanging of tho'ts & affections.[51]

The word "experimental" at that time referred to individual perceptions derived from personal experience, a meaning now expressed with the word "experiential."[52]

The Congregational religion reached its followers primarily through the word—Sabbath meetings and lectures, family prayers, reading of the Scriptures and theological works—though singing played an important role at services. Consistent Calvinists were more analytical than emotional in their observances. There is in Elizabeth Phelps something of the zeal of medieval piety, without the stimulus that came from the visual beauty of stained glass, stone carvings, painted images, and illuminated prayer books. Nor were there the pilgrimages, often made by women unaccompanied by their husbands, that would have served as a channel for her religious fervor.[53]

The Second Awakening provided an outlet for those seeking a more expressive form of worship. Elizabeth participated in the women's prayer groups that began to appear at this time. Her letters to Betsey enthuse about the many conversions that follow in the wake of revivals:

> O what good tidings are constantly saluting our ears respecting the spread of the glorious Gospel of Christ. does not our hearts leap. [54]

Yet her preoccupation with the revival that was sweeping through the Connecticut River Valley did not change her longing for an "endearing interchanging of tho'ts & affections" with her husband. Instead she met with "reserve & distance." Their diverging attitudes toward their personal religion might be seen as analogous to the divergence in late-eighteenth-century thought between the Age of Reason and what Northrop Frye has labeled "The Age of Sensibility." Some women may have dismissed this kind of difference as inevitable between the sexes, but Elizabeth sought a more perfect union with her husband, just as, on Sacrament Days, she longed for a complete union with God.

Chapter XII

~

THE VALLEY
OF THE SHADOW

"I have got all my writing apparatus into the long room."

Dusting her father's desk, Elizabeth stops to look out the south window, resisting the temptation to sit down in the chair and begin a letter to Betsey. She has promised herself to clean the Long Room before she is needed in the kitchen, and then the cheeses must be turned over. How tired she is—bone-tired, and the day is not yet half over. She finds herself staring at the hand that is pushing the duster over the desktop. It is wrinkled, the knuckles swollen, the little finger misshapen. The sight of her hands never ceases to surprise her. She is old! On days when she feels strong and energetic, she forgets her age, unless reminded by her face in the mirror or, today, her dusting hand.

The house is aging more gracefully than I, she muses—like a snake, it has many skins. The fresh coat of paint has brought new life to the hall and the Long Room. Strong new timbers now shore up what was the sagging front entry. The newly whitewashed walls of the kitchen throw back the light from the hearth fire. From the road, the house appears rooted in the ground, hunkered down in January snows, then unfolding to the green growth that laps at the foundations—resilience that she no longer possesses.

It is as if the vitality that once was hers has become part of the structure itself, palpable in the rooms and objects that she has cared for. The house has become an extension of herself—her living gift to those who find shelter beneath its roof.

And now we hang our harps on the willow tree.[1]
ELIZABETH'S LETTER TO BETSEY,
FEBRUARY 4, 1805

I

In this death-denying era in which we live, constant references to dying seem to us morbid, a sign of mental imbalance. At a time when death among friends and relatives was almost a weekly event and the health of one's soul a constant preoccupation, to shy away from the subject of human mortality was to jeopardize the possibility of salvation. *Memento mori,* ever present, served to focus the pious Calvinist on the next life as it had for the early Christian Desert Fathers, who found in the human skull a focus for their meditations.

Both Elizabeth and Charles continued to respond faithfully to calls from families of dying friends and relatives. Charles sat beside the bed of his sister's eldest child Jonathan for the last three days of the young man's life. Between the years 1794 and 1816, Elizabeth recorded births and deaths in Hadley for the church records. Among the twenty-three deaths that she listed for the year 1810, ten were children. Only four reached an age beyond twenty, all of those over fifty. Interestingly, if one lived to be an adult, the chances of living to a ripe old age were good, particularly for men.[2] For women, the challenge was to survive the child-bearing years.

On March 7, 1811, the Reverend Dr. Hopkins appears on Elizabeth's list of deaths, bringing to an end his long tenure in the Hadley pulpit. He had been a frequent visitor to Forty Acres, his house the object of a number of Elizabeth's visits to Hadley. Charles was one of the pallbearers; Elizabeth recorded the event in her diary: "tuesday we attended the funeral of Dr. Hopkins—a dear good friend to us & to all mankind.[3] It may have been a desire to recognize his death with a memorial gift that prompted Elizabeth's presentation of two sterling Communion cups to the Hadley church. The date of the actual presentation was February 1813. The Boston silversmiths, Fletcher and Gardiner, used one hallmark up until November 1811 and another when they moved to Philadelphia after that date. The cups contain the earlier mark, suggesting that Elizabeth purchased them in Boston before the end of 1811, perhaps waiting for the most appropriate occasion to present them, at which time they were engraved.[4] Her handsome gift reflects the resources that Elizabeth could call upon and reveals her independent spirit, not to be outdone by her husband, who headed the building committee for the magnificent new meetinghouse.

The children of aging parents did not avoid the issue of death as a subject of discussion with those who were possibly close to their demise. Concern for the spiritual welfare of her parents appears in Betsey's letters to her mother beginning in 1813:

> You ask why I feel so much anxiety on your account? how can I help it—the length of time that we have been separated has not diminished that affection which I ever felt for my parents—and tho' I hope I am not unmindful of the event which must soon separate us—yet it is natural to feel anxious to have it as far distant as possible.[5]

In a letter written some months later, Betsey was more explicit:

> I do indeed wish that you and my father had more leisure, to read the word of life & to meditate upon it; and as you are drawing nearer to eternity—that you might be drawing nearer to God in holy communion—that you might be less perplexed with the cares of this world and more completely prepared for the rest and joy of the righteous in heaven.[6]

It is not just Betsey who expresses this concern. There are several wistful passages in Elizabeth's diaries and letters, lamenting her lack of time to reflect on spiritual matters. The metaphor of life as a journey in search of salvation runs through the writings of a number of women living in eighteenth- and early-nineteenth-century America. Introspection and self-examination became increasingly important as women approached what they believed to be the end of their life. Pious old women who anticipated their demise with resignation and serenity were held up as models for younger women. Failure to achieve that state of mind implied inadequate preparation for death, a life misspent in its preoccupation with the material world.[7]

Elizabeth was energetic, but not physically strong, judging by the frequency of illnesses recorded in the diaries. Her letters often refer to sick headaches, trouble with breathing in cold weather, and severe pains in her writing hand and arm. Letters from Betsey to Porter before her marriage refer to her mother's chronic ailments and need to travel for her health. The sick headaches were possibly migraines: "one of those blind fits come on," Elizabeth complained to Betsey, "O how my head did pain."[8]

Charles also suffered from a number of ailments whose symptoms, at first mild, became increasingly alarming with the passage of time. The first indications of some kind of affliction appeared in letters written in the fall of 1805, when he complained of "how dolefully his head felt" after pitching large amounts of hay. The next month Elizabeth reported that he felt much better having stopped drinking cider on the advice of his son's Boston physician Dr. Rand.[9] Now, Elizabeth wrote, he drank only water; however, a postscript appears at the end of the letter: "perhaps I expressed myself improperly about the water, he drinks brandy, or old rum, properly mix'd sometimes—but no cider."[10]

References to Charles's health disappear from the letters for several years, though one sentence written early in 1809 suggests that it was an ongoing concern: "I suspect my fear for his head was needless, he is bright as amber tho I hope I place no dependence on that."[11] The following year he experienced an episode of numbness, mental confusion, and difficulty in talking. Elizabeth wrote to Betsey in an attempt to soothe her anxiety about her father:

> indeed he appears remarkably free from even the old head complaint, yesterday he thot he felt some of that pain he felt some years ago, very low in the lower part of his bowels, but a good bed, and

comfortable sleep has restored ease and comfort by this morning—how careful the husbands are, to inform the wives of their pains and aches, while the wives try, how long they can keep the pain, and uneasiness, secret . . . I really think that pains, and aches, are the lot of women more than men, let us try to reap good from it in some way.[12]

When, a year later, Charles had "a lost turn," complaining that he could not remember where he had been, why, or for how long, Elizabeth summoned Dr. Porter to bleed him, "tho' not near so copiously as the blood indicated he needed."[13]

Blood-letting appears to have been regarded as a cure-all. There were multiple sites in the head, arms, and legs from which blood was drawn.[14] The eminent Dr. Benjamin Rush of Philadelphia was an enthusiastic blood-letter, drawing off a quart of blood every forty-eight hours when necessary. It was then the belief that the body contained twelve rather than six quarts of blood.[15] A paper delivered to the Massachusetts Medical Society in 1790 by Dr. Isaac Rand, Jr., the name of the Porter Phelpses' family physician, advocates what seems an appalling use of blood-letting, drawn from a number of veins, along with cathartics and blistering.[16] Such drastic treatment was, according to one study, more apt to be applied in the city than in rural areas, where blood-letting tended to be used in moderation.[17] Elizabeth's admonition to her daughter Betsey "to be ware of Drs" seems a wise course to follow in this period of experimentation.[18]

Theophilus, the Huntingtons' seventh child, was born on July 11, 1811, and six months later, Betsey reported: "I again am in a situation which requires patience, submission, and fortitude."[19] One might expect this perennial event to have strained the relationship between Betsey and Dan. Yet when her fear for her own survival in childbirth was particularly intense, she wrote:

for two or three months, I have enjoy'd more comfort in my husband than common, our hearts seem to have been more united, and we have I think exercised more forberance, and kindness than we ever have done . . . and now a distressing period is near at hand I find my strength less than ever before—I have some reason to fear that it will be hard for me.[20]

Whether Porter's wife Sarah, who ultimately had nine children, experienced similar fears does not appear in letters, perhaps less likely to be confessed to a mother-in-law. Her greater anxiety must have been for the health of her children after the loss of Edward. In December 1809, Porter wrote to his parents of the death of their little Elizabeth on the day after her first birthday. The details of her death stayed with Porter for the rest of his life, preserved in his memoirs:

> Not long after dinner, while we were sitting in the parlor, Elizabeth was taken with a convulsion fit. . . . I carried her about the parlor in my arms nearly 24 hours, while she was screaming in agony almost the whole time. At length she fell gradually into a state of entire exhaustion, in which she lingered till about 5 o'clock in the afternoon of Tuesday the 5th of Dec., when she ceased to breathe, thus closing a short, sickly, and, as it seemed to us, a *suffering* life.[21]

Elizabeth pondered her reaction to this death in a letter to Betsey:

> Elizabeths death, does not cut like Edwards, by any means.—but perhaps the unexpectedness of his death might be one cause of the difference in our feeling, whereas we were constantly in a sort of expectation to hear of fits or death.[22]

II

The same letter brought Betsey news of another death, that of Andries, the Hessian soldier who had come to work at Forty Acres with his wife in 1782.[23] In the fall of 1783 Charles built a house on his property for Andries and his wife, both German. Mary Andries understood very little English, but Elizabeth described visits to see her and recorded what she understood that Mary had said. It was the Andries who introduced the Phelps family to the celebration of Christmas, inviting them to spend Christmas Eve at their home several times. Christmas was not a feast day in the Congregational Church, the greeting "Merry Christmas" a profanation in the ears of its members.

Andries had been ill for some time and family members and friends took turns watching beside his bed. When he died in December 1809, it was Charles and John Morison who laid him out and prepared him for burial. Elizabeth's concern now was for Mary, who was ill. "How should I feel," she wrote to Betsey, "such a poor helpless creature in a strange land without any person to depend on." Elizabeth persuaded her to move to Forty Acres:

> we have got that old great chest which Phyllis died in, and put against the outward east door in the kitchen, put straw at the bottom then a bed—that is her night accomodation she says "all is good, all is good . . . she is assisted in dressing, and undressing, like a child—I was in hopes we should learn her to walk, but prety much despair now.[24]

Mary remained at Forty Acres under Elizabeth's care until she died in October 1810. Charles received $31.50 from the town of Hadley for housing and feeding Mary Andries for twenty-one weeks, a portion of the time that she resided with the Phelpses. Despite the couple's foreign extraction, they were accepted as members of the community.

Enos Hitchcock died on May 5, 1811.[25] Following bankruptcy, the Hitchcocks had moved from Brimfield to Brookfield, the home of Enos's father, Captain David Hitchcock. Captain Hitchcock owned several farms, and may have offered his son one of them. When David Hitchcock died several years later, his will revealed that he had already given his son his portion of his estate, perhaps at the time of Enos's bankruptcy. He remembered Thankful and her two children with a bequest of $100 each (his pair of oxen were valued at $70).[26] The Phelpses' reluctance to put Thankful's specific problems in writing continued. A letter from Elizabeth to Betsey written five months before Enos's death tells of the arrival of Thankful's son Charles to spend the winter with them. "Your father thinks he can be some help to him . . . it is said he will be undone there."[27] Thankful's daughter Martha was to spend the winter with a paternal aunt.

The affection and esteem that Elizabeth felt for Dan Huntington and Sarah Parsons Phelps, whom she often referred to as son and daughter, does not appear in her references to Thankful's husband. When she does mention his name, it is as Mr. Hitchcock, never as her son. Most references to him were related to his episodes of illness or financial difficulties.

Entrusting the children to the care of relatives to avoid being "undone" suggests serious problems. Alcoholism is one possible explanation for his gradual decline, both in health and in business acumen. A cure for that disease might be the "one thing" that Thankful had desired. On hearing of his death, Elizabeth left immediately for Brookfield. One of her purposes was to ask Thankful to return with her children to live at Forty Acres, and in October her possessions were brought back to her childhood home, making Thankful the first to return to the family seat. Once again three generations of the family resided in Moses Porter's house.

Another branch of the family was also experiencing financial concerns. The problems with both France and England reduced drastically the possibilities for foreign trade. Britain cut off all trade with America in November 1807. In December of that year, Jefferson's embargo on all American shipping to foreign ports went into effect.[28] Porter's import-export business was no longer able to support his family, a fact that brought him with his family to Forty Acres. In the spring of 1808, he rented a house and garden on West Street in Hadley Village from his cousin Jonathan Edwards Porter, staying there for fifteen months. Once again he tried to establish a law practice and once again he failed. Clearly, his heart was not in it. Without clients, he passed his time in caring for the house and garden in the summer and, by his own admission, in idleness in the winter. In 1807, Porter had embarked on a new business project, purchasing Havana sugar, which he then exported to Holland, a hazardous undertaking with the threats of piracy and possible attacks from both Britain and France. While in Hadley he heard that his sugar had miraculously arrived and been sold at a high price, making him once again solvent. His original investment of $8,000 realized a profit of above $18,000.[29]

The sudden windfall took him to Boston:

> while there I ventured, on the strength of our recent success to incur a little more expense than had been usual for a year or two past. I procured several articles for my wife and children, and treated myself to the first and only dark suit that I ever owned. I purchased also a horse and chaise, which being *unnecessary*, was in fact an extravagant expense.[30]

Porter's boyhood habit of recording his expenses—neat, precise, and inscribed with an elegant hand—down to the smallest purchase—

continued for the rest of his life. He carefully noted each expenditure, along with traveling expenses, for his trips to Boston, "each costing 10 or 12$ . . . only."[31]

In a number of significant ways, Porter deviated from the values held by his parents. They were committed to one place, to the soil that provided their subsistence and on which the family dwelling stood. They sought the self-sufficiency that had been the primary goal of their parents and grandparents. Thrift was a necessary ingredient in that sufficiency. The house was the pivoting point, the "fixed foot," from which they moved out into an ever-enlarging community and which perpetually pulled them back to its centering presence. "I wanted to set up an Ebeneser in every room," Elizabeth announced at the end of a particularly long journey.[32] The biblical passage that she was referring to was from the Book of Samuel (I, 7:12), when Samuel set up a stone to commemorate the Israelites' victory over the Philistines. One wonders if Elizabeth saw those journeys to Boston as ventures into the land of Mammon.

Porter, on the other hand, changed residences frequently, sometimes in response to the rise and fall of his finances, sometimes to accommodate his growing family. Sarah's relatives occupied substantial houses in fashionable neighborhoods of both Newburyport and Boston, on the corner of Washington and Green Streets in the former, and on Summer Street and Bromfield Lane in the latter. Summer Street, lined with chestnut trees before the Great Fire of 1872, was the site of a number of handsome houses, residences of prosperous citizens. Sarah's uncle, Eben Parsons, leased a house on that street to the young couple at a moderate rent. They lived there for several years. They rented houses at various times on Orange Street and Pearl Street, both in proximity to the Boston Common.[33]

When the embargo was removed in April 1809, it seemed certain that Porter and Sarah would remain in Boston. In 1812, they moved back to Summer Street into a house owned by Judge John Phillips, giving up several unexpired months on their current lease, which Porter duly noted cost him about $350. Once again they were fortunate in a kind landlord who charged them a lower rent than they had been paying. Elizabeth reported to Betsey on this move:

We have had a letter from your brother a few days since has disposed of his house tho' at some lose, & hir'd another at less expence—Sally

[Sarah] told me when we were there that it was much more expence for them to live in such an house, on account of the greater number of servants,—but I cannot think of one of the domesticks, who can be dyspensed with—the Cook certainly must be had—the chamber maid cannot be wanting—a man or boy to do arrands, & split wood etc.[34]

One wonders how Betsey, constantly in search of a young girl to help her in the kitchen, reacted to this letter. The differences in Sarah's and Betsey's situations reflect distinctions between urban and rural living at that time, as well as differences in income. Porter was sensitive to the Huntingtons' financial difficulties, however, and in his periods of affluence bought presents for his sister: a wedding gift of a cask of wine, "a nice chaise," $15 for a silver cream-pot among them.[35]

Porter was able to sustain enough commerce with northern Europe throughout the war with England to continue living in Boston, though his memoirs report family expenditures well in excess of what he considered to be commensurate with his income. In 1810 and 1811 his expenses had amounted to $3,100, and in 1812, $3,600—"a great deal too much," he confessed.[36]

Their seventh child, Louisa, was born in June 1812, "a healthy and promising infant."[37] Porter followed this announcement with the remark that life "seemed to glide smoothly on thro the remainder of the year and the following winter, with scarcely a ripple on its surface." In September of that year they were able to leave Louisa with a wet nurse and set off on a journey to Connecticut, staying with the Huntingtons in Middletown, stopping in New Haven and visiting Professor Silliman at Yale College, then returning to Boston via Hadley, "a very pleasant journey of about 400 miles." Porter's sense of humor, somewhat self-mocking, appears in his description of this journey:

I had hired for the occasion a light carriage, and a pair of horses of Spurr & Holmes, stables of some note in Boston, and Henry Stewart, a black fellow, who had lived in my family several years, and who was one of the best house servants I ever knew, was mounted on my white Hussar charger as a sort of outrider. Thus equipped we made quite a display *for us,* in journeying thro the country.[38]

He clearly enjoyed arriving at his sister's with such a retinue, well aware
of the figure that he and his family cut in the country town of Middletown. His servant Henry was no less pleased with the opportunity to
share his sophistication:

> Henry was very much delighted and wonder struck at the rhap-
> sodies and shoutings of the Methodists, several of whose meetings
> he there attended, and Zack, Brother Huntington's man, and some
> other of his cronies, were astonished at his wonderful knowledge of
> the world, and especialy of the charms of city life, which he nar-
> rated in terms of most fascinating eloquence, he having formerly
> been a denizen of the noted village of Comminapaw on the Jersey
> Shore, somewhere below New York.[39]

The journey cost $176, more than $100 due to Spurr & Holmes for
their stylish equipage.

This halcyon period in the younger Phelps's life came to an end in the
fall of 1813. Theophilus Parsons, now Chief Justice in Massachusetts,
died at the end of October. As Porter's mentor while he was studying law
and Sarah's uncle, with whom she had lived for extended periods of time,
he had occupied an important position in their lives. Following hard on
the heels of this loss, came another death, a harder loss to bear. Little
Louisa, now eighteen months old, died on New Year's Eve of the same
year. There was no warning for this death as she had been unusually
healthy compared to several of her siblings. For approximately five days
her parents watched by her bed as she suffered a high fever and shortness
of breath, "when about 9 o'clock in the evening, her gentle spirit, after a
few faint struggles, was released from suffering." This third loss of a child
left them, once again, "with sad and sorrowing hearts."[40]

IV

Despite the elder Phelpses' advancing age and bouts of sickness, they
continued to work the farm, Charles in the field and Elizabeth in the
kitchen and cheese room: "Tuesday made candles. about .40. doz
Wednesday kill'd hogs .2. Fryday try'd the lard." (December 19, 1813)
Two weeks later they killed more hogs for the Boston market, which

Elizabeth and Charles delivered, followed by their hired man Silas with three hogs on the hoof. Elizabeth sold cheese from the house as well as sending it to Boston, employing a "middleman" to distribute her produce to storekeepers and distant customers.[41] People stopped by to purchase a cheese as late as 1813. In May of that year Charles was injured by the cheese press, apparently assisting his wife in the arduous task of handling thirty-pound wheels of cheese. Embargoes on imports created new tasks; molasses was expensive, but could be made from cider, which Elizabeth did.

Neither the demands of the farm nor failing health kept Elizabeth and Charles away from Middletown when, in 1813, yet another grandchild (the eighth) was expected. The direct route south along the river over a fine powdery snow made a single-day journey possible in a double sleigh with two horses. They arrived two weeks before the actual birth, which had been contemplated by Betsey with trepidation. Betsey's labor began on Tuesday evening, March 16:

> Mrs. Harris (midwife), Dr Tracey—to no avail—early in the morning of Thursday sent for Dr Osburn he came with instruments of dissection—but the Lord was gracious wrought deliverance for his hand maid in the hour of great distress & danger.[42]

After seven apparently normal deliveries (despite Betsey's prenatal anxieties), the possibility of a Caesarean section must have brought to Elizabeth's mind other births that she had witnessed, ending with the loss of either mother or child or both. A year later Betsey wrote to her mother: "You doubtless remember the events of this day a year ago—what gratitude ought I to feel—for the mercy I experienced."[43]

In the same letter Betsey described her husband's conversation with a member of the Church Committee in which he declared "that his salary was by no means adequate to his support in the present state of things." Ten mouths to feed along with hired help certainly contributed to that "state of things." His appeal produced private contributions from a few members amounting to $150, which seemed to stem the tide for the time being, but could not have allayed their fears for the future.

Change on a broader scale had been in the making long before its full impact would be felt in western Massachusetts. The farmer's dream of self-sufficiency had been fading since well before the Revolution. The demands of merchants from the coastal cities were more apt to be heard in the state legislature than those of western Massachusetts farmers. Shays Rebellion was an early sign of the bipartisan politics that would replace the nonpartisanship (with the exception of the Tory faction) that had existed for a brief time during the struggle with Britain.

At the same time, the unity that came from a single community church was on its way out. Divisions within the congregation developed over the siting of the new Hadley meetinghouse, whether it should remain on West Street or be moved to the back street (now Middle Street). Elizabeth's account of the disagreement suggests that the discord ran even deeper:

> I almost fear your fathers head is in danger.—for the town street seemed very spirited and you know their leader must not flinch. . . . there is not I guess more than .10. or .15. men of much conse-quence in the opposition, the rest are prety much the outskirts, and poor sort who live in the back-street, and seldom if ever go to meet-ing anywhere.[44]

Elizabeth did not limit demonstrations of compassion to people of "con-sequence," but this comment reflects the distinction that she makes between those in the center of power and those on the outskirts. The elit-ism that lies beneath these words was undoubtedly a part of Elizabeth's view of the community from her particular "station," but the reference to a ghetto-like area and dismissal of people as a "poor sort" is new to the diaries. The dream of a united community tied together by a covenant to which the entire population was committed had vanished.

V

The fracturing of a once cohesive society was also becoming more pro-nounced on the national level. In a letter to Betsey in March 1812, Eliz-abeth wrote:

> was ever so dark a day in America? I am not very apt to be gloomy, but Democracy is raging to such an enormous height, that unless

the spirit of God lift up a standard against the enemy, who are coming in like a flood, it appears as if disstruction was inevitable.[45]

The word "democracy" had not yet acquired the meaning that it has held
for us since the Jacksonian era. Federalist John Adams was wary of unbridled power in the hands of any group; even a majority of the populace he
believed to be as capable of despotism as were monarchies. While he concurred with Jefferson in endorsing power derived from the people, he felt
that constraints were necessary to control the natural greed inherent in
human beings. Unlike Jefferson, he did not applaud the French Revolution, seeing it as "how not to affect social change."[46]

The Federalist attitude toward those who were then referred to as "Jeffersonian democrats" appears in Elizabeth's letter to Betsey in April 1807.
Ned Upham of Northampton, "one of the worst of Democrats," according to Elizabeth, fell ill and died on the Saturday before the elections:

some say it was really the plague. . . . the following Monday which
was freeman's meeting day he was voted for as a sinator, by a great
many, although they were told he was buried the day before—they
said twas a federal lie. but his words and conduct the whole of the
week in which he died was very shocking—it is said he was excellent at oaths and curses which he employ'd in a most profuse manner upon the federalest's ministers and people—wishing calamities
upon all those that they might be prevented from attending the
meeting on the next monday.[47]

Henry Adams described the contempt with which Federalists
regarded Jefferson's rising democratic following in *The United States in
1800*: "the democrat had no caste: he was not respectable; he was a
Jacobin."[48] For Federalists, linking democrats with the radical supporters
of the French Revolution was the ultimate censure. The extent to which
they viewed these "Jacobins" as pariahs is illustrated in a comment by one
lady who, according to Henry Adams, had "long outlived the time."
"There was no exclusiveness," she reminisced, "but I should as soon have
expected to see a cow in a drawing-room as a Jacobin."[49]

Prominent families such as the Phelpses and the Porters found in Federalism support for their religious, social, and political convictions.
Theophilus Parsons had been the unofficial leader of the conservative

Federalists.[50] The connection with Parsons kept the Phelps family abreast of the views held by this group of Federalists, as did Charles's position as Hadley representative to the state legislature in 1807 and 1808.

New England was the stronghold of Federalism. Leaders such as Timothy Dwight worked hard to keep what was developing into a political party rooted in the Calvinist tradition. Fasts were part of that tradition. The governor of Massachusetts declared several days of "publick fasting and prayer" in the course of the War of 1812. Such proclamations had become controversial in a number of the states. Jefferson, when president, wrote a letter to a Baptist association in Danbury, Connecticut, in response to the group's request that he declare "a fast day of national reconciliation." In the original version, which he did not send, he makes clear that he regarded the duties of the president of the United States as temporal and that such declarations belonged to the heads of the established church, as was true of Britain. At the urging of two New England democratic republicans, Jefferson made deletions to avoid alienating what following he had in New England.[51]

James Madison, president during the War of 1812, attempted to sit on the fence in regard to public fasts. He declared several days to be dedicated to "humiliation and prayer." Elizabeth complained of one of his proclamations as "so frenchified" that she didn't know what to make of it.[52] What Elizabeth saw as "frenchified" (for Federalists a pejorative label) may have arisen from a certain amount of equivocation on Madison's part in his desire to bestride two camps: those who wished to pray and fast in an appeal for God's forgiveness of the country's sins and those who wished to pray for God's blessing on the military campaigns.[53] Fasting, a disapproving Elizabeth noted, was to be a voluntary observance.[54]

Once again, the pulpit became a platform from which ministers addressed political issues. In reference to a fast in September, Mr. Woodbridge, the Reverend Hopkins's successor to the Hadley pulpit, preached to a large gathering "very plain federalism."[55] In Elizabeth's eyes this latest war was a civil affair, "the worst of all wars."[56] By the spring of 1813 her fears intensified:

> we have our saviours express declaration "that a kingdom divided against itself cannot stand"—& surely never was it more exactly accomplished than in this Country at the present time, & pestilence which wasteth the inhabitants of our towns & Villages. & all

manner of iniquities are perpetrated . . . it really appears as if we
were devoted to distruction . . . O what a dreadful prospect there
seem to be for our future generations when our heads are laid low,
in the silent grave, Bonipart is a dreadful hard master—save
Lord—save us, from his cruelty, we tremble for fear of his power—
& the dear friendship their is between our administration &
him . . . how many poor tho'tless wretches will fall probably in the
course of this summer?[57]

Unlike her lack of conviction at the time of Shays Rebellion as to which
side was the just one, her position on the War of 1812 was clear. It was
not because her countrymen were once again fighting the English that
her cry of despair was brought forth; it was the strong division among the
States between those who supported Britain and those who supported
France. She foresaw brothers against brothers arising from the differing
factions: those Federalists who wished to defeat Napoleon and those
Jeffersonian Democrats who desired to quell, once again, the power of
Britain. Most of the Northern involvement in the War of 1812 took
place at sea. No trips to army bases by Charles appear in the diaries, nor
does Elizabeth mention wounded soldiers returning to neighbors' homes
nor prisoners of war being marched through the streets of Hadley, as had
occured during the Revolution. But the horrors of war remained vivid
for her. She perused newspapers and her imagination, always capable of
reconstructing a scene that she had read or heard about, summoned up a
vision of Armageddon: "O that there might be many wrestling Jacobs, &
prevailing Israel's in this hour of publick calamity."[58] She was now thinking of future generations. Her view of events was as if seen from a moun-
taintop. How many would fall in battle? What would happen to the new
"Jerusalem," so dearly bought with two wars and periodic uprisings?

In a letter from Betsey to her mother, written on June 14, 1814, the
family's reaction to the war appears:

Under the impression which the late joyful news has made I take
my pen—You have doubtless heard that peace is restored to
Europe, and that a Convention is to sit at which our Commissioners are invited to attend for the purpose of an amicable settlement
of all difficulties. . . . Little did we think last winter when at Hadley,
that your wish (or toast rather, the downfall of Bonaparte) would

so soon be realized—Is not the glorious millenial day speedily advancing—do we not see the signs of the son of man approaching. . . . What an animating spectacle was that, when such a number of Kings and nobles took off their crowns and kneeling in the open air adored the Lord God of Hosts, who had granted them success.[59]

It was not just Elizabeth who raised her glass in denunciation of Napoleon. On the Fourth of July of the same year, two toasts were offered at the annual Independence Day celebration in Northampton: "The Island of Elba—an Empire of Apes—a fit residence for those who ape the Emperor" (J. H. Lyman, Esq.); "The Abdication of Napoleon. It is the *Magna Charta* of European deliverance, and the second charter of American independence." [60]

The premature announcement of the end of the war may have been prompted by the news of the victory of Alexander, Czar of Russia, over France, with his entry into Paris on March 31, 1814. Federalists saw Alexander as a model leader. Known for his piety, he was also a supporter of evangelical movements, dedicating the traditional corn tithe to the distribution of Bibles among the Russian peasantry.[61] Peace would not be certain for another year, but in the eyes of most Federalists, the defeat of Napoleon had ensured that it would soon be restored to America.

Chapter XIII

~

ENDS AND BEGINNINGS

"longings of soul I tho't I had."

ELIZABETH opens her eyes, her heart pounding. She sits up in bed, trying to identify a familiar shape in the darkness that will tell her where she is. But a minute ago she'd been standing at the foot of the stairs, the front hall filled with morning light. Had she been dreaming? Yes, for she heard her mother calling from upstairs. How many years ago was it that she died? Eighteen or nineteen?

In the dream she had wandered through room after subterranean room, stairs descending from one to another, each room lined with shelves containing pots, jars, boxes. She remembers thinking, "I must go through these, sort them out." How strange, too, that the last room was filled with light, but no shelves, nothing stored there. How peaceful it was. Was it the undercroft of her cathedral house? She had wanted to stay there, but her mother's voice was insistent. The dream is still with her, so vivid that she has to suppress the impulse to investigate the cellar.

Elizabeth lies back on the pillow and thinks about the house. Sometimes it seems to her that it has a life of its own, and she wonders what it will look like in a hundred years, in two hundred. Whose lives will it be sheltering, shaping? Will it escape the devastation of fire and flood? She prays that the house survives to shelter her grandchildren and great-grandchildren and that the farm continues to nourish them.

She imagines musical evenings in the Long Room, weddings in its alcove, harvest after harvest celebrated on the back stoop, the north kitchen redolent with preparations for Thanksgiving.

Elizabeth closes her eyes. The image of that last room drenched in light returns and she wonders as she drifts back into sleep, could it be a foretaste of Bunyan's Celestial City?

How short when past—a tale, a vapour, a shadow, yet big with consequences.

I

Elizabeth experienced moments of pleasure and tranquility in the year 1812, despite her failing health, decrease in hired help, and fears associated with yet another war. The forces at work—both hidden and overt—that were bringing about economic, political, religious, and social change did not disrupt the seasonal and daily round of Forty Acres. References to the dissension between Elizabeth, now sixty-five years old, and Charles, sixty-nine, disappear from the diaries. Just how it was resolved remains a mystery, but a newfound equilibrium between the business of living and the "better part" dedicated to the spirit seems to have come about. One of Elizabeth's letters to Betsey testifies to this peace of mind:

> I do feel that you, & I are exactly in the best place for us, if I did not feel pleased with my situation, still I might be convinced it was best—but now I enjoy all the sweetness, of the appointment of my Lord.[1]

There is more than resignation in these words; they emanate a strong sense of well-being. Nor was it a fleeting state of mind; a letter written a month later reenforces the sense of composure in the previous one: "My situation is so much more agreable than ever before," she wrote.[2]

In May 1812, Elizabeth's constant desire to gather together as many members of the family as possible was realized:

> Jest at night Mr Huntington wife & all their children & a man to drive the coach. 10 in all—at the same moment my son from Boston with his oldest daughter Sarah. . . . Satt: we all up on the mountain but Mrs Hitchcock she stay'd with the babe [Theophilus Huntington]—I rode almost to the top of the mountain—we had a beautiful prospect.[3]

Mount Warner is the "mountain" frequently referred to in Elizabeth's diaries. It provided a vantage point from which to view the roofs of Forty Acres, shaded by tall elm trees, stands of pine and birch, its farmed fields bound by the river—this was the "beautiful prospect" that met the viewers' eyes. The hill appears a number of times as the setting for walks, drives with Charles, apple picking, and nut gathering. Theodore Huntington identified it as the family's source of birch, wintergreen, sassafras, and particularly chestnuts. He recalled walking in the woods on Mount Warner when a small boy:

> there was an air of mystery about them. I could not compass or know them as I did the open fields. And yet they were fascinating. I would not dare explore their depths alone for fear of being lost, but with one who knew their intricacies, a plunge from sunlight, song, and flowers into their overhanging shadows with nothing to break the silence but the distant trill of some solitary wood thrush, was a strange, awe-inspiring, and but for the guide at my side, rather a fearful experience; but with one who knew the way, exhilarating, a sort of tonic.[4]

A large boulder, curious in that its composition differs from the surrounding rock, sits near the top of Mount Warner and came to be called "John's Rock," sharing the Scottish gardener's alien status.[5] It was there that he repaired for his Sunday nap, sometimes to sleep off one of the drinking bouts lamented by both Elizabeth and Charles. From this hill, he could admire his handiwork. Seen from a distance, the order that he had imported from the Old World and imposed on the grounds of Forty Acres would have been all the more striking.

Elizabeth's pleasure in the "beautiful prospect" from Mount Warner and her grandson's description of its mysterious woodland are foretastes of the awakening to the beauty of America's virgin wilderness that was finding expression in American landscape painting.[6] Although the period in which such paintings abounded in this country was some years after Elizabeth Phelps's death, her response to views and prospects provides one example of a development in the American consciousness that would create the audience for these works. Several years before the family excursion to the top of Mount Warner, Elizabeth viewed an eclipse, which elicited from her an awestruck paean to "Nature's God."

> June 15 . . . the greatest eclipse of the sun this day ever seen for many 100 years the shining of the sun was entirely gone about .4. or .5. minutes many stars I saw for some time O what a solemn scene! The middle of it was between .11. & .12. then darkness prevailed— Nature's God, displayed his power, in Majesty divine.[7]

Porter remembers the same "total and remarkable eclipse" in his memoirs from a more practical perspective, "when the day was so dark that the fowls went to roost."[8]

The facility with which the house expanded and contracted in response to the number of people living within is demonstrated by the arrival of the Huntingtons, swelling the numbers to seventeen plus at least one hired helper. Jerusha, formerly employed by the Phelpses, returned to Forty Acres for the duration of the children's stay. The Long Room, usually reserved for formal gatherings—weddings, meetings, court hearings, musical evenings—rose to this occasion as well, providing sleeping accommodation. With the return of Thankful and her children to Forty Acres, the house was once again accommodating the multiple activities generated by the presence of three generations. Porter's son Charles accompanied his father on visits to Hadley. A letter from the five-year old boy to his mother in Boston (written in his father's hand) provides a small vignette of indulgent grandparents:

> After dinner yesterday I went to lecture with grandpa & grandma. & they let me drive the chaise myself, & hold the whip—but they would not let me whip the horse, only shake the bridle.[9]

In the year 1812, Elizabeth recorded extended visits from Betsey's children. To Betsey she boasts of the accomplishments of the nine-year-old Elizabeth and seven-year-old Bethia:

> Elizabeth had spun near .2. run last Satt: but on sunday her fore finger on her left hand begun to have a sore come upon it like Martha's . . . this has been a good chance for B—a She has been very busy trying her possibles—we have been killing Hogs, trying, sewet etc—hitherto this week, & She has work'd out her own way prety much nearly half a run I guess in all, but she inclines to spin too corse Elizabeth spins prety yearn . . . they read, & spell—the catechism . . . B—a has tol me several times be sure tell ma'm "I have learn'd to spin."[10]

Martha, Thankful's ten-year-old daughter, was there with her Huntington cousins. Elizabeth was leading the three little girls along their mothers' footsteps, teaching the skills necessary to become industrious wives of farmers, educated women, and God-fearing members of the pious community that she strove to perpetuate. The proud grandmother reported on their reading and memorizing: "E: has learn'd some parts of what is requir'd, & forbidden, in the Commandments . . . E: has read fifty psalms B:—thirty eight chapters in De[uteronom]y & Joshua." One wonders what seven-year-old Bethia made of all the directions in Deuteronomy for food preparation, haircutting, and clothes making, though the list of curses might have captured her attention.

Certainly the presence of her grandchildren at Forty Acres and the opportunity to instruct them as she had their mothers contributed to her sense of well-being. But there is another possible source of this new serenity, glimpsed in a single sentence in a letter to Betsey: "here by the fireside, in our keeping room, are your father and I sitting."[11] Elizabeth's desire to set the scene for Betsey appears in the sentence's grammatical reversal. With the setting of the October sun, the small room becomes an intimate, warm sanctuary, the fire providing a point of concentration between the shadow-filled corners. One imagines its flickering light cast across the paper on which Elizabeth is writing and on the page that Charles is reading, the sound of the scratching pen and turning page audible in the silence. In the quiet of the evening, the keeping room lends itself to conversation between husband and wife: "we had a good visit" appears from time to time in the diaries.

Moses Porter's design for his new house and the subsequent additions and alterations provided a number of retreats in the midst of a busy, productive farm. The keeping room, close to the working areas of the house, had not been one of those. In these later years of Elizabeth and Charles's life together it took on a new function. A part of the south ell addition to the house, it was directly behind the 1771 kitchen, then after 1799, just across the hall from the present kitchen. This room looks westward through two windows (at that time only one), across fields and the Connecticut River to Hatfield and the setting sun. The walls are covered with pine-board sheathing, originally whitewashed along with the kitchen as part of annual spring cleanings. A cupboard with shelves once existed to the left of the fireplace, but was removed in this century. In the "waste not, want not" ethic of early New Englanders, it was made from what appeared to be a bookcase turned upside down, its feet reaching to the attic floorboards.[12]

The keeping room appears in Elizabeth's diaries as early as 1772, three weeks after the birth of Porter when she moved her bed there in order to remain near the work areas of the house.[13] At that time a door led from this room to the 1771 kitchen. It served as a temporary retreat when she suffered from sick headaches, the room's small size rapidly warmed by the fireplace. Charles may have used this room as well, its position close to the rear entrance to the house making it a likely place to settle accounts with hired hands, particularly if the small desk that seems to belong in its place by the door was put there by the Phelpses.

But this final reference to the keeping room evokes an atmosphere of tranquility, a coming together of Elizabeth and Charles in companionable intimacy in this place that contained so many signs of their mutual labor. It was as if, having passed through the Slough of Despond and climbed the Delectable Mountains, both Phelpses found themselves within sight of the Celestial City.

Another room, no larger than an ample closet, is on the second floor at the east end of the hall. The room serves as a place to house the family's lares and penates; the condition of the two-hundred-year-old books reflects the degree to which they were read and cherished. The small library was created along with other Federal additions to the house in the late 1790s.[14] Three sides of the room are lined with books, most of them religious in nature. There is a desk close to the window from which one can see the hills sloping up to Mount Warner. It is a space designed to fulfill pulpit admonitions to "read, mark, and inwardly digest."

In its present state, the house stands as the realization of a way of life to which the first three generations of the family aspired. First came Moses Porter's innovative and ambitious vision of a new way of living and farming outside the village proper, then the enlargements to the working spaces that accommodated the growing family, as well as the increasing farm production that brought Elizabeth into commercial cheese-making. The long stoop stretching across the west end of the house recalls Southern plantations, providing a dining area for large numbers of harvest workers.

Then came the changes to the front of the house that further define public versus private spaces. The "closet" on the second floor invites solitary reading and reflection. The Long Room, by contrast, accommodates large social gatherings. On May 1, 1814, Elizabeth's diary notes the arrival of twenty friends for tea. Her grandson, Theodore Huntington, remembered one of those teas that took place in the winter:

> Winter was the time for making tea-parties on a large and generous scale. . . . The old-fashioned tea-party, in order to go off well, must not number less than ten or fifteen couples. We were living two miles out, so some one must be sent the day before to give the invitations. Many were the discussions and consultations in respect to the weather, for if a storm should intervene there would be great danger of failure. . . . Brother T. and myself were generally selected to watch for the guests when they should come, so as to care for the horses. Many a time have we stood in the old "Space" fronting the road and listened for the bells and strained our eyes in the duskiness of coming evening, to catch sight of the first gay "cutter" with its complement of the rosy faces buffalo robes, hoods, caps, etc., of the Hadley farmers. And how our pride was touched if the guests came slowly and there was fear lest all the hitching posts would not be occupied![15]

Theodore's account goes on to describe the Long Room with a crackling fire, candles on the mantels and on tables at either end of the room. Multiple candles were essential as well as pleasing, for it has been pointed out that one hundred candles do not produce as much light as a single electric bulb.[16] After the brimming teacups, buttered biscuits, and cakes were brought in, the minister or "some other saintly person" asked a blessing. An hour or so having gone by, the company changed seats to create new conversation circles. Finally apples and nuts were passed among the company and at nine o'clock the guests departed. Then, according to Theodore, came the best time of all when the family sat down in front of the fire and considered their party and the news that they had gathered from their guests. His recollections had acquired a nostalgic patina, but provide the details missing in Elizabeth's many terse diary references to teas at Forty Acres.

Tea drinking in the Long Room explains yet another need for numerous chairs, which inventories mention by the dozen, and for as many teacups. The cupboard in the dining/sitting room still houses small handleless cups made of thin translucent porcelain, identified by one family descendant as Lowestoft, but possibly China export.[17] Purchased by Charles, probably on one of his journeys to Boston, they are an investment in the communal ritual of tea drinking and an elegant testimonial to the Phelps family's prosperity.

II

In January 1814, Charles had a violent attack of the ague, his pulse imperceptible for fifteen minutes, "look'd exactly like a corps," wrote Elizabeth, always surprisingly graphic in her descriptions of the physical manifestations of disease.[18] Nevertheless, Charles recovered and continued to travel to see children, conduct court at Forty Acres, make and receive visits. In the summer, the harvest was gathered in, the harvest cake baked. Porter came to Forty Acres in September to help his father with repairs to the floor of the front entry to the house. An ominous diary entry, October 30, 1814, reports that Charles had been taking mercury for several days. On the following Sabbath, he requested prayers of the meeting, and sent for Dr. Porter, who watched beside his bed. The next day the family from Boston arrived and, several days later, Dan and Betsey Huntington from Middletown. A procession of friends and neighbors began to call. Thanksgiving came and went, Elizabeth's preparations interlaced with prayers for her husband: "Lord may thy supporting rod & staff comfort him thro' the dark & untryed Valley of death."[19]

Porter's autobiography gives a more detailed account of Charles's condition. He found him feeble, but without pain. His mind was clear and, from time to time, he inquired about passing events. He had not seen his son's youngest child Caroline and "gave her a grandfather's blessing," expressing pleasure and gratitude at finding the whole family gathered around his bed. On Saturday, December 3, his condition began to deteriorate rapidly, and all through that night his struggle to breathe could be heard throughout the house.[20] With the same precision with which Elizabeth had recorded the specific moment when she made her wedding vows, she recorded her husband's death:

> twentyfive minutes after four my Husband lost his breath—without one struggle or groan . . . stopt breathing as easy to appearance as one goes to sleep. had his reason to the last, tho't he knew in whom he had believed put all his trust & dependence in the great redeemer of sinners . . . & now Lord here I am a bereav'd widow.[21]

No reference to Charles Phelps having written a will appears among the family papers nor in the Hampshire Court records nor the state archives. Without a will the estate would be divided between his two natural children, following their mother's death. Porter's memoirs mention a "provisional arrangement for a division of the estate" until that time. On his deathbed, Charles expressed his desire that two five-acre pieces of land be deeded to Thankful and her son Charles.[22]

General Porter and Colonel Porter prepared Charles for burial and, three days later, carried his body to the general's house. Large numbers came to Forty Acres to dine before the funeral. As the ground was covered with snow, the procession traveled to General Porter's house by sleigh, and then to the cemetery. The list of pallbearers and coffin bearers comprised the Hadley citizens who had occupied prominent positions in local government. A short sentence appeared in the *Hampshire Gazette*: "Died at Hadley, on Sunday last, Charles Phelps, Esq. aged 71." The following Sunday, Mr. Woodbridge, the pastor, remembered Deacon Charles Phelps during the meeting. In this quiet, dignified way the life of the paterfamilias of Forty Acres came to an end.

Once again Porter men came to Forty Acres, this time to assist in the dividing of the land, which Porter and Dan Huntington measured between them. Porter explained in his memoirs that his mother "held by descent in her own right a very considerable chare of the real estate occupied by my father;" therefore, the final settling of the estate would not take place until her death.[23]

The inexorable demands of farm life continued: "Thursday kill'd Hogs .1. Fryday Betsey Gaylord here to taylour."[24] Elizabeth's attention then turned to her friend since childhood, Penelope Gaylord, who was ill and prayed for at the Sabbath meeting. She lingered until the spring, dying on April 10. "O tis breach upon breach," Elizabeth wrote to Betsey.[25]

III

The same diary entry that records Mrs. Gaylord's death announces a Thanksgiving proclamation, celebrating the return of peace. Settled by British and American commissioners at Ghent on December 24, 1814, President Madison ratified the treaty on February 17 of the following year. Elizabeth's diaries continue to weave together her internal life with the external world of family, community, and nation. No matter how absorbed she was with personal losses, she continued to follow events taking place on a larger stage than the village of Hadley or even western Massachusetts. An heir to the Calvinist preoccupation with millenarian dreams, Elizabeth avoided the insularity that almost seventy years in one house and community might have dictated.

The July harvesting of hay now took place in two stages: "Monday Mr Huntingtons Harvest Day, tuesday finished—wednesday harvest begun for my son."[26] Porter's barn was raised in May 1815. The sheep and cider houses at Forty Acres were moved across the road to his land, an undertaking that required twenty-eight yoke of oxen and "near double that number of hands."[27] In the fall Porter came home to supervise the raising of a "hovel" or cattle shed. He engaged a man from Hatfield to oversee his farm as he continued to live and work in Boston. Despite the return of peaceful relations between the United States and Europe, Porter found the income from his former business slow to recover. He then accepted a major position as cashier of the Massachusetts Bank of which Sarah's uncle was a director.

In the spring of 1816, he journeyed to Hadley to arrange for the construction of a house on his land, across the road and slightly south of his parents' home. It was not with the view of living there in the near future, but rather to prepare a retreat for his and his wife's old age. It is a large house that the couple may have hoped to fill with grandchildren. Raised on July 3, 1816, the building was completed toward the end of November of that year. Porter and Sarah were at Forty Acres to inspect it and to help move Thankful and her children, who were to occupy a portion of the house, from across the road.

Thankful Hitchcock and her children had made their home at Forty Acres since 1811, an arrangement that Elizabeth must have welcomed, particularly following the death of her husband. Frequent mention of "daughter," referring to Thankful, appears in the diaries: "I walk'd over to Hatfield & daughter . . . we walk'd home arriv'd at day light down."[28] Walking to Hatfield was made possible by crossing the bridge completed in 1809, yet another undertaking that had involved the direction of Charles Phelps. The completion of the bridge construction merited a sermon from the Reverend Lyman, who said that "in view of such improvements the millenium could not be far in the future."[29] With such expeditions, Elizabeth was maintaining ties with surrounding communities that she and her husband had established over the years of their marriage.

The new house across the road seemed to please her, perhaps because it provided her with an outward, visible sign of the ultimate return of all the family to their roots. She began to record her visits to the "other house," and the Hitchcocks' reciprocating calls. Thankful's move into Porter's house made way for the Huntingtons' return to Forty Acres. Since 1815, hints as to a change in their situation appeared in Elizabeth's letters. There were allusions to differences in opinion between Dan Huntington and several prominent members of his congregation. No letters to Betsey in Middletown exist among the family papers after May 4, 1815, when Elizabeth wrote begging Betsey to come for a visit so that she could meet her new granddaughter, the Huntingtons' ninth child, Mary. At that time she makes no mention of their possible return to Forty Acres.[30] Beginning in February 1816, however, the diaries record Dan Huntington's preaching almost weekly in the hill towns close to Hadley, and on June 16 she was able to announce the arrival of the entire family at the homestead.

A visit from Mitte appears in the diary of August 25, 1816: "Submit West came here with her child to try to do our kitchen work."[31] In April of the next year, she wrote: "mrs West [Mitte's grandmother] & her husbands sister hannah here brought our Submits child which they have took I hope to keep."[32] Their visit with the child points to Mitte's presence in the house and her intention to remain with the Phelps indefinitely. Elizabeth's use of the word *our* could be either a term of affection or of proprietorship if Mitte were working at Forty Acres, perhaps both. Her hope that Mrs. West would keep the six-year-old child is perhaps an indication of waning energy as Elizabeth approached the age of seventy, for small children in the house had been a source of pleasure until then. Mitte's return to Forty Acres suggests that time had mitigated the offense in Elizabeth's mind, expressed in the words "shocking affair."

Porter was the last of the Phelps children to return to the family seat. He soon discovered that he was ill-suited to the nine-to-three, six-days-a-week existence of the bank. He described the effects of this position:

> I became nervous—irritable—and desponding—till at length, after a wearisome effort of twenty one months, I resigned an office which neither physical energy—technical education—appropriate talents, tact or taste ever enabled me properly to fill.[33]

He did not discuss his intention with Sarah before resigning and did not expect the effect that it had on her:

> On hearing the statement she stood for some moments silent and motionless.—Being informed that Mr. Payson was to be my successor, she remarked that there was at least one person—Mrs. Payson—who would rejoice at my resignation. And from that moment, I have no recollection that she ever opened her lips on the subject.[34]

It was now Sarah who became despondent when the return to Hadley became inevitable. Porter confided in his memoirs that neither of them expected much happiness from country life. His salary from the bank had proved insufficient for the support of his family, and his sporadic attempts to revive his commercial enterprises had resulted in more loss than gain. A return to Hadley seemed the only solution.

In September 1817, Porter and Sarah began to prepare for the move back to Hadley and their house across the road from Forty Acres. In the midst of packing up their belongings Sarah fell ill with what Porter referred to as a "typhous fever." Typhus is a contagious disease, sometimes fatal, carried by fleas, lice, or mites. She was taken to her aunt at Theophilus Parsons's house on Chauncey Street, where she lay ill with a persistent fever for several weeks. After a week in which she seemed much improved, Porter set out for Hadley with two of the children. On the day after his arrival at what he referred to as his "*half* home" (the Hitchcocks occupying a portion of it), a stranger on horseback rode up to the north door where he stood. His errand was to deliver a letter to Porter, who guessed at the contents before unsealing it. On seeing the messenger approach, Porter described his terror: "the blood curdled at my heart. . . . My wife is dead?" he asked. "Yes Sir" was the reply.[35] With her death, the energy that Porter had been able to summon again and again for new enterprises seemed to dissipate. He returned to Boston for Sarah's funeral on October 25. She was interred next to her three deceased children and her father in the Parsons family tomb. The next day, Harvard's President Kirkland preached a sermon that, for Porter, paid homage to Sarah. A few days later, with Sarah's cousin Charlotte Parsons, a nurse, and his six children, he returned to his "new—sad—and disconsolate home."[36] Porter's memoirs reveal remorse as well as grief for her death, remembering her reaction to his resignation from the bank. Not just the loss of his beloved wife, but also the sense that he had not found his vocation, color the story of his life with sadness and disappointment. His academic honors, his love of music, his interest in architecture, and his own writing all suggest that, in another time or place, he might have found a different profession.[37]

IV

With all her children in the vicinity, there was no longer an incentive for Elizabeth to write letters, but she continued the diaries until well into 1817 when her handwriting became less legible, words sometimes obliterated with ink blotches. It was in the spring of that year that Forty Acres was once again the site of a birth, Betsey and Dan's tenth child, Catherine.

After the arrival of the Huntingtons, Elizabeth's references to housework disappear from the diaries. Prayers increase, but with very little of the self-castigation on Communion days that was so prevalent in earlier years. Porter described his mother as "feeble and helpless" on his arrival at Forty Acres at the end of October.[38] Theodore Huntington recalled, as a very young child, being asked to fan his grandmother as she rested in her room on a hot summer day. He remembered feeling that he was performing this task in an awkward fashion, which evoked a smile from her, a sign that delight in children had not disappeared entirely with ill health.

Elizabeth was deeply affected by the death of her daughter-in-law, and her own decline quickened from that time.[39] But certainly a substantial part of her dream of a large family rooted in the soil of the Connecticut River Valley and living as pious Christians was realized, though not in the strict form that she had envisioned. The family numbered twenty-three in the fall of 1817 and there would be more to come before the next generation began.

Theodore Huntington leaves us with an image of Elizabeth Phelps that captures her unquenchable spirit. In describing an expedition to the summit of Mount Holyoke in the summer of 1817 when he was four years old, he refers to his grandmother:

> It was a hot summer morning and I remember the tugging of the younger members of the party to get up the jugs of water and the baskets of provisions. There were stories enough of bears and rattlesnakes to give the expedition a coloring of adventure and our credulity was taxed to the utmost to believe that our Grandmother performed the feat of riding to the summit on horseback.[40]

This mountain is one of the most challenging in the region, for Elizabeth an impressive feat at any age.

Standing on its summit, one looks down on the great Oxbow where the Connecticut River curves at least 240 degrees before pursuing its course southward. To the north, and still within this bird's-eye view from the mountain, the river makes a hairpin turn enclosing the Hadley meadows. The forest has grown up the mountain since the mid–nineteenth century when Thomas Cole climbed its slopes with palette and paint in search of the sublime. But even then and from that height the signs of human encroachment on the wilderness would have been visible, as would the straight lines defining farm lots and Hadley's main street. The spire of the meetinghouse, its construction supervised by Charles Phelps, still rises above the housetops. Across the river to the north, like a reflection, the Hatfield church spire is visible, now partially covered by trees. Surrounding the village of Hadley, plowed and planted fields shimmer in the hot sun. Other towns are visible: Northampton to the west, Amherst to the east, The Mills (now North Hadley) to the north, villages that formed the larger community of which Forty Acres became a geographic and social center.

Roads running north and south, east and west, were then the cart roads and rugged paths that Elizabeth and Charles followed on their journeys, first to Litchfield, later along the river to Middletown, the same road traveled by the Huntingtons returning to Forty Acres. On a hot, sunny day such as the one described by Theodore Huntington, the continuous circle of blue mountains undulates in the mist. Beyond that circle and barely visible, are still higher peaks: Mount Wachusett to the east, Mount Snow in Vermont to the north, Mount Graylock to the west. Their phantom presence is a reminder of the world beyond the Connecticut Valley, much of it on that day still to be settled.

On November 11, 1817, two weeks and a day before her seventieth birthday, Elizabeth Porter Phelps died. The next day, the *Hampshire Gazette and Public Advertiser* published the notice of her death. "Funeral from the meeting-house, tomorrow afternoon, 2 o'clk." With all of her children in the vicinity, no letters remain among the family papers to record the details of her death or her funeral; neither does her daughter's diary for that day nor her son's memoirs provide any information. She is buried next to her husband. The graves of Charles and Elizabeth Phelps are in the oldest section of the Hadley Cemetery, close to that of Elizabeth Porter and next to a marker commemorating the death of Moses Porter in the Bloody Morning Scout. There is a small stone for the infant Charles, who died after his brief life of eight days. Shade trees and rises in the land on the east and west sides shelter the graves. Here and there red sandstone markers give off a warm glow. Stands of trees—pines, hemlocks, spruce, and cedar—mark the original cemetery's boundaries. Not far away from Elizabeth's and Charles's graves are the stones marking the graves of Porter aunts, uncles, and cousins, Warners and Gaylords. John Morison's gravestone tells his story:

a Scotch Highlander, captured with Col. Cambell, in Boston Harbor, June 1776, died in the family of Chas. Phelps, Sept. 13, 1814
aged about 65.

Here lies the community that peopled Elizabeth's diaries and letters.
Missing are markers for the slaves and many of the Hadley workers that
came to Forty Acres, their identity preserved, if at all, only in legal documents and their employer's family papers.

With Elizabeth's propensity to find allegorical meaning in her travels,
the view from Mount Holyoke of the beautiful valley below was for her
a glimpse of the promised land, the New Eden, sought by the first settlers,
her ancestors. On that land her father and her husband had built "a great
cathedral of a house" in the midst of a prosperous farm that drew numerous people across its thresholds and finally pulled all of her children and
grandchildren back. With unremitting labor, Elizabeth, Charles, and
scores of workers established the means by which future generations
might find sustenance. It would not always be the life that they had envisioned for them, nor the kind of sustenance that they intended, but the
family papers and the house continue to serve as material witnesses to a
millennial dream of lives lived out in pursuit of the divine intention.

AFTERWORD

The Prophet's Chamber

Two hundred and fifty years after the roof at Forty Acres was raised on a spring day in May, the house still stands, furnished with possessions brought there by six generations of the family. Now a museum, it testifies to the durability of this family that grew from a single branch, and, in a patriarchal society, a female branch. Is this house then, and the objects within, the sole legacy that comes down from Elizabeth Phelps's dynastic ambitions? Is it possible to pass on a commitment to community, internalized from the original written covenants that were part of these early settlements? Can one generation bequeath to the next and the next, in an unbroken line, strong convictions as to one's relationship to God and to one's neighbor?

Descendants from that brief and tragic union of Moses and Elizabeth Porter now number in the hundreds. Their residences spread across the world. With such a diffusion of family members and multiplicity of offshoots, there are most certainly descendants who know nothing of those early generations of the family nor of the house that nurtured them. But for others, it has continued to serve as a lodestar for personal pilgrimages.

Family lore includes ghost stories, but they are not the kind designed to stand hair on end. The ghosts of Forty Acres have not been chilly ectoplasms, but "solid" presences, their energy felt in firm, staccato footsteps ascending the stairs to the third-floor attic, in the whir of the spinning wheel from the north kitchen, a fleeting impression of a figure bustling by the dining room door, or a child rolling a hoop past the Long Room windows. Over the breakfast table, generations of children have asked about the lady in gray leaning over their bed the night before as if to tuck them in. Only one of these spectral visitors left behind evidence of having been at rest. For several days, despite repeated smoothing, an imprint on Moses Porter's bed appeared and reappeared, indenting the pillow and wrinkling the counterpane.[1]

With family members no longer in residence, the ghosts have departed, and taken that apparently unquenchable energy elsewhere. But the house continues to live. The death of Elizabeth Porter Phelps did not bring to an end the productivity of house and farm, nor the keeping of diaries and account books. With the arrival of the Dan Huntingtons, Forty Acres was once again occupied by several generations. In the room where she was born, Betsey Huntington gave birth to her tenth child in 1817 and eleventh in 1819.

In addition to Betsey's ongoing diary is a wealth of letters to her children as they grew up and left Forty Acres. Those to her sons echo her parents' letters to Porter, admonitions concerning the state of both body and soul, clean clothes and pious prayer. In some letters to her adult children, Betsey recounts her emotional crises, which bring to mind her mother's description of the aberrations experienced by Charlotte Porter and others. Her diary is a more single-minded exploration of her soul's welfare than was her mother's. The pull between the demands of Mary and of Martha does not appear to be the concern for Betsey that it was for Elizabeth. While her mother sought an "experimental" expression of her personal religion, Betsey began to move in the direction of a greater emphasis on the rationalism that was turning large numbers of New Englanders to the Unitarian Church. She shared with her mother, however different their approach, an intense desire for an authentic spirituality.

Her pursuit of that experience led her outside the aegis of the Hadley meeting. When she found that she no longer could concur with all the doctrines of the church in which she grew up, such as that of the Trinity, she was excommunicated—precipitously—at great cost to her position in the community. Both her diary and her letters to children evidence the sea change that she was undergoing. Words and phrases that appear in her diaries evidence her espousal of Unitarian theology, particularly that of William Ellery Channing.

Dan Huntington, an energetic participant in the Second Awakening while in Litchfield, Connecticut, had early gained the reputation for openness to theological debates. In biographical sketches of Yale graduates, he is described as "tinged with liberalism" from the time of his ordination.[2] This reputation is all the more interesting in that he had been under the tutelage of Yale President Timothy Dwight, known for his nurturing of champions of Calvinist orthodoxy. After the Huntingtons' return to Forty Acres, Dan was frequently invited to preach in Congregational pulpits of a number of surrounding villages and hill towns. There is no record of his having been offered a permanent position, his "liberal" tendencies perhaps seen as risky in these rural communities of the Connecticut River Valley.

One hundred and forty-eight years later (June 27, 1968), Elizabeth Whiting Phelps Huntington was formally exonerated by the pastor, the Reverend Stanley J. Parker, and the Board of Deacons of the Hadley church. The accompanying statement noted that, during the preceding thirty years, there had been "a lessening of emphasis on doctrinal differences."[3] No longer are members required to declare their acceptance of specific doctrines in order to become members of the congregation. The exoneration may have pleased Betsey's great-great-grandchildren, but came too late to reunite her with the community in which she had grown up.

The young woman who confessed to Federalist feelings rising in her breast, and who thrilled at the launching of the Constitution, in time turned her attention to the problems of the nation-at-large. To her son Frederic, Betsey wrote of "the abominations of slavery [that] are at the bottom of all our national troubles." (June 10, 1840)[4] To Edward she lamented the "apathy upon this subject [slavery] in this part of the country." (June 10, 1837)[5] She had been reading Channing on slavery, and distributing antislavery pamphlets at The Mills (now North Hadley) that advocated abolition of slavery in the District of Columbia.[6] The family attended meetings of the Anti-Slavery Society in Hatfield.[7]

The Huntington children were dispersing. Forty Acres could not provide a means of living for seven sons. The Huntingtons' eldest son Charles, having graduated from Harvard College, then studied law and set up his practice in nearby Northampton, achieving what his grandfather had desired for his son Porter. He served Massachusetts as both legislator and judge in the supreme court. As a testimonial to the regard with which he was held in Massachusetts, the little town of Norwich was renamed Huntington in his honor. One obituary described him as "a hearty lover of good books. . . . His character was built upon the rock foundations upon which Church and State alike repose," praise that would have satisfied both of his maternal grandparents.

As they had with the previous generation, letters continued to bind the family together. The house remained the magnet that pulled the children home, if not in body, in mind. During his first year at Harvard, sixteen-year-old William Huntington wrote to his mother shortly before Thanksgiving:

I anticipate . . . with pleasure the time when I shall meet you all at the Mansion House fireside. I have pictur'd frequently to myself of

late, the appearance of the Sitting Room, kitchen etc. about Thanksgiving time. and imagination represents these things in colours so
lively that at times, I almost think myself at Forty Acres.[8]

It is William, among the Huntington children, who moves farthest away,
and settles in Illinois, but continues to write letters home, trying to contrive ways to return for a visit. William studied theology after graduating
from Harvard, and was eventually ordained. His abolitionist convictions
took him to the Midwest to preach against slavery in the new territories.

The Huntingtons managed to send three sons to Harvard, although
their finances were always problematic. By the time the third son set off
for Cambridge, Betsey wrote in her diary: "Whiting has gone to college—
how he will be supported seems to be quite uncertain."[9] It was no longer
possible to take a pair of oxen to the Boston market, their sale covering a
semester's tuition. Edward, who had gone into business, paid his younger
brother Whiting's college expenses, despite disappointments in his business enterprises.

In his letters to his niece, Theodore remarks:

> Our family had always to endure the misfortune of being accounted
> wealthy. . . . We, as you know, are not a money-making family and
> perhaps it was ordained that Edward should not make an exception
> to the rule.[10]

Whiting died in 1832, just before the commencement exercises at Harvard. He had planned to continue his studies in theology. Eleven years
later, Edward followed him, dying at the age of thirty-six. In going
through Edward's papers after his death, Betsey found the following testimonial to Whiting:

> By his death I have lost everything that could be comprehended in
> the title of friend and brother—his example of inflexible adherence
> to principle, and sincere endeavour to be actuated by right motives,
> though still before me, have lost the benefit which is attach'd to pre-
> cept by example.[11]

Frederic, the youngest Huntington child, elected to go to Amherst College from which he was able to return home occasionally on foot. He was

the third son to enter the ministry. Like William and Whiting, he then went to Harvard Divinity School, and later accepted a position on the Harvard faculty.

While at Amherst College, Frederic came to know Emily Dickinson's family.[12] Evenings spent with the socially prominent Lymans in Northampton introduced him to a number of people from outside the Connecticut River Valley, including Ralph Waldo Emerson. Some years later, when living in Boston, he passed evenings with people associated with the Transcendental movement, among them Theodore Parker, Bronson Alcott, and Margaret Fuller. "Hawthorne," he reported, "occasionally looked in."[13] The practical farmer in Frederic thought little of the Brook Farm experiment as an agrarian enterprise: "The turnips and potatoes languished while the builders of the Future 'cultivated literature on a little oatmeal.' The weeds grew rank while the unanxious husbandmen discussed the Vedas."[14]

Whether it was tendencies among some of his Unitarian colleagues to espouse ideas of the Transcendentalists, or other latent inclinations of his own, Frederic left the Unitarian Church and joined the Episcopal Church. He resigned his position at Harvard, feeling that it would be wrong to remain in that institution, so closely related to Unitarian thought, when he had changed his church affiliation so radically. He was then ordained in the Episcopal Church, became rector of Trinity Church in Boston, and eventually the first bishop of Central New York.

Frederic lived to the age of eighty-five. He wrote sermons, theological essays, and books, and in the manner of his parents and grandparents, was an inveterate correspondent. In part because he left behind such a wealth of writing, he is one of the most complete examples of the way in which the family's spiritual legacy was passed on to subsequent generations. His love for Forty Acres nourished him during all the months that he was necessarily absent from Hadley. In 1860, he wrote to a friend living in the Berkshires:

> The beauty of the valley is indeed very different from the majesty of your grand elevations; but I cannot allow that there is anything in this world more lovely, more perfect,—in its kind,—than this beloved old homestead where I was born; with the windings of the river,—the "green meadows and still waters" of an earthly Paradise,—the flowing outlines of the distant Western hills,—the

splendid urn-shaped and sheaf-shaped elms around us and over us,—the woods, not far off, at the East,—with large grassy yards and hay-fields on every side.[15]

Frederic and his wife, Hannah Dane Sargent, had seven children. The Phelpses' preoccupation with theological questions, along with their growing endorsement of "good works," found overt expression in succeeding generations. Frederic's two sons graduated from Harvard College and went on to Episcopal seminaries. George was both scholar and clergyman, a member of the Dartmouth faculty and rector of the Hanover church. His younger brother, James Otis, founded the first monastic order of the Episcopal Church in the United States, the Order of the Holy Cross. It was a controversial undertaking, stirring considerable dissension between conservative and liberal factions of the denomination. The monks in this order take the vow of poverty, piety, and celibacy, but do not cloister themselves from the world. James Otis Huntington was fired with missionary zeal, not to go into places where Christianity was unknown, but rather to work for social justice on the streets of New York City, on farms in the Northeast, and among coal miners in Pennsylvania.

This monk, whose work took him away from the quiet river valley of western Massachusetts, left a vivid image of his life in the family homestead. In the attic area above the keeping room he made his own room, which his brother and sisters named "the Prophet's chamber." The 1771 pine sheathing, once whitewashed, remains uncovered. A narrow bed and washstand are the only furnishings except for an improvised lectern before the window looking to the west. A simple wooden cross hangs over the bed. It is a monk's cell transplanted to Forty Acres, a retreat, the place for contemplation so often sought by Elizabeth Phelps.

Father Huntington was also a champion for women's rights, urging them to organize in order to improve the conditions under which women labored: insufficient wages, long hours, and unhealthy environments.[16] He may have been influenced by his older sister Arria, who campaigned for legislation that would increase opportunities for women. It was she who was largely responsible for the establishment of child labor laws in the State of New York; she founded The Shelter for Unprotected Girls in Syracuse. "Her heart was with the poor, the afflicted, the unguided and uninstructed."[17]

Arria's niece, Catherine Huntington, an actress, was on active service with the American Expeditionary Force in France during and following World War I. The family's belief in advanced education for their sons had at last been extended to daughters. Catherine graduated from Radcliffe in 1911. A founder of the New England Repertory Theater and the Provincetown Playhouse, she was also a suffragette. She was arrested while protesting the death sentence for Sacco and Vanzetti, the charge "sauntering and loitering" in front of the Boston State House. She wrote a response to the charges, refusing to plead guilty:

> I am an American citizen by inheritance. . . . When the liberties which my ancestors established are endangered as they have been in Boston during these recent weeks, I consider it peculiarly my duty to protest. . . . If it is unlawful to walk in silence before the State House, carrying a card mutely voicing a great injustice then I *am* guilty. . . . I don't believe that this is the sort of country which my ancestors tried to make,—and that is why I walked in front of the State House yesterday.[18]

Variations on these stories of idealistic, independent thinking, and courageous departures from social norms abound among the family descendants down to the present generation. They do not all find their vocation in the Church, though some, male and female, have done so. It was James Lincoln Huntington, brother of Catherine, who was the last member of the family to live in the house. A physician practicing in Boston, he was able to buy out his brothers' shares in the house and retire to Hadley. It was then that the chaise house was transformed into a year-round residence, and in 1949, he incorporated the main house as a museum.[19]

Across the road still stands the house that Moses Porter Phelps built in 1816, in anticipation of years of retirement with his wife Sarah. His second wife, Charlotte, gave him four children, in addition to the nine born to Sarah. From a third and fourth marriage there were no children. He was to have no descendants beyond two granddaughters, only one of whom married, Ellen Bullfinch, whose other grandfather was the famous architect. She had no children.

Thankful Hitchcock lived to the age of seventy-five. Her son Charles married Sophia Porter, granddaughter of the Honorable Eleazar Porter, thus bringing him into close relationship with a family once numbered among the "River Gods." He was a deacon in the Hadley meeting, a title that testifies to his prominent position in the community, as well as his piety.

A letter to Bishop Huntington from the minister of the Unitarian church in Northampton recounts a visit to Forty Acres, providing an outsider's recollection of Dan and Betsey Huntington, as well as Moses Porter Phelps. He begins with Dan:

> that calm old man, quietly farming and theologizing upon his broad rich meadow, not knowing what a stir the son [Frederic Dan Huntington] who returned on that Saturday for his vacation was destined to make in our Zion; that true Christian woman his wife, that courtly and melancholy and wise and large-minded gentleman under the evergreens in the brown house opposite.[20]

Eventually, Frederic bought Porter's house as a gift for his daughter, Ruth Sessions, mother of the composer Roger Sessions, and it belongs to her descendants to this day.

Forty Acres has outlived its function as the dwelling place for family members. The myriad papers generated by them are safely stowed in the library of Amherst College, accessible to those who wish to learn from them. Fortunately, the family propensity to take pen in hand and send letters back and forth to each other has continued—some descendants have even written memoirs.

The Connecticut River continues to flow by the house on its way to Long Island Sound, enriching the land along its banks. Corn grows in neat rows in the fields between the house and the river. Hatfield church bells still sound the hour and summon the congregation on Sunday morning. Buried in the earth beneath these fields and waiting to be uncovered are remnants associated with those who lived and worked in this house and on this farm. The material world that surrounded this family through six generations and beyond is still there—the structure first dreamed of, then erected by Moses Porter, and transformed by Elizabeth and Charles Phelps. There are numerous stories waiting to be told of family members whose lives reflect the changing forces at work in the nation, and at the same time embody the zeal with which Elizabeth Phelps sought to nourish both her spirit and the community in which she lived.

ENDNOTES

Note: The Porters, Phelpses, and Huntingtons (and for that matter, the Pitkins), like many families then and now, wished to pass on to future generations first names as well as last. In these families, the names Elizabeth and Charles appear again and again. To complicate the matter of distinguishing one generation from another, the women in particular passed along nicknames as well. Two members of the Phelps family changed their first name when they reached adulthood. For the sake of clarity, I use one name for each person throughout the book. When one of the alternate names appears in a quotation from a letter or diary entry, I put the name that I have chosen in brackets.

Elizabeth Porter Phelps begins each week of her diaries with Sunday and the date, and places weekday entries under the particular day. For ease in locating specific entries, I have used the Sunday date in the endnotes.

The abbreviation, AC/PPH, refers to the Porter-Phelps-Huntington Family Papers, housed in the Archives and Special Collections, Robert Frost Library, Amherst College, Amherst, Massachusetts.

There are several sources for the writings of the nineteenth-century historian Sylvester Judd. His *History of Hadley Massachusetts* was completed by L. M. Boltwood in 1863 and first published in 1905. It was reprinted in 1976 and 1993. Judd's handwritten notes recording numerous interviews that he held with elderly Hadley citizens are kept in the Special Collections of the Forbes Library, Northampton, Massachusetts. The Special Collections of the W. E. B. DuBois Library of the University of Massachusetts has a typescript of portions of those notes, *Selected Papers.*

OED refers to the Compact Edition of the Oxford English Dictionary, vols. 1 & 2, Clarendon, U.K.: Oxford University Press, 1971.

Sources for the introductions to each chapter come from Sylvester Judd's interviews of Hadley octogenarians in the first half of the nineteenth century, Elizabeth Porter Phelps's own words, and my observations of the house, its surroundings, and the town of Hadley.

I. A FOUNDATION LAID

1. Kathleen J. Bragdon, *Native People of Southern New England, 1500–1650* (Norman: University of Oklahoma Press, 1998), 23–26, 90. See also Leo Bonfanti, *Biographies and Legends of the New England Indians*, Vol. III (Wakefield, Mass.: Pride Publications Inc., 1972), for his account of the Norwottuck presence in the Connecticut Valley, 47–51.

2. Elizabeth Wheeler, a Congregational minister and a descendant of Elizabeth Phelps, told me that her church in North Adams, Massachusetts, drew up a covenant during her ministry there.

3. Page Smith, *As a City Upon a Hill* (New York: Alfred A. Knopf, 1966), 10. Smith is quoting from Mary Ellen Chase's *Jonathan Fisher, Maine Parson, 1788–1847* (New York: The Macmillan Company, 1948), 74, which contains the complete text of the 1772 covenant for the Blue Hill, Maine, meeting. A fire in 1766 demolished the home of the Hadley pastor, which also housed the church papers. The covenant would have contained similar words, both congregations drawing from works such as Winthrop's sermon aboard the *Arbella*.

4. From "A Model of Christian Charity," a sermon delivered en route to Plymouth, in Perry Miller, *The American Puritans* (New York: Doubleday Anchor Books, 1956), 83.

5. Page Smith, 12–13.

6. Sylvester Judd, *The History of Hadley, Massachusetts* (Somersworth, N.H.: The New Hampshire Publishing Company, 1976), 33. This edition is a photo offset of the 1905 edition by H. R. Huntting & Co., Springfield, Massachusetts, first published in 1863. Judd points out that: "lands were variously distributed in different towns" (23). If house lots were under eight acres, more meadowland made up the deficiency. "Among the original proprietors of Hadley, the largest share of land was only four times greater than the smallest" (25). Judd comments, optimistically, that the distribution among the settlers "must have been the result of friendly consultation and agreement." Judd purchased the Northampton newspaper, *The Hampshire Gazette*, in 1822. While writing for the newspaper, he wrote columns on the early history of the Connecticut Valley,

using information drawn from conversations with elderly people, many of whose recollections went back as far as the 1750s. When he sold the paper in 1834, he turned his attention to local history, ahead of his time in his extensive use of oral accounts obtained from interviewing local residents. See also Roy Hidemichi Akagi, *The Town Proprietors of the New England Colonies* (Gloucester, Mass.: Peter Smith, 1963), who discusses in detail the manner in which the distributions were made, 103–10.

7. Andrew Raymond, "A New England Colonial Family: Four Generations of the Porters of Hadley, Massachusetts," *The New England Historical and Genealogical Register* 129 (July 1975), 198–205.

8. Sylvester Judd, *Manuscripts,* Hadley Series, 1:14. The Judd manuscripts are housed in the Local History Special Collections, Forbes Library, Northampton, Massachusetts.

9. Judd, *History of Hadley,* 283. Samuel and Eleazar Porter's real estate holdings were the only ones among Hadley residents that are represented in three figures (Samuel's valued at 120 pounds, 5 shillings, his brother's, only 6 pounds less).

10. Joseph O. Goodwin. *East Hartford: Its History and Traditions.* (Hartford, Conn.: Lockwood & Brainard Co., 1879), street map on frontispiece. The Pitkin owners of those dwellings during Elizabeth Pitkin's life were Colonel George, Governor William, Timothy, Major Samuel, William, Jr., The Honorable Colonel Joseph, Nathaniel (father of Elizabeth), and Joseph.

11. Charles William Manwaring, ed., *A Digest of the Early Connecticut Probate Records* (Hartford: 1902–1906), Hartford District. Vol. 1, 1635–1700; vol. 2, 1700–29; vol. 3, 1729–50. See also *Collections of the Connecticut Historical Society* (Hartford: 1912), 14:537–38.

12. This grandmother was yet another connection to early Hadley, as she was the third wife of John Russell, the first minister in that settlement. It is Russell who was believed to have sheltered the regicides, Whalley and Goffe, in his home for a number of years.

13. David E. Lazaro, Collections Manager at Historic Deerfield, Inc., "Constructing an Imported Appearance in the Connecticut River Valley: the 1742 Wedding Gown of Elizabeth Pitkin Porter," an unpublished paper delivered at a Porter-Phelps-Huntington Museum Colloquium on September 28, 2002.

14. Judd, *History of Hadley,* 236.

15. Judd, *Manuscripts,* Hadley Series, 3:10.

16. Among the Judd manuscripts, cataloged at the Forbes Library as Judd's Notebooks, is "Dr. Richard Crouch's Medicine Book," in which he mentions having visited a patient at Moses Porter's house, her name variously spelled as Madame Pipkin, Pidkin, Pictkin, 136. Elizabeth Whiting Pitkin is buried in the Hadley cemetery.

17. From Sarah Pitkin Porter's *Interleaved Almanac,* entry of December 7, 1752. "Sister Porter moved into his [Moses] house." The *Almanac* is housed in the Special Collections of the Jones Library, Amherst, Massachusetts.

18. See Hugh MCardle, "Population Growth, Out-migration and the Regulation of Community Size: Hadley, Massachusetts, 1660–1730," 11, Master's Thesis, University of Massachusetts (January 1975). MCardle discusses the impact of the open-field system on religious and social solidarity, as well as the control of population. Roy Hidimichi Akagi explores ways in which the system of land distribution created proprietors who controlled the uses of the open fields, 111.

19. AC/PPH, box 3, folder 8. The 640 acres were valued at 1,016 pounds, 18 shillings, and 10 pence. A comparison of Forty Acres with the holdings of a well-known contemporary of Moses' gives a sense of the unusually large size of the Hadley farm for that time and place. On the death of his father in 1761, John Adams inherited two houses and forty acres, which included ten acres of swampland, becoming "a man of substantial property by the measure of Braintree." David McCullough, *John Adams* (New York: Simon & Schuster, 2001), 53.

20. Lee Nathaniel Newcomer, *The Embattled Farmers: A Massachusetts Countryside in the American Revolution* (New York: King's Crown Press, 1953), 3.

21. Judd, *History of Hadley,* 382–84, 449.

22. Kevin M. Sweeney, "Mansion People: Kinship, Class, and Architecture in Western Massachusetts in the Mid Eighteenth Century," *Winterthur Portfolio,* vol. 19:4 (Winter 1984), 238. Sweeney notes that probate inventories in Connecticut and western Massachusetts contain few references to central-hall houses before 1750.

23. Ibid. Sweeney finds few surviving central-hall plans dated before 1750, one in Middletown, Connecticut, one in Wethersfield, Connecticut, one in Longmeadow, Massachusetts. The last, built after Forty Acres, belonged to Samuel Colton, related to Moses Porter through his mother. See pages 231–55, in which Sweeney examines particular architectural forms such as the central hall and gambrel roof in relation to the social and economic position of the owners. It is from this article that I drew my information concerning the builders and sites of these early central-hall houses.

24. Ibid., 236.

25. Changes in the configuration of the second-story rooms make it impossible to identify with certainty the original number of fireplaces. See Adams and Roy, *Historic Structure Report: Porter-Phelps-Huntington House, Hadley, Massachusetts* (Portsmouth, N.H.: 1988), 13–14.

26. Ibid., 6–7. Adams and Roy's examination of the house exterior revealed this earlier treatment of the surface. My discussion of the rustication of the exterior of the house is based on their description of the original surfaces that they uncovered.

27. Examples of substantial rusticated buildings in New England are the Isaac Royall House in Medford, Massachusetts, built between 1747 and 1750, and the Redwood Library in Newport, Rhode Island, built in 1748.

28. An unidentified traveler from Chesterfield, Massachusetts, passing through the upper Connecticut Valley in 1762, remarked that he had not seen a single example of exterior paint, which would certainly include rustication (Judd, *His-*

tory of Hadley, 377n. Sweeney corroborates this observation in "Mansion People," 241–44). Sweeney numbers among the particular features of "mansion" houses built in the 1750s and 1760s, "painted exteriors." He found only seven of the 100 to 200 houses in Northampton, Massachusetts, to have been painted by 1782.

29. Adams and Roy, drawing 15.

30. Sweeney, "Mansion People," 231–55. Sweeney discusses ways in which specific architectural forms came to represent economic and social status in western Massachusetts.

31. See Roger Chartier, "The Practical Impact of Writing," *A History of Private Life,* vol. 3, Philippe Ariès and Georges Duby, eds. (Cambridge, Mass.: Harvard University Press, 1989), 111–59, for a discussion of literacy in America and comparison between the reading habits of Protestants and Catholics.

32. Ibid., 133.

33. See Kenneth A. Lockridge, *Literacy in Colonial New England* (New York: W. W. Norton & Company, 1974) for his careful study of the circumstances contributing to the development of literacy in the course of the seventeenth and eighteenth centuries in New England.

34. The first Samuel Porter opened the store in 1659, the year in which Hadley was settled. It was operated by members of the family until 1880. This information appears in "A History and Walking Tour of West Street, Hadley, Massachusetts," 3, prepared by Gregory Farmer for the Hadley Historical Commission in 1987.

35. Colonel Williams was a member of the Stockbridge Williams family, but had recently moved to Hatfield. His substantial bequest founded Williams College.

36. Judd, *Manuscripts,* Hadley Series, 3:316. This inventory appears in a court record in which the family of Nathaniel Bart of Springfield, Massachusetts, applies to Governor Shirley for compensation for the loss of these items when the lieutenant was killed in an ambush by the French. *Camblet* was a fabric, a blend of silk and wool. See also John Mollo, *Uniforms of the Seven Years War: 1756–1763* (New York: Hippocrene Books, 1977), 31–32, for illustrations of uniforms worn by various officers, as well as privates. The illustration of an officer from Braddock's regiment is indeed "splendid": red coat lined with gold-colored silk, a vest of the same color, red breeches, and a red sash across one shoulder and tied at the side.

37. AC/PPH, box 3, folder 10, August 9, 1755. The reference to three months as the length of time that Moses Porter would be away may have been the anticipated length of this particular campaign.

38. The battle for Crown Point is discussed in detail in Edward P. Hamilton's *The French and Indian Wars* (Garden City, N.Y.: Doubleday & Co., 1962), 161–70.

39. AC/PPH, box 3, folder 1a, July 22, 1755. The subsequent quotations from the correspondence between Elizabeth and Moses Porter are all from box 3, letters from Moses Porter in folder 1a and from Elizabeth Porter in folder 10.

40. AC/PPH, box 3, folder 1a, August 16, 1755.

41. AC/PPH, box 3, folder 1a, August 22, 1755.

42. Hamilton, 166–67. Also, Judd, *History of Hadley*, 339.

43. James Russell Trumbull, *History of Northampton, Massachusetts, from its Settlement in 1654* (Northampton, Mass.: 1902), vol. 3:269.

44. Theodore Gregson Huntington, "Sketches," written in the form of letters to his niece, Helen Frances Huntington Quincy, 1882, are housed with the family papers, AC/PPH, box 21, folder 5.

45. James Lincoln Huntington, *Forty Acres* (New York: Hastings House, 1949), 5.

46. Judd, *Manuscripts*, Hadley Series, 3:425.

47. AC/PPH, box 8, folder 1, March 16, 1771.

48. AC/PPH, box 3, folder 10, February 18, 1754.

49. Judd, *Manuscripts*, "Dr. Richard Crouch's Medicine Book," 136.

50. The word "hysteric" is defined in the Oxford English Dictionary (compact edition) as "a remedy for hysteria; a medicine efficacious in uterine disorders (New York: Oxford University Press, 1971): 1363. Following this definition are a series of examples of this use of the word from the 1700s.

51. AC/PPH, box 8, folder 2, September 15, 1784.

52. See David T. Courtwright, *Dark Paradise: Opiate Addiction in America before 1940* (Cambridge, Mass.: Harvard University Press, 1982), 43–50.

53. Samuel Lee to Nehemiah Grew, M.D., in "Letters of Samuel Lee and Samuel Sewall Relating to New England and the Indians," 146, quoted by Harold B. Gill, Jr., in *The Apothecary in Colonial Virginia* (Williamsburg, Va.: Colonial Williamsburg Foundation, 1972), 35.

54. Rawleigh Downman to Edward and Samuel Athawes, London, August 14, 1766, in *Joseph Ball Letter Book*, Library of Congress. The letter is quoted by Gill in *The Apothecary in Colonial Virginia*, 35.

55. A letter from R. (an unnamed physician) to the *Boston Medical and Surgical Journal* (1832): 6:156–7, finds only favorable results from treating various ills with opium. He claims never to have seen intoxication, except in those "of an hysterical temperament." He does, however, believe opium to be a powerful anaphrodisiac, producing "all but impotency."

56. Alfred Gordon, M.D., "Insanities Caused by Acute and Chronic Intoxications with Opium and Cocaine," *Journal of American Medical Association* (1908): 51: 97–101.

57. Courtwright, 60. Elizabeth Porter gave birth to one child in thirteen years of marriage, unusual in Colonial families. There were, however, childless couples, and her failure to have more children could be attributed to a number of factors, a possible uterine disorder for one.

58. AC/PPH, box 3, folder 1A, July 22, 1755; folder 10, August 9, 1755.

59. AC/PPH, box 3, folder 9, September 22, 1765.

60. AC/PPH, box 8, folder 1, May 23, 1767.

61. AC/PPH, box 8, folder 1, June 10, 1767; June 30, 1767.

62. Judd, *Manuscripts*, Hadley Series, 3:34.

63. See Roger Chartier's discussion of reading and writing in "The Practical Impact of Writing," in Philippe Ariès and Georges Duby, eds. *A History of Private Life, Vol. 3., Passions of the Renaissance.* See particularly page 115.

64. Judd, *History of Hadley,* 57.

65. Judd, *Manuscripts,* Hadley Series, 3:48. The interesting story of this bequest is told by Margaret Clifford Dwyer in *Hopkins Academy & The Hopkins Fund: 1664–1964* (Hadley, Mass.: Trustees of Hopkins Academy, 1964). A more detailed discussion of the bequest appears in *History of the Hopkins Fund: Grammar School and Academy in Hadley, Mass., 1657–1890,* prepared and published under the direction and authority of the Trustees of Hopkins Academy. (Amherst, Mass.: *The Amherst Record Press,* 1890).

66. *History of the Hopkins Fund,* 72, 84. With the incorporation of Hopkins Academy in 1817, female enrollment increased rapidly. "From that time onward more young women than young men have enjoyed the advantages of the school," 152.

67. Judd, *Manuscripts,* Hadley Series, 3:220.

68. Ibid., 3:339.

69. Judd, *History of Hadley,* 61.

70. Manwaring, *A Digest of the Early Connecticut Probate Records*: Vols. 1–3. See William Pitkin's will, 1:496; Nathaniel Pitkin's, 3:94–96.

71. AC/PPH, box 10, folder 6, December 15, 1796.

II. Pleasures of the Pen

1. AC/PPH, box 5, folder 16, June 11, 1769. This folder holds the correspondence between Elizabeth and Penelope Williams. Penelope, or Miss Pen, as Elizabeth addresses her, had two brothers, younger but close in age, as well as three stepbrothers.

2. Tamara Plakins Thornton, *Handwriting in America: A Cultural History* (New Haven: Yale University Press, 1996), 14–15. Chapter 1, "The Lost World of Colonial Handwriting," explores the multifaceted significance of handwriting for this period.

3. Sarah Pitkin Porter's *Inerleaved Almanac,* Jones Library Special Collections, box 3, Amherst, Massachusetts.

4. Both citations from the Scriptures served as texts for the Hadley minister, the Reverend Hopkins's sermons.

5. See Austin Warren's chapter "Orthodox Parsons of Christ's Church," in *New England Saints.* (Ann Arbor: The University of Michigan Press, 1956), 23–34, for his discussion of eighteenth-century clergy and their preaching.

6. Ibid., 31.

7. The Reverend Hopkins came to Hadley in 1754, the year after the death of his predecessor, the Reverend Chester Williams. See Judd, *History of Hadley,* 318–31, for a discussion of the ministers of Hadley.

8–11. AC/PPH, box 8, folder 1. Box 8 contains the typescript of Elizabeth Porter Phelps's diaries. The original is contained in box 7. The majority of excerpts from the diaries may be found in box 8. When I have had questions as to possible misreadings by the typist or where there are ellipses that I wished to fill in, I have used the original manuscript (which is very fragile).

12. See Jane C. Nylander's discussion of visiting in *Our Own Snug Fireside: Images of the New England Home: 1760–1860* (New Haven: Yale University Press, 1994), 221–25.

13. AC/PPH, box 8, folder 1, September 11, 1768.

14. Laurel Thatcher Ulrich, *A Midwife's Tale* (New York: Random House, 1991), 147–61. See also Carol Hymowitz and Michaele Weismann, *A History of Women in America* (New York: Bantam Books, 1978), 11–14, for their discussion of attitudes toward adultery in Colonial America: "Throughout the colonies sexual transgressions committed by people not planning to marry, or already married, were considered far more serious than such acts by engaged couples. . . . In strongly religious communities there was an attempt to treat male and female adulterers alike. Both were forced to go to church and confess in public. In New England confession was the only punishment demanded from those of high rank, while those of less social distinction often were branded, whipped, or dunked in the river" (11–12). Hymowitz and Weismann refer to a study of the congregation in Groton, Massachusetts, between the years 1761 and 1775; of the 200 members, "about one-third confessed to having engaged in premarital sex. The confession was made by an equal number of men and women" (11). No mention of the humiliating punishments mentioned above are in Elizabeth's diaries; however, Judd's *Manuscripts,* Northampton with Westfield series, 2:372, cites two instances in which citizens carried, first Mrs. Phelps, then Mr. Phelps (distant relatives of the Hadley Phelpses) through town on a rail. In 1761, "a number of persons in Turkey Hills and Southwick 'violently took Mrs Phelps and carried her on a rail, blowing horns and ringing cow bells. The pretense was criminal conduct and ill treatment of her husband.'" Judd took this passage from the diary of a Mr. Ballantine. Twenty-eight years later, it was her husband, Joseph Phelps, who was carried on a rail for abusing his wife. At this time, the rail-carriers were indicted, suggesting that this practice was on its way out. These incidents, however, were related to marital practices rather than premarital.

15. AC/PPH, box 8, folder 1, September 18, 1768.

16. See Michael Zuckerman, "A Different Thermidor: The Revolution Beyond the American Revolution," *The Transformation of Early American History: Society, Authority, and Ideology.* James A. Henretta, Michael Kammon, and Stanley N. Katz, eds. (New York: Alfred A. Knopf, 1991), 189. Zuckerman sees this increase as an indication of growing independence among young people in terms of their choice of mate, pregnancy "out of wedlock," one way of obtaining their wish as to securing their chosen partner. See also Michael Hindus and Daniel Scott Smith, "Premarital Pregnancy in America, 1640–1971: An

Overview and Interpretation," *Journal of Interdisciplinary History,* 5 (1975), 537–70.

17. AC/PPH, box 8, folder 1, February 25, 1775. Elizabeth uses this phrase in reference to a confession by Martha Cook, who gave birth to a child more than nine months after her husband left her.

18. AC/PPH, box 8, folder 1.

19. Ruth Ann McNicholas, in an unpublished study, found evidence of fruit trees dating back to the late eighteenth century. "Porter-Phelps-Huntington House Museum: Restoration of Historic Grounds," Master's Thesis, Amherst Mass,: University of Massachusetts, May 1985. In "Sketches," written in the form of letters to his niece, Theodore Huntington speaks of apple trees near the house, but also in greater abundance on Mount Warner, land that belonged to the farm at the time. AC/PPH, box 21, folder 5, 8.

20. AC/PPH, box 8, folder 1.

21. Walter is quoted in John Atlee Kouwenhoven's article, "Some Unfamiliar Aspects of Singing in New England: 1620–1810," *New England Quarterly* 6:1 (1933): 567–88.

22. Sara Pitkin Porter, *Interleaved Almanac,* February 18, 1768.

23. AC/PPH, box 5, folder 16, March 26, 1787.

24. AC/PPH, box 8, folder 1.

25. AC/PPH, box 5, folder 16, March 19, 1769.

26. AC/PPH, box 5, folder 14, November 6, 1792.

27. Charles Porter Phelps, "Autobiography," PPH/AC, box 10, folder 21, 83.

28. See Christina Marsden Gillis, *The Paradox of Privacy: Epistolary Form in Clarissa* (Gainesville, Fla.: University Press of Florida, 1984), particularly 95–136, for the novels' relevance to the role of letter writing in the life of Elizabeth Phelps.

29. Barbara Benedict, *Framing Feeling: Sentiment and Style in English Prose Fiction, 1745–1800* (New York: AMS Press, 1994), 12.

30. AC/PPH, box 5, folder 16, June 13, 1769. John Cooke married Elizabeth Smith, widow of Josiah Smith, on January 4, 1770. Lucius M. Boltwood, *Genealogies of Hadley Families,* 25, published with Sylvester Judd's *History of Hadley,* Camden Maine, Picton Press, 1993.

31. It was not until 1783 that Noah Webster's spelling book was first published under the title *The First Part of a Grammatical Institute of the English Language.* Endorsed by Ezra Stiles, President of Yale College, it was seen as the first step in unifying the language of the new nation. It would then be "happily free of those provincial dialects that confused social and regional differences in less fortunate countries." *Noah Webster's American Spelling Book,* Introductory Essay by Henry Steele Commager (New York: Columbia University Press, 1958), 1. It is not surprising then that fifteen years earlier Elizabeth expressed uncertainty as to her spelling of certain words. Webster's approach to spelling is interwoven with his stress on pronunciation, and some of Elizabeth's spellings clearly derive from her having sounded out the word.

32. Judd, *Manuscripts,* Hadley Series, 3:289.

33. See Nancy F. Cott, "Sarah Osborn's Religious Conversion," in *Root of Bitterness: Documents of the Social History of American Women,* Nancy F. Cott, ed. (New York: E. P. Dutton & Co., 1972) for Osborn's description of the self-doubt followed by self-chastising that she experienced when young. A generation older than Elizabeth Porter, their use of language is parallel. She struggles against sin, but "the devil and carnal reasoning argued me out of a great part of my resolutions for strict godliness." (86). Marla R. Miller quotes from the diary of Rebecca Dickinson in "My Part Alone: The World of Rebecca Dickinson," *New England Quarterly* (September 1998): 1–38, revealing a similar frame of mind. Dickinson did extensive sewing for the Forty Acres family.

34. This passage from *Memoirs of Doctor Seth Coleman, AM* (New Haven, Conn.: 1817), 18–19, is quoted by Gregory H. Nobles in *Divisions Throughout the Whole: Politics and Diversity in Hampshire County Massachusetts 1770–1775* (Cambridge, Mass.: Cambridge University Press, 1983), 78. Coleman wrote this diary entry in 1765.

35. Judd, *History of Hadley,* 330.

36. AC/PPH, box 5, folder 16, March 18, 1769.

37. Emily Dickinson's letter to her friend Abiah is quoted in George Frisbie Whicher's *This Was a Poet: Emily Dickinson* (Ann Arbor, Mich.: University of Michigan Press, 1965), 76.

38. This rhyming couplet appears to be a quotation, though not identified by Elizabeth, nor have I been able to find its source.

39. See Joy Day Buel and Richard Buel, Jr., *The Way of Duty* (New York: W. W. Norton & Co., 1984) for the letters between Mary and Becca Fish. See also the correspondence in the Appendix of *The Journal of Esther Edwards Burr: 1754–1757,* Carol F. Karlsen and Laurie Crumpacker, eds. (New Haven, Conn.: Yale University Press, 1984), 279–304, and Sarah Prince's Eulogy to Esther Burr, 307–8. In the eulogy, Sarah says of the loss of her friend: "O Desolate World, how Barren art thou *now to me*! A Land of Darkness and a vale of Tears and no . . . lightsome ray is left me—my Earthly joy is gone!" See also Nancy F. Cott, *The Bonds of Womanhood "Women's Sphere" in New England, 1780–1835,* (New Haven, Conn.: Yale University Press, 1977). Cott's study of women's diaries and letters from the late eighteenth and early nineteenth centuries provides numerous examples of close female friendships expressed in the language of Elizabeth's letters to Miss Pen. Cott concludes that the "romantic effusions" of young women living at the end of the eighteenth century became "the common experience of middle-class women" in the early nineteenth century (185).

40. See Carroll Smith-Rosenberg, "The Female World of Love and Ritual: Relations Between Women in Nineteenth-Century America," in *Women's Experience in America: An Historical Anthology,* Esther Katz and Anita Rapone, eds. (New Brunswick, N.J.: Transaction Books, 1980), 259–91. Smith-Rosenberg examines correspondence and diaries of women and men in thirty-five families writing between the 1760s and the 1880s. She considers the problems and dan-

gers that arise in looking at same-sex relationships purely from a psychosexual perspective. "Intimate friendships between men and men and women and women existed in a larger world of social relations and social values. To interpret such friendships more fully they must be related to the structure of the American family and to the nature of sex-role divisions and of male-female relationships both within the family and in society generally." She chooses a focus for her study away from "a concern with deviance to that of defining configurations of legitimate behavioral norms and options." Smith-Rosenberg warns that present-day historians, "influenced by Freud's libidinal theory, have discussed these relationships almost exclusively within the context of individual psychosexual developments or, to be more explicit, psychopathology." She suggests an alternative approach, "one which would view them within a cultural and social setting rather than from an exclusively individual psychosexual perspective." Her approach mitigates the distortion that comes from our cultural bias and illuminates for us the context within which these friendships and the language that they evoke occurred.

41. AC/PPH, box 5, folder 16.

42. Ibid.

43. Hannah T. Emery to Mary Carter, October 17, 1791, Cutts Family Manuscripts, Exeter Institute, quoted by Nancy F. Cott in *The Bonds of Womanhood: "Woman's Sphere" in New England, 1780–1835,* 79, 27n.

44. AC/PPH, box 8, folder 1.

45. Kevin Michael Sweeney, "River Gods and Related Minor Deities: The Williams Family and the Connecticut River Valley, 1637–1790." Ph.D. dissertation, Yale University, 1986. Sweeney first identifies these families in the Introduction, 22, but his discussion of the Williams family frequently includes the other families, many of them relatives.

46. See Andrew Raymond, "A New England Colonial Family: Four Generations of the Porters of Hadley, Massachusetts." *The New England Historical and Genealogical Register* 129 (July 1975), particularly for his discussion of the family's acquisition of land and positions in public office.

47. Kevin Sweeney, in "River Gods in the Making: The Williamses of Western Massachusetts," from *The Bay and the River: 1600–1900,* Peter Benes, ed. (Boston: Boston University Press, 1981), 101–16, argues that the Hampshire County elite differed from the elite in Worcester County and Hartford in significant ways: their close ties to the clergy and the powerful Hampshire Association of Ministers, influential military positions, and ongoing relationships with both eastern Massachusetts and Connecticut to the south. A high percentage of Hampshire County magistrates sent sons to either Harvard or Yale, whereas Worcester County sons favored Harvard, and Hartford County in Connecticut, Yale. Hampshire County's affiliations with the two colleges helped to maintain significant connections with both regions.

48. AC/PPH, box 21, folder 5, Theodore Huntington, "Sketches,"17.

49. From the unpublished diary of Rebecca Dickinson, which is housed at

the Pocumtuck Valley Memorial Libraries, Historic Deerfield, Massacusetts. See Marla R. Miller's unpublished dissertation, "My Daily Bread Depends Upon My Labor: Craftswomen, Community and the Marketplace in Rural Massachusetts: 1740–1820," Ph.D. dissertation, Chapel Hill: University of North Carolina, 1997, for her examination of Dickinson's life, as well as the light that she sheds on the Phelps household. The account book of Samuel Gaylord, joiner, reflects a number of Williams's unpaid debts prior to the period, nearly a year, that he spent in jail. Gaylord's account book is also housed in the Memorial Libraries in Historic Deerfield. Williams was appointed Register of Probate in 1776. While in jail he continued to conduct the business of the court "at the new place of residence." See Trumbull, 521–22, also Note 1, in which the author quotes from the *Hampshire Gazette* of December 6, congratulating the people "in this day of tumultuous opposition to the Courts of Justice that the Court of Probate can be safely holden within the county, those important records (as appears by the Registers sign fronting the gaol) are safely kept within the same place."

50. Judd, *Manuscripts,* Hadley Series, 3:178.

51. AC/PPH, box 8, folder 1, June 7, 1772.

52. Hampshire County Probate Court, box 117, #12.

53. Benjamin Hall, *History of Eastern Vermont* (New York: D. Appleton & Co., 1865), 689.

54. Hampshire County Probate Court Records, book 5, 88. The probate court contains no record of a previous trial, and I have been unable to find the record of the original proceeding, which may have taken place before a justice of the peace. I am indebted to Elizabeth Bouvier, Head of Archives, Massachusetts Supreme Judicial Court for that suggestion, as well as a copy of the appeal.

55. Kevin M. Sweeney, "Mansion People: Kinship, Class, and Architecture in Western Massachusetts in the Mid Eighteenth Century," *Winterthur Portfolio,* vol. 19:4 (Winter 1984), 234.

56. J. Kevin Graffagnino, "Vermonters Unmasked," *Vermont History* (Summer 1989), 57:135. Graffagnino is quoting from Benjamin H. Hall's *History of Eastern Vermont* (New York: D. Appleton & Co., 1865).

57. Ibid.

58. Hall, 682.

59. Judd, *Manuscripts,* Hadley Series, 3:86.

60. Nobles, *Divisions Throughout the Whole,* 83.

61. Sweeney, "River Gods and Related Minor Deities," 577.

62. AC/PPH, box 10, folder 21, Charles Porter Phelps, "Autobiography," 82–3.

63. Judd, *History of Hadley,* 383, 391. Judd mentions seven vehicles on the tax rolls by 1785, including one owned by Charles Phelps. The number in 1770 was undoubtedly closer to that of 1768.

III. Crossing the Threshold

1. AC/PPH, box 8, folder 1.

2. Ibid.

3. Arria S. Huntington, *Under a Colonial Rooftree: Fireside Chronicles of Early New England* (Boston: Houghton Mifflin, 1891), 34.

4. AC/PPH, box 10, folder 21, 83.

5. AC/PPH, box 8, folder 1, March 3, 1771.

6. Ibid.

7. AC/PPH, box 8, folder 1, June 9, 1771.

8. AC/PPH, box 8, folder 1, March 8, 1772.

9. AC/PPH, box 5, folder 4, January 9, 1802.

10. AC/PPH, box 8, folder 1.

11. AC/PPH, box 8, folder 1, June 14, 1772.

12. AC/PPH, box 4, folder 27.

13. AC/PPH, box 4, folders 27–31.

14. Adams and Roy, *Historic Structure Report: Porter-Phelps-Huntington House, Hadley, Massachusetts* (Portsmouth, N.H.: 1988) 45ff.

15. AC/PPH, box 8, folder 1, February 16, 1772.

16. There is a tradition among later members of the family that Charles Phelps, Jr., was a lawyer, having received his commission from Governor Tryon of New York in 1771. It seems likely that that commission was meant for his father, Charles Phelps, Sr., giving him license to practice in the Grants, which was then considered part of New York State. Benjamin Hall mentions having access to Phelps family papers, among them John Phelps's *Family Memoirs,* written in 1849 and published in 1886 (Brattleboro, Vt.: Selleck & Davis). John Phelps refers to Charles Phelps, Sr., as a lawyer. At the same time, Hall lists the commission as going to Charles Phelps without affixing Junior to his name, which he does in all other references to the Hadley Phelpses. I have not found any specific mention of Phelps Junior having served as a lawyer in the State of New York. His connections with the court in Massachusetts appear to be in relation to his numerous civic offices, among them justice of the peace. An early mention of his attending court in Springfield specifies his function there as "Grand-Jury man." His son, Charles Porter Phelps, says of his father: "He was altogether a self made man, having had none of the advantages of education except those of a very common school in his native place [Hadley]." "Autobiography," 53.

17. AC/PPH, box 4, folder 27, July 19, 1770.

18. Charles Phelps, Account Book, vol. 1, Baker Library, Harvard Business School, Boston, Massachusetts.

19. This same system appears in other account books of the time, such as that of the joiner, Samuel Gaylord, which resides in the Special Collection, Pocumtuck Valley Memorial Association Library in Old Deerfield, Massachusetts.

20. AC/PPH, box 4, folder 5, September 26, 1789.

21. Polly Randall was from Pelham. She came in July 1809 and stayed until November of the following year.

22. I am indebted to Marla Miller for reminding me of this diary entry, AC/PPH, box 8, folder 1.

23. Sweeney, "River Gods and Related Minor Deities: The Williams Family in the Connecticut River Valley, 1637–1790," from *The Bay and the River: 1600–1900*. Peter Benes, ed. (Boston: Boston University Press, 1981), 583. He notes that "the equivalent of one quarter to one half of the colony's adult males found themselves in court annually."

24. The comings and goings of clothes workers and domestic help appear in Elizabeth's diary, AC/PPH, box 8, folders 1–4.

25. In "Black Women in Pre-Federal America," Chester W. Gregory quotes from *Clio Was a Woman*, Mabel E. Deatrich and Virginia C. Purdy, eds. (Washington, D.C.: Howard University Press, 1980), 55: "In 1630 there were ten blacks in the North and fifty in the South. By 1780 the number had grown to 56,796 in the North and 518,624 in the South." These statistics refer to enslaved men and women.

26. AC/PPH, box 8, folder 1, October 18, 1767 and February 7, 1768.

27. Adams and Roy, 14.

28. See William D. Piersen, *Black Yankees: The Development of an Afro-American Subculture in Eighteenth-Century New England* (Amherst, Mass.: University of Massachusetts Press, 1988), particularly Chapter 3, "Family Slavery," for his discussion of the relationships between northern slave-owners and slaves. Both Phillis Wheatley and Lucy Prince, once slaves who were educated and achieved fame for their poetry, remembered separate seating for slaves, not always true for white servants, 31–32.

29. AC/PPH, box 8, folder 1, July 12, 1772.

30. In *Franklin: The Apostle of Modern Times* (Boston: Little, Brown & Co., 1929), 226–27, Bernard Fax quotes the Reverend Prince: "O! There is no getting out of the mighty Hand of God! If we think to avoid it in the air, we cannot in the Earth." He believed that there were more lightning rods in Boston than any other place in New England and held them responsible for the frequent earthquakes occuring in that city.

31. AC/PPH, box 8, folder 1, April 3, 1772.

32. AC/PPH, box 8, folder 1, August 25, 1771.

33. Marla Miller, in an unpublished paper, "Eggs on the Sand: Domestic Servants and Their Children in Federal New England, 1620–1920" Dublin Seminar for Massachusetts Folklife, Deerfield, Massachusetts, June 2001, has found references to the couple's desire that their marriage be published by the town clerk, Josiah Pierce. Jonathan Warner resisted giving permission for his slave Pomp to marry, but finally agreed after a year of petitioning from the couple.

34. Lorenzo Johnston Greene, *The Negro in Colonial New England* (New

York: Atheneum, 1969), 167. Greene's study, first published in 1942, uncovers extensive documentation of the social, economic, and political position of people of color in New England in the seventeenth and eighteenth centuries. Drawing upon court records, newspaper advertisements, as well as contemporary memoirs, he succeeds in demolishing long-held beliefs as to the uniformity in status, education, and occupation among slaves. Greene writes that the Massachusetts law of 1641 did not dictate the status of children of slaves. In 1670, however, the legislature revised this law legalizing the selling of slave children into bondage. British common law had decreed that the child's status depended on that of the father. Although Massachusetts did not change this law, "custom and tradition" dictated that the child's status followed that of the mother, 126.

35. The slave's classical name was commonly held by slaves recently brought from Africa. Pierson, 129.

36. All of these diary entries are in AC/PPH, box 8, folder 1.

37. AC/PPH, box 2, folder 2, February 15, 1776.

38. AC/PPH, box 4, folder 32, contains a number of documents for indentured servants. Although the one for Simon Parcus is missing, the form for these indentures is standardized.

39. Greene, 196. See also Joanne Pope Melish's discussion of Cotton Mather's admonitions to slaveholders "'to teach your Negroes the Truths of the Glorious Gospels,' [promising] earthly as well as spiritual results" in *Disowning Slavery: Gradual Emancipation and "Race" in New England, 1780–1860* (Ithaca, N.Y.: Cornell University Press, 1998), 32.

40. Greene, 57. On Samuel Sewell, see 50–51.

41. AC/PPH, box 8, folder 1, June 4, 1775.

42. It will be Elizabeth's daughter Betsey who, on January 22, 1834, writes to the Boston *Liberator,* expressing her support for the abolition of slavery.

43. AC/PPH, box 6, folder 4, December 15, 1809. Elizabeth refers to this use for the chest in a letter written many years after Phillis's death,

44. I have Marla Miller to thank for the identity of Mrs. Alien. Elizabeth consistently used this spelling, but she was Elizabeth Parsons Allen, known as Betty Allen, from Northampton. Born in 1715, she died in 1800. She was believed to have delivered 3,000 babies in the course of her career as midwife. Her trips to Hadley necessitated crossing the Connecticut River by boat, ferry, or walking across the frozen river.

45. Greene, Chapter 9, "Master and Slave."

46. See Melish for her exploration of the "kin/alien contradiction" in New England owner/slave relationships, particularly Chapter 1.

47. Elizabeth Donnan, *Documents Illustrative of the History of the Slave Trade to America,* "New England and the Middle Colonies" (New York: Octagon Books, 1969), 3: 72–78.

48. Despite an act brought before the legislature in 1787 and passed, prohibiting all persons residing in the Commonwealth of Massachusetts from participating in the trading of slaves, cases continue to appear before the court, one

in 1792 involving the ship *Abeona* from Salem (Donnan, 89–91). The act is recorded in *Acts and Resolves of Massachusetts, 1786–87.*

49. Laurel Thatcher Ulrich, "Vertuous Women Found: New England Ministerial Literature, 1668–1735," in *A Heritage of Her Own,* Nancy F. Cott and Elizabeth H. Pleck, eds. (New York: Simon & Schuster, 1979), 58–59. Some of these women wrote. Cotton Mather recognized their eloquence by quoting from their writings in his eulogies. Mather's elegies and sermons, written between 1668 and 1735, recognize the single perceived possibility for equal status between men and women, their hope for salvation. The women celebrated by Mather lived from fifty to a hundred years before Elizabeth Porter Phelps and were from the Boston area where access to a limited formal education for women was more likely. There were, however, striking exceptions such as the daughters of Jonathan Edwards, who grew up in Northampton, Massachusetts.

50. AC/PPH, box 8, folder 1.

51. Ibid.

52. Ecclesiastes 9:10.

53. AC/PPH, box 8, folder 1.

54. Marla Miller kindly called my attention to the presence of Hannah Stockwell, wife of Timothy, at Forty Acres as hired help for a period of time.

55–59. AC/PPH, box 8, folder 1.

IV. CONFLICT AND LOSS

1. Arria Huntington, *Under a Colonial Rooftree: Fireside Chronicles of Early New England.* (Boston: Houghton Mifflin, 1891), 47.

2. James A. Henretta and Gregory H. Nobles, *Evolution and Revolution: American Society, 1600–1820* (Lexington, Mass.: D.C. Heath and Company, 1987), 125–47. See also Lee Nathaniel Newcomer, *The Embattled Farmers: A Massachusetts Countryside in the American Revolution* (New York: King's Crown Press, 1953), Chapter 2.

3. J. Kevin Graffagnino, "Vermonters Unmasked," *Vermont History* (Summer 1989), 57:3:138. Graffagnino is drawing upon Benjamin H. Hall, *History of Eastern Vermont* (New York: D. Appleton & Co., 1865), first published in 1858, for these assessments of the Phelps men.

4. Sylvester Judd, *Manuscripts,* Local History Special Collections, Forbes Library, Northampton, Mass., "Revolutionary Matters," 3.

5. Gregory H. Nobles, *Divisions Throughout the Whole: Politics and Society in Hampshire County, Massachusetts, 1770–1775* (New York: Cambridge University Press, 1983), 160–61.

6. AC/PPH, box 8, folder 1, June 19, 1774.

7. Nobles, 160.

8. Newcomer, 64–65.

9. Theodore Huntington, in a letter to his niece, speaks of his sister's dowry

as consisting of proceeds from "a fine fat ox" and all the flax and wool . . . that she could spin." She was married in 1824. "Sketches," AC/PPH, box 21, folder 5, 45.

10. See Benson J. Lossing, *Seventeen Hundred and Seventy-six or the War of Independence* (Detroit: Singing Tree Press, 1970), first published in 1847 (New York: Edward Walker) for his account of Boston females signing a document in which they vow to abstain from the consumption of tea, 90.

11. AC/PPH, box 8, folder 1, October 23, 1774, August 13, 1775, March 31, 1776.

12. Frank H. Smith, M.D., Notes on the history of Hadley, Hadley Historical Commission, Goodwin Library, Hadley, Massachusetts.

13. Judd, *Manuscripts,* Hadley Series, 3:23. See also Lossing, 100.

14. AC/PPH, box 8, folder 1, July 10, 1774. Mr. Hopkins proposed a fast at the morning Sabbath meeting. Mr. Lyman, Hatfield's pastor, preached on the subject of fasting in the afternoon Sabbath service at the Hadley meeting.

15. Newcomer, 49–50.

16. Nobles, 166–78. Additional incidents of mob action occurred in Hatfield and Northampton. Interestingly, the mobs were made up of outsiders, coming from neighboring communities: Williamsburg and Pelham. In both cases, their targets were leading citizens identified as Tories: Israel Williams and Solomon Stoddard. Nobles argues persuasively that these actions "represent the most visible and violent manifestations of a growing tension between authority and autonomy that pervaded much of pre-Revolutionary America and provided part of the context for the Revolution itself," 186.

17. AC/PPH, box 8, folder 1.

18. In his book *Arming America: The Origins of a National Gun Culture* (New York: Alfred A. Knopf, 2000), Michael A. Bellesiles explodes the theory that all early Americans possessed a gun. Even privately owned guns were subject to seizure by the state in an emergency. See especially Chapter 6, "A People Numerous and Unarmed."

19. William B. Sprague, D.D., *Annals of the American Pulpit* (New York: Robert Carter & Brothers, 1866), 2:521. Sprague is quoting from the Reverend Parsons Cook, who had grown up in Hadley during Hopkins's tenure as minister.

20. AC/PPH, box 8, folder 1.

21. An account of the cruel death of Moses Porter, his uniform "a prey to the savages," survived into the nineteenth century when it appears in several family memoirs. AC/PPH, box 21, folder 5, 16.

22. AC/PPH, box 8, folder 1.

23. Newcomer, 51–56. See also Henretta and Nobles, 152.

24. The number 183 appears in Frank H. Smith's Notes on the history of Hadley. He believed the number to be even greater, close to one third of the "total white population, men, women and children, and nearly forty more than the number of ratable polls as recorded in 1771." This high percentage of the

population seems unlikely. Towns such as Pelham served as places where men came to enlist from neighboring communities.

25. Henretta and Nobles, 154.

26. Robert A. Gross, *The Minutemen and Their World* (New York: Hill & Wang, 1976), 147.

27. Ibid.

28. Lorenzo Johnston Greene, *The Negro in Colonial New England* (New York: Atheneum, 1969), 189–90. According to Greene, there were approximately 3,000 black men fighting in the Revolution.

29. AC/PPH, box 4, folder 12, September 30, 1776.

30. Greene, 201.

31. William D. Pierson, *Black Yankees: The Development of an Afro-American Subculture in Eighteenth-Century New England* (Amherst, Mass.: University of Massachusetts Press, 1988), 35.

32. Judd, *History of Hadley,* 313n.

33. Greene, 237. See Chapter 11, "The Free Negro." See also Melish, 88. Melish points out that the freed slave in the North, "no longer formally a part of the coherent social structure constituted by the interrelationships of household, community, and polity," now became dependent on the (white) population at large, a much less secure position.

34. AC/PPH, box 8, folder 2.

35. AC/PPH, box 8, folder 1, May 7, 1775. Lyman's text was drawn from 2 Chronicles, 20:14–15.

36. AC/PPH, box 8, folder 1, March 17, 1776.

37. James Thacher, M.D. *Military Journal of the American Revolution* (Hartford, Conn.: Hurlbut, Williams & Company, 1862), 41. Thacher's journal covers the duration of the war from 1775 through 1783. He also discusses the various calls upon his skills as army physician.

38. C. Keith Wilbur, M.D., *Revolutionary Medicine: 1700–1800* (Old Saybrook, Conn.: Globe Pequot Press, 1997), 13–14. Dr. Wilbur discusses this method of inoculation, noting that "advanced, contaminated pustules were avoided." One imagines that such a distinction by soldiers with no medical training would be difficult for lay people to make.

39. Judd, *Manuscripts,* "Revolutionary Matters," 14–19.

40. John Clement Fitzpatrick, ed., *The Writings of George Washington from the Original Manuscript Sources, 1745–1799* (Washington, D.C.: Government Printing Office, 1931–44), vol. 4, 162, Washington to president of the council, September 14, 1775. Newcomer cites this letter in a footnote to his discussion of the spread of smallpox in 1775, 197.

41. AC/PPH, box 8, folder 1. Although Elizabeth spells the word "parsons," it is clear that she meant "persons." A gathering of parsons in Hadley on a Sabbath would certainly have elicited further comment from Elizabeth.

42. Judd, *Selected Papers,* Special Collections, W. E. B. DuBois Library, University of Massachusetts, Amherst, Mass., Miscellaneous, 400.

43. AC/PPH, box 8, folder 1.

44. Laurel Thatcher Ulrich, "Vertuous Women Found: New England Ministerial Literature, 1668–1735," in *A Heritage of Her Own*, Nancy F. Cott and Elizabeth H. Pleck, eds. (New York: Simon & Schuster, 1979), 67. Ulrich quotes from John Oliver, *A Present for Teeming American Women* (Boston: 1694), 3. Similar fears persisted through the nineteenth and into the twentieth century. I have been told that my own grandmother, whose four children were born in the 1890s on a farm in Minnesota, laid out her "grave clothes" along with the layette for the baby when her labor pains began.

45. See Laurel Thatcher Ulrich's "The Living Mother of a Living Child: Midwifery and Mortality in Post-Revolutionary New England," *William and Mary Quarterly,* 46 (January 1989), 27–48. See particularly 37 and following, for her discussion of puerperal ("childbed") fever.

46. AC/PPH, box 8, folder 1.

47. AC/PPH, box 8, folder 1, February 2, 1777.

48. Judd, *Manuscripts,* Hadley and Hatfield Series, 1:112.

49. AC/PPH, box 8, folder 1, April 13, 1777.

50. C. O. Parmenter, *History of Pelham, Massachusetts from 1738 to 1898* (Amherst, Mass.: Press of Carpenter & Morehouse, 1898), 348. *History and Genealogy of the Families of Chesterfield, Massachusetts, 1762–1962* (Northampton, Mass.: Gazette Printing Co., 1963), 307. The names of Zebulon and Nathaniel appear in the Chesterfield history as coming there from Pelham. Helen H. Lane's *The History of Dighton, Massachusetts* (1962) contains numerous references to Zebulon's father, Nathaniel, active in Washington's army in 1776, as well as other members of the family active in town government.

51. AC/PPH, box 8, folder 1.

52. Thacher, 44.

53. John Morison's gravestone recounts his capture; "John Morison, a Scotch Highlander captured with Col. Campbell in Boston Harbor June 1776 died in the family of Chas. Phelps September 13, 1814 aged about 65." His grave is located on Cemetery Road in Hadley, where most of the people mentioned in this book are buried.

54. Newcomer, 117. "In some cases, trouble arose; a few of the prisoners released to work on the farms even attempted to escape. But most, like the one hundred and fifty Hessians assigned to Northampton, seemed content to spend the war on a Massachusetts farm."

55. AC/PPH, box 8, folder 1.

56. The indenture document for Simon Baker can be found at AC/PPH, box 3, folder 7.

57. AC/PPH, box 8, folder 1.

58. Thacher, 82–86.

59. AC/PPH, box 8, folder 1.

60. Ibid.

61. AC/PPH, box 21, folders 5, 13. This story is recounted by several peo-

ple, among them Frank H. Smith in his Notes on the history of Hadley, Hadley Historical Commission, Goodwin Library, Hadley, Massachusetts.

62. AC/PPH, box 8, folder 1, February 22, 1778.

63. See Thomas Wood's account of his experience in the army's attempt to defend Ticonderoga and subsequent surrender in *The Revolution Remembered,* John C. Dann, ed. (Chicago: University of Chicago Press, 1980), 91–95. He discusses the role played by the town of Skenesborough (now known as Whitehall) following the battle at Fort Ticonderoga.

64. AC/PPH, box 8, folder 2.

V. A TUMULTUOUS TIME

1. AC/PPH, box 8, folder 2.

2. AC/PPH, box 2, folder 2.

3. Clifford K. Shipton, *Sibley's Harvard Graduates* (Boston: Massachusetts Historical Society, 1970), 15:286–87.

4. AC/PPH, Box 2, folder 8. This letter was written June 28, 1761.

5. See Sara Schechner Genuth's essay, "From Heaven's Alarm to Public Appeal," in *Science at Harvard University: Historical Perspectives,* Clark A. Elliott and Margaret W. Rossiter eds. (Bethlehem, Pa.: Lehigh University Press, 1992), 28–54, for her discussion of the teaching of astronomy at Harvard in the eighteenth century.

6. See discussion of the Reverend Lyon from Sunderland in Chapter 7, 155.

7. AC/PPH, box 8, folder 2, January 4, 1781.

8. Judd, *Selected Papers,* 326.

9. Mary Ann Jimenez, *Changing Faces of Madness* (Hanover, NH: University Press of New England, 1987), 72–73. This book traces the evolving attitudes among early Americans toward mental illness.

10. Ibid. Chapter 4, "The Medical Face of Madness." Jiminez discusses specific cases of insanity in eighteenth-century New England, among them a number of young Harvard graduates destined for the Church. She quotes Cotton Mather on the subject of melancholy. Mather speaks of religious melancholy as "'a common problem' in New England. . . . 'Persons of a melancholy nature and much alone' were most susceptible to this condition," 22. Jiminez is quoting from Mather's "The Case of a Troubled Mind" (Boston, 1717). She points out, however, that Mather links melancholy with sin in his treatise *The Angel of Bethesda.* The numerous examples of this affliction among the clergy at this time suggest an interesting and useful direction for future study.

11. Ibid. Jiminez gives several examples of public resistance to asylums in New England. One example comes from Boston: "Boston's *Independent Chronicle* demonstrated a far less sympathetic attitude than the Boston physicians who had solicited funds for an asylum in 1810, and warned its readers in 1817 that if

an asylum were to be built in Boston, residents would be exposed to a 'malignant distemper' (February 1817)," 81–82.

12. Rebecca Dickinson, Unpublished Diary, Special Collections, Pocumtuck Valley Memorial Association, Deerfield, Massachusetts. July 12, 1789.

13. AC/PPH, box 8, folder 3.

14. Benjamin H. Hall, *History of Eastern Vermont* (New York: D. Appleton & Co., 1865), first published in 1858, 2:692.

15. See Laurel Thatcher Ulrich, *A Midwife's Tale* (New York: Random House, 1991), 300, 308, and 406, n. 24, for her discussion of attitudes toward suicide during the period in which Solomon died.

16. The tombstone of Timothy Phelps (1792–1822), son of Charles Phelps Sr., helps to identify the site of the Phelps farm: "With the first Emigrants He settled in Marlboro April 1761. This plot of ground whose dust mingles with his Was among the first that felt his cultivating care."

17. AC/PPH, Box 8, folder 2, December 31, 1780.

18. AC/PPH, box 8, folder 2.

19. William B. Sprague, D.D., *Annals of the American Pulpit* (New York: Robert Carter & Brothers, 1866), 1:653–57. From Sprague's biography of Jonathan Edward II, husband of Polly. Sprague based his brief biographies of early American pastors on accounts from people who had known the subjects personally.

20. AC/PPH, box 8, folder 2.

21. Ibid.

22. Judd, *History of Hadley,* 345n.

23. AC/PPH, box 8, folder 2.

24. AC/PPH, box 8, folder 2, February 3, 1782. Seventh sons were believed to have second sight, as well as the power to cure diseases in addition to scrofula, beliefs that were carried with the early settlers from Britain. See Edwin Radford and Mona Augusta Radford, *Encyclopedia of Superstitions,* Christina Hole, ed. (London: Hutchison, 1975), 301–2.

25. My understanding of stroking came from a conversation with Professor Frank Ellis, who told me that the Stuarts "stroked" a number of people with this disease. Their successor, William IV, did so once, but followed his stroking with yet another, saying that it should cure the sick person of the illusion that such a treatment would cure his disease.

26. AC/PPH, box 8, folder 2, May 4, 1783.

27. Lorenzo Johnston Greene, *The Negro in Colonial New England* (New York: Atheneum, 1969), 222–30. Greene draws his conclusions as to the clothing of slaves from newspaper advertisements for runaway slaves describing their apparel when last seen.

28. Ibid., 34–35.

29. J. Kevin Graffagnino, "Vermonters Unmasked," *Vermont History* (Summer 1989) 57:136. Graffagnino's examination of the role played by the senior Charles Phelps in the conflict over the question of Vermont statehood uncovers a great deal of the state's history that has been ignored. His article provides a

much-needed counterbalance to the mythologizing of Vermont history around
the saga of the Green Mountain Boys.

30. Hall, 682.

31. AC/PPH, box 4, folder 13.

32. Hall, 763–65.

33. Ibid., 693.

34. AC/PPH, box 8, folder 2.

35. Graffagnino, 147–49.

36. Ibid., 152.

37. AC/PPH, box 8, folder 2, February 22, 1784.

38. Hall, 537; see also Graffagnino, 155.

39. Graffagnino, 136.

40. Ibid., 133–61.

41–48. AC/PPH, box 8, folder 2.

49. Marquis de Chastellux, *Travels in North America in the Years 1780–81–82,*
Howard C. Rice, Jr., trans. (New York: A. M. Kelley, 1970), 36. The marquis also
reports on the quality of the meals and the beauty of the young serving women,
in that order, in both taverns and houses in which he spends the night.

50. A number of these almanacs exist in the Jones Library Special Collections, Amherst, Massachusetts, and a particularly large collection in the Antiquarian Society of Worcester, Massachusetts.

51. AC/PPH, box 8, folders 1 and 2.

52. Charles Phelps's account book (volume 1), is housed in the Baker Library
of Harvard Business School, Boston, Massachusetts, along with four additional
account books kept by his son, Charles Porter Phelps. Baker Library also possesses
ledgers, cash books, waste books (discarded assets) and a journal related to Porter's
business partnership with Edward Rand, beginning with the year 1805. All references that follow concerning his account books come from the Baker Library.
Vol. 1 records the Phelpses being paid by lodgers on December 5 and 8, 1814.
The lodgers that appear in Elizabeth's diaries are usually unnamed, reflecting a different relationship with the mistress of the house than that of the named guests.

53. AC/PPH, box 8, folder 2, January 4, 1784.

54. AC/PPH, box 8, folder 2.

55. AC/PPH, box 6, folder 1, September 13, 1802.

56. AC/PPH, box 8, folder 1.

57. AC/PPH, box 8, folder 2.

58. Christopher Clark, *The Roots of Rural Capitalism: Western Massachusetts,
1780–1860* (Ithaca: Cornell University Press, 1990), 56–57.

59. Douglas Lamar Jones, "The Strolling Poor: Transiency in Eighteenth-
Century Massachusetts" *Journal of Social History* 8 (Spring 1975) 3:47–49. Jones
discusses the gradual evolution of laws pertaining to transients in the eighteenth
century and the eventual redefining of that portion of the population as
"deviants from the cultural and economic norms of family life, residential stability, and secure employment," thus opening the door to newcomers who did not

deviate from those norms. Josiah Henry Benton in *Warning Out in New England* (Boston: W. B. Clarke Co., 1911) finds substantial evidence that the practice continued in Massachusetts into the 1790s. Worcester County records, for example, show that between 1737 and 1788, 6,764 people were excluded from forty of its towns, 59–60.

60. AC/PPH, box 4, folder 32.

61. Josaiah Holland, *History of Western Massachusetts* (Springfield, Mass.: Samuel Bowles and Company, 1855), 231–32. See the whole of Chapter 16, "The Shays Rebellion—Its Origin and Progress," for his not unbiased, but colorful account of this eruption in western Massachusetts. He spells out the amount of state and national debts, as well as the lengthy list of grievances put together at the Hatfield Convention that met in August 1786. Averse to mob action, he nevertheless, perhaps unwittingly, provides compelling reasons for resistance to authority. Holland mistakenly identifies the sheriff as Elihu Porter. He was Elisha Porter, Elizabeth Phelps' second cousin, once removed. He was first colonel, then general in the Revolutionary forces.

62. David P. Szatmary, *Shays' Rebellion: The Making of an Agrarian Insurrection* (Amherst, Mass.: University of Massachusetts Press, 1980), 29. Szatmary's first chapter, "The Two Worlds of New England," gives an overview of the roots of the rebellion.

63. Ibid., 66.

64. AC/PPH, box 8, folder 2.

65. AC/PPH, box 8, folder 2, December 10, 1786.

66. Clark, 34. On pages 28–38, Clark discusses the implications of distant trade versus local exchange.

67. Charles Phelps, Account Book: vol. 1. 1805–1815, Baker Library of Harvard Business School, Boston, Massachusetts. The cash values listed in Charles's account books appear to serve merely as a means of exchange, rather than implying that the debt would be redeemed in specie. In his account with Pomeroy, he sells rye for a dollar a bushel, beef for $4.00 a hundredweight, but drops 17 cents from a bushel of rye in order to round the total to the dollar value of the furniture.

68. Clark, 44–50. Another perspective on the causes of Shays Rebellion appears in Winifred Barr Rothenberg, *From Market-Places to a Market Economy: The Transformation of Rural Massachusetts, 1750–1850* (Chicago: University of Chicago Press, 1992). See particularly 234–37. She also briefly explores the impact of climate on economic issues of this period, quoting from the work of climatologist William R. Baron, who identifies 1750–1850 as a "change-over period," one in which the unpredictability of weather increased the farmers' need to maximize production for the market when the opportunity arose, "weather permitting." 238–40.

69. See Rothenberg, 234–37, for her discussion of "anti-Shay towns" and "pro-Shay towns," related to their relative prosperity.

70. AC/PPH, box 8, folder 2, January 28 and February 4.

71. AC/PPH, box 8, folder 2.
72. Szatmary, 105, and AC/PPH, box 8, folder 2, February 4, 1787.
73. Szatmary, 111.
74. Clark, 50.

VI. FOSTERING HEIRS

1. AC/PPH, box 8, folder 2.
2. Karin Calvert, *Children in the House: The Material Culture of Early Childhood, 1600–1900* (Boston: Northeastern University Press, 1992), 92–94. See chapters 3 and 4 for her discussion of children between 1750 and 1830.
3. AC/PPH, box 8, folder 1, June 15, 1777.
4. Teachers at the Hadley school are listed in *History of the Hopkins Fund*. A diplomatic comment at the end of the list may explain the Phelpses' decision to send their son away for his education: "It appears that these teachers with few exceptions, were young men, recent graduates of College. Many of them afterwards distinguished. Their terms of service were short for the most part. Very few of them made teaching their life work. Hence the quality of their work, though excellent, would not be what it might have been, had it been their permanent choice," 75. In 1754, Israel Williams wrote to a member of the Hadley School Committee, complaining that the "English scholars," as opposed to the grammar scholars occupied the greatest part of the masters' attention, 76. This tendency appears to have continued through the remainder of the eighteenth century. See also Margaret Clifford Dwyer, *Hopkins Academy and the Hopkins Fund: 1664–1964* (Hadley, Mass.: Trustees of Hopkins Academy, 1964), 76–77, 84.
5. *History of the Hopkins Fund*, 77.
6. William B. Sprague, D.D., *Annals of the American Pulpit* (New York: Robert Carter & Brothers, 1866), 2:11.
7. AC/PPH, box 8, folder 2, September 27, 1784, April 30, 1786.
8. AC/PPH, box 4, folder 5.
9. AC/PPH, Moses Porter Phelps's Account Book, box 10, folder 8.
10. AC/PPH, box 8, folder 2.
11. AC/PPH, box 10, folder 9, contains the notice of tuition fees for Porter's first year, 1786–87. Room and board were in addition to tuition.
12. AC/PPH, box 8, folder 2, April 19, 1789.
13. The first of these citations provided the text for Jonathan Edwards's famous sermon "Sinners in the Hands of an Angry God." First preached in Enfield, Connecticut, in 1741, it was also preached in Northampton. I am indebted to Patricia Tracey for that information. Although the actual sermon occurred before Elizabeth was born, she knew his sermons, a copy of them in the family library.
14. AC/PPH, box 10, folder 21, 83.
15. AC/PPH, box 4, folder 5.

16. Ibid.

17. Clifford K. Shipton, *Sibley's Harvard Graduates,* 15:96. The definition of "detur" comes from OED, 1:706.

18. See the discussion of Harvard's curriculum when Solomon Phelps studied there, Chapter 5, 99.

19. Samuel Eliot Morison, *Three Centuries of Harvard: 1636–1936* (Cambridge, Massachusetts: Harvard University Press, 1970), 68, 84.

20. *Hampshire Gazette,* Northampton, Massachusetts, July 30, 1794. Up until 1772, class rank at Harvard was based on qualifications other than academic. Clifford K. Shipton describes the system in "Ye Mystery of Ye Ages Solved, or, How Placing Worked at Colonial Harvard and Yale," *Harvard Alumni Bulletin,* December 11, 1954, 258–63. "Until 1767 at Yale and 1772 at Harvard the students in each class were placed in an arbitrary order in which they recited, helped themselves at the table, fell in to form academic processions, and were listed in the Triennial Catalogue. . . . This order was, in the language of the Overseers of 1770, that of the 'supposed Dignity of the Families' to which the students severally belonged." Presumably, when this system came to an end, academic achievement provided the basis for rank. Porter Phelps's election to Phi Beta Kappa establishes superior achievement. "In course" refers to the work done after receiving the bachelor's degree, which normally leads to a master's degree in three years. It may be done away from Cambridge, as in the case of Porter, who was articled to Theophilus Parsons in Newburyport.

21. AC/PPH, box 10, folder 2.

22. See Thomas Woody, "Early Education of Girls in New England," in *A History of Women's Education in the United States,* vol. 1 (New York: Octagon Books, 1980) for his carefully researched survey of women's education in the different regions of the United States. Nathan Hale reported teaching girls at those hours in New London in 1774. Girls in Newburyport attended school in the summer for an hour and a half after the boys' classes had ended. David McClure opened a school for girls in Portsmouth, New Hampshire, in 1773, "the only female school (supported by the town) in New England," he claimed, 144–45.

23. Judd *Manuscripts,* Hadley Series, 3:34, 187, 339.

24. AC/PPH, box 8, folder 3, August 7, 1791. On Amherst schools, see George R. Taylor, "The Rise and Decline of Manufactures and Other Matters," in *Essays on Amherst's History* (Amherst, Mass.: Vista Trust, 1978), 67. Taylor notes that females were excluded from the academy by 1824, necessitating the establishment of a school for females that continued until 1838.

25. See Chapter 9 for examples of both young women's writing, particularly poetry.

26. The house was moved in 1838 halfway down the hill away from the center of town. Paul F. Norton, *Amherst: A Guide to Its Architecture* (Amherst Historical Society: 1975), 65.

27. Robert Cutler, *Memoirs,* 1811, Lucius M. Boltwood Historical and

Genealogical Collection, Jones Library Special Collections, Amherst, Massachusetts, microfilm reel B22.

28. Ibid., Reel B21.

29. Woody, 145–46.

30. AC/PPH, box 13, folder 1, August 30, 1797.

31. Jane Austen, *Selected Letters,* R.W. Chapman, ed. (Oxford, England: Oxford University Press, 1985), 4.

32. AC/PPH, box 13, folder 1, December 18, 1797. The word "pudding" applied to a type of neck scarf may have derived from the nautical use of the word: "a wreath of plaited cordage placed around the mast. . . to prevent chafing." The word is also used to describe anything with the consistency of a pudding. OED, vol. 2, 2351.

33. AC/PPH, box 13, folder 1, August 30, 1797. The instrument acquired by Porter for his sister was actually a mandola, a larger variety of the mandolin.

34. AC/PPH, box 13, folder 1, October 4, 1797.

35. AC/PPH, box 8, folder 3.

36. Gerald W. R. Ward and William N. Hosley, Jr., eds. *The Great River: Art and Society of the Connecticut Valley, 1635–1820,* Hartford, Conn.: Wadsworth Atheneum, 1985, 259.

37. An advertisement in the Hampshire Gazette of July 10, 1799, lists a number of fabrics for sale at J&R Breck in Northampton. Along with camblets and nankins appears "wild bores," an alternative spelling for boar (OED, vol. 1, 238).

38. AC/PPH, box 8, folder 3, November 24, 1799.

39. AC/PPH, box 8, folder 2, April 12, 1789.

40. AC/PPH, box 4, folder 6.

41. AC/PPH, box 5, folder 3, August 20, 1794.

42. AC/PPH, box 4, folder 6.

43. AC/PPH, box 5, folder 14, September 16, 1799.

44. AC/PPH, box 10, folder 21, 17–19.

45. AC/PPH, box 12, folder 15.

46. AC/PPH, box 12, folder 14, July 1, 1796.

47. AC/PPH Papers, box 12, folder 14, September 11, 1796.

48. AC/PPH Papers, box 12, folder 14.

49. AC/PPH, box 8, folder 3.

50. The early Puritans had rejected all rituals associated with the Anglican Church, except those based on scriptural direction: Baptism and the Lord's Supper. Therefore both weddings and funerals were civic affairs. Elizabeth Phelps attended those ceremonies, sometimes in the home, sometimes in the meetinghouse, reflecting the gradual change in custom taking place during the latter half of the eighteenth century. See Horton Davies, *The Worship of the American Puritans, 1629–1730* (New York: Peter Lang Publishing, 1990), Chapter 8, "The Sacraments," 157–86, and Chapter 9, "Weddings and Funerals," 187–212.

51. AC/PPH, box 8, folder 3, October 23, 1796.

52. Edward Maeder, *An Elegant Art: Fashion and Fantasy in the Eighteenth Century* (New York: Harry N. Abrams, 1983), 237.

53. Elizabeth Phelps's diary records Porter's arrival as occurring on Friday, clearly a mistake made in haste, as it precedes the Thursday entries.

54. A hanging for an altar or bed, OED, vol. 1, 569.

55. AC/PPH, box 10, folder 7. A bumper refers to "a cup or glass of wine etc., filled to the brim, esp. when drunk as a toast." OED, vol. 1, 294.

56. AC/PPH, box 8, folder 3, April 2, 1797 and April 16, 1797.

57. Judd, *Manuscripts,* Hadley Series, 3:18.

58. AC/PPH, box 12, folder 15, March 13, 1798.

59. See Laurel Thatcher Ulrich's *A Midwife's Tale* (New York: Random House, 1991), particularly pages 254–58, for her discussion of the relationships between male doctors and midwives in the period encompassing the late eighteenth and early nineteenth centuries.

60. AC/PPH, box 8, folder 3, April 8, 1798.

61. AC/PPH, box 12, folder 15, April 23, 1798.

62. AC/PPH, box 8, folder 3. Mitte is subsequently given the last name of West in diaries and letters. As her mother is referred to as Susannah Whipple until a later marriage, it is clear that Mitte was illegitimate, her father possibly a member of the Hadley Wests listed in Lucius M. Boltwood's "Family Genealogies" included in Sylvester Judd's *History of Hadley* (Springfield Mass.: H. R. Huntting & Co., 1905), 152.

63. AC/PPH, box 6, folder 1, August 20, 1794.

64. Ibid.

65. Ibid.

VII. SOME NEW SORROWS

1. AC/PPH, box 6, folder 2, July 31, 1805.

2. AC/PPH, box 8, folder 2, April 27, 1788.

3. OED, vol. 1, 341. Sexual connotations appear under b. of the third definition.

4. See OED, vol. 2, 1198, fifth meaning.

5. OED 2:3112.

6. First and second causes are explicated in a sermon by Urian Oakes, delivered in Cambridge, Massachusetts, in 1677. Oakes states emphatically "that God is the absolute first cause of all the causal power and virtue that is in creatures." Second causes lie with the free will possessed by human beings. See Urian Oakes, "The Sovereign Efficacy of Divine Providence," in *The American Puritans,* Perry Miller, ed. (Garden City, N.Y.: Doubleday Anchor Books, 1956), 192–213.

7. AC/PPH, box 8, folder 2, which contains the succeeding 1788 entries as well.

8. Ibid.

9. See Chapter 2, page 45 of this book, for Rebecca Dickinson's account of Lois Dickinson Williams's death. Rebecca and Lois were distant cousins, sharing the same great-great-grandfather, Nathaniel Dickinson, one of the first settlers in Hadley, who died in 1676. The poet Emily Dickinson descended from this same common ancestor.

10. AC/PPH, box 5, folder 16, March 25, 1787.

11. Elizabeth corrected the last digit in the year of the letter, making it unclear as to whether it is a 6 or 7. Her diary reference to Mr. Hopkins's sermon text matches a reference in the letter to that sermon, however, establishing the date as March 25, 1787.

12. AC/PPH, box 8, folder 3, June 5, 1791.

13. AC/PPH, box 8, folder 3, July 20, 1794.

14. AC/PPH, box 8, folder 3, November 23, 1794.

15. Lamentations, 3:19–20.

16. Kevin Sweeney, "River Gods and Related Minor Deities, The Williams Family and the Connecticut River Valley, 1637–1790." (PhD. dissertation, Yale University, 1986), 590–91. The author was referring in particular to the 1750s and 1760s.

17. Judd *Manuscripts,* Hadley Series, 3:55. "Confessions for fornication were made by married people till after Dr. Woodbridge was settled perhaps ceased about the time of revival 1816."

18. AC/PPH, box 8, folder 3, June 14, 1795.

19. AC/PPH, box 8, folder 3.

20. AC/PPH, box 5, folder 13, April 24, 1802. The underlining is Elizabeth's.

21. AC/PPH, box 7, folder 3, July 12, 1807.

22. AC/PPH, box 7, folder 3.

23. AC/PPH, box 8, folder 2, June 11, 1786.

24. AC/PPH, box 5, folder 13, October 22, 1802.

25. See, for example, AC/PPH, box 8, folder 3, November 20, 1796.

26. Eliza Haywood, in the essays that she published in *The Female Spectator,* endorses education for women, but does not question their subordinate position. "She recommends compliance to husbands, for the practical reason that women have no other plausible recourse, given legal and social actualities." This statement is from an introductory essay to *The Female Spectator: Eliza Haywood,* Patricia Meyer Spacks, ed. (New York: Oxford University Press, 1999), xv.

27. AC/PPH, box 8, folder 3, August 25, 1793.

28. AC/PPH, box 8, folder 3, September 22, 1793.

29. John Montague Smith, *History of the Town of Sunderland, Massachusetts* (Greenfield, Mass.: Press of E. A. Hall & Co., 1899), 72.

30. John P. Manwell, *A History of the Hampshire Association of Congregational Churches and Ministers* (Amherst, Mass.: The Newell Press, 1941), 17.

31. Such behavior was a crime according to a Massachusetts law of 1784: "if

any man or woman, married or unmarried shall be guilty of open gross lewdness and lascivious behaviour, and being thereof convicted before the Justices of the Supreme Judicial Court, shall be punished by setting in the pillory, whipping, fining, imprisonment and binding to the good behaviour." *Acts and Resolves of Massachusetts, 1784–85,* Chapter 40, 118. There is no record in the Sunderland histories of Mr. Lyon having been brought before a civil court. Perhaps matters pertaining to the clergy were felt to be the concern of the Church when handled by the Association of Ministers, a remnant of the former theocracy.

32. The Hampshire Association of Congregational Churches and Ministers, Notes, November 7, 1787—November 6, 1794, are housed in the Local History Special Collections of the Forbes Library, Northampton, Massachusetts. The case against the Reverend Asa Lyon appears on pages 81–88 under the year 1793. The source of this system for resolving conflicts within the meeting congregation may have derived from a seventeenth-century procedure described by Cotton Mather and designed to restore the all-important consensus essential for a covenanted community. See Michael Zuckerman, *Peaceable Kingdoms* (New York: W. W. Norton & Co., 1970) 61, for his summary of Mather's description in *Ratio Disciplinae Fratrum Nov-Anglorum* (Boston: 1726) 148–49.

33. A brief biography of the Reverend Mr. Lyon appears in John Montague Smith, *History of the Town of Sunderland, Massachusetts,* 440. The "mutual council" attended by Elizabeth Phelps is described as a "six-day session." I am grateful to William Hubbard for this information.

34. Judd, *Manuscripts,* Hadley Series, 3:187. This assessment of Elizabeth Phelps comes from a conversation between Sylvester Judd and Mrs. Allen Clark that took place on September 12, 1859. She told Judd that nearly all the women of Hadley worked and "were in the kitchen and elsewhere," though she digresses to say that "Windsor Smith's family despised labor as much as any & were above work. He & some daughters have died poor."

35. AC/PPH, box 10, folder 21, 83.

36. AC/PPH, box 5, folder 3, June 13, 1801.

37. AC/PPH, box 4, folder 3; both letters were written in September 1801.

38. AC/PPH, box 8, folder 3, March 26, 1797. Hadley did not possess a town hall, where hearings could take place, until 1840. Until then they occurred in houses, in the church or in school.

39. Samuel Freeman, Esq., *The Massachusetts Justice: Being a Collection of the Laws of the Commonwealth of Massachusetts Relative to the Power and Duty of Justices of the Peace* (Boston: 1795). A copy of this work exists in Charles Phelps's personal library, inscribed with his name.

40. James Russell Trumbull, *History of Northampton, Massachusetts from Its Settlement in 1654,* vol. 2 (Northampton, Mass.: 1902), 337–38.

41. See *History of Transportation in the United States before 1860,* Balthasar Henry Meyer, director (Carnegie Institute of Washington, Washington, D.C.: 1948), particularly Chapters 1, 2, 5, and 12, for the discussion of transportation facilities in New England.

42. AC/PPH, box 6, folder 1, September 13, 1802.

43. AC/PPH, box 6, folder 1, May 29, 1796.

44. AC/PPH, box 6, folder 1, September 7, 1800.

45. See Karen V. Hansen's *A Very Social Time* (Berkeley, Calif.: University of California Press, 1994), Chapter 4, for her discussion of visiting in antebellum New England.

46. AC/PPH, box 8, folder 3.

47. Stanley Elkins and Eric McKitrick, *The Age of Federalism* (New York: Oxford University Press, 1993), 581–82.

48. Charles Ellis Dickson, "Jeremiads in the New American Republic: The Case of National Fasts in the John Adams Administration," *The New England Quarterly* 2 (June 1987), 60:188. See also Horton Davies, *The Worship of the American Puritans: 1629–1730* (New York: Peter Lang Publishing, 1990), 58–63, for his discussion of the origins of this attitude toward fasting.

49. Dickson, 189.

50. "Federalist" flags may never have flown in New England. Neither Marilyn Ziodis of the Smithsonian Institution nor the Newburyport Historical Society was able to find any reference to such a flag for the Federalist party. Newburyport was the original home of Theophilus Parsons, a prominent leader within the party, who later moved to Boston.

51. AC/PPH, box 12, folder 19. Elisabeth Nichols discusses the linguistic significance of this letter in "'Pray Don't Tell Any Body That I Write Politics': Private Expressions and Public Admonitions in the Early Republic." Ph.D. dissertation, Durham, University of New Hampshire, 1997. See particularly Chapter 4, 216 ff. In this use of the word Federal, Betsey is most certainly referring to the party endorsed by her parents.

52. AC/PPH, box 8, folder 3, September 30, 1798. The details of Elizabeth Porter's death and funeral appear in this diary entry.

53. AC/PPH, box 14, folder 1, October 7, 1798.

54. AC/PPH, box 8, folder 3, November 25, 1798.

VIII. "THIS GREAT CATHEDRAL OF A HOUSE"

1. AC/PPH, box 5, folder 15, December 15. The present whereabouts of Moses Porter's desk is believed to be in the home of a descendant of the family.

2. AC/PPH, box 8, folder 2.

3. For the following discussion of the work done on the interior of the house, I have drawn extensively on Adams and Roy, *Historic Structure Report: Porter-Phelps-Huntington House, Hadley Massachusetts* (Portsmouth, N.H.: 1988) as well as references in Elizabeth Phelps's diaries. An archaeological dig has yet to take place on the grounds. When that happens, it will make possible a more complete picture of the entire farm as it existed into the early twentieth century. James Lincoln Huntington, the last member of the family to live in the house,

took down a number of the outbuildings that had fallen into disrepair and arranged for the barn to be removed to Hadley as a farm museum.

4. Adams and Roy, 76.

5. AC/PPH, box 8, folder 2, February 11, 1787.

6. AC/PPH, box 4, folder 5, December 31, 1794.

7. AC/PPH, box 8, folder 3, May 17, 1795.

8. AC/PPH, box 13, folder 1.

9. A passageway through the middle of this building to the back stoop includes a privy. It is not certain when it was placed in this position, but it would have been a welcome convenience, particularly in the winter, as opposed to the customary site at some distance from the house.

10. Investigations conducted by Adams & Roy Consultants, make clear that the south ell kitchen and pump room, woodshed, and corn barn were erected at the same time, *Historic Structure Report,* 58–59. Theophilus Parsons's barn in Newburyport is no longer standing.

11. AC/PPH, box 12, folder 15, Sunday evening, May 1796.

12. AC/PPH, box 10, folder 21, 22.

13. These speculations on the uses of the kitchen and connecting rooms are made by the Adams & Roy consultants who base them on plausible evidence from close examination of the structures and layers of paint covering them, Adams and Roy, 64.

14. AC/PPH, box 175, folder 1. This room appears on a map drawn in 1820 by a member of the family.

15. Adams and Roy, 61. Adams and Roy believe that Elizabeth's use of the plural implies that all of the hearthstones were replaced at this time.

16. AC/PPH, box 6, folder 1, November 4, 1797.

17. Gambrel roofs appear in East Hartford, on the Longmeadow house of Samuel Colton, a relative of Elizabeth's, in Deerfield, and on the homes of Timothy Dwight and Solomon Stoddard in Northampton, all places visited by the Phelpses.

18. Kevin Sweeney, in "Mansion People: Kinship, Class, and Architecture in Western Massachusetts in the Mid Eighteenth Century," *Winterthur Portfolio,* vol. 19:4 (Winter 1984), 231–55 notes that a number of prominent citizens who served as justices of the peace held court in their gambrel-roofed houses, further linking this structure with authority, 242. Elizabeth Phelps's diary records several sessions of the court held at Forty Acres, one such meeting on January 1, 1804 (AC/PPH, box 8, folder 4).

19. One example of Benjamin's work is the William Coleman house, completed in 1796. Sitting on a promontory at the town's center, it is a striking example of the architect's early work. His first book, *The Country Builder's Assistant,* was published in 1797. Charles would have known of both the house and the book. Like Forty Acres, the Coleman house is an amalgam of Georgian and Federal features.

20. AC/PPH, box 8, folder 3, June 2, 1799.

21. Judd, *Manuscripts,* Hadley Series, 3:19. This information came from Judd's conversation with Thankful Hitchcock.

22. AC/PPH, box 6, folder 2, November 15, 1805.

23. AC/PPH, box 21, folder 5, 33–35.

24. AC/PPH, box 8, folder 4, May 20, 1804.

25. Mac Griswold, "Garden Notebook," *New York Times,* June 3, 1999, F10. Griswold has written a book, *Washington's Gardens at Mount Vernon: Landscape of the Inner Man* (New York: Houghton Mifflin, 1999).

26. Judd, *History of Hadley,* 366 and note and *Manuscripts,* 3:21. Judd notes that early New England gardens contained vegetables, medicinal herbs, and "a small plot of flowers." "All old ladies whom I have questioned, and some were born before 1760, told me that they and others had little flower beds when young. But there was nothing like the present fondness for flowers." See also Ruth Ann McNicholas, "Porter-Phelps-Huntington House Museum: Restoration of Historic Grounds," Master's thesis, Amherst, University of Massachusetts, May 1985, 11, for her sketch of the garden as it would have appeared during the time in which Morison worked for the Phelpses. She found evidence of a large square with a rose garden at the center and two bisecting paths dividing the square into four smaller squares. The east and west boundaries of the square were planted with fruit trees, according to Judd, "apples, peaches, pears and plums."

27. Timothy Dwight, *Travels in New-England and New-York* (Cambridge, Mass.: Harvard University Press, 1969), vol. 1, 259–60. Dwight's *Travels* were first published in 1821 in four volumes. The particular section devoted to the Connecticut River Valley was written in 1810.

28. In "Mansion People," Kevin Sweeney finds in architectural details of the houses built by the "River Gods," declarations of the occupants claim to a "genteel life-style" that "put social distance between themselves and their neighbors," 231. The article is especially interesting, as well as convincing, in its recognition of the forces that lie behind architectural developments. The houses that he discusses antedate the late eighteenth-century changes made by the Phelpses, but coincide with Moses Porter's construction in 1752.

29. See letter quoted in Chapter 6, 134.

30. AC/PPH, box 10, folder 21, 22–23. Porter is referring to the spring of 1800.

31. AC/PPH, box 8, folder 3.

32. AC/PPH, box 12, folder 19, July 18, 1799.

33. AC/PPH, box 11, folder 7.

34. Ibid.

35. AC/PPH, box 14, folder 1, January 13, 1799.

36. AC/PPH, box 12, folder 13, September 28, 1800.

37. Charles Phelps's account book of 1814 continues to record exchanges of labor for produce, though the final settlement sometimes includes a balance paid in cash.

38. See Christopher Clark, *The Roots of Rural Capitalism: Western Massachusetts, 1780–1860* (Ithaca, N.Y.: Cornell University Press, 1990), particularly pages 64–71, for his discussion of means of exchange in the Connecticut Valley.

39. AC/PPH, box 8, folder 3.

IX. ONCE AGAIN THE PLEASURES OF A PEN

1. AC/PPH, box 5, folder 4, September 13, 1802.

2. Quoted in June Sprigg's *Domestick Beings* (New York: Alfred A. Knopf, 1984), 37.

3. AC/PPH, box 5, folder 3, March 16, 1801.

4. AC/PPH, box 6, folder 1, March 2, 1801.

5. Karen V. Hansen, *A Very Social Time* (Berkeley, Calif.: University of California Press, 1994), Chapter 4.

6. AC/PPH, box 6, folder 1, February 26, 1801.

7. Ibid.

8. AC/PPH, box 13, folder 5, March 14, 1801.

9. AC/PPH, box 6, folder 1, February 7, 1801.

10. AC/PPH, box 6, folder 1, March 16, 1801.

11. AC/PPH, box 6, folder 1, June 13, 1801.

12. AC/PPH, box 6, folder 1, February 26, 1801.

13. AC/PPH, box 13, folder 1, July 22, 1801.

14. Ibid.

15. AC/PPH, box 6, folder 1, July 5, 1801.

16. Ibid.

17. AC/PPH, box 6, folder 1, August 13, 1801.

18. I have drawn upon Theodore Huntington's "Sketches" for this description of the rye harvest (AC/PPH, box 27, folder 5). "Shouting" the harvest home most likely came from Britain with John Morison. It is described in Flora Thompson's reminiscences of her childhood late in the nineteenth century near Oxfordshire, England, as an ancient practice: *Lark Rise to Candleford* (Baltimore: Penguin Books, 1974), 237.

19. AC/PPH, box 13, folder 1.

20. I have appreciated my conversations with C. Keith Wilbur, M.D. (author of *Revolutionary Medicine: 1700–1800*), on the subject of smallpox vaccines. He finds it extraordinary that the knowledge of the kine pox serum had traveled so rapidly from England to western Massachusetts.

21. AC/PPH, box 6, folder 1, March 16, 1801.

22. AC/PPH, box 8, folder 4, April 12, 1801.

23. AC/PPH, box 8, folder 4, May 10, 1801.

24. AC/PPH, box 12, folder 23.

25. Ibid. Sylvester Judd reports that whippoorwills would occasionally come into the garden at Forty Acres. Judd, *Manuscripts,* Hadley Series, 3:43.

26. For a discussion of Elizabeth Phelps Huntington's writing style and the particular "voices" with which she addressed different members of her family, see Elisabeth B. Nichols's, "'Attached and Loving Sister,' 'Constant Unalterable Friend,' and 'Loving and Dutiful Daughter:' Elizabeth Phelps Huntington Conceptualizes Her Identity." Unpublished, it was presented at a symposium at Forty Acres, September 13, 1994, a copy of which resides in the Archives and Special Collections of the Frost Library, Amherst College. Nichols further examines this subject, along with several other contemporary letter writers in her dissertation, "'Pray Don't Tell Any Body That I Write Politics': Private Expressions and Public Admonitions in the Early Republic." Ph.D. dissertation (Durham, N.H.: University of New Hampshire, 1997).

27. AC/PPH, box 13, folder 1, June 20, 1801.

28. AC/PPH, box 13, folder 1, February 17, 1802. Like her mother, Betsey's references to reading in her diary are confined to "uplifting" reading: the Bible, John Newton's sermons, for example. In one letter she does mention a novel, Fanny Burney's *Camilla,* who was also prone to tears. "She gave vent to her tears, and thought herself the most wretched of human beings." On the next page, "She started and rose; she strove to chace the tears from her eyes without wiping them, and asked what he had done with Dr. Orkborne?" *Camilla or a Picture of Youth,* Edward A. Bloom and Lillian D. Bloom, eds. (New York: Oxford University Press, 1983), 542–43.

29. AC/PPH, box 12, folder 13, Excerpts from two of Elizabeth Phelps Huntington's poems, "The Whip Poor Will" and [Lines] Written February 25, 1802.

30. AC/PPH, box 6, folder 1, February 26, 1801.

31. AC/PPH, box 5, folder 14, November 6, 1792.

32. Hansen, 102–6. In Chapter 4, Hansen examines the function of gossip in the community, describing it as "information tinged with judgment," but as a force in the establishment of what was acceptable behavior.

33. AC/PPH, box 6, folder 1, February 26, 1801.

34. AC/PPH, box 6, folder 5, April 18, 1813.

35. AC/PPH, box 6, folder 1, January 24, 1802.

36. AC/PPH, box 6, folder 2, February 26, 1804.

37. AC/PPH, box 7, folder 3, February 3, 1811.

38. This map appears as one of several frontispieces in Joy Day Buel and Richard Buel, Jr., *The Way of Duty* (New York: W. W. Norton & Co., 1984), preceding Chapter 1. It was engraved by Amos Doolittle in 1795 and is housed in the Yale University Map Collection.

39. AC/PPH, box 6, folder 1, June 10, 1803.

40. AC/PPH, box 6, folder 4, December 15, 1811.

41. AC/PPH, box 6, folder 1, January 16, 1802.

42. AC/PPH, box 6, folder 1, March 2, 1801.

43. AC/PPH, box 6, folder 1, March 16, 1801.

44. AC/PPH, box 6, folder 1, July 21, 1801.

45. AC/PPH, box 6, folder 1, December 17, 1801.

46. AC/PPH, box 13, folder 1, February 17, 1802.

47. AC/PPH, box 5, folder 17.

48. AC/PPH, box 5, folder 18.

49. Ibid.

50. AC/PPH, box 6, folder 1, August 13, 1801.

51. AC/PPH, box 6, folder 1, June 13, 1801.

52. AC/PPH, box 10, folder 21, 23.

53. AC/PPH, box 10, folder 21, 25.

54. AC/PPH, box 10, folder 21, 27. No mention of Edward Rand's grave exists in the Granary Burial Ground records, though the secrecy with which he was interred would make that unlikely. Their choice of cemetery may have had to do with the number of Rands already buried there. There is, however, another grave in the Granary that contains the body of a victim of a duel that took place on the Boston Common in 1728. Benjamin Woodbridge's grave is marked, though there is no mention of the cause of death. Robert Baldick, *The Duel: A History of Duelling* (London: Chapman & Hall, 1965), 118.

55. Baldick, 115–16.

56. Joanne B. Freeman, *Affairs of Honor: National Politics in the New Republic* (New Haven, Conn.: Yale University Press, 2001), 180.

57. AC/PPH, box 10, folder 21, 26. Porter's underlining of the words "may" and "may not" gives significance to Miller's intention, which would determine whether or not he was guilty of murder.

58. In *Affairs of Honor,* Joanne B. Freeman explores particularly men in politics. She examines a number of disputes, some resulting in duels, such as that between Hamilton and Burr. Her thorough and incisive examination of this subject sheds light on the motivating forces that lay behind this and other duels, which were not simply rash actions undertaken in the heat of the moment. She argues convincingly that challenges to one's honor and the consequences of those challenges were very much present in the turbulent years of the late–eighteenth and early–nineteenth centuries.

59. This duel took place at Weehawken, New Jersey, on July 11, 1804. Hamilton's son had also lost his life in a duel that took place at the same site on November 24, 1801. See Don C. Seitz, *Famous American Duels* (Freeport, New York: Books for Libraries Press, 1966).

60. Freeman, *Affairs of Honor,* xvi.

61. Timothy Dwight, "A Sermon on Duelling, Preached in the Chapel of Yale College, New Haven, September 9, 1804, and in the Old Church, New York, 1805" (New York: 1805), 14.

62. Timothy Dwight, *Travels in New-England and New-York, in Four Volumes* (Cambridge, Mass.: Harvard University Press, 1969, first published 1821), vol. 4, 325.

63. Stephen E. Berk, *Calvinism Versus Democracy* ([Hamden, Conn.]: Archon Books, 1974), 108.

64. Dwight, *Travels,* vol. 1, 368–69.

65. AC/PPH, box 6, folder 1, June 13, 1801.

66. AC/PPH, box 6, folder 1, August 26, 1801.

67. AC/PPH, box 6, folder 1, undated, presumably written September 18, 1801.

68. See Hansen, 102–6.

69. William Buchan, M.D., *Domestic Medicine: or, a Treatise on the Prevention and Cure of Diseases by Regimen and Simple Medicines. Adapted to the Climate and Diseases of America* by Isaac Cathrall (Philadelphia: Robert Campbell & Co., 1797), 362–63.

70. AC/PPH, box 6, folder 1, undated.

71. AC/PPH, box 13, folder 1, March 18, 1801.

72. AC/PPH, box 13, folder 1, June 12, 1801.

73. AC/PPH, box 13, folder 1, September 27, 1801.

74. AC/PPH, box 13, folder 1, October 22, 1801.

75. AC/PPH, box 13, folder 1.

76. AC/PPH, box 13, folder 1, June 20, 1801.

77. AC/PPH, box 13, folder 1, July 22, 1801.

78. AC/PPH, box 6, folder 1, August 13, 1801, and June 13, 1801.

79. AC/PPH, box 6, folder 1, December 17, 1801.

80. Judd, *Selected Papers,* 252, quoting from Sarah Porter's *Interleaved Almanac,* 1752 and 1756.

81. AC/PPH, box 8, folder 2, March 25, 1787.

82. AC/PPH, box 6, folder 1, August 6, 1802. My information about the process of whitening came from *Encyclopaedia Britannica* (11th ed.), III:49. The system was developed in Holland and exported to England. Jacob van Ruisdael, the Dutch artist, has painted low-lying fields near Amsterdam covered with linen cloth bleaching in the sun.

83. William Cobbett, *Journal of a Year's Residence in the US of A* (Gloucester, England: Sutton, 1983, first published 1819), 193.

84. AC/PPH, box 8, folder 3, November 23, 1794, and January 4, 1795.

85. AC/PPH, box 6, folder 1, August 6, 1802.

86. AC/PPH, box 6, folder 1, July 5, 1801.

87. AC/PPH, box 6, folder 1, August 6, 1802.

X. BINDING THE TIES

1. AC/PPH, box 13, folder 1, March 18, 1801.

2. In a lively unpublished paper, "Mothers and Daughters: Different Codes of Behavior," Miriam Christman finds in Betsey's letters to her mother, cries for help in veiled references to her husband's "unwearied attention and tender regard" for her. Elizabeth reassures her that "the love and friendship of your husband will continue as long as you live, I trust, but that very particular attention

will likely in some degree abate." Presented to the Friends of the William Allen Neilson Library, Smith College, Northampton, Mass., April 11, 1997.

3. AC/PPH, box 13, folder 1.

4. AC/PPH, box 6, folder 1, December 17, 1801.

5. AC/PPH, box 13, folder 1, March 13, 1802.

6. AC/PPH, box 6, folder 1, July 25, 1802.

7. Ibid.

8. AC/PPH, box 6, folder 1, September 13, 1802.

9. AC/PPH, box 6, folder 1, October 22, 1802.

10. Daniel Scott Smith, "Differential Mortality in the United States Before 1900," 13:4 *Journal of Interdisciplinary History* (Spring 1983), 735.

11. AC/PPH, box 6, folder 1, December 20, 1802.

12. AC/PPH, box 13, folder 1, March 7, 1803.

13. AC/PPH, box 13, folder 1, September 3, 1802.

14. AC/PPH, box 8, folder 4, August 14, 1803, September 18, 1803, and October 16, 1803.

15. AC/PPH, box 8, folder 4.

16. AC/PPH, box 6, folder 1, December 8, 1803.

17. Ibid.

18. AC/PPH, box 6, folder 2, November 18, 1804.

19. AC/PPH, box 8, folder 4. The descriptions of Edward's illness first appear in Elizabeth's diary during the week of February 5, 1804, and continue through the remainder of the young Phelpses' stay at Forty Acres until their departure for Boston in the week of September 2, 1804. The "garlic steeped in brandy" was administered on April 22.

20. AC/PPH, box 6, folder 1, September 13, 1802.

21. AC/PPH, box 13, folder 1, February 9, 1803.

22. AC/PPH, box 6, folder 1, February 7, 1803.

23. AC/PPH, box 13, folder 7, June 7, 1803.

24. Dr. Buchan stated that "females generally begin to menstruate about the age of fifteen, and leave it off about fifty." He adds, "In America generally about forty-five." William Buchan, M.D., *Domestic Medicine* (Philadelphia: Robert Campbell and Co., 1797), 356.

25. AC/PPH, box 13, folder 4, January 6, 1804.

26. AC/PPH, box 6, folder 1, December 8, 1803.

27. Lucius M. Boltwood's "Family Genealogies" lists only one Ruth Dickinson who would have been a young girl at this time. She was the daughter of Perez Dickinson of Amherst. She died unmarried in 1843 at the age of forty-nine, so would have been nine years old at the time of Elizabeth's letter.

28. AC/PPH, box 8, folder 4.

29. AC/PPH, box 7, folder 3, February 11, 1810.

30. AC/PPH, box 7, folder 3, February 18, 1810.

31. I am indebted to Laurel Thatcher Ulrich for this information.

32. AC/PPH, box 11, folder 6, February 16, 1810.

33. *Acts & Resolves of Massachusetts: 1786–87,* Chapter 3, 10.

34. Oscar Reiss, *Blacks in Colonial America* (Jefferson, N.C.: McFarland & Co., 1997), 182–83. See also Greene, *The Negro in Colonial New England,* 204–8, and Melish, *Disowning Slavery,* 29–30, 63, 122–29 for their discussion of the incidence of miscegenation and the circumstances surrounding its occurrence.

35. In a diary entry of 1788, Elizabeth refers to Thankful's brothers and sisters, then living in Goshen, Massachusetts. Still apparently transient, Zebulon Richmond is mentioned in the Goshen town history as having been "warned out" in 1790, "in order to prevent his 'gaining a settlement.'" Hiram Barrus, *History of the Town of Goshen, Hampshire County, Massachusetts, from Its First Settlement in 1761 to 1881* (Boston: 1881), 23.

36. In *Under a Colonial Rooftree: Fireside Chronicles of Early New England* (Boston, Mass.: Houghton Mifflin, 1891), Arria S. Huntington says that Mitte eventually made a "respectable marriage," had children and grandchildren and continued working for the family. I have not been able to find any record of that marriage. "Respectable" implies a white husband.

37. AC/PPH, box 13, folder 2, February 10 1804.

38. AC/PPH, box 13, folder 10, November 20, 1806.

39. AC/PPH, box 13, folder 3, January 28, 1813.

40. AC/PPH, box 13, folder 9, June 8, 1805.

41. AC/PPH, box 13, folder 1, March 7, 1803. Betsey was not alone in her pessimistic view of the outcome of pregnancies. As Laurel Thatcher Ulrich points out in *A Midwife's Tale,* mortality rates related to childbirth continued high into the 1930s with one mother dying of every 150 births in the United States, 170.

42. AC/PPH, box 13, folder 9, August 14, 1805.

43. Laurel Thatcher Ulrich, *A Midwife's Tale* (New York: Random House, 1991), 309.

44. Ibid., 172. Ulrich is quoting from Edmund Chapman, *A Treatise on the Improvement of Midwifery* (London, 1759, 1st ed., 1733), xx.

45. AC/PPH, box 13, folder 9, September 9, 1805.

46. AC/PPH, box 13, folder 2, November 1, 1805.

47. AC/PPH, box 13, folder 2, December 1, 1810.

48. AC/PPH, box 13, folder 9, December 15, 1805 and January 10, 1806.

49. AC/PPH, box 6, folder 4, November 28, 1809.

50. AC/PPH, box 16, folder 11.

51. Franklin Bowditch Dexter, *Biographical Sketches of the Graduates of Yale College,* vol. 5, June, 1792–September, 1805 (New York: Holt & Company, 1911), 110–11.

52. AC/PPH, box 6, folder 3, June 10, 1807.

53. AC/PPH, box 6, folder 2, June 5, 1805.

54. AC/PPH, box 6, folder 3, May 21, 1807.

55. AC/PPH, box 6, folder 5, October 13, 1813.

XI. SEEKING THE CELESTIAL CITY

1. AC/PPH, box 6, folder 1, March 13, 1802.

2. AC/PPH, box 7, folder 3.

3. AC/PPH, box 6, folder 1, December 8, 1803.

4. In Chapter 1, I discuss the continuing signing of covenants in certain communities well into the nineteenth and twentieth centuries.

5. These qualifications appear in most New England town histories. See for example the town histories of Amherst and South Hadley, Massachusetts.

6. William Root Bliss, *Side Glimpses from the Colonial Meeting-House* (Boston, Mass.: Houghton Mifflin and Co., 1894), 90.

7. Judd, *History of Hadley*, 312.

8. Judd, *Manuscripts*, Hadley Series, 3:344.

9. Judd, *History of Hadley*, 313.

10. See Gregory H. Nobles, *Divisions Throughout the Whole*, "The Politics of Parochialism," 132–54, for his discussion of the effects on the community of these separatist movements.

11. Stephen E. Berk discusses at length Dwight's role in launching the Second Awakening, as well as his influence on the Connecticut government, in *Calvinism Versus Democracy* ([Hamden, Conn.] Archon Books, 1974).

12. Ibid., 39. See also Joseph Ellis, *Passionate Sage: The Character and Legacy of John Adams* (New York: W. W. Norton & Company, 1994), 132–36, for his discussion of Adams's misgivings about the rising democratic movement. Although Adams's religious views were not a focus of Ellis's biography, the second president's belief in the flawed nature of humankind was clearly derived from Calvinist doctrine.

13. I owe the following discussion of Dwight's understanding of means to Berk's discriminating analysis of the Yale president's departures from early Calvinist views of the Elect. Berk explains the distinctions, some of them subtle, among the branches of Calvinism and its offshoots in Chapter 1 of his book. See especially pages 11–17. Orthodox Calvinists at this time referred to themselves as "Consistent Calvinists."

14. Timothy Dwight, *Travels in New-England and New-York* (Cambridge, Mass.: Harvard University Press, 1969), first published in New Haven, 1821, 1:256. His use of "Presbyterianism" in this passage refers to church governance by elders rather than the particular denomination stemming from the Church of Scotland. See OED, 2:2283–84.

15. Ibid., 258–59.

16. Ibid., 230.

17. Ibid., 78.

18. See Berk, 10–11, for his definitions of the various factions within the Congregational Church, including the Consistent Calvinists.

19. Nobles, 113.

20. William B. Sprague, D.D. *Annals of the American Pulpit* (New York: Robert Carter & Brothers, 1866), 8:263.

21. AC/PPH, box 10, folder 1, March 5, 1807.

22. AC/PPH, box 10, folder 21, 54.

23. AC/PPH, box 13, folder 1, August 30, 1797.

24. AC/PPH, box 10, folder 21, 83–84.

25. Sprague, 8:278.

26. Ibid., 8:269.

27. Ibid., 8:281.

28. AC/PPH, box 6, folder 2, January 14, 1804.

29. AC/PPH, box 6, folder 2, March 16, 1807.

30. AC/PPH, box 13, folder 2, January 10, 1806.

31. AC/PPH, box 13, folder 2, October 16, 1807.

32. AC/PPH, box 10, folder 21, 34–35.

33. AC/PPH, box 7, folder 3, March 15, 1807.

34. AC/PPH, box 6, folder 3, April 4, 1807.

35. AC/PPH, box 13, folder 3, February 26, 1807.

36. See, for example, AC/PPH, box 7, folder 4, May 17, 1812, where, in her diary, she prays that her family may be members of the elect.

37. Sprague, 1:523.

38. AC/PPH, box 5, folder 5, December 8, 1803.

39. Berk discusses this publication in some detail in Chapter 9 of *Calvinism Versus Democracy*.

40. AC/PPH, box 5, folder 5, August 17, 1803.

41. AC/PPH, box 6, folder 1, January 4, 1802.

42. Ibid.

43. See discussion of mental illness in Chapter 5.

44. AC/PPH, box 6, folder 2, November 29, 1804.

45. Lucius M. Boltwood, "Family Genealogies," 68. George Hibbard is listed as having sixteen children. His son John's wife had fourteen. Elizabeth was younger than the former and older than the latter. Whichever of the two wives was her particular friend, Mrs. Hibbard had given birth frequently and in rapid succession, a feat that must have taken both a physical and emotional toll. Certainly postpartum depression would be a possible reason for her state of mind.

46. Rose Ann Lockwood, "Birth, Illness, and Death in 18th-Century New England," *Journal of Social History* 12:1 (Fall 1978), 115.

47. See for example, *The Journal of Esther Edwards Burr: 1754–1757*. Although Burr's diary was begun and ended in the decade preceding the first entry in Elizabeth's, there are a number of similar phrases that each writer utilizes to express her Sabbath reflections on Communion Day: "I thought I felt a little more alive than I do commonly, but O my deadness!" 61; "I was in great hopes of meeting Christ in some extreordinary manner at his Table, but alas God has dissappointed me! Perhaps to shew me tis not in *means,* nor *ordinances*—but I desire to be found waiting at the *Pool,*" 131. She, too, speaks of being "*carnel, fleshly, Worldly minded,*" 127.

48. AC/PPH, box 13, folder 8, November 10, 1804.

49. AC/PPH, box 13, folder 2, October 16, 1807.

50. *History of the Town of Litchfield, Ct.: 1720–1920* (Litchfield, Conn.: Litchfield Historical Society, 1920), 32–33.

51. AC/PPH, box 7, folder 3, June 14, 1807.

52. See Berk, 14–15, for his discussion of experimental religion. This use of the word was current through the first half of the nineteenth century, OED 1:930.

53. Margery Kempe was one of these pilgrims, whose many pilgrimages are described in Louise Collis's *Memoirs of a Medieval Woman: The Life and Times of Margery Kempe* (New York: Harper & Row, 1983).

54. AC/PPH, box 6, folder 6, folder 4, December 15, 1811.

XII. THE VALLEY OF THE SHADOW

1. In a diary entry, Elizabeth rewrites a line from Psalm 137: "We hanged our harps on the willows in the midst thereof."

2. See Daniel Scott Smith, "Differential Mortality in the United States Before 1900," 13:4 *Journal of Interdisciplinary History* (Spring 1983), 735.

3. AC/PPH, box 7, folder 3, March 10, 1811.

4. My information about the Communion cups comes from Karen Parsons's unpublished paper "How did my heart burn within me: Sacred and Secular Meanings, Elizabeth Porter Phelps's Gift of Communion Silver," presented at a Symposium, Porter-Phelps-Huntington Museum, Hadley Massachusetts, September 13, 1994. In this paper she develops her argument for the cups as a memorial gift from Elizabeth Phelps in honor of the Reverend Hopkins.

5. AC/PPH, box 13, folder 3, October 21, 1813.

6. AC/PPH, box 13, folder 3, February 28, 1814.

7. In *Winter Friends: Women Growing Old in the New Republic, 1785–1835* (Chicago: University of Illinois Press, 1990), Terri L. Premo discusses the role played by spirituality in the lives of women in this period, particularly aging women. She also considers the paradox that these women face after a lifetime of connections with the community and close relationships in their need for withdrawal and meditation, a radical switch from an active to inactive life. See particularly Chapters 5 and 6.

8. AC/PPH, box 6, folder 3, November 12, 1807.

9. AC/PPH, box 6, folder 2, October 11, 1805.

10. AC/PPH, box 6, folder 2, November 15, 1805.

11. AC/PPH, box 6, folder 4, January 21, 1809.

12. AC/PPH, box 6, folder 4, November 13, 1810.

13. AC/PPH, box 6, folder 4, December 15, 1811.

14. C. Keith Wilbur, M.D., *Revolutionary Medicine: 1700–1800* (Old Saybrook, Conn.: Globe Pequot Press, 1997), 11. Wilbur notes that "George Washington died of his infected throat—with the help of his physician—after nine pints were taken in twenty-four hours!" 10.

15. Ibid.

16. Joseph Carvalho III, "Rural Medical Practice in Early 19th Century New England," *Historical Journal of Western Massachusetts* 4 (Spring, 1975), 5. Carvalho quotes from Rand's paper "Observations on the Hydracephalus Internus," *Medical Papers Communicated to the Massachusetts Medical Society* 1 (Boston, 1790), 75–76. Two Dr. Isaac Rands, one Junior, are listed in the 1813 Boston City Directory. As Dr. Rand Junior delivered his paper, based on treatments of his own patients, in 1790, it seems likely that Dr. Rand Senior would have been retired by the second decade of the nineteenth century. I am indebted to the Boston Historical Society for the information concerning the Doctors Rand.

17. Carvalho, 5.

18. See Chapter 10 of this book, page 213.

19. AC/PPH, box 14, folder 6, February 4, 1812.

20. AC/PPH, box 14, folder 6, February 6, 1813.

21. AC/PPH, box 10, folder 21, 39.

22. AC/PPH, box 6, folder 4, December 15, 1809.

23. AC/PPH, box 8, folder 2, December 15, 1782.

24. AC/PPH, box 6, folder 4, December 15, 1809.

25. AC/PPH, box 7, folder 3.

26. The Last Will and Testament of David Hitchcock, April 22, 1812, and the Inventory of the Real & Personal Estate of Capt. David Hitchcock, October 25, 1814, both filed with the Court of Probate, County of Worcester, Massachusetts.

27. AC/PPH, box 6, folder 4, December 19, 1810.

28. Reginald Horsman, *The Causes of the War of 1812* (Philadelphia: University of Pennsylvania Press, 1962), 42, 110.

29. AC/PPH, box 10, folder 21, 36–37.

30. AC/PPH, box 10, folder 21, 38.

31. Ibid.

32. AC/PPH, box 6, folder 2, February 4, 1805.

33. AC/PPH, box 10, folder 21, 42.

34. AC/PPH, box 6, folder 5, March 31, 1812.

35. See AC/PPH, box 13, folder 1, June 20, 1801; box 14, folder 6, June 24, 1810; box 12, folder 14, August 14, 1809, for Betsey's mention of these gifts.

36. AC/PPH, box 10, folder 21, 42.

37. Ibid.

38. AC/PPH, box 10, folder 21, 43–44.

39. Ibid.

40. AC/PPH, box 10, folder 21, 46–48. Porter describes these two deaths in these pages.

41. I am indebted to an unpublished paper by Anne Poubeau for her interpretation of this passage from Elizabeth's diary. In "'You did not mention whether you had a cow . . .': Cheese Making at the Porter Phelps farm, Hadley, MA, 1770–1815" (University of Massachusetts, Fall, 1999), she finds corrobo-

ration for this interpretation in Sally Ann McMurry, *Transforming Rural Life* (Baltimore: Johns Hopkins University Press, 1995), 47.

42. AC/PPH, box 7, folder 4, March 14, 1813.

43. AC/PPH, box 13, folder 3, February 28, 1814.

44. AC/PPH, box 6, folder 4, January 21, 1809.

45. AC/PPH, box 6, folder 5, March 31, 1812.

46. Joseph Ellis, *Passionate Sage: The Character and Legacy of John Adams* (New York: W. W. Norton & Company, 1994), 92. See also 128–36 for Ellis's discussion of Adams versus Jefferson on the question of popular sovereignty.

47. AC/PPH, box 5, folder 9, April 4, 1807.

48. Henry Adams, *The United States in 1800* (Ithaca: Cornell University Press, 1957, first published in 1883), 56.

49. Ibid., 65–66.

50. See Benjamin W. Labaree, *Patriots and Partisans: The Merchants of Newburyport* (Cambridge, Mass.: Harvard University Press, 1962), 45–55, for his discussion of Parsons's authorship of *The Essex Result,* the Federalist manifesto, and his influence on other Federalists, such as John Adams and John Hancock.

51. See Laurie Goodstein, "Fresh Debate on 1802 Jefferson Letter," *New York Times,* May 30, 1998, A20. See also, "One of Jefferson's Enigmas, So Finally the F.B.I Steps In," *New York Times,* September 10, 1998, B10.

52. AC/PPH, box 6, folder 5, July 27, 1813.

53. See William Gribbin, *The Churches Militant: The War of 1812 and American Religion* (New Haven, Conn.: Yale University Press, 1973), Chapter 1, for his discussion of the various stances on fast days.

54. AC/PPH, box 7, folder 4, August 16, 1812.

55. AC/PPH, box 7, folder 4, September 5, 1813.

56. AC/PPH, box 6, folder 5, June 29, 1812.

57. AC/PPH, box 7, folder 5, April 10, 1813.

58. Ibid.

59. AC/PPH, box 13, folder 3, June 14, 1814.

60. *Hampshire Gazette,* (July 6, 1814), 28:1453.

61. Gribbin, 51–55.

XIII. ENDS AND BEGINNINGS

1. AC/PPH, box 6, folder 5, June 29, 1812.

2. AC/PPH, box 6, folder 5, July 27, 1812.

3. AC/PPH, box 7, folder 3, May 10, 1812.

4. AC/PPH, box 21, folder 5, 9.

5. Ibid.

6. John Wilmerding describes these developments in the American consciousness in "Themes and Places," *American Views: Essays on American Art* (Princeton, N.J.: Princeton University Press, 1991). Barbara Novak discusses the

link between the beautiful and the good in the American mind in the first half of the nineteenth century in her essay on Thomas Cole in *American Painting of the Nineteenth Century* (New York: Harper & Row, 1979), 61–79. "The American in love with nature approximated the aesthetic contemplation of a landscape painting with 'the contemplation of virtuous deeds.'" Novak is quoting from the *North American Review*, 81 (1855), 220. One can imagine minds trained in the Calvinist mode of thought forging this link to explain the attraction to these works.

7. AC/PPH, box 7, folder 3, June 15, 1806.

8. AC/PPH, box 10, folder 21, 34.

9. AC/PPH, box 11, folder 11, July 2, 1806.

10. AC/PPH, box 6, folder 5, December 14, 1812.

11. AC/PPH, box 6, folder 5, October 21, 1814.

12. Adams and Roy, *Historic Structure Report: Porter-Phelps-Huntington House, Hadley Massachusetts* (Portsmouth, N.H., 1988), 50.

13. See Jane Nylander, *Our Own Snug Fireside: Images of the New England Home: 1760–1860* (New Haven: Yale University Press, 1994), 26–30, for her discussion of the customs surrounding childbirth in "lying-in" or "borning" rooms.

14. Adams and Roy, 20.

15. AC/PPH, box 21, folder 5, 36–38. In his "Sketches," Theodore Huntington describes a tea party given by his parents Betsey and Dan Huntington at Forty Acres, around the year 1820. It seems likely that Betsey's manner of entertaining followed traditions established by her parents.

16. Witold Rybczynski, *Home: A Short History of an Idea* (New York: Penguin Books, 1986), 138.

17. Lowestoft china does not bear factory marks of their own; therefore, the lack of marking does not disqualify it as a Lowestoft product. Their designs are based on Chinese porcelains, but Americans had begun to trade directly with China in 1784, making it more difficult to determine the source of the Phelpses' teacups. See Geoffrey A. Godden, *British Porcelain* (London: Barrie Jenkins, 1974), 284–85; Marshall B. Davidson, ed., *American Heritage: Three Centuries of American Antiques* (New York: Bonanza Books, 1967), 1:255–58.

18. AC/PPH, box 7, folder 4, January 23, 1814.

19. AC/PPH, box 7, folder 4, November 27, 1814.

20. AC/PPH, box 10, folder 21, 51–52

21. AC/PPH, box 7, folder 4, December 4, 1814.

22. As adoptions were not yet legalized, Thankful would not be automatically included in the distribution of Charles Phelps's estate. A five-acre piece of land seems a small bequest in relation to the division in two of the estate. Enos Hitchcock was also omitted from his father's will, which mentions that he had received his portion before Captain Hitchcock's Death (Worcester County Probate Records, Docket 29703/29729). It is also possible that Charles Phelps arranged for some financial support for Thankful at the time of her return to Forty Acres following her husband's death.

23. AC/PPH, box 10, folder 21, 54.

24. AC/PPH, box 7, folder 4, December 11, 1814.

25. AC/PPH, box 6, folder 5, April 5, 1815.

26. AC/PPH, box 7, folder 4, July 30, 1815.

27. AC/PPH, box 7, folder 4, August 13, 1817.

28. AC/PPH, box 7, folder 4, October 15, 1815.

29. AC/PPH, box 21, folder 5,11.

30. AC/PPH, box 5, folder 12, May 4, 1815.

31. AC/PPH, box 7, folder 4.

32. AC/PPH, box 7, folder 4, April 13, 1817.

33. AC/PPH, box 10, folder 21, 62–63.

34. AC/PPH, box 10, folder 21, 80–81.

35. AC/PPH, box 10, folder 21, 73–76.

36. AC/PPH, box 10, folder 21, 77–78.

37. Porter seems to have had a strong interest in architecture. Rybczynski discusses architecture as an interest of dilettantes in England at that time. No formal architectural education was available in England until 1850 (126–27 and note). In New England, men who functioned as architects, such as Samuel McIntyre and Asher Benjamin, were first and foremost builders.

38. AC/PPH, box 10, folder 21, 78.

39. AC/PPH, box 14, folder 11, November 11, 1817. Betsey Huntington made this remark in her diary.

40. AC/PPH, box 21, folder 5, 5. Interestingly enough, both bears and rattlesnakes are once again making appearances in the vicinity of the Holyoke range.

AFTERWORD

1. The ghost stories are recounted in two works written by members of the family: Arria S. Huntington, *Under a Colonial Rooftree* (Boston: Houghton Mifflin & Company, 1891) and James Lincoln Huntington, *Forty Acres,* (New York: Hastings House, 1949).

2. Franklin Bowditch Dexter, *Biographical Sketches of the Graduates of Yale College: June, 1792–September, 1805* (New York: Holt & Company, 1911), 5:110–111.

3. AC/PPH, box 12, folder 21, "The Matter of the Exoneration and Acceptance of Elizabeth W. P. Huntington." This two-page statement issued by the pastor, the Reverend Stanley J. Parker, and the Board of Deacons of the Hadley United Church reviews the case against Elizabeth Phelps Huntington and rescinds her excommunication of 1828.

4. AC/PPH, box 12, folder 8.

5. AC/PPH, box 12, folder 4.

6. AC/PPH, box 14, folder 9, August 16, 1835.

7. AC/PPH, box 14, folder 9, August 16, 1835 and January 14, 1838.

8. AC/PPH, box 19, folder 5.

9. AC/PPH, box 14, folder 7.

10. AC/PPH, box 21, folder 5, 59.

11. AC/PPH, box 12, folder 9, October 26, 1843.

12. Arria S. Huntington *Memoir and Letters of Frederic Dan Huntington* (Boston: Houghton Mifflin & Co., 1906), 41.

13. Ibid., 69.

14. Ibid., 70.

15. Ibid., 236.

16. AC/PPH, box 58, folder 1. This folder contains a number of obituaries describing Father Huntington's work with the poor as well as selections of his own writing.

17. *Post Standard,* Syracuse, New York, March 25, 1921.

18. AC/PPH, box 94, folder 38, August 22, 1927.

19. The story of James Lincoln Huntington's purchase and preservation of the house as a museum is told in his book *Forty Acres.*

20. Arria Huntington is quoting from *Memoir of Rufus Ellis* in *Memoir and Letters of Frederic Dan Huntington,* 63.

BIBLIOGRAPHY

Primary Sources

Acts and Resolves of Massachusetts: 1784–85, 86–87.

Austen, Jane. *Selected Letters.* R. W. Chapman, ed. Oxford, England: Oxford University Press, 1985.

Benjamin, Asher. *The Country Builder's Assistant; Containing a Collection of New Designs of Carpentry and Architechture, Which Will Be Particularly Useful to Country Workmen in General.* New York: Da Capo Press, 1972.

Boston Medical and Surgical Journal (1832). 6:56–57

Buchan, William, M.D. *Domestic Medicine: or, a Treatise on the Prevention and Cure of Diseases by Regimen and Simple Medicines: Adapted to the Climate and Diseases of America by Isaac Cathrall.* Philadelphia: Robert Campbell and Co., 1797.

Burr, Esther Edwards. *The Journal of Esther Edwards Burr: 1754–1757.* Carol F. Karlsen and Laurie Crumpacker, eds. New Haven, Conn.: Yale University Press, 1984.

Collections of the Connecticut Historical Society. Vol. 14. Hartford, Conn.: 1912.

Chastellux, Marquis de. *Travels in North-America in the Years 1780–81–82,* Howard C. Rice, Jr., trans. New York: A.M. Kelley, 1970.

Cobbett, William. *Journal of a Year's Residence in the US of A.* Gloucester, England: Sutton, 1983, first published 1819.

Cutler, Robert. *Memoirs,* 1811. Lucius M. Boltwood Historical and Genealogical Collection, Jones Library Special Collections, Amherst, Massachusetts.

Dann, John C., ed. *The Revolution Remembered: Eyewitness Accounts of the War for Independence.* Chicago: University of Chicago Press, 1980.

Dickinson, Rebecca. Unpublished Diary. Special Collections, Pocumtuck Valley Memorial Association, Deerfield, Massachusetts.

Dwight, Timothy. "A Sermon on Duelling, Preached in the Chapel of Yale College, New Haven, September 9, 1804, and in the Old Church, New York, 1805" (New York: 1805), 14.

————. *Travels in New-England and New-York, in Four Volumes.* Cambridge, Mass.: Harvard University Press, 1969. First published in New Haven, 1821.

Edwards, Jonathan. *Letters and Personal Writings.* George S. Claghorn, ed. New Haven, Conn.: Yale University Press, 1998.

Fitzpatrick, John Clement, ed. *The Writings of George Washington from the Original Manuscript Sources, 1745–1799,* Vol. 4. Washington, D.C.: Government Printing Office, 1931–44.

Freeman, Samuel, Esq. *The Massachusetts Justice: Being a Collection of the Laws of the Commonwealth of Massachusetts Relative to the Power and Duty of Justices of the Peace.* Boston: 1795.

Gaylord, Samuel. Account Book. Special Collection, Pocumtuck Valley Memorial Association Library, Deerfield, Massachusetts.

Hampshire Association of Congregational Churches and Ministers, Notes, November 7, 1787—November 6, 1794, Forbes Library, Local History Special Collection.

Hampshire Gazette, Northampton, Massachusetts, July 30, 1794, July 10, 1799, and June 15, June 22, July 6, December 7, 1814.

Hampshire Gazette and Public Advertiser, November 12, 1817.

Haywood, Eliza. *The Female Spectator.* Patricia Meyer Spacks, ed. New York: Oxford University Press, 1999.

Housman, Mrs. *The Power and Pleasure of the Divine Life Exemplify'd in the Late Mrs. Housman.* Richard Pearsall, ed. London: 1755.

Huntington, Arria S. *Memoir and Letters of Frederic Dan Huntington.* Boston: Houghton Mifflin & Co., 1906.

Judd, Sylvester. *The History of Hadley: Including the Early History of Hatfield, South Hadley, Amherst and Granby Massachusetts.* Bound with Lucius M. Boltwood's "Genealogies of Hadley Families Embracing the Early Settlers of the Towns of Hatfield, South Hadley, Amherst and Granby." Camden, Maine: Picton Press, 1993; first published in Springfield Mass.: H.R. Hunting & Company, 1905. I use a shortened form of the title in the endnotes.

————. *Manuscripts.* Hadley and Hatfield, Hadley, Miscellaneous, Northampton and Westfield, "Revolutionary Matters," Medicines, etc., Including Dr. Crouch's Practice. Local History, Special Collections, Forbes Library, Northampton, Massachusetts.

————. *Selected Papers* (typescript). Special Collections, W. E. B. DuBois Library, University of Massachusetts, Amherst, Massachusetts.

Manwaring, Charles William, ed. *A Digest of the Early Connecticut Probate Records.* Vols. 1, 2, 3. Hartford, Conn.: 1904.

Newton, Reverend John. *An Authentic Narrative of Some Remarkable and Interesting Particulars in the Life of ** ****, Communicated in a Series of Letters to the Rev. Dr. Haweis.* London: Ogle, Duncan, and Co., 1822.

Oakes, Urian. "The Sovereign Efficacy of Divine Providence," *The American Puritans*. Perry Miller, ed. Garden City, N.Y.: Doubleday Anchor Books, 1956.

Phelps, Charles. Account Book, Vol. 1, 1805–1815. Baker Library, Harvard Business School, Boston, Massachusetts.

Phelps, John. *Family Memoirs* (Brattleboro, Vt.: Selleck & Davis, 1886, written in 1849).

Pierce, Josiah. Diaries in Almanacs. Jones Library Special Collections, Amherst, Massachusetts.

Porter-Phelps-Huntington Family Papers. Archives and Special Collections, Robert Frost Library, Amherst College, Amherst, Massachusetts

Porter, Sarah Pitkin. *Interleaved Almanac*. Jones Library Special Collections, Amherst, Massachusetts.

Sprague, William B., D.D. *Annals of the American Pulpit*, Vols. 1, 2, 4, 8. New York: Robert Carter & Brothers, 1866.

Thacher, James, M.D. *Military Journal of the American Revolution*. Hartford, Conn.: Hurlbut, Williams & Company, 1862.

Webster, Noah. *Noah Webster's American Spelling Book*, Introductory Essay by Henry Steele Commager. New York: Columbia University Press, 1958.

Secondary Sources

Adams, Henry. *The United States in 1800*. Ithaca: Cornell University Press, 1957, first published 1883.

Akagi, Roy Hidemichi. *The Town Proprietors of the New England Colonies* Gloucester, Mass.: Peter Smith, 1963.

Bachelard, Gaston. *The Poetics of Space*. Trans. by Maria Jolas. Boston: Beacon Press, 1969.

Baldick, Robert. *The Duel: A History of Duelling*. London, England: Chapman & Hall, 1965.

Barrus, Hiram. *History of the Town of Goshen, Hampshire County, Massachusetts, from Its First Settlement in 1761 to 1881*. Boston: 1881.

Bartlett, Irving H. *William Ellery Channing: Unitarian Christianity and Other Essays*. New York: Liberal Arts Press, 1957.

Bellesiles, Michael A. *Arming America: The Origins of a National Gun Culture*. New York: Alfred A. Knopf, 2000.

Benedict, Barbara. *Framing Feeling: Sentiment and Style in English Prose Fiction, 1745–1800*. New York: AMS Press, 1994.

Benton, Josiah Henry. *Warning Out in New England*. Boston: W. B. Clarke Co., 1911.

Berk, Stephen E. *Calvinism Versus Democracy*. [Hamden, Conn.] Archon Books, 1974.

Bliss, William Root. *Side Glimpses from the Colonial Meeting-House*. Boston: Houghton Mifflin and Co., 1894.

Boltwood, Lucius M. "Genealogies of Hadley Families Embracing the Earlty Settlers of the Towns of Hatfield, South Hadley, Amherst and Granby," bound with Sylvester Judd's *History of Hadley*. Springfield, Mass.: H. R. Huntting & Company, 1905.

Bonfanti, Leo. *Biographies and Legends of the New England Indians,* Vol. 3. Wakefield, Mass.: Pride Publications, 1972.

Bragdon, Kathleen J. *Native People of Southern New England, 1500–1650.* Norman, Okla.: University of Oklahoma Press, 1996.

Buel, Joy Day, and Richard Buel, Jr. *The Way of Duty.* New York: W. W. Norton & Co., 1984.

Burney, Fanny. *Camilla or a Picture of Youth.* Edward A. Bloom and Lillian D. Bloom, eds. New York: Oxford University Press, 1983.

Calvert, Karin. *Children in the House: The Material Culture of Early Childhood, 1600–1900.* Boston: Northeastern University Press, 1992.

Chartier, Roger. "The Practical Impact of Writing." Philippe Ariès and Georges Duby, eds. *A History of Private Life: Vol. 3, Passions of the Renaissance.* Cambridge, Mass.: Harvard University Press, 1989.

Clark, Christopher. *The Roots of Rural Capitalism: Western Massachusetts, 1780–1860.* Ithaca, N.Y.: Cornell University Press, 1990.

Collis, Louise. *Memoirs of a Medieval Woman: The Life and Times of Margery Kempe.* New York: Harper & Row, 1983.

Cott, Nancy F. *The Bonds of Womanhood: "Women's Sphere" in New England, 1780–1835.* New Haven, Conn.: Yale University Press, 1977.

———, ed. "Sarah Osborn's Religious Conversion." In *Root of Bitterness: Documents of the Social History of American Women.* New York: E. P. Dutton & Co. Inc., 1972.

Courtwright, David T. *Dark Paradise: Opiate Addiction in America Before 1940.* Cambridge, Mass.: Harvard University Press, 1982.

Dann, John C., ed. *The Revolution Remembered.* Chicago: University of Chicago Press, 1980.

Davidson, Marshall B., ed. *American Heritage: Three Centuries of American Antiques.* New York: Bonanza Books, 1967.

Davies, Horton. *The Worship of the American Puritans, 1629–1730.* New York: Peter Lang Publishing, 1990.

Deatrich, Mabel E., and Virginia C. Purdy, eds. *Clio Was a Woman.* Washington, D.C.: Howard University Press, 1980.

Dexter, Franklin Bowditch. *Biographical Sketches of the Graduates of Yale College, Vol. 5: June, 1792–September, 1805.* New York: Holt & Company, 1911.

Donnan, Elizabeth. *Documents Illustrative of the History of the Slave Trade to America,* Vol. 3, "New England and the Middle Colonies." New York: Octagon Books, 1969.

Draper, Theodore. *A Struggle for Power: The American Revolution.* New York: Vintage Books, 1997.

Dwyer, Margaret Clifford. *Hopkins Academy and the Hopkins Fund: 1664–1964.* Hadley, Mass.: Trustees of Hopkins Academy, 1964.

Elkins, Stanley, and Eric McKitrick. *The Age of Federalism* (New York: Oxford University Press, 1993), Chapter 13.

Ellis, Joseph. *Passionate Sage: The Character and Legacy of John Adams.* New York: W. W. Norton & Company, 1994.

Essays on Amherst's History. Amherst, Mass.: The Vista Trust, 1978.

Farmer, Gregory. "A History and Walking Tour of West Street, Hadley Massachusetts." Hadley, Mass.: Massachusetts Historical Comission, 1987.

Fax, Bernard. *Franklin: The Apostle of Modern Times.* Boston: Little, Brown & Co., 1929.

Fox, Early Lee. *The American Colonization Society 1817–1840.* Baltimore: Johns Hopkins Press, 1919.

Freeman, Joanne B. *Affairs of Honor: National Politics in the New Republic.* New Haven, Conn.: Yale University Press, 2001.

Frye, Northrop. "Towards Defining an Age of Sensibility." *Eighteenth Century English Literature.* James L. Clifford, ed.

Genuth, Sara Schechner. "From Heaven's Alarm to Public Appeal." In *Science at Harvard University: Historical Perspectives.* Clark A. Elliott and Margaret W. Rossiter, eds. Bethlehem, Pa.: Lehigh University Press, 1992.

Gill, Harold B., Jr. *The Apothecary in Colonial Virginia.* Williamsburg, Va.: Colonial Williamsburg Foundation, 1972.

Gillis, Christina Marsden. *The Paradox of Privacy: Epistolary Form in Clarissa.* Gainesville, Fla.: University Press of Florida, 1984.

Godden, Geoffrey A. *British Porcelain.* London: Barrie Jenkins, 1974.

Goodwin, Joseph. *East Hartford: Its History and Traditions.* Hartford, Conn.: Lockwood & Brainard Co., 1879.

Greene, Lorenzo Johnston. *The Negro in Colonial New England.* New York: Atheneum, 1969.

Gribbin, William. *The Churches Militant: The War of 1812 and American Religion.* New Haven, Conn.: Yale University Press, 1973.

Gross, Robert A. *The Minutemen and Their World.* New York: Hill & Wang, 1976.

Hall, Benjamin H. *History of Eastern Vermont.* New York: D. Appleton & Co., 1865.

Hamilton, Edward P. *The French and Indian Wars.* Garden City, N.Y.: Doubleday & Co., 1962.

Hansen, Karen V. *A Very Social Time.* Berkeley, Calif.: University of California Press, 1994.

Henretta, James A., and Gregory H. Nobles. *Evolution and Revolution: American Society, 1600–1820.* Lexington, Mass.: D. C. Heath and Company, 1987.

History and Genealogy of the Families of Chesterfield, Massachusetts, 1762–1962. Northampton, Mass.: Gazette Printing Co., 1963.

History of the Hopkins Fund: Grammar School and Academy in Hadley, Mass., 1657–1890. Prepared and published under the direction and authority of the Trustees of Hopkins Academy. Amherst, Mass.: *The Amherst Record Press,* 1890

History of the Town of Litchfield, Ct.: 1720–1920. Litchfield, Conn.: Litchfield Historical Society, 1920.

History of Transportation in the United States before 1860. Balthasar Henry Meyer, director. Washington, D.C.: Carnegie Institute of Washington, 1948.

Holland, Josiah. *History of Western Massachusetts.* Springfield, Mass.: Samuel Bowles and Company, 1855.

Horsman, Reginald. *The Causes of the War of 1812.* Philadelphia: University of Pennsylvania Press, 1962.

Huntington, Arria S. *Under a Colonial Rooftree: Fireside Chronicles of Early New England.* Boston: Houghton Mifflin, 1891.

Huntington, James Lincoln. *Forty Acres.* New York: Hastings House, 1949.

Hymowitz, Carol, and Michaele Weismann, *A History of Women in America.* New York: Bantam Books, 1978.

Jedrey, Christopher M. *The World of John Cleaveland.* New York: W. W. Norton & Company, 1979.

Jimenez, Mary Ann. *Changing Faces of Madness.* Hanover, N.H.: University Press of New England, 1987.

Kerber, Linda K. "Reinterpretation of the Revolution," *Women in the American Revolution.* Charlottesville, Va.: University Press of Virginia, 1989.

Labaree, Benjamin W. *Patriots and Partisans: The Merchants of Newburyport.* Cambridge, Mass.: Harvard University Press, 1962.

Lane, Helen H. *History of the Town of Dighton, Mass.: The South Purchase, May 30, 1712.* Dighton: 1962.

Lesage, Alain Renais. *The Adventures of Gil Blas of Sanatillane.* trans. by Tobias Smollett, London: 1766.

Lockridge, Kenneth A. *Literacy in Colonial New England.* New York: W. W. Norton and Company, 1974.

Lossing, Benson J. *Seventeen Hundred and Seventy-Six or the War of Independence.* Detroit: Singing Tree Press, 1970 (reprint of 1847 edition).

Maeder, Edward. *An Elegant Art: Fashion and Fantasy in the Eighteenth Century.* New York: Harry N. Abrams, 1983.

Manwell, John P. *A History of the Hampshire Association of Congregational Churches and Ministers.* Amherst, Mass.: Newell Press, 1941.

Marx, Leo. *The Machine in the Garden: Technology and the Pastoral Ideal in America.* New York: Oxford University Press, 1964.

Melish, Joanne Pope. *Disowning Slavery: Gradual Emancipation and "Race" in New England: 1780–1860.* Ithaca, N.Y.: Cornell University Press, 1998.

Miller, Perry. *The American Puritans.* New York: Doubleday Anchor Books, 1956.

———. *Jonathan Edwards.* New York: Meridian Books, 1959.

Mollo, John. *Uniforms of the Seven Years War: 1756–1763*. New York: Hippocrene Books, 1977.

Morison, Samuel Eliot. *Three Centuries of Harvard: 1636–1936*. Cambridge, Mass., Harvard University Press, 1970.

Newcomer, Lee Nathaniel. *The Embattled Farmers: A Massachusetts Countryside in the American Revolution*. New York: King's Crown Press, 1953.

Nobles, Gregory H. *Divisions Throughout the Whole: Politics and Society in Hampshire County, Massachusetts, 1770–1775*. New York: Cambridge University Press, 1983.

The Northampton Book: chapters from 300 Years in the Life of a New England Town, 1654–1954. The Tercentenary Committee, comp. and ed., Northampton, Massachusetts: 1954.

Norton, Paul F. *Amherst: A Guide to Its Architecture*. Amherst, Mass.: Amherst Historical Society, 1975.

Novak, Barbara. *American Painting of the Nineteenth Century*. New York: Harper & Row, 1979.

Nylander, Jane C. *Our Own Snug Fireside: Images of the New England Home: 1760–1860*. New Haven, Conn.: Yale University Press, 1994.

Parmenter, C. O. *History of Pelham, Massachusetts from 1738 to 1898*. Amherst, Mass.: Press of Carpenter & Morehouse, 1898.

Piersen, William D. *Black Yankees: The Development of an Afro-American Subculture in Eighteenth-Century New England*. Amherst, Mass.: University of Massachusetts Press, 1988.

Premo, Terri L. *Winter Friends: Women Growing Old in the New Republic, 1785–1835*. Chicago: University of Illinois Press, 1990.

Quint, Wilder Dwight. *The Story of Dartmouth*. Boston: Little, Brown, and Co., 1922.

Radford, Edwin and Mona Augusta Radford. *Encyclopedia of Superstitions*, Christina Hole, ed. London: Hutchison, 1975.

Reiss, Oscar. *Blacks in Colonial America*. Jefferson, N.C.: McFarland & Co., 1997.

Rothenberg, Winifred Barr. *From Market-Places to a Market Economy: The Transformation of Rural Massachusetts, 1750–1850*. Chicago: University of Chicago Press, 1992.

Rybczynski, Witold. *Home: A Short History of an Idea*. New York: Penguin Books, 1986.

Seitz, Don C. *Famous American Duels*. Freeport, New York: Books for Libraries Press, 1966.

Shipton, Clifford K. *Biographical Sketches of Those Who Attended Harvard College in the Classes 1761–1763*. Boston: Massachusetts Historical Society, 1970.

———. *Sibley's Harvard Graduates*, Vol. 15. Boston: Massachusetts Historical Society, 1970.

Sloan, Irving J. *The Law of Adoption and Surrogate Parenting*. New York: Oceana Publications, 1988.

Smith, John Montague. *History of the Town of Sunderland, Massachusetts*. Greenfield, Mass.: Press of E. A. Hall & Co., 1899.

Smith, Page. *As a City Upon a Hill*. New York: Alfred A. Knopf, 1966.

Smith-Rosenberg, Carroll. "The Female World of Love and Ritual: Relations Between Women in Nineteenth-Century America," in *Women's Experience in America: An Historical Anthology*. Esther Katz and Anita Rapone, eds. New Brunswick, N.J.: Transaction Books, 1980.

Sorin, Gerald. *Abolitionism: A New Perspective*. New York: Praeger Publishers, 1972.

Sprigg, June. *Domestick Beings*. New York: Alfred A. Knopf, 1984.

Sweeney, Kevin. "River Gods in the Making: The Williamses of Western Massachusetts." in *The Bay and the River: 1600–1900*. Peter Benes, ed. Boston: Boston University Press, 1981

Szatmary, David P. *Shay's Rebellion: The Making of an Agrarian Insurrection*. Amherst, Mass.: University of Massachusetts Press, 1980.

Taylor, George R. "The Rise and Decline of Manufactures and Other Matters," in *Essays on Amherst's History*. Amherst, Mass.: Vista Trust, 1978.

Thompson, Flora. *Lark Rise to Candleford*. Baltimore: Penguin Books, 1974.

Thornton, Tamara Plakins. *Handwriting in America: A Cultural History*. New Haven: Yale University Press, 1996.

Trumbull, James Russell. *History of Northampton, Massachusetts from Its Settlement in 1654*, Vol. 2. Northampton, Mass.: 1902.

Ulrich, Laurel Thatcher. *A Midwife's Tale*. New York: Random House, 1991.

———. "'Daughters of Liberty': Religious Women in Revolutionary New England." in *Women in the Age of the American Revolution*. Ronald Hoffman and Peter J. Albert, eds. Charlottesville: University Press of Virginia, 1989.

———. "Vertuous Women Found: New England Ministerial Literature, 1668–1735," in *A Heritage of Her Own*. Nancy F. Cott and Elizabeth H. Pleck, eds. New York: Simon & Schuster, 1979.

Ward, Gerald W. R., and William N. Hosley, Jr., eds. *The Great River: Art and Society of the Connecticut Valley, 1635–1820*. Hartford, Conn.: Wadsworth Atheneum, 1985.

Warren, Austin. "Orthodox Parsons of Christ's Church," in *New England Saints*. Ann Arbor: University of Michigan Press, 1956.

———. "Jonathan Edwards," in *The New England Conscience*. Ann Arbor: The University of Michigan Press, 1966.

Whicher, George Frisbie. *This Was a Poet*. Ann Arbor: University of Michigan Press, 1965.

Wilbur, C. Keith, M.D. *Revolutionary Medicine: 1700–1800*. Old Saybrook, Conn.: Globe Pequot Press, 1997.

Wilmerding, John. "Themes and Places," in *American Views: Essays on American Art*. Princeton: Princeton University Press, 1991.

Woody, Thomas. *A History of Women's Education in the United States*. New York: Octagon Books, 1980.

Zuckerman, Michael. *Peaceable Kingdoms*. New York: W. W. Norton & Co., 1970.

———. "A Different Thermidor: The Revolution Beyond the American Revolution," in *The Transformation of Early American History: Society, Authority, and Ideology*. James A. Henretta, Michael Kammon, and Stanley N. Katz, eds. New York: Alfred A. Knopf, 1991.

Journals

Boston Medical and Surgical Journal 16 (1832): 156–57. Letter from "R."

Carvalho, Joseph III. "Rural Medical Practice in Early 19th Century New England." *Historical Journal of Western Massachusetts* IV (Spring, 1975): 1–15.

Dickson, Charles Ellis. "Jeremiads in the New American Republic: The Case of National Fasts in the John Adams Administration," *The New England Quarterly* 2 (June 1987) 60: 187–207.

Dole, Vincent P. "Addictive Behavior." *Scientific American* 243 (December 1980): 138–54.

Dussinger, John A. "Conscience and the Pattern of Christian Perfection in *Clarissa*." *Proceedings of the Modern Language Association* 81(June 1966): 36–245.

Gordon, Alfred, M.D. "Insanities Caused by Acute and Chronic Intoxications with Opium and Cocaine." *Journal of the American Medical Association* (1908) 51: 97–101.

Graffagnino, J. Kevin. "Vermonters Unmasked." *Vermont History* (Summer 1989) 57:133–61.

Hindus, Michael, and Daniel Scott Smith. "Premarital Pregnancy in America, 1640–1971: An Overview and Interpretation," *Journal of Interdisciplinary History*, 5 (1975).

Huntington, James O. S. "Philanthropy and Morality." *International Journal of Ethics* (October 1892).

Jones, Douglas Lamar. "The Strolling Poor: Transiency in Eighteenth-Century Massachusetts." *Journal of Social History* 8 (Spring 1975): 28–54.

Juster, Susan. "'In a Different Voice:' Male and Female Narratives of Religious Conversion in Post-Revolutionary America." *American Quarterly* 41 (March 1989): 34–62.

Kouwenhoven, John Atlee. "Some Unfamiliar Aspects of Singing in New England: 1620–1810." *New England Quarterly* 6:1 (1933).

Lockwood, Rose Ann. "Birth, Illness, and Death in 18th-Century New England." *Journal of Social History* 12:1 (Fall 1978): 111–28.

Metropolitan Museum of Art Bulletin. (Fall 1987): 45:2.

Miller, Marla. "My Part Alone: The World of Rebecca Dickinson," *New England Quarterly* (September 1988): 1–38.

Raymond, Andrew. "A New England Colonial Family: Four Generations of the Porters of Hadley, Massachusetts." *The New England Historical and Genealogical Register* 129 (July 1975): 198–220.

Shipton, Clifford K. "Ye Mystery of Ye Ages Solved, or, How Placing Worked at Colonial Harvard and Yale." *Harvard Alumni Bulletin* (December 11, 1954): 258–63.

Smith, Daniel Scott. "Differential Mortality in the United States Before 1900." *Journal of Interdisciplinary History* 4 (Spring 1983): 735–59.

Sweeney, Kevin M. "Mansion People: Kinship, Class, and Architecture in Western Massachusetts in the Mid Eighteenth Century," *Winterthur Portfolio* 19, 4 (Winter 1984): 231–55.

Ulrich, Laurel Thatcher. "The Living Mother of a Living Child: Midwifery and Mortality in Post-Revolutionary New England," *William and Mary Quarterly* 46 (January 1989): 27–48.

Unpublished Sources

Adams and Roy. *Historic Structure Report; Porter-Phelps-Huntington House, Hadley Massachusetts*. Portsmouth, N.H.: Adams & Roy Consultants, Inc., 1988. A copy of this report is available at the Archives and Special Collections of the Robert Frost Library, Amherst College (AC/PPH, box 178).

Christman, Miriam. "Mothers and Daughters: Different Codes of Behavior." Paper presented to the Friends of the William Allen Neilson Library, Smith College, Northampton, Massachusetts, April 11, 1997.

Lazaro, David E. "Constructing an Imported Appearance in the Connecticut River Valley: The Wedding Gown of Elizabeth Pitkin Porter." Paper presented at the Porter-Phelps-Huntington Museum Colloquium on September 28, 2002.

McCardle, Hugh. "Population Growth, Out-migration and the Regulation of Community Size: Hadley, Massachusetts, 1660–1730." Master's Thesis, Amherst, Mass.:University of Massachusetts, January 1975.

McNicholas, Ruth Ann. "Porter-Phelps-Huntington House Museum: Restoration of Historic Grounds." Master's Thesis, Amherst, Mass.: University of Massachusetts, May 1985.

Miller, Marla. "Eggs on the Sand: Domestic Servants and Their Children in Federal New England, 1620–1920." *Women's Work in New England 1620–1920*, Dublin Seminar for Massachusetts Folklife, Deerfield, Massachusetts, June 2001.

———. "My Daily Bread Depends Upon My Labor: Craftswomen, Community and the Marketplace in Rural Massachusetts: 1740–1820." Ph.D. dissertation, Chapel Hill: University of North Carolina, 1997.

Nichols, Elisabeth B. "'Attached and Loving Sister,' 'Constant Unalterable Friend,' and 'Loving and Dutiful Daughter': Elizabeth Phelps Huntington

Conceptualizes Her Identity." Paper presented at Symposium, Porter-Phelps-Huntington Museum, Hadley, Massachusetts, September 13, 1994.

———. "'Pray Don't Tell Any Body That I Write Politics': Private Expressions and Public Admonitions in the Early Republic." Ph.D. dissertation, Durham, N.H.: University of New Hampshire, 1997.

Parsons, Karen. "How did my heart burn within me: Sacred and Secular Meanings, Elizabeth Porter Phelps's Gift of Communion Silver." Paper presented at Symposium, Porter Phelps Huntington Museum, Hadley, Massachusetts, September 13, 1994.

Poubeau, Anne. "'You did not mention whether you had a cow . . .': Cheese Making at the Porter-Phelps-Huntington Museum, Hadley, Massachusetts, 1770–1815." Paper, Amherst, Mass.: University of Massachusetts, Fall 1999.

Smith, Frank H., M.D. Notes on the history of Hadley. Hadley Historical Commission, Goodwin Library, Hadley, Massachusetts.

Sweeney, Kevin Michael. "River Gods and Related Minor Deities: The Williams Family and the Connecticut River Valley, 1637–1790." Ph.D. dissertation, New Haven, Conn.: Yale University, 1986.

Acknowledgments

The making of this book began in 1763 when Elizabeth Porter Phelps first put pen to paper to keep a diary. Judithe Speidel sent me to the Archives and Special Collections at the Amherst College Frost Library with a research project that introduced me to the Porter-Phelps-Huntington papers. Daria D'Arienzo, Head of the Special Collections at Amherst College, and her staff provided access to those papers for the last decade, patiently digging out files and copying documents, as well as photographing several documents for me. Susan Lisk, Director of the Porter-Phelps-Huntington Museum, has been a constant and enthusiastic support in numerous ways. Elise Feeley at the Forbes Library in Northampton, Massachusetts, led me to Sylvester Judd's journals containing his interviews of Hadley octogenarians in the first half of the nineteenth century.

Several scholars have read my manuscript, correcting me where I went astray and guiding me to sources that I had not discovered. If I have, nevertheless, strayed again, the fault is entirely mine. Christopher Clark, Patricia Tracey, and Laurel Ulrich commented upon the entire manuscript. Mary Flesher, Marla Miller, and Paul Norton advised me on chapters related to their fields of study. Medievalist Penelope Johnson helped me in multiple ways: in her careful reading of the manuscript and her suggestions for ordering the abundant material available to me. It was she who led me to Victoria Sanders, agent extraordinaire, who in turn placed me with Scribner, where I have been fortunate to have the scrutiny of two fine editors, Gillian Blake and Sarah McGrath. The latter's assistants, Erin Curler and Diana Tejerina, have helped me with numerous details of the publishing process. I appreciated Dan Cuddy's careful supervision of the production process and Kyoko Watanabe's creative response to the text in her design for the book. Rebecca Jerome guided me patiently through computer crises and designed a comprehensible family tree.

Librarians have assisted me at the University of Massachusetts W. E. B. DuBois Library in the Reference Department and Special Collections; the Pocumtuck Valley Memorial Association Library of Old Deerfield; the Harvard Business School's Baker Library; the Jones Library Special Collections, Amherst, Massachusetts; the Graves Memorial Library in Sunderland, Massachusetts; and the Beacon Street Congregational Library of Boston. The late Dorothy Russell, a member of the Hadley Historical Society, gave me access to its records and answered many questions herself. Archivists have responded promptly to numerous requests for documents: Elizabeth Bouvier of the Supreme Judicial Court of Massachusetts, Brian Sullivan of the Harvard University Archives, and Richard Kaplan, Reference Archivist of the Commonwealth of Massachusetts. The Hampshire County and Worcester County Court offices made available to me inventories from wills. Several people associated with historical societies provided me with valuable information: Douglas Southard of the Boston Historical Society, Janet Nelson of the Bostonian Society, Catherine Fields of the Litchfield, Connecticut, Historical Society, and Augusta Bartlett, a member of the Marlboro, Vermont, Historical Society, who served as a lively guide through the Vermont woods to the Phelps family cemetery. I found useful road and lodging information at the American Antiquarian Society of Worcester, Massachusetts.

Joseph Bartlet, Esquire, allowed me to browse through eighteenth-century volumes of Massachusetts laws in his library. The Reverend Leo Hourihan, present Pastor of the First Congregational Church of Hadley, responded to my questions and directed me to the Beacon Street Congregational Library in Boston. Shirley Parsons's detective work secured permission for me to use the drawing of the church. Dark Horse Photographics of Florence, Massachusetts, printed with painstaking care Elliott Carlisle's photographs of the house and Hadley Common. Penny Leveritt, photographer for Historic Deerfield, Massachusetts, procured a copy for me of "The Battle of Bloody Morning Scout." Mary Lou Cutter of the Hatfield, Massachusetts, Historical Society uncovered a sermon by the Reverend Joseph Lyman that shed light on his character. Several people have responded to numerous queries: Ned Lazaro on eighteenth-century dress; Dr. Keith Wilbur on medical matters; Robert Schuyler, an American history aficionado, on geographical settings of particular battles in the American Revolution.

Loyal friends have encouraged me along the way and allowed me to bend their ears with each new discovery that excited me. Thank you. My children, occupied with their own pursuits, have nevertheless found time to cheer me on. Constance Pendergast, my sister who died eight years ago, read the first paper that I wrote about Elizabeth Phelps and responded with many questions that sent me back to the papers. A demanding, disciplined writer, she taught me that the arduous process of writing can be joyful as well. Finally, Elliott Carlisle. His unflagging interest in this project has endured for many more years than I had a right to expect. He has followed me, camera in hand, in pursuit of visual images that would enhance this story of the life of Elizabeth Phelps and Forty Acres, photographing the house over and over again in search of the ideal light. He has been both champion and critic, reading numerous renditions of my manuscript. He continues to accompany me on my search for Mitte West's grave. It is his book, too.

INDEX

Page numbers of illustrations appear in italics.